THE PRINCETON REVIEW

STUDENT ACCESS
GUIDE TO

THE
BEST
BUSINESS
SCHOOLS

1996 Edition

Books in The Princeton Review Series

Cracking the ACT
Cracking the ACT with Sample Tests on Computer Disk
Cracking the GED
Cracking the GMAT
Cracking the GMAT with Sample Tests on Computer Disk
Cracking the GRE
Cracking the GRE with Sample Tests on Computer Disk
Cracking the GRE Psychology Subject Test
Cracking the LSAT
Cracking the LSAT with Sample Tests on Computer Disk
Cracking the MCAT
Cracking the MCAT with Sample Tests on Computer Disk
Cracking the SAT and PSAT
Cracking the SAT and PSAT with Sample Tests on Computer Disk
Cracking the SAT II: Biology Subject Test
Cracking the SAT II: Chemistry Subject Test
Cracking the SAT II: English Subject Tests
Cracking the SAT II: French Subject Test
Cracking the SAT II: History Subject Tests
Cracking the SAT II: Math Subject Tests
Cracking the SAT II: Physics Subject Test
Cracking the SAT II: Spanish Subject Test
Cracking the TOEFL with Audiocassette

SAT Math Workout
SAT Verbal Workout

Don't Be a Chump!
How to Survive Without Your Parents' Money
Trashproof Resumes

Grammar Smart
Math Smart
Reading Smart
Study Smart
Word Smart: Building an Educated Vocabulary
Word Smart II: How to Build a More Educated Vocabulary
Writing Smart

Grammar Smart Junior
Math Smart Junior
Word Smart Junior
Writing Smart Junior

Student Access Guide to America's Top Internships
Student Access Guide to College Admissions
Student Access Guide to the Best Business Schools
Student Access Guide to the Best Law Schools
Student Access Guide to the Best Medical Schools
Student Access Guide to the Best 309 Colleges
Student Access Guide to Paying for College
Student Access Guide to Visiting College Campuses
Student Access Guide: The Big Book of Colleges
Student Access Guide: The Internship Bible

Also available on cassette from Living Language

Grammar Smart
Word Smart
Word Smart II

THE **PRINCETON** REVIEW

STUDENT ACCESS
GUIDE TO

THE
BEST
BUSINESS
SCHOOLS

By Nedda Gilbert

Random House, Inc. New York 1995

1996 Edition

ISSN 1067-2141
ISBN 0-679-76147-0
Includes indexes

Manufactured in the United States of America on paper using partially recycled fibers

9 8 7 6 5 4 3 2

Revised Edition

FOREWORD

In the late '80s, The Princeton Review began working with Fortune 500 companies to provide their employees with on-site preparation classes for the GMAT. In the course of our work, it became clear that most of these prospective business school students were lacking critical information about the business school admissions process on which they were about to embark. Over and over, students asked:

- "How many times should I take the GMAT?"
- "If I take it twice, which score will they count?"
- "How high does my score need to be?"
- "What points do I need to make in my essays?"
- "What if all I've done is work? I don't have any extracurriculars to write about."
- "Should I interview?"
- "How much do my grades count?"
- "Who should write my recommendation—an immediate boss who knows me well or a senior V.P. who's a power alum of the school?"
- "When's the best time to send in the application—early or close to the deadline?"

These students were confused, with good reason. Unlike high-school students—who can turn to guidance counselors and professional advisors for help navigating the undergraduate admissions process—prospective MBAs have almost nowhere to turn for advice on selecting and applying to the right business school. Even the information that is available—mainly guidebooks and magazine rankings—is obscure and contradictory. What, then, is a B-school applicant to do?

Read This Book

We surveyed 15,500 current students, hundreds of admissions officers, and dozens of recruiters and business school grads to bring you the real scoop on B-school.

Want to know what really happens to the applications you toiled, sweated, and bled over? This book gives you an exclusive inside look at the deliberations of a top admissions committee and shows you what they're looking for in an applicant. Ever wonder who actually reads your essays? We not only tell you, we show you what they liked about fifteen essays submitted to twelve top schools. This book tells you what admissions officers are looking for, what your life as a business school student will be like, what to talk about in your interviews, when to apply, and more. But, most important, this book gives you essential facts, unique insights, and up-to-the-minute information on the nation's top 70 B-schools, so you can make an educated decision about where you should apply.

Why These 70 Schools?

For several years now, two leading magazines have been trying to tell you which school is number one, which is number eight, which is number thirty-seven. These rankings make headline news and sell millions of magazines. Business schools take these lists very seriously. But these rankings are too precise, to the point of being arbitrary, and, if you think about it, they really don't reveal much about the schools in question. One magazine says a school is number five. Another says the school is number eleven. With that knowledge, you can deduce one thing: these magazines are obviously using different criteria. But aside from the numbers "five" and "eleven," do you know anything useful about the school? Not much.

We are not completely debunking the idea that there are better and worse schools. After all, this book is called *Student Access Guide to the Best Business Schools*. There are about 900 graduate business programs offered in the United States. Of these, roughly 250 are accredited by the American Assembly of Collegiate Business Schools. Of these, we determined that about 70 are, on the basis of reputation, curriculum, quality of professors, and student opinion, the top schools in the country. Those schools are included in this book—with three exceptions. Rice University is not accredited by the AACBS but is included in this book because of its excellent programs and the national reputation it enjoys, and deserves, as an exceptional business school. The University of Florida and State University of New York–Albany graduate business programs are both among the finest in the country. We were unable to poll students at these schools because of difficulty obtaining permission to come on campus. We regret that we could not include them in this edition of *Student Access Guide to the Best Business Schools*, and hope to bring you full profiles of these schools in next year's edition.

After arriving at our list, we decided that any rank ordering of the schools would be pointless: every school in this book is top-notch. We've chosen to list schools in our book alphabetically. We believe our profiles highlight each program's major strengths and weaknesses as well as capture its personality. The profiles take into account the reputation, prestige, and status of a school. The question is, which school is best for you? We hope this book helps you make the right choice.

Good luck!

ACKNOWLEDGMENTS

This book absolutely would not have been possible without the help of my husband, Paul. His insights and support were invaluable—this book is as much his as it is mine.

The following people were also instrumental in the completion of this book: my father, Dr. Irving Buchen, for his razor's-edge editorial suggestions; David Ro Hall—proofreader. Julian Ham, who designed this book; Rob Zopf, for his tireless phone interviews with business school administrators; Bruno Butler, Andrew Dunn, Joe Keith, Bruce McAmis, Joe Pelletier, Mark Stein, and Thane Thomsen, who gathered all manner of facts and figures and processed the endless flood of surveys; Cynthia Brantley, Lee Elliott, and Kristin Fayne-Mulroy for putting all the pieces together; Alicia Ernst and John Katzman, for giving me the chance to write this book; and to the folks at Villard, who helped this project reach fruition. Special thanks go to Andy Goldfarb and to all those section-A mates, HBS-92, who lent a hand and provided valuable feedback.

Thanks are also due to the business school folks who went far out of their way to provide essential information:

Will Makris, Director of Admissions—Babson University

David Irons—University of California, Berkeley

John Gould, outgoing Dean, and Allan Friedman, Director of Communications—University of Chicago

Meyer Feldberg, Dean, and Ethan Hanabury, Director of Admissions—Columbia Business School

Skip Horne, Director of Admissions, and Elaine Ruggieri, Director of Public Relations—University of Virginia

Pat Wetherall, Assistant Director of Communications—Dartmouth College

Cathy Cassio and her staff at the News and Publications Office—Stanford University

CONTENTS

ALL ABOUT B-SCHOOL

CHAPTER ONE:

Picking the Right Business School for You:
How to Use This Book

CHAPTER TWO:

Suspenders and Power Breakfasts:
What Does an MBA Offer?

CHAPTER THREE:

What B-School Is Really Like

HOW TO GET IN

CHAPTER FOUR:

Preparing to Be a Successful Applicant

CHAPTER FIVE:

Admissions

CHAPTER SIX:

The Right Stuff: Filing a Winning Application

CHAPTER SEVEN:

Essays That Work: Writing Your Way into Business School

THE SCHOOLS

CHAPTER EIGHT:

Schools Rated by Category

CHAPTER NINE:

Profiles of the Best Business Schools

INTRODUCTION

The MBA - Back in Business at the Elite Schools

Just when you thought it was getting easier to get in...

The MBA, often seen as the golden passport to power and wealth, has taken some hard knocks lately. First, there were all those business scandals in the 80's that made MBA's look smarmy. Then downsizing shrunk middle management (*the* destination for grads) and the degree no longer held the promise of great jobs, much less huge payoffs. Then, to make matters worse, corporate recruiters, the primary consumers of the MBA, became critical of MBA programs in the media, claiming that the graduate education added no measurable value to the business skills of those it was graduating. Unsurprisingly, potential candidates swung to professions in which there was renewed interest - teaching, medicine, and public service. The bottom line? The number of individuals taking the Graduate Management Admission Test (GMAT), dropped by twenty percent since it's peak in 1990-1991.

B-Schools fell upon tough times. Even top tier programs couldn't count on a bottomless cup of applications, much less their yield of the best and the brightest. To fill their spots, the schools had to work harder. Applicants were wined and dined, provided 800 numbers and Saturday interviews, and treated to personal calls from the dean and faculty—all intended to convince the future MBA their school was best.

... It got tougher at the top schools

Many schools are still hustling for students. But the decline in would-be tycoons is short-lived. At the nations elite schools— programs such as Stanford, Wharton, Columbia and Michigan— applications have recently swung back to levels not seen since the 80's. Indeed, for two dozen or so of the nations most selective programs, applications are up a generous twenty percent.

"Everyone refers to the early to mid-80's as the long gone heyday for MBAs," says Ethan Hanabury, the Associate Director of Admissions and Administration at Columbia Business School. "But the myth that the MBA is no longer essential has been thoroughly debunked by double digit increases at the top schools.

This extraordinary year was no surprise to us; it represents a trend that began three years ago. *Our applications have increased sixty-seven percent to an all-time high of 4,600."* Applications at the University of Chicago mirror the trend. "We are seeing an increase in the percentage of applicants who are accepting our offers of admission," comments Donald Martin , Director of Admissions at the University of Chicago Graduate School of Business. "The increased number of applications combined with the higher matriculation rate clearly indicates a strong interest in business education."

What's driving the boom? Gurus can only speculate. First, insiders now believe fewer people took the GMAT because they were waiting out recessionary changes. Now, more MBAs than ever are being granted to young hopefuls like yourself. And the numbers are expected to increase as potential candidates from nations such as China, India and Eastern Europe weigh in. Second, the demand for quality MBAs is once again, sky high. Led by the consulting firms, industry flagships are rushing B-Schools for the best and brightest. A "glut " may have been more perception than reality. As a result, a shrinking U.S. MBA applicant pool is targeting the elite schools and researching job prospects *before* they matriculate. MBAs from top programs consistently fare better than their counterparts at lower tier schools. Finally, applicants to Law School have begun to trade in their dreams of the courtroom for those of the boardroom.

What does this mean? Basically this: if you plan on applying to the most competitive programs this year, brace yourself. Perhaps you were a sure shot in previous years. But this time around, you'll enter a far more competitive pool. As for the second and third tier schools, many are also reporting increases in applications. But whatever school you end up at, remember, your success will have more to do with you, than the piece of paper you get framed on your wall.

Getting In

So now you know, admission to the top programs will require your absolute best shot. Thousands and thousands of prospective MBA candidates spend loads of time and money making sure they select, and are in turn admitted to, the "best" school. Their time and money go toward working in jobs they think will impress a B-school, studying and preparing for the GMAT, writing essays, interviewing, visiting prospective schools, and buying guides like —but not as good as—this one.

This book is your best bet. It takes you into the heretofore secret deliberations of the admissions committees at the top schools. You get a firsthand look at who decides your fate. More important, you learn what criteria are used to evaluate applicants. As we found out, it isn't always what you expect. You also get straight talk from admissions officers—what dooms an application and how to ace the interview.

In addition to getting inside information on the application process, you learn when the best time is to apply, how to answer the most commonly asked essay questions and the key points to make in your essays. There's also loads of information on what you can do before applying to increase your odds of gaining admission.

We've also given you the facts—from the most up-to-date information on major curricula changes and placement rates to demographics of the student body—for the seventy best B-schools in the country. And we've included enough information about them—which we gathered from admissions officers, administrators, and students—to let you make a smart decision about going there.

Why These 70 Schools?

For several years now, two leading magazines have been telling you who's hot and who's not. They've smooshed together objective and subjective data into a quantified format to create the perception of precise numerical rankings. But the rankings are as imprecise as they are arbitrary. One magazine says a school is number five. Another says it's number eight. The weighting of different criteria leads to dramatically different interpretations of a program. While the rankings make news and sell a lot of magazines, in real-life prospective students are as much, if not more, interested in those characteristics that distinguish one school from another. What makes a program tops?

To find the answers, we took a more holistic approach and gathered input from a variety of sources. First on our list was student opinion. Mass-interview style, we surveyed over 12,500 currently matriculated B-school students. We surveyed hundreds of admissions officers and administrators. In addition, we also looked at more traditional measures, including a school's acceptance rate, average GPA, average GMAT scores, placement rate, curriculum, learning environment, and caliber of student body. As we progressed, we learned that many lesser-known schools belonged in this book because of their regional reputation, star faculty, "bang for the buck," or unique course offerings. Finally, we sought to focus on those schools that are accredited by the American Assembly of Collegiate Business Schools (of the approximately 900 business programs in the nation, roughly 250 are so accredited). All of the schools included in this book are accredited by the AACBS with the exception of Rice University. Rice University is included in our book because of its special programs and the national reputation it enjoys and deserves as a top business school. In a few cases, schools which might have met our criteria for inclusion had to be omitted because they wouldn't allow us to poll their students.

A final note: As you might have expected, we've chosen to list schools in our book alphabetically, rather than rank them. We believe our profiles highlight each program's major strengths and weaknesses, as well as capture their distinct personalities. The profiles take into account the reputation, prestige, and status of a school without ranking it.

The GMAT has changed: The GMAT is continuing its evolution this year, with slightly shorter reading sections. It's too early to tell if schools are paying any real attention to scores on the new AWA (Analytic Writing Assessment). But if you need some advice about the test, our book *Cracking the GMAT* has the latest information available on the restructured GMAT and, of course, our techniques and tips on how to beat the test (have you ever heard of *How to Succeed in Business Without Really Trying*? We have.). You can also call us at 1-800-REVIEW-6 or you can reach us by e-mail at info@review.com. We'd also be happy to tell you about our intensive six-week GMAT course. Whatever you do, we wish you good luck in b-school and beyond.

B-SCHOOL ADMISSION GOES ELECTRONIC

Business school admission is finally moving onto the "information superhighway." Here are a couple of ways to use your computer to best effect.

Looking For B-schools On-line

First off, *we've* put up a lot of information about business schools and business school admissions through our on-line services on the Internet, America Online, eWorld, and the Microsoft Network.

The Internet is the most interesting of all on-line information services, because the B-schools themselves have posted information there. You can connect to the 'net through an *Internet service provider* or through America Online, CompuServe, or Prodigy (if you've never played with the Internet, you'll find these last three companies the easiest way). Once you're on the Internet, you can reach the schools directly (provided they post one, we've listed each B-school's address at the bottom right of its entry).

Note that the Internet changes every day—content is added or deleted, and sites change their look and feel regularly. Addresses (known as URLs) change; some sites disappear completely. All of the URLs that we have provided here were accurate and functioning at the time of publication, but the best way to find schools is through our own World Wide Web (also known as the Web, this is the graphical interface to the internet) page. (For those without a speedy PC, we have a text-only gopher server, too.) We've set up a search engine, and posted some of the information in this book, so you can access virtually every college and university Internet site by just clicking. We've also posted useful (we hope) career and internship advice, info about all of our books and software, an extensive phone list of useful numbers, and hotlinks to our favorite educational sites on the Internet.

Our boards on America Online and eWorld offer more information, and a very different look and feel. One of the most popular features of these boards is our Student Message areas, where you can create your own topic folders and post questions for other students and for our own on-line admissions and testing experts. We also schedule live on-line forums where you can get answers in real time to your questions about admission, testing, and just about anything else to do with grad school direct from our experts and special guests. By the time you read this, we will have launched our newest on-line board on the Microsoft Network, set to debut with the release of Windows 95.

To reach The Princeton Review at any of these sites, or to eMail us, use the following addresses:

- eMail: info@review.com
- World Wide Web: http://www.review.com
- America Online: keyword "student"
- eWorld: shortcut "test prep"
- Gopher: bloggs.review.com
- Microsoft Network: eMail us for the address

Applying To B-school Via Electronic Application

Once you've gathered all the information that you need about the schools and have decided where to apply, you may not need to leave your keyboard. Just a handful of years ago electronic applications were *never* going to happen. Today, business schools are scrambling to make electronic versions of their applications available. The B-schools that currently accept electronic applications are identified in our write-ups by the icon you see at right.

There happen to be two excellent packages for electonic applications, and we've convinced both companies to give you a small discount on their software because you bought this book. Each is available for the Mac and Windows, and each allows you to fill out your applications on screen, print, and submit directly to the admissions offices. Each allows you to enter common information only once, saving you some time and hassle (moreover, do you even *have* a typewriter anymore?).

One is called *Apply!*. It supplies you with an exact duplicate of each school's application both on screen and in hard copy, complete with logos and graphics. To order, call (800) WE-APPLY or (212) 245-4558, email them at apply@aol.com, fax them at (212) 245-4808, or write them at *Apply Software*, 440 West 47th St, New York, NY 10036.

The other package is called *MBA Multi-App*. In addition to printing out perfect duplicates of the regular applications, it has an easy data entry mechanism. To order, call *MBA Multi-App* at (800) 516-2227 or (610) 544-9358, email them at mcs@pond.com, fax them at (610) 544-9877, or write them at MCS, 635 North Chester Road, Swarthmore, PA 19081.

Pricing on both *Apply!* and *MBA Multi-App* are the same; single applications are available for $15; the full package including every school is $36, plus shipping. (By the way, the prices on the full packages include a 10% discount. Make *sure* to mention this book, and don't say we never got you anything.)

A final note of advice: no matter which form of electronic application you choose, you must still contact the admissions office for an application packet. This is the *only* way that you can be sure to have all the information and materials that you need to put together the strongest candidacy possible. Despite the increasing on-line presence of business schools and the convenience of the electronic medium, "snail mail" remains an integral part of the process.

■   ■   ■

If you have any questions, comments, or suggestions, please e-mail your insights to us over the Internet at Books@review.com. We appreciate your input and want to make our books as useful to you as they can be.

CHAPTER ONE

Picking the Right Business School for You

How to Use This Book

Making the Decision to Go

The first step for you may be B-school. Indeed, armed with an MBA you may journey far. But the success of your trip and the direction you take will depend on knowing exactly why you're going to B-school and just what you'll be getting out of it.

The most critical questions you need to ask yourself are: Do you really want a career in business? What do you want the MBA to do for you? Are you looking to gain credibility, accelerate your development, or move into a new job or industry?

Knowing what you want doesn't just affect your decision to go. It also affects your candidacy; admissions committees favor applicants who have clear goals and objectives. Moreover, once at school, students who know what they want make the most of their two years. If you're uncertain about your goals, opportunities for career development—such as networking, mentoring, student clubs, and recruiter events—are squandered.

You also need to find a school that fits your individual needs. Consider the personal and financial costs. This may be the single biggest investment of your life. How much salary will you forego by leaving the work force? What will the tuition be? How will you pay for it? If you have a family, spouse, or significant other, how will getting your MBA affect them?

If you do have a spouse, you may choose programs that involve partners in campus life. If status is the be-all and end-all, you may simply choose the most prestigious school you can get into.

The MBA presents many opportunities, but no guarantees. As with any opportunity, you must make the most of it. Whether you go to a first-tier school, or to a part-time program close to home, you'll acquire the skills that can jump start your career. But your success will have more to do with you than with the piece of paper your MBA is printed on.

Why the Rankings Aren't a Useful Guide to School Selection

All too many applicants rely on the magazine rankings to decide where to apply. Caught up with winners, losers, and whoever falls in between, their thinking is simply: Can I get into the top five? Top ten? Top fifteen?

But it's a mistake to rely on the rankings. Mark Twain once said, "There are lies, damn lies, and statistics." Today, he'd probably add B-school rankings. Why? Because statistics rarely show the whole picture. When deciding on the validity of a study, it's wise to consider *how* the study was conducted and *what* exactly it was trying to measure.

First, the rankings have made must-read news for several years. Not surprisingly, some of the survey respondents—current B-school students and recent grads—now know there's a game to play. The game is this: Give your own school the highest marks possible. The goal: that coveted number-one spot. Rumor has it that some schools even remind their students of how their responses will affect the stature of their program. This kind of self-interest is known as respondent bias, and the B-school rankings suffer from it in a big way.

The rankings feature easy-to-measure differences such as selectivity, placement success, and proficiency in the basic disciplines. But these rankings don't allow for any intangibles—such as the progressiveness of a program, the school's learning environment, and the happiness of the students.

To create standards by which comparisons *can* be made, the rankings force an evaluative framework on the programs. But this is like trying to evaluate a collection of paintings—impressionist, modern, classical, and cubist—with the same criteria. Relying on narrow criteria to evaluate subjective components fails to capture the true strengths and weaknesses of each piece.

The statistically measurable differences that the magazines base their ratings on are often so marginal as to be insignificant. In other words, it's too close to call the race. Perhaps in some years two schools should be tied for the number-one spot. What would the tie-breaker look like? A rally cry of "We're number one" with the loudest school winning?

A designation as the number-one, number-five, or number-ten school is almost meaningless when you consider that it changes from year to year—and from magazine to magazine. (At least Olympic medalists enjoy a four-year victory lap.)

Judging for Yourself

Depending on what you're looking for, the rankings may tell you something about the B-schools. But it's wise to use them as approximations rather than the declarations of fact they're made out to be.

The rankings don't factor in *your* values or all of the criteria *you* need to consider. Is it selectivity? The highest rate of placement? The best starting salary? Surprise! The number-one school is not number one in all these areas. No school is.

The best way to pick a program is to do your homework and find a match. For example, if you have limited experience with numbers, then a program with a heavy quantitative focus may round out your résumé. If you want to stay in your home area, then a local school that's highly regarded by the top regional companies may be best for you. If you know that you want to go into a field typified by cutthroat competition, or a field in which status is all-important . . . well, obviously, keep your eyes on those rankings.

You also need to consider your personal style and comfort zone. Suppose you get into a "top ranked" school but the workload is destroying your life or the mentality is predatory. It won't matter how prestigious the program is if you don't make it through. Do you want an intimate and supportive environment or are you happy to blend in with the masses? Different schools will meet these needs. Lecture versus case study, specialization versus broad-based general management curriculum, and heavy finance versus heavy marketing are other kinds of trade-offs.

One last thing to consider is social atmosphere. What is the spirit of the student body? Do students like each other? Are they indifferent? Perhaps a bit hostile? If you go through graduate school in an atmosphere of camaraderie, you'll never forget those two years. But if you go through school in an atmosphere of enmity . . . OK, you'll still remember those two years. It's up to you to decide *how* you want to remember them.

Remember when you applied to college? You talked to friends, alumni, and teachers. You visited the campus and sat in on classes (or should have). It's not all that different with B-school. Here are some of the things you should check out:

ACADEMICS

- Academic reputation
- International reputation
- Primary teaching methodology
- Renown and availability of professors
- General or specialized curriculum
- Range of school specialties
- Opportunities for global/foreign study
- Emphasis on teamwork
- Fieldwork/student consulting available
- Student support—extra study sessions, accessible faculty, tutoring
- Academic support—libraries, computer facilities and expertise

- Grading/probation policy
- Workload/hours per week in class
- Class and section size
- Pressure and competition

CAREER

- Summer and full-time job placement (number of companies recruiting on and off campus)
- Placement rate
- Average starting salaries
- Salaries at five-year mark
- Career support—assistance with career planning, résumé preparation, interview skills
- Networking with visiting executives

QUALITY OF LIFE

- Location
- Campus
- Orientation
- Range of student clubs/activities
- Diversity of student body
- Housing
- Social life
- Spouse/partner group
- Recreational facilities

EXPENSE

- Tuition
- Books, computer
- Cost of living
- Financial aid

How to Use This Book

Each of the business schools listed in this book has its own two-page spread. Each spread has eight components: two "sidebars" (the narrow columns on the outside of each page that contain charts and statistics) and four "boxes" (the big boxes in the middle that contain text). Look at the sample page below:

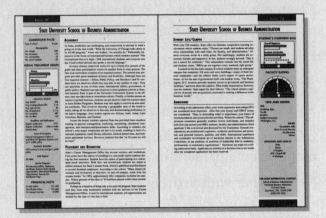

Here's what's in each section.

The Sidebars

The sidebars contain various statistics that were gathered either from the questionnaires we sent to the schools or from our own surveys.

■ Type of School
Whether the school is public or private.

■ No. Men, No. Women, No. Minorities, No. International Students
The demographic breakdown of last year's entering class.

■ Equality Meter
Based on the opinions of the students we surveyed at the schools, these graphs reveal whether women and minorities feel they are afforded equal treatment as compared to the white, male majority. Their responses are compared to the national average (also based on our student survey).

■ **Admissions Statistics**

Gives the average GMAT score, average undergraduate GPA, average age at entry into business school, number of applicants, number of students accepted, and number of students enrolled for last year's entering class.

■ **Deadlines and Notification**

Gives the application deadline and acceptance notification dates.

■ **Focus of Curriculum**

Those academic areas the school is particularly noted for.

■ **Academic Specialties**

This will either read "general" or "specialized." A business school with a general curriculum gives students very broad coverage of all functional areas. A specialized curriculum allows students to major in or specialize in one or two areas.

■ **Joint Degrees**

Lists any special graduate degrees offered by the school.

■ **Special Programs**

Lists any exchange, internship, or job programs.

■ **Financial Facts**

Gives in-state tuition, out-of-state tuition, and costs of on-campus housing.

■ **Students' Overview Box**

At each school, the students we surveyed were asked to rate their overall happiness and their satisfaction with their school's program. The results are shown on a scale of 50 to 100, and are compared with the national average (also gathered from our student surveys).

■ **Faculty Rating**

Our survey asked students how they would rate their professors as teachers. The results are shown on this scale. The national average is also shown.

■ *Hits and Misses*

Summarizes the results of our survey. The lists show what students felt unusually strong about, both positively and negatively, at their schools. Following are the categories:

- Gym—if this appears under the "hits" list, the students at the school love the gym facilities; if it appears under the "misses" list, the students are dissatisfied with the facilities.

- Helping Other Students—if this appears under the "hits" list, the students feel that students are willing to help each other; if it appears under the "misses" list, the students feel that their classmates aren't willing to help each other.

- Accounting Dept.—students rated their improvement in the area of accounting. If this listing appears under the "hits" list, the students were happy with the quality of accounting instruction; if it appears under the "misses" list, they were not satisfied.

- Finance Dept.—same as above, only for finance skills.

- Marketing Skills—same, only for marketing skills.

- Quantitative Skills—same as above, *mutatis mutandis*.

- Placement—a rating of the efficiency of the school's job placement office.

- Ethnic and Racial Diversity—students were asked whether their school is ethnically and racially diverse. If it is, this rating appears in the "hits" list; if not, it appears under "misses."

- Classmates are smart/classmates are stupid—reveals students' opinions about the intelligence of their classmates.

- Recruiting—rates students' satisfaction with their school's recruiting efforts.

- Social Life—if students have active social lives, this rating appears in the "hits" list; if not, it appears in the "misses" list.

- Diverse Work Experience—this rating appears in the "hits" list if students said their classmates had come from diverse work backgrounds; if it appears in the "misses" list students came mostly from the same type of company.

- Off-campus Housing—students' rating of the quality of off-campus housing.

- On-campus Housing—students' rating of the quality of on-campus housing.

- Library—a rating of the usefulness of the library.

- Location—this is a rating of whether or not students like the town their school is in.

- Cozy Student Community—students were asked whether they liked to hang out with their classmates. If they did, "Cozy student community" appears in the "hits" list; if not "Don't like classmates" appears in the "misses" list.

- School Clubs—a rating of the breadth and number of extracurricular clubs and organizations on campus.

- Staying in Touch—students were asked whether their classmates were the kind of people they'd want to stay in contact with after business school. If this rating appears in the "hits" list, they did want to stay in touch with their classmates; if it appears in the "misses" list, they felt they wouldn't stay in touch.

■ **Applicants Also Look at**
Lists other schools applicants also consider.

■ **For More Information, Contact:**
The address and phone number of the school's admissions office can be found here.

The Boxes

Academics

This section describes the academic atmosphere of each school, what the professors are like, where the curriculum is headed, and what students think about the education they are receiving.

Placement and Recruiting

One of the most important issues to MBAs is the quality and efficacy of their school's recruiting and placement offices. This box explains the programs each school offers.

Student Life/Campus

From dating to off-campus housing, this box describes the social atmosphere and quality of life at each campus.

Admissions

This box tells you what aspects of applications are most important to the school's admissions officers. We used the admissions officers' responses to our questionnaire, as well as telephone interviews with many admissions officers, to write these boxes.

A Glossary of Insider Lingo

You've probably already noticed this, but business school students, graduates, and professors—like most close-knit, somewhat solipsistic groups—seem to speak their own weird language. With that in mind, here's one last set of tools that will help you on your way through this book and into the business world: a list of MBA jargon (with English translations):

Air Hogs: students who monopolize classroom discussion and love to hear themselves speak.

Air Time: a precious opportunity—speaking or making comments in class.

Analysis Paralysis: not being able to make a decision because you've gotten lost in the thicket of your own analysis.

Back of the Envelope: an abbreviated analysis of the numbers.

Barriers to Entry: conditions that prevent entry into a particular market.

Beta of a Stock: the inherent volatility of a stock.

Bottleneck: the point in a plant or process that determines or blocks the pace.

Burn Rate: amount of cash a company consumes each day.

Case Cracker: a comment in class that gets to the essence of case.

Case Study Method: popular teaching method that uses real-life business cases for analysis.

Chip Shots: unenlightening comments made during class discussion for the sole purpose of getting credit.

Cold Call: unexpected, often dreaded request by the professor to open a case.

Core Courses: courses in the basic disciplines of business, usually mandatory.

Corner Office: office location that all MBAs aspire to and the exclusive province of partners, managing directors and senior executives.

Cost Benefit Analysis: calculating whether something is worth doing on the basis of the real dollar cost versus real dollar benefit. This is often used as a shortcut in analyzing the numbers.

Cycle Time: how fast you can turn something around.

Deliverable: what your end product is.

Finheads: finance heads. See also sharks.

Four P's: elements of a marketing strategy—Price, Promotion, Place, Product.

Fume Date: date the company will run out of cash reserves.

Functional Areas: the basic disciplines of business.

Globalization: trend of the '80s and '90s; expanding the definition of your market to include the challenges of operating in a multicountry, multiconsumer market.

Hard Courses: anything with numbers.

HP12-C: the calculator of choice for number crunching.

I-Bankers: investment banking analysts coming out of the two-year training programs and into B-school.

Incentivize: a bastardized version of the word *incentive*, used as a verb.

MBA Weenies: students who believe that once they get their MBAs they'll be masters of the universe.

Net Net: End result.

OOC: out of cash.

Opportunity Costs: the cost of pursuing an opportunity, i.e., for B-school, tuition and loss of income for two years.

Poets: students with little quantitative skills or experience (numerically challenged).

Power Naps: quick, intense in-class recharge for the continually sleep deprived.

Power Tool: someone who does all the work and sits in the front row of the class with his hand up.

Pre-enrollment Courses: commonly known as MBA summer camp—quantitative courses, generally offered in the summer before the first year to get the numerically challenged up to speed.

Pro Forma: financial presentation of hypothetical events; for example, how much new debt would a company require if it grows ten percent a year?

Quant Jock: a numerical athlete who is happiest crunching numbers.

Quick and Dirty: an abbreviated analysis, often involving numbers.

Run the Numbers: analyze quantitatively.

Sharks: aggressive students who smell blood and move in for the kill.

Shark Comment: comment meant to gore a fellow student in class discussion.

Soft Courses: touchy-feely courses such as human resources and organizational behavior.

Soft Skills: conflict resolution, teamwork, negotiation, oral and written communication.

Slice and Dice: running all kinds of quantitative analysis on a set of numbers.

The Five Forces: Michael Porter's model for analyzing the strategic attractiveness of an industry.

Three C's: the primary forces—Customer, Competition, Company.

Total Quality Management: the Edward Demming method of management that caught on with the Japanese and is now "hot" in American business—managing the quality of products, service, work, process, people and objectives.

Valuation: adds up projected future cash flows into current dollars.

Value-Based Decision Making: values and ethics as part of the practice of business.

Suspenders and Power Breakfasts

What Does an MBA Offer?

Nuts-and-Bolts Business Skills

Graduate business schools teach the applied science of business. The best business schools, the ones in this book, combine the latest academic theories with pragmatic concepts, hands-on experience, and real-world solutions.

To equip students with the broad expertise they need to be managers, most business schools start new MBAs off with a set of foundation or "core" courses in what are known as the "functional areas": finance, accounting, management, marketing, operations, and economics. These courses introduce you to the basic vocabulary and concepts of formal business culture. They also develop your practical skills—ones you'll be able to use immediately in your new career.

Your learning occurs on three levels: You become familiar with *concepts*. For example, in finance you learn that a company's cost of equity is greater than its cost of debt. You acquire *tools* such as ratio analysis, valuations, and pro formas. Finally, you experience *action-based learning* by applying your skills and knowledge to case studies, role plays, and business simulations. Over the course of this three-tiered study, you will explore the complete business cycle of many different kinds of organizations.

B-schools also teach the analytical skills used to make complicated business decisions. You learn how to define the critical issues, apply analytical techniques, develop the criteria for decisions, and make decisions after evaluating their impact on other variables.

After two years, you're ready to market a box of cereal. Or prepare a valuation of the cereal company's worth. You'll speak the language of business. You'll know the tools of the trade. Your expertise will extend to many areas and industries. In short, you will have acquired the skills that open doors.

The Fast Track and Big Bucks

Applicants often have big bucks in mind when they decide to go to business school, believing that earning an MBA is equivalent to winning the lottery. At some schools, this is (sort of) the case. The top talent at elite schools are commonly offered salaries from $50,000 to $90,000. In fact, thirty percent of all Harvard B-school graduates accept positions in the six figure range. But this is hardly a common experience.

Many factors have an effect on a student's first-job-out-of-school salary. First, there's a correlation between school reputation and average starting salary. The better the school (or the better the current perception of the school), the better the compensation. Second, compensation varies by industry. For example, consulting and investment banking are at the high end of the salary spectrum these days. Some companies in these industries even offer students "sign-on bonuses" and reimbursement of their second-year tuition. By contrast, advertising firms and small businesses offer smaller compensation packages and fewer perks.

Third, previous work experience and salary will boost or deflate your perceived value. A clear track record of success before school is likely to secure a bigger package after graduation.

Another common reason for pursuing an MBA is to get on the proverbial "fast track." Many students do find that the degree allows them to leapfrog several notches up the ladder. But the guaranteed fast track is something of an illusion.

B-school students these days are older than they used to be: the average age is twenty-seven, as opposed to twenty-two twenty years ago. This indicates that students typically spend more time working after college before entering a graduate degree program. Their age, maturity, and previous work experience allow these graduates to move into substantive, responsible positions right after completing their programs. In contrast, twenty years ago a recent MBA's first job out of school was in a management development track, but at a fairly low level in the organization.

All that said, the MBA can lead to accelerated career development. But like your salary, much of this depends on the industry you enter and the program you graduate from.

Access to Hundreds of Recruiters, Entry to New Fields

Applicants tend to place great emphasis on "incoming" and "outgoing" statistics. First they ask, "Will I get in?" Then they ask, "Will I get a job?"

If the first is getting tougher to accomplish, then the second is getting easier. MBAs are back in style and hot again, thanks in part to the renewed interest in hiring from consulting firms and investment banks. Students graduating from the class of '94 are awash with offers. Consulting firms who traditionally offer generous packages, are making more offers at higher starting salaries than ever before. Starting salaries are weighing in at the $80,000 mark, and that doesn't include the $20,000 newly minted MBAs get as a sign-on bonus. The majority also receive a generous relocation package. Indeed, if you were fortunate enough to have spent the summer in between your first and second year at the consulting company,

then you will in all likelihood also receive a "rebate" on your tuition. These companies pick-up student's second year tuition bill. The big enchilada however goes to those MBA students who worked at the firm *before* B-School. **These lucky capitalists get**

RECRUITER SPELLS IT OUT

David Tanzer,
Booz-Allen & Hamilton

"It may be kind of self-limiting, but we hire MBAs from the Business Schools that use the case method. Students trained in this methodology get exposure to a wide variety of business situations. They learn to quickly figure out what's truly important and focus on that. This is an important part of the consulting process.

"As a recruiter, when you read a résumé, you look for some continuity: that what you're hiring an MBA for is some logical progression of what they've done before. The MBA will allow you to switch careers, but it's still a good idea to build on prior experiences.

"In general, the MBA is a screening device. Somebody who got into a good business school has something going for him or her. You find in an MBA the level of maturity you're looking for and the interpersonal skills of someone who has had several years of work experience."

their whole tuition paid for.

A survey of placement offices reveals that salaries are up an average of seven percent this year with salary and bonus packages ranging from $40,000 to $80,000. At the twenty or so most selective schools, the prime hunting grounds for consultants, thirty to forty percent of the graduating classes have heard the siren call of big money and signed on the dotted line with the consulting firms.

What will all this talent be doing? Many of them will be flying around the country to client companies to help them skinny-down and get more competitive. In boardrooms all across America this year, reengineering and restructuring management are big again. But to institute these changes, companies often require the help of outside consultants. Because of the breadth of companies and industries that MBAs as consultants are exposed to , consulting is seen as "MBA finishing school." Most new MBA hires will stay for only three years before joining industry as strategic planners and managers.

Where are the remainder of MBAs headed? Wall Street is taking a big chunk of the remaining students. Investment banking, sales and trading, and venture capital offer packages comparable to consulting. While the numbers going to Wall Street from the class of 1995 won't be available until past this book's publication date, over 45% of Harvard's 1994 class headed to The Street. That's up more than 25% over the year prior. The pendulum of Wall Street hires saw smaller entering classes in the early 90's as the deal flow shrank. But with mergers and acquisitions back in vogue, a slew of companies going public, and a boom in the equity and bond markets, Wall Street is opening its doors to MBAs again.

Mainstream industry also wants its share of MBAs. Like Wall Street, years of downsizing needs to be replenished with fresh hires and talent. For many companies, it's cheaper to

hire new MBAs through on-campus recruiting than through other means. MBAs are also attractive because they bring fresh, state-of-the-art ideas, are eager to implement them, can tackle the grittier, more complex problems of the modern business world, and most important, can make immediate contributions. As a MBA might put it, that's a solid return on one's investment.

Getting a Job

For most would-be MBAs, B-school represents a fresh beginning—either in their current profession or in an entirely different industry. Whatever promise the degree holds for you, it's wise to question what the return on your investment will be.

As with average starting salary, several factors affect job placement. School reputation and ties to industries and employers are important. At the top programs, the lists of recruiters read like a "Who's Who" of American companies. These schools not only attract the greatest volume of recruiters, but consistently get the attention of those considered blue chip.

Not to be overlooked are lesser-known, regional schools that often have the strongest relationships with local employers and industries. Some B-schools (many of them state universities) are regarded by both academicians and employers as number one in their respective regions. In other words, as far as the local business community is concerned, these programs offer as much prestige and pull as a nationally ranked program.

Student clubs also play a big part in getting a job, because they extend the recruiting efforts at many schools. They host a variety of events that allow you to meet leading business people, so that you can learn about their industries and their specific companies. Most important, these clubs are very effective at bringing in recruiters and other interested parties that do not recruit through traditional mainstream channels. For example, the high-tech, international, and enter-tainment student clubs provide career opportunities not available through the front door.

Another important factor is the industry you enter. Newly rediscovered fields such as marketing and manufacturing are red hot. Consulting and investment banking are popular, because salaries have stayed high. Brand management positions in packaged-goods companies are always appealing; you get to manage a product as though you were a mini-CEO. Companies off the

RECRUITER SPILLS THE BEANS

Liz Tunkiar,
Senior V.P. - Director of Personnel,
Ogilvy and Mather

"We've gone back and forth on whether we should hire MBAs. We've finally come to the conclusion that from an account point of view, they fit well into our organization.

"Many of our clients have MBAs—Kraft, General Foods, Unilever—so it makes sense that we hire MBAs to work on those businesses. They tend to have instant credibility with the client.

"MBAs have an advantage over BAs in that they bring a certain maturity to the account work. They also bring marketing knowledge and problem-solving and analytical skills.

"MBAs cost us more. We pay them higher salaries. In return we expect them to understand the business much more quickly than non-MBAs. We also expect them to move quickly up the learning curve and make immediate contributions.

"Obviously, this puts them on a faster track."

beaten track, such as start-up ventures, offer unique opportunities but many more unknowns.

Your background and experiences also affect your success in securing a position. Important factors are academic specialization (or course of study), academic standing, prior work experience, and intangibles such as your personal fit with the company. These days, what you did before B-school is particularly important; it helps establish credibility and gives you an edge in competing for a position in a specific field. For those using B-school to switch careers to a new industry, it's helpful if something on your résumé ties your interest to the new profession. It's smart to secure a summer job in the new area.

Finally, persistence and initiative are critical factors in the job search. Since the beginning of this decade, many fast tracks have been narrowed. Increasingly, even at the best schools, finding a job requires off-campus recruiting efforts and ferreting out the hidden jobs.

Friends Who Are Going Places, Alumni Who Are Already There

Most students say that the best part about B-school is meeting classmates with whom they share common goals and interests. Many students claim that the "single greatest resource is each other." Not surprisingly, with so many bright and ambitious people cocooned in one place, B-school can be the time of your life. It presents numerous professional and social opportunities. It can be where you find future customers, business partners, and mentors. It can also be where you establish lifelong friendships. And after graduation, these classmates form an enduring network of contacts and professional assistance.

Alumni are also an important part of the B-school experience. While professors teach business theory and practice, alumni provide insight into the real business world. When you're ready to interview, they can provide advice on how to get hired by the companies recruiting at your school. In some cases, they help secure the interview and shepherd you through the hiring process.

B-schools love to boast about the influence of their alumni network. To be sure, some are very powerful. But this varies from institution to institution. At the very least, alumni will help you get your foot in the door. A résumé sent to an alum at a given company, instead of "Dear Sir or Madam" in the personnel department, has a much better chance of being noticed and acted on.

After you graduate, the network continues to grow. Regional alumni clubs and alumni publications keep you plugged into the network with class notes on who's doing what, where, and with whom.

Throughout your career, an active alumni relations department can give you continued support. Post-MBA executive education series, fund-raising events, and continued job placement efforts are all resources you can draw on for years to come.

CHAPTER THREE

What B-School Is Really Like

The Changing Face of Business

In the last decade, B-schools have been taken to task. A recent article in *The Chronicle of Higher Education* observed, "Hardly a month passes without a new article in the business press lamenting the narrow, overly quantitative focus of graduate business curricula, the irrelevant research done by business schools' faculty members, and the inability of graduates to grapple successfully with the nation's economic problems. Reporters gleefully interview unemployed graduates of business schools and pump corporate executives for unflattering comments about their employees with Masters Degrees in Business Administration."

Things have certainly changed. In the 1980s, for example, Wall Street was the place to be. Investment bankers surfed on a monster wave of mergers and acquisitions. Students studied finance with an eye toward mega-deals. Today, with a soft Wall Street job market, high finance falling into discredit, and an economy besieged by invigorated foreign competitors, the focus is on building and delivering better products and services. Jobs may be easier to find in the Rust Belt than on Wall Street.

B-schools are responding to these challenges by carving out a new image for themselves. Many programs have sprouted social consciences. The '90s MBA student hardly resembles the Gordon Gekko stereotype (remember that evil arbitrager from the movie *Wall Street*?) of the '80s. Gone is the tolerance for avaricious, self-important MBAs. B-schools are recruiting students with broader, more humanitarian outlooks—students interested in contributing as much as in profit-taking. And, importantly, schools are trying to break down the rich-white-male stronghold on the business world by actively recruiting women and minorities.

Schools are also training students differently, both in content and in style. There's a move toward the medical-school model of education—learning by doing. Business "residencies," product "laboratories," and fieldwork augment classroom instruction with real-world experiences. Greater emphasis is being placed on public service and citizenship. Professional ethics classes are now mandatory in many schools. Outward Bound–style orientation and leadership programs are in vogue. Interpersonal communication skills, such as negotiation, conflict resolution, and team playing, have moved to the forefront. In short, the "bottom line" is no longer the bottom line.

Much has been made in recent years of the rise of a global economy. To make sure MBAs have the skills necessary to be effective in this economy, leading business programs have developed courses on global business operations and international economics. To teach sensitive leadership in an increasingly multicultural work force, they've enhanced offerings on cultural diversity and human resources.

One other change is worth noting. The reason that the average age of the business school student has steadily increased to the current high of twenty-seven is that B-schools have sought older students to satisfy the new demands of the marketplace. Recruiters want graduates with more than a degree; they want the skills that come with maturity, and the maturity that comes with several years of work experience.

An Academic Perspective

The objective of all MBA programs is to prepare students for a professional career in business. One business school puts it this way:

Graduates should be

1. Able to think and reason independently, creatively, and analytically

2. Skilled in the use of quantitative techniques

3. Literate in the use of software applications as management tools

4. Knowledgeable about the world's management issues and problems

5. Willing to work in and successfully cope with conditions of uncertainty, risk, and change

6. Astute decision makers

7. Ethically and socially responsible

Sound like a tall order? Possibly. But this level of expectation is what business school is all about.

All MBA programs feature a core curriculum that focuses students on the major disciplines of business: finance, management, accounting, marketing, manufacturing, decision sciences, economics, and organizational behavior. Unless your school allows you to place out of them, these courses are mandatory. Core courses provide broad functional knowledge in one discipline. For example, a core marketing course covers pricing, segmentation, communications, product line planning, and implementation. Electives provide a narrow focus that deepens the area of study. For example, a marketing elective might be entirely devoted to pricing.

Students sometimes question the need for such a comprehensive core program. But the functional areas of a real business are not parallel lines. All departments of a business affect each other every day. For example, an MBA in a manufacturing job might be asked by a financial controller why the company's product has become unprofitable to produce. Without an understanding of how product costs are accounted for, this MBA wouldn't know how to respond to a critical and legitimate request.

At most schools, the first term or year is devoted to a rigid core curriculum. Some schools allow first-years to take core courses side by side with electives. Still others have come up with an entirely new way of covering the basics, integrating the core courses into one cross-functional learning experience, which may also include sessions on '90s topics such as globalization, ethics, and managing diversity. Half-year to year-long courses are team-taught by professors who see you through all the disciplines.

Teaching Methodology

Business schools employ two basic teaching methods: case-study and lecture. Usually, they employ some combination of the two. The most popular is the case-study approach. Students are presented with either real or hypothetical business scenarios and are asked to analyze them. This method provides concrete situations (rather than abstractions) that require mastery of a wide range of skills. Students often find case studies exciting because they can engage in spirited discussions about possible solutions to given business problems and because they get an opportunity to apply newly acquired business knowledge.

The other teaching method used by B-schools is lecturing, in which—you guessed it—the professor speaks to the class and the class listens. The efficacy of the lecture method depends entirely on the professor. If the professor is compelling, you'll probably get a lot out of the class. If the professor is boring, you probably won't listen. Which isn't necessarily a big deal, since many professors make their class notes available on computer disc or in the library.

The Classroom Experience

Professors teaching case methodology often begin class with a "cold call." A randomly selected student opens the class with an analysis of the case and makes recommendations for solutions. The cold call forces you to be prepared and think on your feet.

No doubt, a cold call can be intimidating. But unlike law school, B-school professors don't use the Socratic method to torture you, testing your thinking with a pounding cross-examination. They're training managers, not trial lawyers. At worst, particularly if you're unprepared, a professor will abruptly dismiss your contributions.

Alternatively, professors ask for a volunteer to open a case, particularly someone who has had real industry experience with the issues. After the opening, the discussion is broadened to include the whole class. Everyone tries to get in a good comment, particularly if class participation counts heavily toward the grade. "Chip shots"—unenlightening, just-say-anything-to-get-credit comments—are common. So are "air hogs," students who go on and on because they like nothing more than to hear themselves pontificate.

Depending on the school, sometimes class discussions degenerate into wars of ego rather than ideas. But for the most part, debates are kept constructive and civilized. Students are competitive, but not offensively so, and learn to make their points succinctly and persuasively.

Your First Year

The first six months of B-school can be daunting. You're unfamiliar with the subjects. There's a tremendous amount of work to do. And when you least have the skills to do so, there's pressure to stay with the pack. All of this produces anxiety and a tendency to overprepare. Eventually, students learn shortcuts and settle into a routine, but until then much of the first year is just plain tough. The programs usually pack more learning into the first term than they do into each of the remaining terms. For the schools to teach the core curriculum (which accounts for as much as seventy percent of learning) in a limited time, an intensive pace is considered necessary. Much of the second year will be spent on gaining proficiency in your area of expertise and searching for a job.

The good news is that the schools recognize how tough the first year can be. During the early part of the program, they anchor students socially by placing them in small sections. You take many or all of your classes with your section-mates. Sectioning encourages the formation of personal and working relationships and can help make a large program feel like a school within a school.

Because so much has to be accomplished in so little time, getting an MBA is like living in fast-forward. This is especially true of the job search. No sooner are you in the program than

A RECENT GRAD LOOKS BACK

"I went to work for IBM straight out of undergraduate school. Within a year or two, I decided to get my MBA—part-time. I never considered going full-time. Not having any money? I couldn't deal with that. Unfortunately, after one year in the program I quit because I didn't have clear goals for myself. Several years later I returned. This time I was ready.

"Depending on your background, some of the core courses are not exactly pleasant or stimulating. If you don't have a business background, you'll benefit from them tremendously. They provide a good foundation. I had some waived because I had taken them as an undergrad. The courses I really enjoyed were advanced electives like strategic management.

"Most of my professors left successful careers in business to teach. They brought their practical experience into the classroom. You know the expression, 'Those who can do—do. Those who can't—teach.' This isn't so at business school.

continued on the next page

recruiters for summer jobs show up, which tends to divert students from their studies. First-years aggressively pursue summer positions, which are linked with the promise of a permanent job offer if the summer goes well. At some schools the recruiting period begins as early as October, at others in January or February.

In Your Second Year

Relax, the second year is easier. By now, students know what's important and what's not. Second-years work more efficiently than first-years. Academic anxiety is no longer a factor. Having mastered the broad-based core curriculum, students now enjoy taking electives and developing an area of specialization.

Anxiety in the second year has to do more with the arduous task of finding a job. For some lucky students, a summer position has yielded a full-time offer. But even those students often go through the whole recruiting grind anyway, because they don't want to cut off any opportunities prematurely.

Most MBAs leave school with a full-time offer. Sometimes it's their only offer. Sometimes it's not their dream job. Which may be why most grads change jobs after just two years.

One University of Chicago Business School student summed up the whole two-year academic/recruiting process like this: "The first-year students collapse in the winter quarter because of on-campus recruiting. The second-years collapse academically in the first quarter of their second year because it's so competitive to get a good job. And when a second-year does get a job, he or she forgets about class entirely. That's why pass/fail was invented."

Life Outside of Class

Business school is more than academics and a big-bucks job. A spirited student community provides ample opportunities for social interaction, extracurricular activity, and career development.

Much of campus life revolves around student-run clubs. There are groups for just about every career interest and social need—from "MBAs for a Greener America" to the "Small Business Club." There's even a spouse group for significant others on most campuses. The clubs are a great way to meet classmates with similar interests and get in on the social scene. They might have a reputation for throwing the best black-tie balls, pizza and keg events, and professional mixers. During orientation week, these clubs aggressively market themselves to first-years.

Various socially responsible projects are also popular on campus. An emphasis on volunteer work is part of the overall trend toward good citizenship. Perhaps to counter the greed of the '80s, "giving back" is the B-school style of the moment. There is usually a wide range of options—from tutoring in an inner-city school to working in a soup kitchen to renovating public buildings.

Still another way to get involved is to work on a school committee. Here you might serve on a task force designed to improve student quality of life. Or you might work in the admissions office and interview prospective students.

For those with more creative urges there are always the old standbys: extracurriculars such as the school paper, yearbook, or school play. At some schools, the latter takes the form of the B-school follies and is a highlight of the year. Like the student clubs, these are a great way to get to know your fellow students.

Finally, you can play on intramural sports teams or attend the numerous informal get-togethers, dinner parties, and group trips. There are also plenty of regularly scheduled pub nights, just in case you thought your beer-guzzling days were over.

Most former MBA students say that going to B-school was the best decision they ever made. That's primarily because of non-academic experiences. Make the most of your classes, but take the time to get involved and enjoy yourself.

"Females at my school were well-represented. But in terms of minority ethnic groups—Black and Hispanic, and that applies to myself—these were underrepresented. I could count on my two hands how many minorities were in that program. This is not an indictment of the school, it's just that as a minority, you have to be comfortable with the numbers.

"There's a lot of press out there that says the MBA is not the golden ticket it's cracked up to be. But it does make you more competitive. I remember interviewing for a job in one of the other IBM offices. I had just started the MBA program again, and this manager said, 'It's really good you're doing that. All the other people who work for me have MBAs. Every one of them.' So I can see the degree helping with my short- and long-term career goals.

"The MBA gave me credibility. It helped me understand my customers' needs better. Business school changes HOW you think about a problem. And I've made better business decisions because of that."

Female MBA, Graduate School of Business, Claremont College, 1991 Manager, IBM

A DAY IN THE LIFE OF A STUDENT

Male MBA, First Year
Kenan-Flagler Business School,
The University of North Carolina at Chapel Hill

7:00 am: Review notes for my first class.

7:30 am: Eat some high-energy flake cereal; read *The Wall Street Journal*—professors like to discuss news items that relate to the class topics.

8:00 am: Read review for quantitative methods exam; do practice problems; reread case on control systems for organizational behavior class.

9:00 am: Arrive at school. Go to "reading room" to hang out with everyone. Check student mailbox for invitations to recruiter events.

9:30 am: Integrative Management Class: Guest speaker from case-study discusses how the company approached problems.

10:45 am: Hang out.

11:00 am: Organizational Behavior Class: Get in a couple of good comments; debate the effectiveness of a management decision with another student in class.

12:15 pm: Grab some lunch and sit with friends. Talk about the lousy cafeteria food and who's dating whom.

1:00 pm: Go back to reading room to review for 2:00 class.

2:00 pm: Microeconomics Class: Listen to lecture on monopolistic competition.

3:15 pm: Arrive at home, change into work-out clothes. Go running, lift weights—relax.

6:00 pm: Eat dinner; watch the news. Read the next day's case.

7:30 pm: Head back to campus for study group.

7:45 pm: Discuss cases, help each other with homework problems on interpreting regression statistics; discuss how to account for capital leases versus operating leases.

10:00 pm: Back at home. Review more cases, read next class assignment in textbook, work on problem set.

Midnight: Sports on ESPN till I fall asleep. Boardroom dreams.

Female MBA, Second Year
The Fuqua School of Business, Duke University

6:45 am: Get dressed, listen to CNN and pick up *The Wall Street Journal* on way to school.

8:00 am: Arrive at school. Bargaining and Negotiations class. Perform role play on conflict resolution.

10:15 am: Hang out—grab a bagel.

10:30 am: Intermediate Accounting Class—Discussion on cash flow statements—nothing exciting.

12:45 pm: Arrive at admissions office to review résumé of applicant to B-school.

1:00 pm: Conduct interview of applicant.

1:45 pm: Write evaluation of candidate. Hand in to admissions secretary.

2:00 pm: Attend quality advisory board meeting—discuss creation of corporate survey.

3:30 pm: Competitive Strategy class. Lecture on barriers to entry.

5:45 pm: Attend recruiter event. Tell the recruiter how interested I am in the industry (I know nothing about it).

7:45 pm: Over to the health club for aerobics.

8:45 pm: Drive home, eat dinner, and finally read *The Wall Street Journal*—of course, it's not news by now.

9:30 pm: Study class notes, prepare next day's case.

11:45 pm: Quality phone time with my boyfriend.

12:30 pm: Boardroom dreams.

CHAPTER FOUR

Preparing to Be a Successful Applicant

Get Good Grades

If you're still in school, work on getting good grades. A high GPA says you've not only got brains, but discipline. It shows the admissions committee you have what you need to make it through the program. If you're applying directly from college, or have limited job experience, your grades will matter even more. The admissions committee has little else on which to evaluate you.

It's especially important that you do well in courses such as economics, statistics, and calculus. Success in these courses is more meaningful than your success in classes like "Monday Night at the Movies" film appreciation. Of course, English is also important; B-schools want students who communicate well.

Strengthen Math Skills

Number-crunching is an inescapable part of B-school. Take an accounting or statistics course for credit at a local college or B-school. If you have a liberal arts background, did poorly in math, or got a low GMAT math score, this is especially important. Get a decent grade and this will go a long way toward convincing the admissions committee you can manage the quantitative challenges of the program.

Work for a Few Years—But Not *Too* Many

Business schools favor applicants who have worked full time for several years. There are three primary reasons for this: 1) With experience comes maturity. 2) You're more likely to know what you want out of the program. 3) Your experience enables you to bring real-work perspectives to the classroom. Since business school is designed for you to learn from your classmates, each student's contribution is important.

How many years of work experience should you have? Two to five seems to be the preferred amount, although there is no magic number. The rationale is that at two years you've worked enough to be able to make a solid contribution. Beyond four or five, you may be too advanced in your career to appreciate the program fully. You may also have reached a salary level too pricey for most recruiters.

If your grades are weak, consider working at least three years before applying. The more professional success you have, the greater the likelihood the admissions committee will overlook your GPA.

Let Your Job Work for You

Many companies encourage employees to go to B-school. Some of these companies have close ties to a favored B-school and produce well-qualified applicants. If their employees are going to the kinds of schools you want to get into, these may be smart places to work.

Other companies, such as investment banks, feature training

programs at the end of which trainees go to B-school or leave the company. These programs hire undergraduates right out of school. They're known for producing solid, highly skilled applicants. Moreover, they're full of well-connected alumni who may write influential letters of recommendation.

Happily, the opposite tactic—working in an industry that generates few applicants—can be equally effective. Admissions officers look for students from underrepresented professions. Applicants from biotechnology, health care, not-for-profit, and even the Peace Corps are viewed favorably.

One way to set yourself apart is to have had two entirely different professional experiences before business school. For example, if you worked in finance, your next job might be in a different field, like marketing. Supplementing quantitative work with qualitative experiences demonstrates versatility.

Finally, what you do on your job is important. Seek out opportunities to distinguish yourself. Even if your responsibilities are limited, exceed the expectations of the position. B-schools are looking for leaders.

March from the Military

A surprising number of business school students hail from the military (although the armed forces probably had commanders in mind, not CEOs, when they designed their regimen).

Military officers know how to be managers because they've held command positions. And they know how to lead a team under the most difficult of circumstances.

Because most have traveled all over the world, they also know how to work with people from different cultures. As a result, they're ideally suited to learn alongside students with diverse backgrounds and perspectives. B-schools with a global focus are particularly attracted to such experience.

The decision to enlist in the military is a very personal one. However, if you've thought of joining those few good men and women, this may be as effective a means of preparing for business school as more traditional avenues.

Check Out Those Essay Questions *Now*

You're worried you don't have interesting stories to tell. Or you just don't know what to write. What do you do?

Ideally, several months before your application is due, you should read the essay questions and begin to think about your answers. Could you describe an ethical dilemma at work? Are you involved in anything outside the office (or classroom)? If not, now is the time to do something about it. While this may seem contrived, it's preferable to sitting down to write the application and finding you have to scrape for or, worse, manufacture situations.

Use the essay questions as a framework for your personal and professional activities. Look back over your business calendar and see if you can find some meaty experiences for the essays in your work life. Keep your eyes open for a situation that involves questionable ethics. And if all you do is work, work, work, get involved in activities that round out your background. In other words, get a life.

Get involved in community-based activities. Some possibilities are being a big brother/big sister, tutoring in a literacy program, or even initiating a recycling project. Demonstrating a concern for others looks good to admissions committees, and hey, it's good for your soul, too.

It's also important to seek out leadership experiences. B-schools are looking for individuals who can manage groups. Volunteer to chair a professional committee or get elected to an office in a club.

It's a wide-open world; you can pick from any number of activities. The bottom line is this: The extracurriculars you select can show that you are mature, multifaceted, and appealing.

We don't mean to sound cynical. Obviously, the best applications do nothing more than describe your true, heartfelt interests and show off your sparkling personality. We're not suggesting you try to guess which activity will win the hearts of admissions directors and then mold yourself accordingly. Instead, think of projects and activities you care about, that maybe you haven't gotten around to acting on, and act on them now!

Pick Your Recommendors Carefully

By the time you apply to business school, you shouldn't have to scramble for recommendations. Like the material for your essays, sources for recommendations should be considered long before the application is due.

How do you get great recommendations? Obviously, good work is a prerequisite. Whom you ask is equally important. Bosses who know you well will recommend you on both a personal and professional level. They can provide specific examples of your accomplishments, skills, and character. Additionally, they can convey a high level of interest in your candidacy.

There's also the issue of trust. Business school recommendations are made in confidence; you probably won't see what's been written about you. Choose someone you can trust to deliver the kind of recommendation that will push you over the top. A casual acquaintance may fail you by writing an adequate, yet mostly humdrum letter.

Cultivate relationships that yield glowing recommendations. Former and current professors, employers, clients, and managers are all good choices. An equally impressive recommendation can come from someone who has observed you in a worthwhile extracurricular activity.

Left to their own devices, a recommendor may create a portrait that leaves out your best features. You need to prep them on what to write. Remind them of those projects or activities in which you achieved some success. You might also discuss the total picture of yourself you're trying to create. The recommendation should reinforce what you're saying about yourself in your essays.

About "Big Shot" recommendations: don't bother. Getting some golf pro who's a friend of your dad's to write you a recommendation will do you no good if he doesn't know you very well, even if he is President of the Universe. Don't try to fudge your application—let people who really know you and your work tell the honest, believable, and impressive truth.

Prepare for the
Graduate Management Admission Test (GMAT)

Most B-schools require you to take the GMAT. The GMAT is a three-and-a-half-hour standardized multiple-choice exam with math and verbal sections. It's the kind of test you hate to take and schools love to demand of you.

Why is the GMAT required? The B-schools believe it measures your verbal and quantitative skills and predicts success in the MBA program. Some think this is a bunch of hooey, most notably the Harvard Business School, which does not require the exam. But for most other schools, the GMAT is weighed heavily in the admissions decision. If nothing else, it gives the school a frame of reference with which to compare you against other applicants.

Most people feel they have no control over the GMAT. They dread it as the potential bomb in their application. But you have more control than you think. You can take a test-preparation course which reviews the math and verbal material, teaches you test-taking strategies, and builds your confidence. Test-prep courses can be highly effective. But if the course you select won't guarantee you a score improvement of at least 70 points, don't take it. You haven't found the best test-preparation course out there.

How many times should you take the GMAT? More than once, if you didn't ace it on the first try. But watch out: Multiple scores that fall in the same range make you look unprepared. Don't take the test more than once if you don't expect a decent increase, and don't even think of taking it the first time without serious preparation. Two tries is best. Three, if there were unusual circumstances or you really need another shot at it. If you take it more than three times, the admissions committee will think you have an unhealthy obsession with filling in dots. A final note: If you submit more than one score, most schools will take the highest. Otherwise, they'll take the average.

If you don't have math courses on your college transcript or numbers-oriented work experience, it's especially important to get a solid score on the quantitative section. There's a lot of math between you and the MBA.

CHAPTER FIVE

Admissions

HOW THE ADMISSIONS CRITERIA ARE WEIGHTED
What They Count

Admissions requirements vary from institution to institution.
Most rely on the following criteria (not necessarily in order):
GMAT score, college GPA, work experience, essays, letters of
recommendation, interviews, and extracurriculars, of which the
first four are the most heavily weighted. The more competitive the
school, the less room there is for weakness in any one of these areas.

Most applicants suspect that the GMAT score or GPA pushes their application into one of three piles: "yes," "no," or "maybe." But that's not the way it is. Unless one or more of your numbers is so low it forces a rejection, the piles are "looks good," "looks bad," "hmmm, interesting," and all variations of "maybe." In B-school admissions, the whole is greater than the sum of the parts. Each of the numbers has an effect but doesn't provide the total picture.

What's fair about the system is that you can compensate for problem areas. Even if you have a low GMAT score, evidence of a high GPA, quantitative work experience, or the completion of an accounting or statistics course will provide a strong counter-balance.

As we've said, no one single thing counts more than everything else. Your scores, work experience, and essays should give the admissions committee a clear idea of your capabilities, interests, and accomplishments. Any particular weakness can be overcome by a particular strength in another area—so make sure you emphasize whatever strengths you have and don't take them for granted.

The GMAT and GPA

The GMAT score and GPA are used in two ways. First, they're used as "success indicators" for the academic work. In other words, if admitted, will you have the brain power and discipline to make it through the program? Second, they're used to compare applicants against the larger pool. In particular, the top schools like applicant pools with high scores. They think that having an incoming class with high score and grade profiles is an indicator of their program's prestige and selectivity.

Some schools look more closely at junior and senior year grades than the overall GPA. Most consider the academic reputation of your college and the difficulty of your curriculum. A transcript loaded with courses like "Environmental Appreciation" and "The Child in You" isn't valued as highly as one with a more substantive agenda.

Work Experience

Of all the criteria, your work history is perhaps the most crucial to acceptance. It provides tangible evidence of your performance in the business world thus far and hints at your potential. This helps B-schools determine if you're going to turn out to be the kind of graduate they'll be proud to have as an alum. Your work experience also reveals whether you've progressed enough (or too far) to benefit from a B-school education. Last, your experience sheds light on the industry perspective you'll bring to the program.

Five elements are considered. First, the stature of your company: Does it have a high reputation? Does it produce well-qualified applicants?

Second, diversity of work experience. Have you started your own business, invented a new software program, or worked in an industry that is underrepresented at the prospective school?

Third, your advancement: Did you progress steadily to ever-more-responsible positions, or did you just tread water? Do your salary increases prove that you are a strong performer? Did you put in your time at each job, or just jump from company to company?

Fourth, your professional and interpersonal skills: Did you get along well with others? Work as part of a team? Do your recommendors see you as future manager material?

Fifth (and this is critical), your leadership potential: Did you excel in your positions, go beyond the job descriptions, save the day, lead a team?

The Essays

Admissions committees consider the essays the clincher, the swing vote on the "admit/deny" issue. Essays offer the most substance about who you really are. The GMAT and GPA reveal little about you, only that you won't crash and burn. Your work history provides a record of performance and justifies your stated desire to study business. But the essays tie all the pieces of the application together and create a summary of your experiences, skills, background, and beliefs.

The essays do more than give answers to questions. They create thumbnail psychological profiles. Depending on how you answer a question or what you present, you reveal yourself in any number of ways—creative, witty, open-minded, articulate, mature—to name a few. Likewise, your essay can reveal a negative side, such as arrogance, sloppiness, or an inability to think and write clearly. In essence, the essays don't just complete the picture. They are the inside picture.

The Recommendations

Admissions committees expect recommendations to support and reinforce the rest of the application. They act as a sort of reality check. When the information from your recommendor doesn't match up with the information you've provided, it looks bad.

Great recommendations are rarely enough to save a weak application from doom. But they might push a borderline case over to the "admit" pile.

Mediocre recommendations are potentially harmful: an application that is strong in all other areas now has an inconsistency that's hard to ignore.

Bad recommendations—meaning that negative information is provided—cast doubt on the picture you've created. In some cases they invalidate your claims. This can mean the end for your application. Again, be careful whom you ask for recommendations.

The Interview

Like the recommendations, the interview is used to reinforce the total picture. But it is also used to fill in the blanks, particularly in borderline cases.

A great interview can tip the scale in the "admit" direction. How do you know if it was great? You were calm and focused. You expressed yourself and your ideas clearly. Your interviewer invited you to go rock climbing with him next weekend. (O.K., let's just say you developed a solid personal rapport with the interviewer.)

A mediocre interview may not have much impact, unless your application is hanging on by a thread. In such a case, the person you're talking to (harsh as it may seem) is probably looking for a reason *not* to admit you, rather than a reason to let you in. If you feel your application may be in that hazy, marginal area, try to be inspired in your interview.

Did you greet your interviewer by saying, "Gee, are all admissions officers as pretty as you?" Did you show up wearing a Karl Marx tee-shirt? Did you bring your mother with you? If so, it's probably safe to say you had a poor interview. A poor interview can doom even a straight-A, high-GMAT, strong-work-history candidate. Use good taste, refrain from belching, avoid insulting the interviewer's tie, and you'll probably be O.K.

Not all B-schools attach equal value to the interview. For some, it's an essential screening tool. For others, it's used to evaluate borderline cases. Still others strongly encourage, but do not require, the interview. Some schools make it simply informative. If you can't schedule an on-campus interview, the admissions office may find an alum to meet with you in your hometown.

If an interview is offered, take it. In person, you may be an entirely more compelling candidate. You can further address weaknesses or bring dull essays to life. Most important, you can display the kinds of qualities—enthusiasm, sense of humor, maturity—that often fill in the blanks and sway a decision.

In general, B-school interviews are not formulaic. The focus can range from specific questions about your job responsibilities to broad discussions of life. Approach the interview as a conversation to be enjoyed, not as a question-and-answer ordeal to get through. You may talk more about your hobbies or recent cross-country trip. This doesn't mean that it won't feel like a job interview. It just means you're being sized up as a person and future professional in *all* your dimensions. Try to be your witty, charming, natural self.

Interviews are conducted by students, faculty, admissions personnel, and alumni. Don't dismiss students as the lightweights; they follow a tight script and report back to the committee. However, because they're inexperienced beyond the script, their interviews are most likely to be duds. You may have to work harder to get your points across.

Prepare for the interview in several ways: Expect to discuss *many* things about yourself. Be ready to go into greater depth than you did in your essays (but don't assume the interviewer has read them). Put together two or three points about yourself that you want the interviewer to remember you by. Go in with examples, or even a portfolio of your work, to showcase your achievements. Practice speaking about your accomplishments without a lot of "I did this, I did that's." Finally, be prepared to give a strong and convincing answer to the interviewer's inevitable question, "Why here?"

How to Blow the Interview

1. Wear casual clothes.

This is an automatic ding. Wearing anything but professional attire suggests you don't know, or want to play by, the rules of the game.

2. Bring your mom or dad. Or talk about them.

Business schools value maturity. If Mom or Dad brings you to the interview, or your answer to the question "Why an MBA," begins with "Dad always told me . . . ," the interviewer is going to wonder how ready you are for the adult world of business school.

3. Talk about high school.

Again, they'll question your maturity. Stories about high school, and even college, suggest you haven't moved on to more mature, new experiences.

Exceptions: Explaining a unique situation or a low GPA.

4. Show up late.

This is another automatic ding at some schools. Short of a real catastrophe, you won't be excused.

5. Say something off the wall or inappropriate.

No doubt, the conversation can get casual and you may start to let your guard down. But certain things are still off-limits: profanity, ethnic jokes, allusions to sex, your romantic life, and anything else that might signal the interviewer that the cheese fell off your cracker.

6. Forget to write a thank-you note to your interviewer.

Sending a thank-you note means you know how to operate in the business world, and it goes a long way toward convincing the interviewer you belong there.

MAKING THE ROUNDS: WHEN TO APPLY

You worked like a dog on your application—is there anything else you can do to increase your odds of getting accepted? Perhaps. The filing period ranges anywhere from six to eight months. Therefore, the *timing* of your application can make a difference. Although there are no guarantees, the earlier you apply, the better your chances. Here's why:

First, there's plenty of space available early on. As the application deadline nears, spaces fill up. The majority of applicants don't apply until the later months because of procrastination or unavoidable delays. As the deadline draws close, the greatest number of applicants compete for the fewest number of spaces.

Second, in the beginning, admissions officers have little clue about how selective they can be. They haven't reviewed enough applications to determine the competitiveness of the pool. An early application may be judged more on its own merit than how it stacks up against others. This is in your favor if the pool turns out to be unusually competitive. Above all, admissions officers like to lock their classes in early; they can't be certain they'll get their normal supply of applicants. Admissions decisions may be more generous at this time.

Third, by getting your application in early you're showing a strong interest. The admissions committee is likely to view you as someone keen on going to their school.

To be sure, some admissions officers report that the first batch of applications tend to be from candidates with strong qualifications, confident of acceptance. In this case, you might not be the very first one on line; but closer to the front is still better than lost in the heap of last-minute hopefuls.

Of course, if applications are down that year at all B-schools or—thanks to the latest drop in its ranking—at the one to which you are applying, then filing later means you can benefit from admissions officers desperately filling spaces. But this is risky business, especially since the rankings don't come out until the spring.

Conversely, if the school to which you are applying was recently ranked number one or two, applying early may make only a marginal difference. Swings in the rankings from year to year send school applications soaring and sagging. From beginning to end, a newly minted number-one or -two school will be flooded with applications.

Rounds and Rolling Admissions

Applications are processed in one of two ways—rounds admissions or rolling admissions. With rounds, the filing period is divided into three to four timed cycles. Applications are batched into the round in which they are received and reviewed competitively with others in that grouping. A typical round might go from February 15th to March 15th.

With rolling admissions, applications are reviewed on an ongoing basis as they are received. The response time for a rolling admissions decision is usually quicker than a decision with rounds. And with rolling admissions, when all the spaces are full, admissions stop.

QUOTAS, RECRUITMENT, AND DIVERSITY

Business schools don't have to operate under quotas—governmental or otherwise. However, they probably try harder than most corporations to recruit diverse groups of people. Just as the modern business world has become global and multicultural, so too have the B-schools. They must not only preach diversity in the classroom but make it a reality in their campus population and, if possible, faculty.

Schools that have a diverse student body tend to be proud of it. They tout their success in profiles that demographically slice and dice the previous year's class by sex, race, and geographic and international residency. Prospective students can review these data and decide whether the school will provide them with the experience they desire: a cosmopolitan, international group of classmates.

But such diversity doesn't come naturally from the demographics of the applicant pool. Admissions committees have to work hard at it. While they don't have quotas per se, they do target groups for admission. Most notably, these are women and minorities. In some cases, enrollment is encouraged with generous financial aid packages and scholarships.

But those targeted for admission are not limited to women and minorities. The committees seek demographic balance in many areas. Have they admitted enough foreign students, marketing strategists, and liberal arts majors? Are different parts of the country represented?

Only toward the end of the admissions filing period do shortages in different categories emerge. Although you can't predict, women and minorities are almost always on the short list.

WHO ARE THOSE ADMISSIONS OFFICERS?
One School's Committee Revealed

Just who are those nameless, faceless people who pore over thousands of applications and determine the future of budding CEOs like you?

Most applicants picture a committee of white male MBAs in blue suits and power ties. But that's not the whole picture. Although many admissions officers do hold MBAs, they represent a wider slice of the demographic spectrum than do the business school classes they admit. There are more women. And more studied liberal arts and worked in fields such as human resources and teaching. In short, they're a diverse group.

But as diverse as they are in background, they share a certain perspective: they believe that *qualities*, such as drive and discipline, rather than *skills*, such as financial analysis, are the true and enduring engines of success. In other words, at least as much value is placed on who you are as on your accomplishments.

Why does knowing this help you? Because in writing your application you need to consider your audience. Admissions officers aren't necessarily the people you thought they were. Moreover, they don't necessarily share your love of business. Their role in the business world is different from yours: They sustain the profession by launching inductees, while you actually practice business. Many officers, even some with MBAs, have limited business experience.

Remember, they're not only admissions officers, they're daughters, sons, mothers, fathers, and grandparents too—in other words, regular people. Would you write the same kind of essay for them that you would for your boss? The essays for B-school should be a combination of the two: strong on substance and heavy on personality.

Here's who reads your application at the Columbia B-school:

THE DIRECTOR OF ADMISSIONS

Gender: Male
Race/Ethnicity: White
Age: Mid-30s
Marital/Family: Single
College Major: Accounting/Economics
Graduate Degree: MBA
First Job out of Graduate School: Brand Manager

> "In the '80s, applications were just flowing in. But now, admissions is a real marketing challenge. I enjoy it; I'm out meeting students, helping them identify their goals, and talking about how our school might be right for them. Because I went through this program, I have an understanding of what it takes to be successful in this environment. I can gauge how realistic the applicant's expectations of B-school are."

ADMISSIONS OFFICER

Gender: Female
Race/Ethnicity: African-American
Age: Mid-30s
Marital/Family: Married/Mother
College Major: French/Political Science
Graduate Degree: M.A. in French, M.S. in Law and Diplomacy
First Job Out of Graduate School: French instructor; developing public policy for higher education

> "My previous work in undergraduate admissions gives me a unique point of view in reviewing MBA applications: I expect an applicant to be able to fully articulate why getting the degree is important. If the reasoning isn't clear, it's a problem. I also look for applicants who can bring something special to the student community—really add to the program and yet take advantage of all that we have to offer."

ADMISSIONS OFFICER

Gender: Female
Race/Ethnicity: White
Age: Late 40s
Marital/Family: Married, Grandmother
College Major: English
Graduate Degree: One year in law school—dropped out to be "ski bum"; M.S. in Reading; Candidate for Ph.D. in philosophy
First Job Out of Graduate School: Teacher in an inner-city high school

"Based on my experiences as a teacher, I can see how some applicants will succeed even with a weak academic history. I err on the side of 'wait—don't reject this student just because the GMAT or academic cum isn't high on the charts.' Other things will refocus me on their application: a unique job experience, compliments that people made about the applicant that are very telling, or something that alludes to depth or potential."

ADMISSIONS OFFICER

Gender: Female
Race/Ethnicity: Indian
Age: Late 20s
Marital/Family: Married
College Major: Art History/Asian Studies
Graduate Degree: MBA
First Job out of Graduate School: Strategic Planning and Financial Manager

"As a recent graduate, I try to bring several perspectives to the admissions process: that of an applicant, a matriculant, and a young professional. Because of my international background, I understand the importance of diversity. I look for applicants who show this in both their professional and personal experiences."

ADMISSIONS OFFICER

Gender: Female
Race/Ethnicity: White
Age: Early 30s
Marital/Family: Married
College Major: English
Graduate Degree: M.A. in Writing
First Job Out of Graduate School: English teacher for grades 9–12

"Admission to B-school is not the experiment of science nor game of roulette that people often think it is. When I review an applicant's profile, I don't fill in columns and rows with data. Making a decision is a very difficult, thought-filled, and time-intensive process. I'm always aware that I'm working with the summary of a person's intellect, talent, culture, and aspirations. On Commencement Day, it's a fact that after the students, the admissions officers are the second happiest group in the school. On that day, everyone knows the decision and the relationship was successful!"

ADMISSIONS CONSULTANT

Gender: Female
Race/Ethnicity: White
Age: Mid-30s
Marital/Family: Married
College Major: Stage and Theater
First Job Out of School: Actress
Career Prior to Admissions: Stage Director/Administrative Consultant

"I look for clear goals that are realistic and born of experience. When applicants can't articulate why they want the MBA, it's a concern. They don't have to have all the answers, but they should have a sound reason for wanting to be here. I'm also looking for people who have a sense of personal responsibility in the world. It's not a bad thing when a candidate says 'the MBA will help me strengthen the family business.' But I'd like to see somewhere else in the application that their universe is greater than themselves."

WHO DO YOU THINK READS YOUR ESSAYS?

Now that you know who those admissions officers are, here's the next surprise. Many top business schools farm out the essays to paid readers. Why would the schools use readers instead of trained admissions officers to evaluate the essays? The answer is volume. As the number of applications to top business schools has soared, it has become cost-effective to hire part-timers to do the most time-intensive work. Admissions officers are then free to make the higher-level admissions decisions.

Most applicants wouldn't be pleased to know that the essay they worked on for two weeks isn't being read by an admissions officer. But admissions committees couldn't be more pleased. Now instead of an enormous pile of unread essays—some terrific, some not—they have a pile that's been evaluated. Moreover, they point out, the essays are now read in greater depth than before.

But what you need to know is this: How do readers affect the admissions decision?

At most schools readers make general recommendations, then pass them on to other members of the committee for other opinions. They don't have the authority to make a final judgment. They're trained to evaluate essays in the same way admissions officers do—writing style, content, message, etc. More than one staff member usually reads them, often a combination of reader and admissions officer, so a reader's opinion is not the only one. Also, readers don't examine or have input into the evaluation of the applicant's total candidacy.

INSIDE BABSON'S ADMISSIONS DEPARTMENT:
What Really Happens to Your Application

Are specific weights or scores assigned to each component of the application?

Do admissions committees get together and read them at one big table—or do they take them home and cover them with coffee stains?

How many people read your essays? How do they decide if they're good or terrible? If there is a system for standardizing the reading of the essays? Are they graded? Are there disagreements? How are they resolved?

Who are the surprise admits, the surprise rejects? Why are some students put on the wait list? What can be done to pull them off?

These are just a few of the questions surrounding an admissions process that often operates with the concealment strategies of the CIA. But all is not lost. The Babson Graduate School of Business agreed to open its files for our review. And while this is only one school's admissions process, there are certainly some interesting conclusions to be drawn. Here's a flow chart of their process:

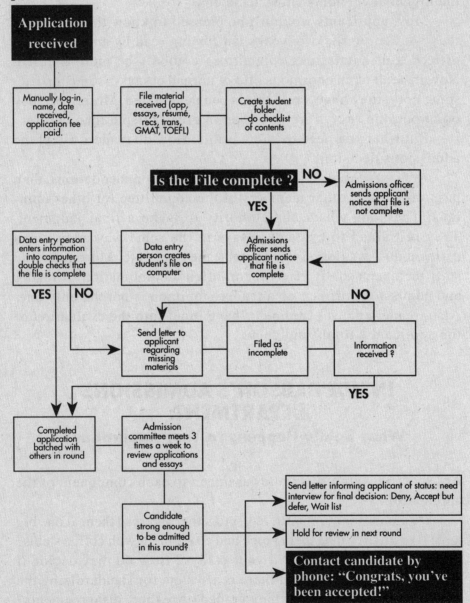

NOW WE CAN TAKE A CLOSER LOOK:
The Babson Admissions Challenge

The Babson admissions committee define their challenge in four ways:

First, will they be presented with the right types of applicants for their program? Second, will they yield enough applications that year to give the committee room for choice? Third, will the applicants they admit make it through the program, and will they be competitive in the marketplace because of the MBA when it's time to get a job? Fourth, will they be the kind of graduate the institution will be proud to have among its alumni?

Sorting Out Candidates

Even before reading the applications, Babson expects applicants will fall into three general categories: those who have exactly what the institution is looking for, those who fall below standard admissions requirements, and the intriguing group—those who possess qualities that capture the attention of the committee yet are short of securing initial and clear acceptance.

Timing Can Make a Difference

Babson batches applications based on when they are received. Early applicants have the advantage; they're reviewed earlier when more spots are available.

No Homework Allowed

At some schools, admissions officers "sign" applications out to be read at home. But at Babson, applications are read on-premises in regularly scheduled "group reads" attended by admissions staff. The aim is to ensure that all applications receive the committee's comprehensive and equal attention and that, as a result, decisions are consistent. The sessions take place in a long rectangular conference room. There are no windows or phones. A DO NOT DISTURB sign hangs on the door. In short, there are no distractions.

At least three admissions officers read each application, essays and all.

An officer spends approximately 30–45 minutes on each. Essays are judged on how well they answer the question, style, writing ability, overall content and message, and maturity; also, if the applicant appears to be trying too hard to impress or has obtained help from a ghost writer. They try not to form opinions on the views expressed in the essay. Because the committee shares the same standards of evaluation, these assessments are qualitative. Essays are not subjected to an internal grading system or checklist of criteria.

Decisions, Decisions, Decisions

Occasionally there is disagreement about a particular essay. But since the admissions decision is based on the entire package, agreement on one essay is not as important as agreement on the overall candidacy of the applicant. When the committee doesn't agree on this, a lengthy discussion about the applicant takes place. If a consensus isn't reached, one of two steps is taken. Either the application is placed into a pile of "rereviews" to be read again against each other at a later date (up to two weeks) or, depending on the problem area, the applicant is asked to have an additional interview with a dean or faculty member, do some extra coursework, or retake the GMAT. Applicants in the latter category may be put on conditional admit or wait lists. If they satisfy the additional requirements and a place is available, they're in.

After the "group read" and review session, the three admissions officers are joined by the remaining admissions staff for a presentation of the applicant's candidacy.

CASE STUDIES

Here are the dossiers of four hopeful applicants to Babson, and the admissions committee's evaluation:

Applicant I is an undergraduate finance major from the University of Connecticut. She has a B grade point average and scored in the high 500s on the GMAT. Her work experience is substantive: five years, including two spent in the Peace Corps. The essays are descriptive and full of enthusiasm for her Peace Corps experience. The admissions committee learned she was up against major odds trying to secure loans from various funding sources for native African business people.

The committee used the interview with this applicant to obtain further insight into why she chose to go into the Peace Corps rather than pursue her original career. A small but important point the applicant had overlooked—what had motivated her decision? In the interview, the admissions officer found her poised, well prepared, and able to articulate why she wanted the MBA. Her clarification of her job experience helped the committee better understand why she made the career decision she made.

Decision: *Admit*

> **Applicant II** is a pharmaceutical salesman for a major international firm. His GMAT score is borderline, his GPA from a small liberal arts school in Maine is a low B. In reviewing his file, however, the committee found that he played a star position on his college's varsity hockey team and held a leadership position in student government. This helped explain and balance his marginal grades.

This applicant requested an interview early in the admissions process (this showed initiative even though interviews are required). He communicated clear expectations of the degree and what he wanted to accomplish. His essays also reflected a concise and persuasive presentation of his ideas. The letters of recommendation strongly supported his candidacy. His successes at work (many of them involving quantitative skill) also gave weight to his future business potential.

Decision: *Admit*

> **Applicant III** is an art major from the Art Institute in Chicago. In addition to her current position as a marketing assistant at a special events planning company, she has been recognized as one of the most creative students in the school and won the opportunity to present her work in the gallery at the museum. The committee felt a gallery show in such a prominent institute is a great accomplishment, particularly for a recent undergraduate.

This applicant took a "risky" approach to the essays, disclosing very personal information about emotional challenges she faced as a young adult. The essays were forthright, strong, and well structured. Most compelling was that her art exhibit was a pictorial essay of young women experiencing the same emotional challenges. The committee saw this as evidence that she had moved beyond the limitations of her emotional issues.

The greatest concern for this applicant was whether she would be able to manage the quantitative demands of the program. She has performed poorly on the math section of the GMAT. Her undergraduate coursework and limited work history provide no evidence of quantitative experience. For her benefit and the benefit of her classmates, she needs to bolster her skills before she can begin.

Decision: *Denied. Needs to retake the GMAT, quantitative courses, and reapply.*

Applicant IV is a Venezuelan banker, one of many applying to the school because of its program's ties to Latin America.

This applicant was visiting Boston on a business trip and thought she would use the opportunity to come in for an interview before she applied. She was outstanding interpersonally. Her application later revealed an undergraduate GPA of a B+, eight years of work experience, and a mid-400 GMAT score. She has progressed in her job from being an economist with a bank to a senior loan officer—a nice progression. But her low GMATs blocked a clear "accept." Moreover, the committee needed to balance the number of students so there was not a predominant presence in any class from any one country.

Decision: *Hold her application for review in the next round and within the Latin American pool of candidates; ask her to retake the GMAT.*

CHAPTER SIX

The Right Stuff
Filing a Winning Application

No one ever said it was going to be easy. Depending on where you're applying and how prolific a writer you are, a B-school application will take anywhere from 50 to 100 hours to complete. Sound excessive? Go ahead and try it. You'll probably scrap and rewrite an essay many times over. It takes time for thoughts to gestate. Indeed, it might feel like a fine wine ages faster than it takes you to write an essay.

This chapter should speed the process along. It deciphers some of the most commonly asked essay questions. It also provides you a list of mistakes applicants most often make.

COMMON ESSAY QUESTIONS:
What They're Really Asking

Each school has its own set of essay questions. Although posed differently, all search for the same insights. Here's a list of commonly asked questions and what's behind them.

1. Theme: Career Goals and the MBA

Describe your specific career aspirations. How will your goals be furthered by an MBA degree, and our MBA program in particular?

How do you feel the X school MBA degree can help you attain your specific career and personal goals for the five years after you graduate?

Discuss your career progression to date. What factors have influenced your decision to seek a general management education? Based on what you know about yourself at this time, how do you envision your career progressing after receiving the MBA degree? Please state your professional goals, and describe your plan to achieve them.

Translation:

"What do I want to be when I grow up, and how will the MBA get me there?"

This may be the most important essay question. It lays out the reasons why you should be given one of the cherished spots in the program. Even if your post-MBA future is tough to envision, this question must be answered.

A good way to frame this essay is to discuss how the MBA makes sense in light of your background, skills, and achievements to date. Why do you need this degree? Why now? One common reason is being stymied in your work by a lack of skills that can be gained in their program. Or you may want to use the MBA as a bridge to the next step. For example, an actress wants an MBA to prepare for a career in theater management. The more specific, the better.

It may be easier to provide specifics by breaking your plans into short- and long-term objectives.

Don't be afraid to present modest goals. If you're in accounting and want to stay there, say so. Deepening your expertise and broadening your perspective are solid reasons for pursuing the degree. On the other hand, feel free to indicate you'll use the MBA to change careers; seventy percent of all students at B-school are there to do just that.

If you aspire to lofty goals, like becoming a CEO or starting your own company, be especially careful that you detail a sensible, pragmatic plan. You need to show you're realistic. No one zooms to the top. Break your progress into steps.

Finally, this essay question asks how a particular program supports your goals. Admissions committees want to know why you've selected their school. That means you not only have to know, but also show, what's special about their program and how that relates specifically to your career aspirations.

(Hint: Many admissions officers say they can tell how much someone wants to go to their school by how well their essays are tailored to the offerings in their program.)

2. Theme: Extracurriculars and Social Interaction: Our nonwork side

What do you do for fun?

What are your principal interests outside of your job or school?

What leisure and/or community activities do you particularly enjoy? Please describe their importance in your life.

Translation:
Would we like to have you over for dinner? Do you know how to make friends? What are your special talents—the B-school Follies needs help. Are you well balanced, or are you going to freak out when you get here?

B-school is not just about business, case studies, and careers. The best programs buzz with the energy of a student body that is talented and creative, and that has personality. You won't be spending all your time in the library.

Are you interesting? Would you contribute to the school's vitality? Are you the kind of person other MBAs would be happy to meet? Describe activities you're involved in that might add something to the B-school community.

Are you sociable? B-school is a very social experience. Much of the work is done in groups. Weekends are full of social gatherings. Will you participate? Initiate? Get along with others? Communicate that people, not just your job, are an important part of your life.

Can you perform at a high level without being a nerd?

B-school can be tough. It's important to know when to walk away and find some fun. Do you know how to play as hard as you work?

How well rounded are you? Business leaders have wide-angle perspectives; they take in the whole picture. How deep or broad are your interests?

(A warning: Don't just list what you've done. Explain how what you've done has made you unique.)

3. Theme: The Personal Statement

Does this application provide the opportunity to present the real you?

The admissions committee would welcome any additional comments you may wish to provide in support of your application.

What question should we have asked you?

Translation:
What did we miss? Appeal to us in any way you want; this is your last chance. Be real.

If you have an experience or personal cause that says something interesting about you, and it hasn't found a place in any other essay, this is the time to stick it in. Keep in mind that you are hoping to present yourself as unique—so show some passion!

4. Theme: Whom You Most Admire

If you were able to choose one person from the business world, past or present, to be your personal professor throughout the MBA program, who would this person be and why?

Describe the characteristics of an exceptional manager, using an example of someone whom you have observed or with whom you have worked. Illustrate how his or her management style has influenced you.

Translation:
What are your values? What character traits do you admire?

This is the curve-ball question. The committee isn't looking to evaluate your judgment in selecting some famous, powerful person in your firm or in the world. What they're really after, which you reveal in your selection of the person, is the qualities, attributes, and strengths you value in others, as well as in yourself. Some important qualities to address: drive, discipline, vision, ethics, and leadership. As always, provide specific examples, and avoid choosing anyone too obvious.

Since whom you select is not as important as what you say about him or her, your choices can be more humble. You might write about a current boss, business associate, or friend. Bad choices are your mother or father.

If you like, it's perfectly fine to go for a famous figure. Indeed, there may be someone whose career and style you're passionate about. Make sure your essay explains why you find this person so compelling.

5. Theme: Ethics

Describe an ethical dilemma you have experienced and discuss how you handled the situation.

Can ethics be taught? How would you teach it?

Translation:
Do you know what an ethical dilemma looks like? Are you a sleazeball? What kinds of decisions and judgments might you make in your future practices as a business professional?

The last decade brought great attention to the ethics of the business world. In the aftermath of the BCCI, savings and loan, and insider-trading scandals, B-schools don't want to turn out graduates who are fast into their suspenders, fast into a deal, and fast to swindle their clients and partners.

While the above two questions are not identical, they get at the same issues: your judgment and integrity. In the first question, it's important to present a real ethical dilemma. Applicants often write about the dilemma of obeying or not obeying a supervisor's orders because they knew a better way. But this is not an ethics problem (unless the order was improper or illegal). This is a management problem. Also, it doesn't showcase your sense of honor and conduct, which is what the essay is about.

Write about an ethical dilemma in which there was no easy course—one that entailed costs either way. For example, you sold a product to a client and later discovered the product was faulty; your employer wants you to keep mum. You've built your sales relationships on trust and personal attention, so you want to be forthcoming. What did you do?

The second question requires some imagination. Ethics is indeed tough to teach. And if you teach it, is it enough?

Like the essay above, this essay should communicate your sense of values. A lesson in ethics might include an exploration of the reasons behind business principles and practices. It might also include role plays and simulations to tease out different perceptions of what's right and wrong.

SUMMARY
General Suggestions for the Essays

- In writing about your achievements, distinguish between those that are task oriented and problem oriented.

- Communicate that you're a proactive, can-do sort of person.

- Put yourself on ego alert: stress what makes you unique, not what makes you great.

STRAIGHT TALK FROM ADMISSIONS OFFICERS:
Fifteen Sure-Fire Ways to Torpedo Your Application

1. Write about the high school glory days.
Unless you're right out of college or you've got a great story to tell, resist using your high-school experiences for the essays. What does it say about your maturity if all you can talk about is being editor of the yearbook or captain of the varsity team?

2. Submit essays that don't answer the questions.
An essay that does no more than restate your résumé frustrates the admissions committees. After reading 5,000 applications, they get irritated to see another long-winded evasive one.

Don't lose focus. Make sure your stories answer the question.

3. Fill essays with industry jargon and detail.

Many essays are burdened by business-speak and unnecessary detail. This clutters your story. Construct your essays with only enough detail about your job to frame your story and make your point. After that, put the emphasis on yourself—what you've accomplished and why you were successful.

4. Write about a failure that's too personal or inconsequential.

Refrain from using breakups, divorces, and other romantic calamities as examples of failures. What may work on a confessional talk show is too personal for a business-school essay.

Also, don't relate a "failure" like getting one "C" in college (out of an otherwise straight "A" average). It calls your perspective into question. Talk about a failure that matured your judgment or changed your outlook.

5. Reveal half-baked reasons for wanting the MBA.

Admissions officers favor applicants who have well-defined goals. Because the school's reputation is tied to the performance of its graduates, those who know what they want are a safer investment.

If business school is just a pit stop on the great journey of life, admissions committees would prefer you make it elsewhere. However unsure you are about your future, it's critical that you demonstrate that you have a plan.

6. Exceed the recommended word limits.

Poundage is not the measure of value here. Exceeding the recommended word limit suggests you don't know how to follow directions, operate within constraints, organize your thoughts, or all of the above.

Get to the crux of your story and make your points. You'll find the word limits adequate.

7. Submit an application full of typos and grammatical errors.

How you present yourself on the application is as important as what you present. While typos don't necessarily knock you out of the running, they suggest a sloppy attitude. Poor grammar is also a problem. It distracts from the clean lines of your story and advertises poor writing skills.

Present your application professionally—neatly typed, and proofed for typos and grammar. And forget gimmicks like a videotape. This isn't "America's Funniest Home Videos."

8. Send one school an essay intended for another— or forget to change the school name when using the same essay for several applications.

Double check before you send anything out. Admissions committees are (understandably) insulted when they see another school's name or forms.

9. Make whiny excuses for everything.

Admissions committees have heard it all—illness, marital difficulties, learning disabilities, test anxiety, bad grades, pink slips, putting oneself through school—anything and everything that has ever happened to anybody. Admissions officers have lived through these things, too. No one expects you to sail through life unscathed. What they do expect is that you own up to your shortcomings.

Avoid trite, predictable explanations. If your undergraduate experience was one long party, be honest. Discuss who you were then and who you've become today. Write confidently about your weaknesses and mistakes. Whatever the problem, it's important you show you can recover and move on.

10. Make the wrong choice of recommendors.

A top-notch application can be doomed by second-rate recommendations. This can happen because you misjudged the recommendors' estimation of you or you failed to give them direction and focus.

As we've said, recommendations from political figures, your uncle's CEO golfing buddy, and others with lifestyles of the rich and famous don't impress (and sometimes annoy) admissions folk—unless such recommendors really know you or built the school's library.

11. Letting the recommendor miss the deadline.

Most recommendors are busy. They require plenty of lead time to write and send in their recommendation. Even with advance notice, a well-meaning but forgetful person can drop the ball.

It's your job to remind them of the deadlines. Do what you have to do to make sure they get there on time.

12. Be impersonal in the personal statement.

Each school has its own version of the "Use this space to tell us anything else about yourself" personal statement question. Yet many applicants avoid the word "personal" like the plague. Instead of talking about how putting themselves through school lowered their GPA, they talk about the rising cost of tuition in America.

The personal statement is your chance to make yourself different from the other applicants, further show a personal side, or explain a problem. Take a chance and be genuine; admissions officers prefer sincerity to a song and dance.

13. Make too many generalizations.

Many applicants approach the essays as though they were writing a newspaper editorial. They make policy statements and deliver platitudes about life without giving any supporting examples from their own experiences.

Granted, these may be the kind of hot-air essays that the application appears to ask for, and probably deserves. But admissions officers dislike essays that don't say anything. An essay full of generalizations is a giveaway that you don't have anything to say, don't know what to say, or just don't know how to say whatever it is you want to say.

14. Neglect to communicate that you've researched the program and you belong there.

B-schools take enormous pride in their programs. The rankings make them even more conscious of their academic turf and differences. While all promise an MBA, they don't all deliver it the same way. The schools have unique offerings and specialties.

Applicants need to convince the committee that the school's programs meet their needs. It's not good enough to declare prestige as the primary reason for selecting a school (even though this is the basis for many applicants' choice).

15. Fail to be courteous to employees in the admissions office.

No doubt, many admissions offices operate with the efficiency of sludge. But no matter what the problem, you need to keep your frustration in check.

If you become a pest or complainer this may become part of your applicant profile. An offended office worker may share his/her ill feelings about you with the boss—that admissions officer you've been trying so hard to impress.

CHAPTER SEVEN

Essays That Work

Writing Your Way into Business School

Case Examples:
Admissions Officers Critique Winning Essays

To show you how some applicants have answered the essay questions, we asked the B-schools for samples of "winning" essays. To show you what worked, we also asked the admissions officers to provide a critique.

As you read through the essays, keep in mind that each was but one of several submitted by an applicant for admission. Moreover, they were part of a package that included other important components. One essay alone did not "win" admission.

One other reminder. The purpose of including essays in this book is to give you a nudge in the right direction, not to provide you with a script or template for your own work. It would be a mistake to use them this way.

Obviously, this collection is by no means all-encompassing. There are thousands of winning essays out there; we just couldn't include them all.

A final note: Because Harvard features a whopping ten-essay application, we especially wanted it in this section. Harvard declined our request. So to access what apparently is guarded as closely as FBI files, we contacted the students and grads directly. To our delight, everyone was eager to supply an essay. We selected those we believe the admissions officers would also have considered "winning."

BOSTON UNIVERSITY

Essay #1:

Imagine a straight line of infinite length, stretching out of sight in two directions. Assuming the line represents time, one can stand at any present moment and simultaneously look back at past experience and project one's sight into the future.

The time line is an assumption that makes planning possible. Though it may someday be proven a false, or at least incomplete model, it can be useful for both personal and professional planning. For this essay, I'll limit myself to the latter.

Where I Stand

Looking back at what I have done, and ahead to what I'd like to do, I can find great sense in beginning a graduate management program.

I have: a foundation of experience in the administration of educational and cultural institutions. Past jobs have ranged from directing a college admissions office to promoting an opera company, to managing a modern dance company, to running a day care center, to editing a weekly newspaper.

I have: an understanding of how groups function, what makes an organization healthy, and various ways people can organize to accomplish a goal. This has come from work experience as well as graduate study in organization theory and design at Harvard and at M.I.T.

I have: dreams and plans for a range of jobs and enterprises that extend ahead through my life.

From Here to There

Among many goals, I would like to direct a major cultural institution. I would also like to head a major educational institution, run a major foundation, and start and run my own cultural or educational organization—not necessarily all at the same time.

To achieve the above, there are skills and arenas of knowledge and experience that I'd like to have in my grasp. Some of these are presently out of reach, others are at my fingertips, but none are firmly in hand.

Financial management is, for me, perhaps the largest arena of knowledge in which I want, but do not have, agility. A course of study that refreshes my quantitative skills and teaches me principles of economics, fiscal planning and other financial management skills would be very useful.

Another such arena includes management information systems and computer programming. I presently work on word processing equipment with comfort and joy. I hope, with time and guidance, to do the same with other systems at an even deeper level.

I would also like more personal contact with professional peers, particularly in the Boston and New England region. The public management program appears to offer that.

Some of my more obvious strengths and weaknesses should be evident from the above. I have confidence in myself. I have a great deal of curiosity. I generate ideas and I develop interests, and can usually turn these into realistic, well-organized and flexible plans. These I consider strengths.

I can also stretch myself too thin, which can be a problem. Though I realize taking on the new demands some letting go of the old, I also believe experience increases capacity. There seems to me a need for more trained generalists to protect against overspecialization and fragmentation.

One great tool for that kind of protection is humor. My own sense of the comic can be quite dry and subtle, or broad and bizarre. Regardless of the form in which it spills out, it provides me perspective, balance and spontaneity.

Cooperation, too, is a central motivation for me, and I am glad to see it stressed in the public management literature.

Arrivals

To accept two accomplishments and label [sic] these significant runs counter to my way of assessing substance. I try to resist measuring my achievement by individual moments of arrival. Still, when pressed, I can come up with a few.

Performing professional theater at the age of 17 is an accomplishment that seems more significant now than it did at the time. Being appointed a college admissions director at 23 seems similarly significant. Both provided a sense of competence at a young age, and both provided a peer experience with people older and more experienced than myself.

Doing well in a graduate program at Harvard feels notable in that the school was an environment very different from any in which I had worked before. The program became a test of adaptability as well as intellect. Other accomplishments might include a few backpacking ventures taken in severe conditions, some of which became life threatening. These provided dramatic tests of my reserves, and gave me confidence in my capacity for survival.

Less dramatic, and not quite finished, is a quilting project that I have worked on for more than six years. I have just completed the top sheet, a multipieced pattern in fabric. Still ahead is the quilting process itself, stitching the top sheet to a sturdy backing, with a layer of batting between the two. When done, the quilt takes on an identity greater than the sum of its many parts.

The work on this piece has been a teacher of patience and harmony. The quilt, with its assortment of shapes and fabric, can serve as a model for the organization of one's life and the people and activities in it.

Now, imagine a fine thread of infinite length weaving in and out of all those pieces.

Critique: Admissions officers review several hundreds or thousands of applications each year. Due to this high volume, any given applicant should formulate a creative approach in composing the essay to attract attention to its quality and content. Unfortunately, many applicants write essays that are similar to a detailed résumé or cover letter. This not only discourages a thorough review but also eliminates the opportunity for the individual to express his or her own uniqueness. The admissions officers are also usually interested in how an applicant responds to a specific question, rather than a general statement.

This essay creatively suggests the applicant's general outlook on his life, what he hopes to achieve, and how he will do it. He does not go into great detail about any of these issues but allows what he does say to have a powerful impact. Reading this essay gives the evaluator the opportunity to get to know the values as well as interests and accomplishments the candidate has. This is particularly helpful when applying to a school that does not have evaluative interviews as part of the application process.

The essay is also brief and concise and makes an effort to link all the topics mentioned in the essay to create a well-defined image. The use of subtitles introduces the outline and scope of the essay.

BRIGHAM YOUNG UNIVERSITY

Essay #1

Donald J. Buehner
January 23, 1991

MBA Admissions Committee
640 TNRB
Brigham Young University
Provo, UT 84602

Dear Members of the BYU MBA Admissions Committee:

In response to your request, I am writing to inform you of my intentions for this coming year as well as to describe my employment experience acquired during the past year.

I plan to attend the MBA program commencing in September, 1991. You should have already received my Bishops Form.

During the past year I have had extensive international and national work experience. In February of 1990 I was promoted by Franklin International Institute Inc. to assist in opening a European Distribution Center in England. My specific assignment was to establish and manage the order entry and customer service departments as well as to hire and train British employees in the various operational functions. Inclusive with this training assignment was to implement the corporate values, philosophies, and quality, and to instill in our employees the high standards of excellence and consumer satisfaction for which the Franklin International Institute strives. During my six-month assignment, I worked under pressured time constraints.

The international exposure in Europe during historic times as Britain and the other eleven continental countries prepare for the economic union in 1992 was extremely beneficial for me. Combined with my work experience in Japan and my mission to South Africa, as well as my ability to speak Japanese, Dutch and Afrikaans, working in the British Isles increased my confidence and desire to pursue a career in international business.

My next promotion came in September last year, which was to help open and manage the first Franklin Day Planner Retail Center to be situated in a mall. This opportunity is providing me with more valuable experience in hiring, training, and management skills, as well as useful retail understanding including sales, stock control, and profit and loss flows. Working with the extremely qualified and professional upper management of Franklin International has been valuable in shaping my career goals.

Regarding my decision to defer attendance at Brigham Young for one year, I believe Dr. Pete Clarke's counsel that additional exposure in the work force would only enhance my graduate experience was wise advice. I feel better prepared to both learn from and be a progressive participant in the Master of Business Administration program at Brigham Young University. I request admittance for the fall of 1991.

Essay #2

Dean of the Business School
Brigham Young University
Provo, Utah 84601

Dear Sir,

In preparation for a career as an International Businessman, I am seeking entrance into the graduate program at Brigham Young University. This letter will provide the requested information regarding my wish to study at BYU.

My family experience has significantly influenced my preparation for a career in business administration. As the youngest of six children I have shared family responsibilities of managing our 45 acre farm. Because my father worked full-time, my brothers and I learned at a young age to operate the farm. At fourteen, being the only son left at home, I learned to creatively utilize my resources and to seek expert advice from local farmers in managing the farm. I learned other important business principles such as hard work, commitment, and honesty. I also learned frugality by saving a portion of my earnings in order to attend University and in addition, support myself for two years as a volunteer missionary in South Africa.

I have actively sought for balance by being involved in school plays, learning to play the trumpet and the guitar, and to sing. I have sought excellence in athletics: baseball, football, track and field, and swimming. I was actively involved in scouting and obtained the Eagle Scout award and the Order of the Arrow, an award earned through leadership, service and courage. Such activities taught me self-discipline and team unity.

At sixteen, I was selected to go for one year as a High School Rotary International Exchange student to South Africa. My responsibility was to represent America while there, and then upon returning home, to be an ambassador for South Africa to enhance world peace and understanding. In this effort, I made presentations about America to business clubs, high schools, and social groups. I also became immersed in South African culture by learning to speak Afrikaans, play their sports, enjoy their food, and listen carefully to their interesting and unique perspectives. From this experience in such a diverse land, I learned to respect foreign cultures, and I feel I developed a special talent to communicate with and relate to a wide variety of people.

As a missionary to South Africa, I served as a district and Zone leader, and Assistant to the President. As an Assistant, I became responsible for the mission's 52 car fleet, the supply and distribution of mission products, and the transportation arrangements for over 130 missionaries. Working both in an intimate and business level in a foreign country was exciting and challenging. On my mission I decided I could best serve my fellow men as an international businessman. This decision was based on my passion for South Africa and my ability to relate with and influence a variety of people for good.

During the summer of my sophomore year at Brigham Young University, I decided to enhance my international marketability by going to Japan and learning Japanese. After arriving in Japan, I negotiated to establish and to teach an English program to an expanding Japanese company. Through this experience, I became excited and confident in my ability to learn languages, and to conduct business in foreign cultures by being understanding and alert to their traditions and values.

One of my major accomplishments has been financing and completing a college education. In this pursuit, I demonstrated creativity in my capacity to see business opportunities and make them profitable. For example, I installed security door-viewers in apartment complexes in exchange for rent by discovering existing trends of vacancy of various apartments, as well as installing door-viewers in a cost effective manner. While working ten to thirty hours a week, I maintained an average of fifteen credit hours, and achieved an overall 3.61 GPA with a 3.74 GPA in my major. I feel this reflects my commitment to achieving excellence under challenging situations.

In addition to the university curriculum I have had valuable experience in the work field. As a salesman for an insulation company in San Francisco, I succeeded at and learned to love honest sales by being competent in my service and by discovering the true needs of the people. My marketing experience as a sales rotator for Karl Lagerfeld products in Utah included direct selling as well as overseeing advertising displays in department stores such as Nordstrom's.

As a full-time employee of Franklin International, I have demonstrated total commitment. I have also sought creative ways to better the company through my organizational behavior training at BYU. Recently, I helped restructure the leadership responsibilities in my department in order for more on-going training and less busy-work. As a result of the confidence of my superiors, I have been offered positions of trust and leadership. In March until August, I will be establishing the customer service/order entry department for our company in England. My responsibilities will include hiring, training, and managing a British team of fifteen employees.

I am extremely enthusiastic about the future of international business administration. I believe there are major breakthroughs yet to be made in the field. After completing an MBA, I hope to gain practical experience and exposure with a major international business firm. Eventually, I intend to establish resorts, clinics and camps in which to motivate and train people of all cultures to incorporate values and thought patterns conducive to healthier, happier and more productive life styles. Such training would include a physical appreciation of body and environment, as well as a spiritual appreciation of fundamental values such as honesty and integrity. I envision training focused at salvaging youth from drug abuse and inspiring them to become producers. I believe this personal passion can best be accomplished as a professional and competent businessman.

I want to attend the graduate program at BYU for many reasons. I understand the working relationship between local corporations and the business school is conducive to consistent business exposure and experience combined with serious academic study. I desire a top quality accredited program that incorporates high moral values as part of the curriculum. I am also impressed with the close working association with professors and students at the Business School. I look forward to a challenging and stimulating relationship with professors and peers and feel my unique exposure to business in South Africa, Japan, England and America will allow me to contribute interesting insights and comparisons.

Thank you for your consideration.

Critique: What the Admissions Committee Looks For In Letter of Intent at Brigham Young University's Marriott School of Management

A Complete Individual

Don's letter of intent gives us a picture of a well-rounded human being. He talks about his preparation in terms of his work experience as a youth as well as an adult, his high school activities in music, sports, and travel, his community experience in scouting and service to his church, as well as his academic preparation.

International Experience

Since eighty-five percent of our students speak second languages and thirty-five percent speak third, we are interested in international experiences which enrich the class. Don mentions four experiences of significance.

The first was his high school exchange student experience in South Africa. He not only explains how he presented information about America to business clubs and social groups, he also talks about what he has learned individually in playing South African sports, learning Afrikaans, and relating to people of different cultures.

The second experience was Don's voluntary mission for the Church of Jesus Christ of Latter-Day Saints to South Africa. The admissions committee is well aware of the growth and maturity which occurs on a mission, but Don chose to elaborate by explaining his specific responsibilities as a leader and manager for the mission's fleet of cars.

The third was a choice Don made as a college student to learn Japanese and Japanese ways. He explains his work with a Japanese company in helping to expand their English program.

The fourth experience was Don's assignment in England to open a new branch of the Franklin International (now Franklin Quest) office.

Work Experience

Don shows valuable work experience from his youth. He supports his assertion that he learned how to work early with specifics about being in charge of a farm at fourteen because his brothers had grown up, looking to neighboring farmers for advice, and saving his earnings for his own future plans.

Don financed his own college education. He mentions creative part-time work—installing door-viewers.

After college Don gained marketing and sales experience with some well-known companies before he joined Franklin International and was promoted to management positions.

Leadership
Evidence of Don's leadership skills is shown in his experience as District and Zone leader and eventually Assistant to the President on his church mission in South Africa.

Future Plans
Don has some definite ideas about what he would like to do in international business administration. He presents his plan to establish resorts and camps to train people. This information gives the admissions committee some idea about whether our program can contribute to what he has in mind.

Good Writing Skills
Don's writing indicates an ability to express himself well and reflects on his undergraduate preparation. He frames his letter in the first paragraph by telling us what the letter is about and he concludes in the final paragraph by pulling together the reasons the Marriott School of Management is attractive to him. This indicates he has done his homework to find out what our program is about. Within the framing are clear paragraphs explaining Don's experiences which make him a viable candidate.

What the Student Brings to the Class
Don shows he has something to contribute to his peers. He shows diversity in his experiences, a teachableness, some definite goals, and an ability to work hard. His international experiences show an ability to cooperate and get along with people and demonstrate good problem-solving skills.

This area is very important. The Admissions Committee works at building a class with diversity in backgrounds and educational experiences which will enrich and contribute to the whole class.

UNIVERSITY OF CALIFORNIA—BERKELEY

Question #1: *What seminal influences, broadly defined, have especially contributed to your personal development? What correlation, if any, has your personal development to your professional goals? In your response to this question, please do not discuss the influence of members of your immediate family, athletic endeavors, or professional experiences.*

Essay #1:

Bangkok, Vientiane, Malaysia, Singapore, Tokyo, Washington DC., Manhattan, Boston, Camden, and San Francisco are the places where I have grown up. My father was a diplomat, my mother a teacher, and I am the youngest of four children. Together, my family moved every two or three years to a new city. Growing up was an adventure: as children, my brothers, sister, and I did not choose to move so frequently, but we became accustomed to it. We learned to assimilate quickly, make new friends, adjust to unfamiliar customs, even speak foreign languages.

The diverse cultural experiences that are part of my childhood have shaped the way I think about the world and my purpose in it. Living abroad cultivated my curiosity in politics and international relations, and moving frequently developed my interpersonal skills and created a strong personal motivation to make the best of a new situation.

Living abroad and moving frequently influenced who I am today, yet they are facts about my life that I have had little control over. When I think about who I am today, I focus on the choices I have made, the actions I have taken, and the guidance I have received from relatives and friends through various struggles. One choice I made stands out as an important influence because it resulted in challenges that stretched me in new directions and dramatically changed my perspective.

*   *   *   *

Following high school graduation, I worked as a roustabout out on an offshore oil rig in the Gulf of Mexico, 125 miles off the coast of Louisiana. For graduation, my family had pitched in for a round trip plane ticket to Europe. I had been preparing for a trip across the continent when my oldest brother called about a job opportunity on an oil rig. I opted for the job because it was both an adventure and an opportunity to earn a lot of money for college (my savings amounted to one year at Harvard).

Within a week I was in a helicopter heading for Block 352, an oil field leased from the government by Chevron. I have several lasting impressions of the experience. The first is primarily sensory as I recall the physical conditions under which we lived and worked. The incessant noise of power generators and welding machines hummed in our ears day and night. Every species of dirt and grime thrived on the rig. The platform was characterized by its oppressive heat, magnified by the flames from the acetylene torches and welding rods and by the exhaust from the welding machines. The only activity we looked forward to was mealtime in an air-conditioned bunkhouse.

The work was dangerous, and if it were not for luck and the other hands who kept a close eye on me, I certainly would have been injured. That summer seven people died in Block 352, four in a helicopter accident, two in a crane accident; the seventh was a close friend of mine. At twenty-one, Eric was the closest person to my age. When I first started, he and I worked closely together and he explained everything he knew about work on the rig. Eric was related in one way or another to many of the people in our crew, and as Eric's friend, I became one of the clan. Most of the older hands looked out for me as they did for Eric.

One day Eric was hurrying around a corner when he tripped on the extra slack of his torch line and he fell through a hole he had just cut in the deck. He fell 200 plus feet, hit the structure before landing, and drowned, taken swiftly under either by the current or the barracuda that circle below waiting for kitchen trash.

The lawyers and the search party came and went, and work began as usual the next morning. I was struck by two reactions to Eric's death. The first was that the other hands barely spoke of it. It was as though the danger of the job was something they had all accepted and put behind them so they could carry on. I will never know if I could have helped Eric if I were there, but I still wonder why it wasn't me. The other response was an unusual step taken by our foreman that morning: someone still needed to descend through the hole that Eric had fallen through and climb out to the very end of the structure to attach a cable. Without a word, our foreman joined us, climbed through the hole, attached the cable, and was back before we realized the spell was broken. His action made me realize that to earn respect as a leader, never ask another person to attempt what you might not try yourself.

Another lasting impression I have of work on the rig, in direct contrast to the harsh conditions, is the strong personal relationships that made the experience memorable. The men I worked with from 5:00 a.m. to 10:00 p.m. were an extraordinary crew, all Cajuns from southern Louisiana, all hard working, all part of a team. On my first day, one of the hands later told me, they thought I was an engineer because I came dressed with a new Chevron hard-hat, clean Levi's, and clean T-shirt. Far from an engineer, I was worse than a 'worm' (someone new on a rig) because I had no training. As a young kid from Maine who did not know how to cut, weld, fit, grind, or stack steel pipe, I had a lot of ground to cover. The interests that had been a strong part of my identity in high school: student athlete, leader, etc. were suddenly irrelevant. Where I had come from and where I was going at the end of the summer had no bearing in the context of working offshore. All that mattered was what I could accomplish during that summer. The way to join this crew was straightforward: work hard, learn quickly, and interact during mealtime.

Initially I was a 'rigger,' someone who supports welders by hauling steel and creating safe, makeshift platforms for welders to stand on as they weld. Early in the summer I asked our foreman, Henry Calais, if I could learn to weld. I did not know about the months of training it takes to become a certified pipe welder, but Henry was kind and offered instead to have me work with Charlie Reitenger as his assistant. Charlie was the crew's 'fitter' and, after Henry, was the most experienced person on the platform. A fitter measures and cuts pipe to length so that when the ends of two sections meet, they are adjacent, plumb, and square.

Charlie never wore a shirt, just a jeans jacket with cut-off sleeves. Charlie was an intense man with a subtle sense of humor; on the morning of our first day working together, immediately after a healthy breakfast (at an unhealthy 5:00 a.m.) Charlie opened his first can of Skoal Long cut, pinched a lip-full of tobacco, and then offered me the can. We were hanging mid-air, about 200 feet above the water, and descending rapidly toward the workboat below as the crane operator lowered us. I smiled declining: 'Thanks, no, maybe after a second cup of coffee.' This exchange became a morning routine with us.

Charlie and I did not start off with a lot in common. I was not sure how to create common ground between us, but I began by showing interest in what he had to teach me. For the first week I hauled steel all over the platform for Charlie to measure and cut. Over time Charlie taught me everything there is to know about cutting and fitting pipe, and I, in turn, taught him some of the basic concepts of trigonometry. I was less successful with physics. One day I was trying to calculate how high we were above the water by dropping a welding rod and counting how many seconds it took to reach the water. For a moment Charlie thought that I was an idiot. He argued that my methodology was flawed because a heavier object would fall faster.

I tried to explain that gravity exerts the same force on all objects, but as our discussion progressed other hands took an interest, and Charlie prevailed by the sheer weight of popular opinion. Galileo would have been empathetic; we eventually conducted an experiment from the heliport, which is the highest level on the rig. We dropped several objects of varying mass before the debate was finally resolved and a basic law of physics restored. It was quite a revelation, and I was surprised by how it consumed the conversation that evening, interrupting the usual ribald dinner talk.

The summer spent offshore was unique preparation for college and for life. I still have not taken a summer off to travel in Europe, but I have never regretted passing up that opportunity to work on the oil rig. The experience exposed me to the human drama of a working class that I had not had contact with. The extreme working conditions and contact with a much older group of peers accelerated a period of growth and maturity for me. Working on the rig gave me an opportunity to reexamine what I wanted to accomplish in college and who I wanted to become. When the summer was over I felt like a completely changed person. In the helicopter heading back to Morgan City, Louisiana, I realized how fortunate I was to have the opportunity to go to college.

Critique: In reviewing Haas MBA application essays, the admissions committee places considerable weight on intellectual performance and potential; a sense of purposiveness; evidence of ethical character; and skill in the development, organization, and presentation of thoughts and ideas. We seek candidates who demonstrated initiative, creativity, thoughtfulness, receptiveness, and resourcefulness in the conduct of their personal and professional lives. We look for individuals who can provide a satisfactory account of who they are, what they have accomplished within the context of their own experiences and opportunities, and what they intend to accomplish during graduate school and beyond. Most compelling are those candidates whose reflections on their experiences and on their record of accomplishments, however defined, suggest an ability to make significant contributions to their class and to the Haas School.

The previous essay ostensibly describes a summer job following graduation from high school. Although the nature of the job may be unusual by MBA-application standards, it is not merely the novelty or drama of the situation that makes this essay successful. Its principal strengths are the degree of thought and writing skill the author exhibits in his composition. The essay is compelling because the author imparts with deep insight, wry humor, and seemly modesty an ability to work successfully with people of widely differing backgrounds, education, and cultures to the mutual benefit of all concerned. It is exceptional because while the author suggests that he was the principal beneficiary of that summer job on an oil rig in the Gulf, it is clear that his account is as instructive to the reader as his participation was to his colleagues.

CASE WESTERN RESERVE UNIVERSITY

Question #1: *Describe the most difficult personal or professional challenge that you have faced in the past five years. What did you learn from that experience?*

Essay #1:

In 1990, I formed my own company, Asian Profiles, Inc., to conduct research on the automotive industry, focusing primarily on East Asian markets. The compiled research is stored in a computer database system which allows me to analyze the data and forecast future automotive trends. Through the evaluation of automotive markets, I am able to construct "profiles" of East Asian nations and determine their relative potential as manufacturing sites and/or consumer markets for American automobile manufacturers and suppliers. My position as a research consultant and president of the company has given me the opportunity to test my professional and personal strengths as well as verify my leadership abilities.

Asian Profiles, Inc., has created a multitude of professional challenges for me. Running a small business of any kind requires a great deal of resourcefulness and ingenuity. When I started my business, my company had a database system with zero information. Four of the major management decisions I was confronted with at the time were: assessing the type of information my clients required, determining the availability of such information, selecting appropriate sources for the information, and choosing the methods for retrieving such information. I take pleasure in the fact that my company now has an extensive operating database. However, I am still faced with the above management decisions in addition to the daily challenge of determining the speed at which I need to retrieve information and the price I am willing to pay for it. I have to constantly ask myself, "Is there a better, quicker, more cost-effective way to find this information?" Often the answer is yes, and I have found that local resources can offer more practical means of information retrieval than other sophisticated sources such as computer network systems and expensive publications. Ultimately, though, I have come to realize that people are the most valuable resource in business. Since incorporating my company, I have carefully developed useful contacts whom I can call upon for professional advice. (To date) my company has enjoyed great success primarily because I have learned when to seek advice, when to give it, and when to solve a problem on my own. During this period I have learned that networking is an important part of any successful business career.

Being self-employed is a true test of one's personal character. When I first made the decision to go into business for myself, many questions ran through my mind. I wondered where I was going to find reliable data, how I was going to compile it, and when I would find time to learn new computer programs. One thing I never questioned, though, was whether I was capable of attaining my goals. From the outset I understood that being self-employed would require incredible self-discipline and emotional maturity. Because I did not have the years of work experience behind me, I have had to learn to rely on my own judgment. For example, soon after incorporating Asian Profiles, Inc., I was faced with the challenge of negotiating business contracts, setting up the company's finances, and deciding which computer system to purchase. With advice from experts and personal research, I found that lack of experience did not have to be a stumbling block to success but, rather, was a challenge to overcome. As company president, I have had to become my own supervisor and supporter, which has been the most challenging aspect of the position. Employing a healthy level of self-judgment has allowed me to improve my job performance by acknowledging and working with my strengths and weaknesses.

In addition to the professional challenges Asian Profiles, Inc., has created for me, it has also given me the opportunity to test my leadership abilities. Although I perform all the research and manage the company myself, I am fortunate to have the support of two secretaries. Being a manager has been a novel and rewarding experience for me. I have learned that in any working relationship, being a good manager is more about leading people and less about being a boss. I have worked hard to establish a consistent and professional management style for dealing with my clients and employees. With the personal and professional responsibilities required of a small business manager, I have had the opportunity to realistically assess my leadership capabilities. I am confident that I do possess leadership potential, but I recognize the need for expanded experience and new challenges. Asian Profiles, Inc., has fostered in me a tremendous amount of self-reliance and business know-how which I will continue to draw upon in my future endeavors.

Critique: We gave this essay high marks on the following dimensions:

Style: Well-constructed essay; gave succinct but sufficient background information about the experience, then described the challenge, how she met the challenge, and what she learned. Tone of the essay was honest and eminently readable.

Content: Situation was unique and interesting to the reader. Descriptions provided specifics, which made the challenge more believable. Cause and effect between the situation and the learning process were made clear.

Reader would have liked to have seen reference to any measurable success resulting from meeting the challenge and learning from the experience.

DARTMOUTH

Question #1: *Discuss your career progression to date. What factors have influenced your decision to seek a general management education? Based on what you know about yourself at this time, how do you envision your career progressing after receiving the MBA degree? Please state your professional goals, and describe your plans to achieve them.*

Essay #1:

As a senior, my initial goal was to gain a thorough education in finance, which I could then apply in a field related to my personal interest in the outdoors. The most efficient way to achieve this education was as an analyst at a major investment bank. Most of the available positions were in New York. Although I was offered an analyst position there, I realized that I was unwilling to sacrifice my personal interest in order to move into the city. Instead I headed West and dedicated a year to fulfillment of these interests before beginning my professional career.

I spent the summer and fall as a professional river guide on the Snake River in Wyoming. Guiding over 2,000 people in Class IV white water rafting and fly-fishing trips taught me to interact comfortably with clients and to effectively promote myself and my abilities. I often draw upon these marketing skills in my current career when soliciting new clients. I then spent the following winter and spring in California managing a cross-country ski touring center. In this position, I gained valuable experience managing people and an appreciation for the numerous responsibilities of running a business, regardless of its size and purpose. More importantly, both experiences instilled within me an appreciation for our natural environment and an obligation to help preserve it.

Shortly thereafter, I began my professional career at Drexel Burnham Lambert in San Francisco. I was one of the first junior members to join its innovative debt restructuring group. The culture was highly entrepreneurial. Since we were the first group on Wall Street to enter the debt restructuring field, we had no standard operating procedures to rely on and therefore created our own. Our success has been a function of our creativity in developing innovative restructuring techniques as well as our cooperative group dynamics. All members of the team are encouraged to contribute to the creative process, regardless of their position. I performed well in this environment and was rewarded with a promotion from analyst to associate, a position usually reserved for MBA graduates. As the business flourished and the group expanded, I had the opportunity to train and manage several second and third year associates who were new to the group and therefore junior to me in experience. When Drexel entered bankruptcy in early 1990, I was the only one out of ten junior members invited to join the senior group in their move to another investment bank, Smith Barney. Our group's continued success at Smith Barney has allowed me to further expand my responsibilities. We recently closed the largest public debt restructuring ever completed, which resulted in the sale of one of America's oldest and largest publishing companies. In this transaction I led our team of ten associates and analysts from Smith Barney and two other investment banks representing the buyer in a comprehensive financial review and valuation of our client. In collaborating with senior team members, I presented these analyses to our client's Board of Directors, who relied upon them in determining the viability of the offer.

In the last four and a half years, I have gained a solid background in finance, experience in line management, and strong negotiating skills by executing numerous transactions in a wide variety of industries. Clearly, I have surpassed the original goal I set as a senior in college. I now plan to pursue other professional goals that I have developed during my tenure at Drexel and Smith Barney.

My next professional goal is to combine my desire to run my own business with my passion for mountaineering, as a manufacturer of outdoor recreational equipment. Mountaineering has advanced at such a rapid pace that athletes in several technical disciplines have exceeded the limits of the equipment available to them. Modern technologies have only been applied to improve the equipment in such recently popular areas as technical rock climbing where sufficient demand has justified the cost of implementation. My focus would be on product development through technology-based innovation in other areas of mountaineering that are gaining popularity, such as back country skiing. I believe that the increased costs of such technology can be offset by more efficient production management. For example, back country ski boots are still made of leather, which freezes when wet and must be hand-stitched. A lightweight plastic boot with a removable synthetic liner, however, would not only improve performance but reduce production costs as well through automation of the manufacturing process. I plan to enter the outdoor recreational equipment market with a product innovation such as this one and then expand into other product lines through a) additional technological innovations, b) joint ventures with or acquisitions of other specialty manufacturers, and c) leveraging my brand recognition to promote related clothing and accessories which typically yield a higher profit margin.

Clearly, my goal is not to run a Fortune 500 company. I believe the future of American manufacturing lies in small, highly specialized companies that can not only quickly respond to technological change but also help direct the public's shifting values regarding our natural environment. To create this type of enterprise, I plan to assemble a small team of individuals with diverse skills but common interests. The structure of this enterprise will combine the many positive organizational aspects of my current organization. I will create a "meritocracy" in which personal and professional growth will be rewarded with increased responsibility. All members of the team will be encouraged to contribute to the creative process regardless of their position. Compensation will be based strictly on performance rather than tenure, so that all members who share the responsibilities may also share the profits. Personal profit, however, will not be the sole motivation. The team will also be motivated by a common interest in environmental protection.

My mentor in the outdoor is Yvon Chouinard, founder of Patagonia, a leading manufacturer of outdoor equipment and clothing. Through product innovation he has advanced the sport of mountaineering and achieved a position at the forefront of the outdoor industry. As an industry leader, he has become a vocal proponent of "sustainable development," which encourages managers to balance economic growth with environmental concerns. I agree with his thesis that our country's current business practices are generally not sustainable. In the past several years, I have witnessed the effects of irresponsible growth at Drexel and at many of its clients' that I helped restructure. Currently we are all witnessing the effects of irresponsible growth on our natural environment. Through the success of my own company, I could fulfill the obligation to the environment I developed years ago as a river guide. As an industry leader, I would be in a position to promote responsible and sustainable growth at all levels—by example within my own organization and industry, by communication with other industry leaders, and by volunteering my time and skills to increase public awareness of the need to protect the wilderness areas on which my industry and interests depend.

I understand that, in order to pursue my entrepreneurial interest in manufacturing, I will need the skills to manage across an entire organization, from finance and production to sales and marketing. I have developed strong financial skills and gained experience in line management in my current career. An MBA education is clearly not a perfect substitute for experience, but I believe it would provide me with the framework necessary for effective decision-making in these areas. An MBA program would also allow me to further research my business ideas through the experiences of my peers, independent study, and related summer employment. Education and experience may not change my goals, but they may well change the means by which I achieve them. Finally, since I will not be able to create this organization alone, I look forward to the opportunity to meet other individuals who share my interests in entrepreneurship, manufacturing and sustainable development.

Critique: The admissions essay is a critical component in an application to the Amos Tuck School's MBA program. Throughout the process of reviewing an application, which includes careful reading of essays, the admissions committee will seek compelling reasons to admit the applicant. Although writing an excellent essay will not guarantee an applicant admission into

Tuck, submitting a poorly organized or badly written essay as part of an otherwise good application will significantly reduce his or her chances for acceptance.

In addition to meeting our more immediate and obvious expectations of a well-organized, articulate presentation of his candidacy, the applicant who wrote our example essay offers (1) compelling reasons for the admissions committee to accept him and (2) convincing evidence that he would both thrive in, and contribute to, the academic and social environment at Tuck. In evaluating any essay, however, keep in mind that we judge neither the experiences nor the goals an applicant presents. Instead, we judge (1) how well the applicant presents these experiences and goals, (2) how well the applicant's accomplishments support his long-term goals, and (3) how the applicant's rationale for wanting an MBA fits into his or her overall career plan.

There are a number of indicators throughout the example essay that the writer possesses attributes that Tuck seeks: (1) the types of experiences and interests that demonstrate sufficient intellectual preparation for a rigorous curriculum of professional study, (2) a high motivational level for achievement, (3) a creative approach to problem solving, (4) a blend of leadership skills to successfully manage multiple aspects of an organization, (5) the interpersonal skills needed to work successfully with diverse groups of people, and (6) an appreciation of the need to balance one's professional and personal lives.

The applicant demonstrates these attributes in describing his career progress, relating each stage to long-term goals. He explains why general management training, central to Tuck's educational mission, is essential for implementing the next stage of his plan toward reaching those goals. The applicant knows what he wants—skills to manage an R&D-based manufacturing operation in close proximity to the great outdoors—and has a clear-cut idea of how to get it. In his essay, he indicates that he made a steady progression of conscious choices that supported his long-term goals by strategically identifying: (1) Where to live and work (on a river in Wyoming, near a ski area in California, then in a major financial center in California), (2) What types of industries were most valuable to gain experience in for his personal and professional interests (an outdoor excursions outfit, a customer service oriented sports operation, an investment banking firm), (3) What roles would prove useful for the future (leader of white-water rafting trips, general manager of a cross-country ski touring center, member of a team in an investment bank's new debt-restructuring group), and (4) Which issues to monitor (the environmental consequences of commercial land development, growth pattern of technological innovations in the sports-equipment industry, how manufacturing factors into the overall national economy).

The applicant asserts that he is management material and backs up this assertion in describing how his superiors at Drexel Burnham Lambert promoted him to a level of responsibility normally reserved for MBAs. He also demonstrates familiarity with current consequences of a slow economy by showing successful adjustment to a new position in another company after his own employer went bankrupt. This flexibility, along with his varied experiences, will enable him to offer an interesting perspective in class discussions.

In conclusion, this particular applicant's attitude, experience, goals, and interests all provided a close match with what Tuck seeks in prospective MBAs. The admissions committee was confident that his interests and abilities provided a close fit with our requirements and that he would be happy in the type of environment that Tuck offers: a rural, residential lifestyle; small classes emphasizing cooperative, highly interactive group learning; a close-knit and cohesive community that welcomes people from diverse backgrounds; and the ability to take full advantage of the career placement services and connections one would expect from an Ivy League business school.

HARVARD

Question #1: *Discuss a change you would make in your work environment and how you would implement that change.*

Essay #1:

The Gillette Personal Care Division is in financial difficulty having severely missed its *profit* objectives in the last half of 1989. The Division responded to its profitability problems by giving the sales force a more aggressive *sales* quota. To control escalating costs, the corporate Controller took over P&L responsibility from the divisional Marketing department.

I feel the above divisional and corporate responses to raising profitability were ill-considered and create new problems. First, the way in which a Sales Representative will respond to an aggressive new sales quota can, ironically, exacerbate the profitability problem. To achieve the aggressive new sales quota, the sales force will push high volume brands (i.e. White Rain) that contribute little to profit. This short term volume increase comes at the expense of the field's promoting and building smaller, high margin brands.

Second, the Controller cut out advertising and field discretionary funds, showing his insensitivity to market considerations and trade issues; an immediate spike in profits comes at the expense of future consumer pickup.

The change I propose is to make the field more responsible for Divisional profitability. This can be done by giving the Sales Reps new Business Development Funds and more profit "accountability." With the funds, the Reps would be better able to respond to opportunities to develop and build the brands.

However, "accountability" would present implementation problems. How do you define and enforce accountability? The field cannot control many of the variables that impact on profitability: production costs, advertising commitments, price increases, and the size of trade allowances. Nor can the field break out different regions on a P&L basis, because developing or maintaining some accounts will be more expensive than others. It might cost more to develop more promising markets where P&G, for example, is also trying to make inroads.

The best solution for field profit accountability is a dual quota system: by sales and by brand. A brand quota would force the Rep to promote a more profitable mix of product regardless of whether he understood the profitability concerns. With the Business Development Fund, he would be able to build the profitable brands emphasized in the new brand quota.

These funds would encourage the Rep to be much more entrepreneurial. The Rep could design trade push and consumer pull programs that best suit his territory. Sales Planning would represent the interests of the sales force in determining fair brand quotas with the marketing department. Ultimately, this change would help balance Divisional and Corporate needs. With the Business Development funds, Reps would better be able to respond to local opportunities. With brand quotas, Corporate could better control product profit mix.

The downside is that the trade will come to expect these additional allowances and give little incremental promotional support. Further, career Reps might not adapt well to the new entrepreneurial demands and may develop ineffective programs. While the immediate solution would be to give the Business Development funds to the Reps who could use the funds most effectively, this would create resentment. The longer term solution is to recruit and build a sales force of entrepreneurial Reps who could run their own "franchises."

Question #2: *Describe your avocations and hobbies.*

Essay #2:

My most passionate nonacademic pursuit is athletics. I have learned invaluable lessons through playing on the Harvard Varsity Water-polo and Squash teams. As goalie in the Water-polo team, I learned the importance of teamwork. During a fast paced game, a goalie must be able to quickly identify potential problems and solve them in an effective manner. Collective responsibility is integral to teamwork. One cannot lay the blame on another player without jeopardizing team unity.

Squash taught me that progress can only be achieved through diligence and patience. Hitting a small black ball thousands of times for hundreds of hours in a small room can be perceived as a meaningless pursuit—or a disciplined process of developing precision and control. There are no shortcuts to improvement in the game of squash.

I have found these valuable lessons of teamwork and discipline to be easily transferable to other areas. Working with others in a competitive and tense environment can only be successfully achieved through proper teamwork. The discipline which I developed on the squash court has (similarly) enabled me to focus in other pursuits with equal determination.

Question #3: *Describe your most substantial accomplishments and explain why you view them as such.*

Essay #3:

1) Last spring I exported nearly $100,000 worth of exercise equipment to Japan. This shipment saved my company over $250,000, due to the price discrepancies between the United States and Japan. I was solely responsible for selecting the equipment, negotiating the price, arranging the insurance, and packing and shipping the equipment to Japan. The first step of the process of selecting the equipment and the company involved inspecting manufacturing facilities based in California, Maryland, Texas, Vermont, and Colorado. I researched the legitimacy of the companies by calling their previous clients, checking credit records, and calling the Better Business Bureau. After exporting the equipment to Japan, I flew to Japan to facilitate the import process. This involved meeting with Japanese customs, as well as assisting in the domestic transportation and installation of the equipment.

I consider this a major accomplishment for three reasons. Firstly, I was solely responsible for the entire project. Secondly, it was a complicated process which involved many unrelated details. Finally, and not least of all, the fact that it was successful also contributes to my sense of pride.

2) When the Japanese company opened its third health club in Japan in July, 1988, it was a great sense of personal satisfaction. Two summers ago, I participated in the planning and design of this club. I saw many of my substantive recommendations implemented, including the installation of a racquetball court system which has movable glass walls to allow squash, racquetball, basketball, and volleyball to be played on the same court. My idea more effectively utilizes very limited and costly space and also provides greater recreational variety for the users. I have previously discussed my export deal that provided over half of the equipment for the club, which was another source of personal satisfaction. In addition to helping design the club, I was actively involved in sales and marketing. I also conducted club tours for prospective members, and designed a new marketing strategy targeting foreigners living in the area. My combined efforts resulted in over 150 new members.

These accomplishments demonstrate my ability to work successfully in a large group setting as well as in an entirely different language and culture. In addition to the satisfaction of seeing my design recommendations actually implemented, I also enjoyed the challenges of sales and marketing.

3) I am currently co-teaching a Harvard college freshman seminar focusing on the economic development of Japan with Professor X. As a teacher, I had to design a reading list which would provide sufficient information without overwhelming the freshmen who have had no background on the topic. A reading list has to have an overall argument with weekly topics to provide specific examples. Teaching in a seminar format presents a tremendous intellectual challenge of stimulating and guiding a discussion. I try to give only directive or stimulative comments rather than to lecture. In this manner students will ask questions and I will try to steer the discussion so that the student is able to answer his/her own question.

Teaching the Seminar represents the cumulative total of my academic career. My studies have largely revolved around Japanese economics and Japanese history. In addition, my practical experience of working in a Japanese company in Japan complements my academic understanding and has further enhanced my abilities as a teacher.

UNIVERSITY OF MARYLAND

Essay #1:

My multi-page application answered the question, "Who am I?" Now it is time to answer another one— "Why am I here, in the pool of applicants to the Maryland MBA program?" That's a question many people have asked me.

My friends' confusion is understandable—why would a graduate student who enjoys doing research and teaching, with an expertise in a politically important part of the world and who allegedly would be able to get full funding in any school if he chose to go all the way to the Ph.D. in political science, want to change his career to take an unknown road in business? Quite a legitimate question. Let me explain why I chose to apply to the Maryland MBA Program and not to do something else, first revisit my life history.

In 1990 I joined the analytical division of a trading firm in Moscow—International Secondary Resources Exchange. I discovered consulting as a career and developed an interest in assessment of market potential, including a degree of political risk. At the time, Russia and other former communist countries were opening their markets and it was fascinating, but also very important to try to predict how promising the Russian market was. So I decided to get my master's in political science in order to be able to competently assess such important categories for estimating market potential as government capacity, public administration competence, political risk (legal and other obstacles to foreign investment), entrepreneurial culture and economic training of the population.

Still working on projects with the Exchange, I started a graduate program with concentration in international relations, comparative politics (Europe), and economics. It has been an important part of my education, given the importance of the political situation and, therefore, political forecasting for the business future of the former communist world.

My education now has to enter its most critical stage — actual study of business. This would let me have a deep understanding, as I hope, of financial and other market structures, competitiveness, and other factors that a consultant needs to take into account when recommending whether to conduct business in a foreign country.

Taking advantage of my bi-cultural background, long study of international relations and foreign languages, and business experience, I plan to pursue a career as an international business consultant. The UMCP certainly has a focus on global business. I am attracted by the Center for International Business Education and Research—I work for CIBER at the University of Utah and my colleagues spoke highly of the Maryland Program. At the same time the School offers a strong general management program—something I need, coming from a country with no free market traditions.

These are the "career" reasons to apply to Maryland. But there is also a "character" reason. It is critically important for me to be challenged. Only when sufficiently challenged, can I work at full capacity and deliver results. Without doubt, Maryland provides enough challenge, without mentioning that an application process itself is very stimulating.

Business schools' quality criteria are no secret. From these I pay special attention to location. The Washington-Baltimore metropolitan area is a perfect location for somebody interested in an international business career. It is also the place to be for a person, who, coming from Utah, is just hungry for student body diversity and cultural attractions. I visited the area on two occasions during my first year in this country and just fell in love with the place.

Add to these advantages a critical one for me—generous financial aid options. Unfortunately, without financial aid, I will not be able to attend school.

The Program's diverse environment is of special importance for me. I appreciate diversity and think I could add something myself to the already culturally rich Maryland MBA Program—after two years in the U.S. I am a walking example of cultural interaction. I picked up a lot of American practices, keeping at the same time some of my old ones. I do not protest any more when my friends take me out dinner around my birthday, but on my birthday itself I, as the Russian tradition goes, have them over for dinner. I try not to go with the flow and never say "how are you?" when I do not care and "nice to meet you" when I do not mean it, but sometimes I am supposed to say these meaningless phrases. I still pass with my face, rather than my back, to people sitting in a theater. I use Kleenex tissues, but still have a handkerchief in my pocket just in case. I kept my main dining habit—never putting down a knife when having salad and a main course. I changed, on the other hand, the way I approach desert, when I dine by myself; I still eat it with a spoon, as the Russians do. And I drink both hot tea and coke.

From my Russian background I keep moral integrity, industriousness, strong attachment to my family, self-reliance, cooperative spirit, sense of humor, strong interest in spending time with children, and my three other hobbies—movies, soccer, and travel. My American present made me friendly, punctual, conscientious, self-disciplined, law-abiding, determined to help people who are less lucky than I am (first of all, my fellow Russians), and two more pastimes—basketball and hiking. I hope that a person combining two cultures will be a good addition to the School's environment.

I believe that the Maryland MBA Program will provide me with a training I need and enough challenges to launch me to a new intellectual orbit. And, also, it would just be nice to be back East.

Critique: One important way MBA programs strengthen their international focus is by attracting talented students from different parts of the world. Indeed, a priority of the Maryland Business School is actively to recruit such students, because they increase both the breadth and depth of the school's international perspective.

In addition to fulfilling the basic requirement of every application's essay section—i.e., *answer the questions asked* (a surprising number of people fail to do this)—"Andrei's" statement also provided the admissions director with a vivid glimpse into his personality. And though English is obviously not his first language, his command of "Americanisms" is impressive and his sense of humor engaging. He comes across as a bright, self-motivated, high-energy individual. Just the type for Maryland.

He also did his homework. For instance, he mentions Maryland's Center for International Business Education and Research and the fact that the university is located in the culturally rich Washington, D.C., area. To the admissions director, this means he is serious about his application to the program; that he is not using the shotgun approach in applying to graduate school.

Had he wanted to make an even stronger impression, however, "Andrei" should have asked a native English speaker to read over his essay. Or two native speakers, for that matter. They would have helped him smooth out some of his sentences with proper punctuation and usage. For though his message is clear to the reader, his occasional lapses into fractured English somewhat detract from his many fine qualities.

UNIVERSITY OF MICHIGAN

Question #1: *During your years of study in the Michigan MBA program, you will be part of a diverse multicultural, multi-ethnic community within both the Business School and the larger University. What rewards and challenges do you anticipate in this campus environment, and how do you expect this experience to prepare you for a culturally diverse business world?*

Essay #1:

High return on investment . . .

One quality I have always admired is independent thinking. I always strive to be different and befriend those who share this same goal. I see conformity as a moral deficiency. "Group think" is the enemy of creativity and innovation. In contrast, diversity in thought is the key to any successful endeavor. I want to be a part of creative concepts proposed from a wide array of sources. These creative concepts can only be reached by assembling individuals with discordant views and from varying backgrounds. For this reason, I find the growing diversity of Michigan's student body to be one of its greatest selling points. I feel that understanding a wide range of views, opinions, and judgments on a variety of subject matter broadens the base of experience from which effective solutions may be derived. Therefore, learning, sharing, and growing within the context of diverse individuals is an avenue for developing a successful manager.

While there will be rewards from this melting pot, there is always the potential for difficulty when assembling people with divergent views and from different cultures. As a member of an international exchange program, in both training and travel, I was able to witness the glaring problems of cultural bias, prejudice, and close-mindedness. One thing I learned through this experience is that nobody is above prejudice of some kind, myself included. Everyone has some innate sense that they are superior to other individuals in some manner. When people feel superior because of their intellect, we call them arrogant. When people feel superior because of their nationality or culture, we call them elitists. And when people feel superior because of their race, we call them racists. The first step in understanding each other is to better understand ourselves and develop an understanding of our own prejudices. This will be the challenge facing every student in the melting pot. For some this challenge will be great and for some it may be overcome easily, but in either case I feel that the rewards from integration of people and ideas provide a great return on the time and energy invested to make it so.

Beyond the hallowed halls . . .
I expect my time at Michigan to enhance my understanding and appreciation of the benefits of mixing ideas and opinions among people from different backgrounds. The business community I will enter is a global, multinational, multicultural based body. Any business manager willing to shun certain peoples or ideas because they are foreign will be injuring his company. And yet, I have every reason to believe that I will inevitably encounter these types of individuals.

While universities are taking the lead in cultural and ethnic diversification, the business world is somewhat behind. The reasons for this are twofold: those people who are fearful of new ideas tend to fight diversity, while those individuals in favor of diversity often find developing it a daunting task. For this reason, many companies concede to the status quo, to the old way of doing business. Yet there are firms willing to shift paradigms of current thinking. These are the companies that will prosper in the future. The company that takes the initiative to broaden its personnel base will find that any short term expenses it may incur in this diversification process are easily offset by the long term benefits of having a dynamic, progressive, and enterprising staff. This is the type of firm I would like to associate with. Just as I expect to do at Michigan, I hope in the business community to be an active part of the melting pot of ideas, developing creative concepts, and forcing new paths by engaging divergent viewpoints.

Critique: Originality, insight, and graceful writing immediately capture the reader of this essay. Tackling the topic directly and substantively, the author effectively relates the subject to past personal experiences and future career aspirations. The writer avoids the platitudes that slide all too easily into application essays. With admirable honesty, he acknowledges the challenges posed by a multicultural environment, admits the prejudices he has felt, and identifies the personal rewards of being part of the Michigan community.

The essay goes beyond any superficial treatment of the issue and reveals how the author thinks. Indeed, the independent thinking admired by the writer emerges from the piece. The reader finds clear evidence of the analytical reasoning skills so critical to success and leadership in management. Finally, the writing style, characterized by flowing, balanced prose and apt word choice, is eloquent. The essay convinces the reader that this is someone whose thinking and ability to convey thoughts will enrich the learning process in and out of the classroom.

UNIVERSITY OF NOTRE DAME

Question #1: *As a Notre Dame student, what contributions would you make to the life of the program, both inside and outside the classroom? How will an MBA from Notre Dame help you achieve your short-term career goals and your long-term professional aspirations?*

Essay #1:

As a Notre Dame M.B.A. student there are many contributions I will make to enhance the excellence of the program. These contributions include attributes such as professional insight, an inquisitive mind, and innovative ideas along with high moral and ethical standards.

My two years' experience with Sikorsky Aircraft has given me a good understanding of multifunctional disciplines within American aerospace firms. I have grown from these experiences, and I will bring them to the classroom in the form of anecdotes. My job has helped me to gain a good perception of some of the best and worst ways to run a business. These experiences are ones you could never pick up from a textbook, but they will enhance the lessons found in one.

To the classroom I also bring an inquisitive mind. I am never satisfied with the statements of "that's the way it is" or "if it's not broke don't fix it." I feel that if you do not ask why or try to completely appreciate a theory or technique you may never truly understand it. There is always an alternative to any method or theory, and questioning is a way of developing new understandings.

Outside the classroom I bring innovation. I enjoy adding to the competitiveness of the organization of which I am a part, and I am always willing to try new things. For example, while at Michigan State I assisted in developing the first annual Materials and Logistics student/faculty retreat. This retreat is now an event supported by both the University and the professional world. In the same respect, as an intern at Sikorsky Aircraft, I worked in our Overhaul and Repair facility (O&R). One of my first observations was that O&R had no definitive way of tracking our suppliers' performance. Every individual department had a different tracking system. I combined the best attributes of each system to form a consolidated tracking run which is now used throughout the entire 600-person facility.

Two other contributions I will bring to Notre Dame cannot be labeled either inside or outside of the classroom because they pertain to both. Number one, I am a good team player. I have a good disposition which helps me not only get along with many different types of people but to enjoy working with them. Number two, through my business trips and experience of serving on M.S.U.'s Anti-Discrimination Judicial Board I have developed a unique appreciation of others' cultures and beliefs. I enjoy learning about other people and what makes them tick.

A Notre Dame M.B.A. will help me to obtain my short-term and long-term goals by providing a solid foundation and set a direction from which I can build. Before choosing the M.B.A. programs to which I would apply, I sat down with a former professor to obtain his insight into this decision. He told me that when choosing an M.B.A. program, I am choosing a label to carry with me throughout my career. This label aligns me with beliefs and practices of my M.B.A. institution. I chose to apply to Notre Dame because of the school's strong stand on ethics and the International Market. At Notre Dame I will be exposed to people not only from the Midwest but from around the world. This will further help me to broaden my horizons and understanding of people.

My long-term professional aspiration is to enter into the field of management consulting. An M.B.A. from Notre Dame in Interdisciplinary Studies will enhance my understanding of all aspects of business. This will contribute significantly to becoming effective in the consulting profession.

In conclusion, as a Notre Dame M.B.A. candidate I will bring a sincere attitude to succeed in the classroom, high ethical standards, and the willingness to go the extra mile. Upon graduation from Notre Dame, I will represent the University as a sign of the excellence a Notre Dame M.B.A. portrays in the professional world.

Critique: We chose Ed's essay because it was clearly and concisely written, using examples from college and career to make his points. For example, he used his experience in O&R at his current employment to highlight his technical and analytical abilities with the establishment of a tracking system now used throughout the facility. He backed up his claim for being innovative by citing his assistance in developing the first faculty and student retreat in his college department.

He dealt with both the short-term and long-term orientation of the program. In seeking advice from his professor, he showed seriousness about making his choice of schools. He wanted an international thrust to his studies and chose Notre Dame because of its reputation in that area as well as its commitment to ethics in business. That fit in nicely with what he learned from his experience on the Anti-Discrimination Judicial Board of his university. And his choice of Interdisciplinary Studies reinforces Notre Dame's focus on preparing students for General Management. Finally, his choice of consulting for a career flows naturally from his prior experiences and his curricular choices.

We like Ed's essay because it was to the point, responded to the essay question, and in a subtle but concrete way "sold" the candidate to the admissions committee. Ed managed to weave in accomplishments on the job with commitments he planned to make to the Notre Dame program. He demonstrated college leadership in a large, public, "anonymous" kind of school in which students often get lost. Based on his experience, his career goals and aspirations appear to be realistic. While he has high ideals, they do not seem to be "pie in the sky" notions, and he displayed a certain kind of maturity and sensitivity which we liked.

STANFORD UNIVERSITY

Question #1: *Tell us about those influences that have significantly shaped who you are today.*

Essay #1:

I am a descendant of a long line of Quaker business people. My family, the ...., have been Quaker since 1630. The common punch line about this group, at gatherings of Friends, is that Quaker business people set out to do good and ended up doing very well. I am just beginning to emerge as a Quaker in business.

Relating some background about my Quaker heritage should help to illustrate how values of the Religious Society of Friends (the official name of "Quakers") have shaped my sense of who I am. Quakers have particular ethics which I try to develop in myself and live out. Quakers believe there is that of God in every person—they often call it the "Inner Light"—and that all people, regardless of rank and position, should be treated with dignity and integrity. This vision has helped me to see the potential in other people, even those who may be difficult to work with. It has also helped me to relate comfortably to people of every rank; in my current job, I enjoy friendships with everyone from secretaries to the president. In addition, a belief in my own Inner Light has helped my self-confidence, especially in those situations where intuition must complement facts and objective measures in making decisions.

This faith in the Inner Light has many other implications, of course, but two of the most important ones involve how group decisions should be made, and the equality of women.

As a way of doing business, Quakers believe in consensus decision-making; in fact they don't believe in hiring or paying ministers. All administration for Quaker Meeting is done by voluntary committees. From participating in consensus decision-making, I have learned to work with diverse groups of people, to negotiate between individual agendas, and to build effective teamwork between people. Consensus decision-making gives everyone a chance to contribute, and helps all members of the group to understand and articulate both the problem and solution.

Because of the Quaker belief that all people possess an Inner Light, they have traditionally believed in the full equality of men and women. In fact, Quakers held separate business meetings for men and women until about 50 years ago, because it was felt that otherwise women would be overshadowed by the men. This separation allowed Quaker women to develop leadership skills in speaking and administration. Strong Quaker women like Lucretia Mott, a leader in the movement to abolish slavery, and Elizabeth Cady Stanton, a leader among the suffragettes, were products of this culture.

Several other characteristic Quaker beliefs are placing a high value on simplicity, and on speaking and living the truth. For example, Quakers refuse to swear to anything, even at a trial or for a marriage license, because it implies that at other times one might not tell the truth. Being practical and "grounded" are Quaker values that discourage otherworldly or naive thinking. As a general rule, Quakers don't proselytize or even talk very much about their religion. They believe that their lives should speak of their convictions.

Quaker values can interact with business priorities in many ways, mostly positive, but some potentially negative as well. For example, because Quakers didn't limit their business contacts to the highest social echelon, they found opportunities for more customers and a wider circle of business associates. As Quaker women developed leadership skills, their ingenuity contributed to the success of Quaker businesses. Quaker businesses put a high value on providing products that truly add value for consumers, rather than devising ways to trick them into buying something. In the days before *Consumer Reports*, people saw many advantages to doing business with Quakers, because it was widely known that they wouldn't cheat you. Since Quakers were known to try to speak the truth regardless of the cost to themselves or whether the news was welcome, their word was trusted. Of course, being honest didn't prevent Quakers from being shrewd business people.

But although Quakers tend to be highly ethical, they can also be somewhat naive. Consensus decision-making can be far too slow and unwieldy for some decisions, and it runs a risk that people will feel coerced by the group into settling for less than they want. Rather than making everyone responsible, it can end up making no one responsible. Even people with an Inner Light can behave badly. "Speaking truth to power," to use the common catch-phrase for Quakers, can either increase long-run credibility or can be a cover for venting harsh feelings at inappropriate times.

My mother has told me that she married my father partially because he had been raised Quaker and was comfortable with strong, independent women. During my senior year of college, I was disheartened to find that many men of my own age found me intimidating. It was also a time when my mother was diagnosed with serious and potentially life-threatening breast cancer. Now I'm happily married, and my mother has at least survived the chemotherapy, but I still keep and re-read a letter I received from my father that year about the strong women in my family. Here's an excerpt [sic].

"Let's start with this generalization: Highly articulate, handsome, intelligent women are not terribly rare. No doubt you yourself have many friends that would easily fit such categorization. But if you add two further adjectival phrases, then such women are very rare indeed. Namely, passionate commitment and courageous. (I'm willing to concede that these may even be redundant . . . they, in your case, certainly go together.) Obviously these same characteristics are very rare in men too.

"The problem arises primarily for women. These characteristics scare the bejabbers out of others . . . they may be admired by some, vilified by others, and wholly misunderstood by the majority. But even those that admire them generally want to do it at a safe distance. Let's face it—sparks are given off by such people. The prudent man usually decides that the warmth and excitement isn't worth the high risk of being consumed in a conflagration set off by so many sparks.

"You are the fourth in a line of such women."

I am enclosing a photocopy of this letter with application (Attachment I) because it illuminates the way Quakers like my father can support and encourage women in leadership. Also, it provides some insight into my family.

Another important influence is my new husband, Timothy .... We were married July 6 of this year. Tim is the managing editor of the *Journal of Economic Perspectives*, which is based at Stanford. My husband's background in economics informs and counterbalances my perspectives.

My career has forced me to balance the idealistic qualities of Quakerism with real-life experience, where the rubber meets the road. My first job out of college was as editor and then executive director for a nonprofit foundation called Fellowship in Prayer (FIP), whose purpose was to "encourage the practice of prayer or meditation among people of all faiths." This nonprofit was a rare one: it actually had an endowment that grew from $2.7 to 3.5 million during my three-year tenure. My job was to organize the programs and facilities from complete chaos to something more effective and methodical. I managed the budgets so that operating expenditures came only from the interest on the endowment, not from the capital. I also learned some lessons that went well beyond business. I was sexually harassed by two members of the Board of Trustees, and had to face the problem of other Board members stealing from the endowment.

Perhaps my biggest lesson from Fellowship in Prayer was that systems—the way information is transferred, decisions are made and reporting relationships defined—largely determine the effectiveness of the organization. When I started working there, the organization had no functioning systems in place, and no objectives or strategies beyond the general mission statement quoted a moment ago. I had previously looked on things like standard operating procedures and methods of reporting and accountability as necessary evils. But I found that it's not nearly enough to have an operating budget and some staff. An organization also needs definite goals, strategies for achieving them, and ways of measuring success. While working at FIP, I came to understand that structure is enabling: without it, people spend too much time wondering what they are supposed to be doing or reinventing the wheel. Now I appreciate the need to organize structures, and the significance when such systems work well.

My position as Executive Director at FIP forced me to learn a wide range of business skills and responsibilities. I wrote the annual budget and the annual report, and oversaw expenditures. I bought a $300,000 property for the headquarters of the foundation (previously, it had rented space), arranged for $20,000 of structural repairs and another $20,000 for redecorating and furnishing, and moved the office. I edited the bimonthly magazine for nine months, until I became Executive Director. I supervised other staff. I tried to create a counterbalance to the power of the Board of Trustees, some of whom had been stealing from the foundation, by recruiting a lawyer with financial expertise to the Board. I also formed an advisory board composed of Christians, Jews, Baha'is, Buddhists, a Mohawk Chief, and others to improve the programs and create a balance of power with the Board of Trustees. Also, this group helped in generating ideas for programs, like lectures and retreats.

I also worked on developing my own speaking and writing skills; I gave lectures, workshops, and retreats myself. I have continued to pursue my interest in designing programs and giving talks that help people deepen their spirituality and fulfill their potential. During the past few years, for example, I have led retreats at the Quaker center in Ben Lomond, California, and for Faith at Work, a national ecumenical group with which I continue to do volunteer work. With my application, I have enclosed some flyers publicizing these retreats (Attachment II). I wrote the ones for Quaker Center.

Critique: *General Guidelines*—The strongest essays give us a real sense of who the applicant is. Because we do not offer interviews, this is the applicants' only opportunity to provide insight into who they are; in a way, it is like an interview on paper. But it should be more personal and less résumélike. Ideally, after reading the essay, we should have a good idea of what this person would like to discuss if we (hypothetically) met over coffee. We're looking for *who* someone is rather than *what* he or she has done. *This is the fundamental distinction we make:* we want to get to know the person behind the grades, scores, and job accomplishments—what are his or her passions, values, interests, and goals? We expect applicants to get beyond the standard "I did this, I did that" model to share with us what they care about and what has shaped them. We look for an honest and natural tone, hoping to find essays that are engaging and immediate rather than dry and distant—ideally, a conversation on paper.

Evaluation of This Essay: For this student, being Quaker has been the most significant influence in her life. She does a good job of focusing deeply on that single influence, extracting specific insight from its effect on her. She ties it in to her values (simplicity, truthful living, living one's convictions), her social/emotional experiences (dating, equality of women), and even her philosophy of business (consensus decision-making, honesty). For her, being Quaker is more than a religious faith; it is a life choice, and by explaining its influences on her she provides insight into who she is and why she developed that way.

This essay is honest and immediate; she opens up about personal matters in a way that allows us to get to know the real her; for example, she shares a personal and emotional letter her father sent her during a difficult time for her family. She has analyzed the positives and negatives that her Quaker upbringing has fostered, further showing intelligent self-analysis and thoughtfulness. Overall, she presents a picture of a smart, committed woman who has thought hard about who she is and is able (and willing) to communicate what she cares about and why.

Toward the end of the essay she shifts from the personal to the professional (from the "who" to the "what"), but does so relatively effectively. We learn how she puts her passions into action, as well as some key lessons she has learned from her initial work experiences. There is a bit too much "I did this, I did that" at the end of the essay; it would have been stronger had she let her résumé tell us her accomplishments, focusing here only on personal introspection. However, as a whole the essay is strong because some of that introspection is present, and even the "what" section tells us something about her.

TULANE UNIVERSITY— A. B. FREEMAN SCHOOL OF BUSINESS

Question #1: *Why are you seeking a Tulane MBA at this time? In your answer, please include critical academic and professional experiences that led to your decision, a self-assessment of your suitability for graduate management school, your career goals and your specific interest in the Freeman School.*

Essay #1:

I am seeking a Tulane MBA because the curriculum and international programs offered by the A. B. Freeman School of Business at Tulane University will expand my knowledge of core business concepts while allowing me to focus on the area in which I plan to make my career: international business. As the national accounts officer at ABC Bank, I serve as the account handling officer for the bank's national and multinational corporate customers, such as General Motors Acceptance Corporation, Anheuser-Busch, and Westinghouse Electric. In working with these firms, both now as an officer and previously as a credit card analyst, I have observed that many of them plan to increase their international presence, especially in Mexico and Europe. My career objective is to work for a multinational firm for several years to gain the experience needed to ultimately establish my own international service-related firm. The knowledge needed and experience offered by the programs at the Freeman School will help me achieve this goal.

After working at ABC Bank for three years, I have decided that I need more academic training in order to pursue a more challenging career. The will and drive to succeed has characterized my tenure at ABC Bank. I attribute my success to two of my personal strengths that will be equally important in future careers: persistence and interpersonal skills.

After graduating from the University of XYZ in August of 1986, my goal was to secure a credit analyst position with ABC Bank. I believed the analyst position would help me build a foundation for making credit decisions as a lender, as well as allow me to study the operations of many industries. Upon applying for the position, however, I was told that no analyst positions were available and that the bank preferred to hire internally for such jobs. With this guideline in mind, I asked for any available job at the bank. I was offered a commercial vault teller position and accepted it. Although the work of processing commercial deposits for eight hours a day was monotonous, I kept my strategy in mind: perform my teller duties well, be persistent with credit management, and thereby earn the credit analyst job. After nine months in the vault, my determination was rewarded; the credit manager offered me the position that I sought. As an analyst, I was responsible for writing detailed analyses of a firm's operations to assist the commercial lenders with credit decisions. After working only eleven months in the credit area (the normal tenure is eighteen to twenty-four months), I was elected national accounts officer, thus becoming the bank's youngest officer. Although I wrote very good credit reviews, I was not promoted for this reason; there were several other analysts who also wrote good reviews. I was promoted largely because of my strong interpersonal and communications skills, since the National Accounts position requires an officer who can work well with both current and prospective customers. The National Accounts position entails handling the lending and cash management needs of the bank's national customers.

At ABC Bank, I have moved from a teller to an officer position in a short time. I have used my intelligence, persistence, and interpersonal skills to move up rapidly and now I wish to pursue a more challenging career. I am ready to use my past experience, combined with my strengths that I have discussed above, to obtain a graduate management degree and then excel in the area of international business.

Goal: Career in International Business

I want to build on my three years of banking experience and my travels, literally around the world, in preparation for an international management position either within the U.S. or abroad. My travels to Australia, Latin America, and South Africa on behalf of my family's cattle ranch first stimulated my interest in international business and trade. This interest has subsequently evolved during my three years in the banking business.

While I was a credit analyst, I learned much more about the international direction in which many firms are increasingly moving. Some of the firms that I reviewed are aggressively pursuing opportunities in Mexico because of their proximity to the border, the probable free trade agreement between the United States and Mexico, and the burgeoning maquiladora industry along the international border. The common denominator among these firms is a desire to take advantage of Mexico's abundance of labor and natural resources. I believe these two resources, coupled with Mexico's progressive government and an increasing interest in Mexico by U.S. businesses, will provide great opportunity in this emerging area of trade.

In addition, the National Accounts position has afforded me the opportunity to travel nationwide to call on my customers' home offices, and, in the course of conducting the bank's affairs, inquire about each firm's international operations. Although noting the obstacles, political and economic, many customers have eagerly outlined their plans to expand into Latin America, Eastern Europe, and China. They made it clear to me that trends such as the movement toward common markets and the increasing capability of long distance communication via satellite will further encourage foreign trade. Furthermore, most noted their company's need to employ more personnel in the international area; the general consensus among my contacts is that there will be an increasing demand for international managers in the next decade.

At present, I am undecided as to which career path I will choose in international business. Some possibilities that I have considered are finance-related and should capitalize on my lending and cash management experience with a multinational bank. Another option I am considering is to establish a firm that provides translation services to companies wishing to conduct business abroad. As more firms enter the international market, the language barrier could be an obstacle to many U.S. businesses. A translation service would overcome this problem and innovations such as video teleconferencing make this idea quite feasible.

Why a Tulane MBA?

Clearly, there are a number of options available to someone pursuing a career in international management, but I realize that I first need a more substantive grasp of the basics of management and the specifics of international business in order to be an effective manager. The Freeman School's curriculum provides the opportunity for me to obtain this knowledge.

The program's first year of required core courses, such as Financial Accounting and Marketing Management, followed by a flexible course schedule in the second year appeals to my desire to expand my knowledge in the areas of finance and accounting, and then focus on international topics. I also hope to take advantage of the school's international internship program or the study abroad program. It is important that I take advantage of one of these programs, since I believe one should have a sense of the culture and economic climate of a region if she or he hopes to conduct business in that area.

Since I will spend almost two years in a Masters program and the school I choose could well determine my career options, I have treated the selection of schools to which I will apply with great care. I am quite aware of the Freeman School's outstanding reputation for international studies. Furthermore, since New Orleans is one of the nation's largest ports, I will have the opportunity to obtain firsthand knowledge about international commerce. Finally, several of the school's alumni have highly recommended the Freeman School to me due to its significant global focus.

In summary, the combination of my three years of banking experience, international travels, and completion of the MBA program at Tulane should prepare me quite well to succeed as an international manager. As you can see, I have demonstrated both motivation and initiative during my tenure at ABC Bank. I realize that my grade point average is below the published median 3.1 for a recent entering class. I attribute my relatively low GPA to lack of career focus and immaturity during my undergraduate years. I want to assert my belief, however, that I have as much character, determination and will to succeed as any student in the MBA program. I might note that there are several credit analysts who obtained their jobs before I did mainly due to higher GPA's; most of these analysts are still in the credit department writing reviews while I travel nationwide representing the bank. I can successfully complete the MBA program at Tulane and would certainly like the opportunity to do so.

Critique: Our admissions committee felt that this was an extremely strong essay. Many applicants have the tendency to treat this as an open-ended "Tell us about yourself . . ." kind of question and write very general essays that elaborate on their backgrounds without providing adequate rationale regarding their suitability for MBA studies, an outline of their goals, or how a Freeman MBA can help them attain these goals. Although often cleverly written, such essays do not help the committee in making an admissions decision.

This essay is well structured, well written, and gives us a clear picture of the applicant as an individual who is both motivated and focused. The description of his rapid progression at ABC Bank from commercial vault teller to credit analyst (his initial goal) to national accounts officer clearly shows that the applicant is able to assess his options, set goals and successfully develop and execute a strategy to reach them. These are characteristics we seek in our MBA students. The essay also shows that the applicant has gained important knowledge and insights along the way which have helped him formulate his goals for the future. Those goals include a Freeman MBA and a career in international business.

Although this applicant confesses that he is still weighing two options in the area of international business (rather refreshing, since many of the very specific career goals we read about are obviously contrived or not well supported in the essay), he makes a convincing case for his interest in the field. He also explains his interest in the Freeman School well, citing our global focus, location in one of the nation's largest port cities, and some of our specific international programs. The applicant shows a strong interest in the Freeman MBA program. He has researched the program and has clearly taken the time to speak with alumni.

Finally, the applicant acknowledges a weakness (his GPA), and, without making excuses, emphasizes the characteristics he has which he believes will make him a strong candidate for our program. These characteristics were amply demonstrated throughout the essay, but he does a nice job of summarizing them and "closing the sale" at the end.

UNIVERSITY OF VIRGINIA

Question #1: *What is the most difficult ethical dilemma you have faced in your professional life? Articulate the nature of the difficulty. Upon present reflection, would you have resolved this dilemma in a different manner?*

Essay #1:

Upon graduation from college, my sense of adventure and quest for learning continued when I accepted a nontraditional position with the Bank of Credit and Commerce International (BCCI). I accepted a position with BCCI with the understanding that overseas placements were the requirement, given the bank's limited US presence. BCCI was founded in 1972 by Pakistani financier Agha Hasan Abedi, whose goal was to create the first multinational bank for the Third World. Its shareholders were rich Middle Eastern oil sheiks. Healthy growth fueled by increased international trade helped BCCI expand to $20 billion in assets that circled the globe in a 70 country branch network.

After completing BCCI's international trade finance training program with distinction at Pace University in New York, I received my first placement in London, England, working as a trainee in bank branch operations and special country analysis projects. After quickly completing my London assignment in three months, BCCI management promoted me to a marketing role at their main offices in the United Arab Emirates (UAE). The ruling sheiks of each of the emirates were BCCI's major stockholders and had enormous international political and economic clout.

By quickly absorbing the local culture and the basics of the Arabic language, I earned the respect of my peers at the bank and in the local business community. Through my efforts, I marketed and received commitments for trade financing and investing from many multinational businesses operating in the UAE.

It was right after my third month working in the UAE that I was faced with a major ethical dilemma. During my search for new business, I learned from a contact at the government ministry of trade that a European sportswear manufacturer had applied for permission to start up a business in the UAE. (An application to do business is required of all foreigners along with the requirement to find a local partner.) I immediately informed bank management of the prospect and began my research into the company. After an initial meeting with the company in the UAE a few weeks later, I learned that the firm required a $30 million line facility. I requested the necessary financial information from the company and began my analysis of the company to assess its creditworthiness. My recommendation to bank management was not to proceed any further with the company, given its losses over the past three years and very high leverage. The risks posed by the company's profile were too great.

My manager, who had always valued my credit skills, mysteriously ignored my recommendations and ordered me to negotiate a loan facility with the company. I was puzzled by my manager's action, especially since he offered no explanation. I structured a smaller facility at a premium interest rate with adequate primary and secondary fallback collateral to protect the bank from any credit risks. After presenting the new proposal to my bank manager, he dismissed it without comment and made the necessary arrangements to grant the company a $30 million unsecured line of credit at an interest rate reserved for the bank's highest creditworthy clients. A new provision was added, though. A finder's fee of one percent of the loan ($300,000) was due. Even though the fee was paid, there existed no mention of it in the loan documents. Through a search of the bank's accounting records, I learned that the fee was transferred out of the UAE to my manager's personal account abroad. I was naive to think that the manager did not have his contacts in the bank who would report my inquiring.

My manager explained that the fee was not to be considered extorted funds, rather it was his finder's fee. Further, he explained that this was a customary practice. In fact, to show goodwill, he offered to share this fee with me and suggested $50,000. The only stipulation was that I had to keep the matter quiet from "jealous" employees.

My dilemma was whether to accept part of my manager's illegally obtained funds and keep quiet or to report the matter to a higher level of bank management. Being only 23 years of age and in a foreign country 8,000 miles away from home, I was scared. If this was a customary practice and the branch was covering up for him, then my reporting this incident would put my job in jeopardy as well as my life. I was always taught by my family to practice high ethical and moral standards and to obey the law. This was my guiding principle in refusing the illegal funds and notifying the bank's London headquarters of this serious matter. Immediately, I was transferred back to London within 48 hours; and no mention of the incident was ever made to me either in the UAE or in London. My newly assigned job in London was nonmarketing related and consisted of counting checks in a windowless basement room. Even though it felt like BCCI management was punishing me for good ethical conduct, I still believed that my decision was right. I resigned from the bank one month later and returned to the U.S., where I obtained a banking job with an organization that, I feel proud to state, has never presented me with the choice of compromising my ethics and moral standards.

If, in the future, I am unfortunately presented with an ethical dilemma of any degree, I feel confident in holding my ethical and moral standards as a priority.

Critique: What makes an application to the Darden School stand out from among the thousands received each year? One important key is well-written essays. As with many business school applications, the essay portion is the applicant's chance to showcase his or her writing talents while at the same time communicating a lot of explicit (and sometimes implicit) information to the admissions committee.

Many B-schools offer the first-year student traditional courses in such functional areas as accounting, marketing, and operations, but Darden was one of the first to include required, graded courses in both communications and ethics. Nowhere at Darden do these two disciplines dovetail more perfectly than in Essay #4 of Darden's application, which asks: "What is the most difficult ethical dilemma you have faced in your professional life? Articulate the nature of the difficulty. Upon present reflection, would you have resolved this dilemma in a different manner?"

While this essay question often prompts the most reflection and introspection on the part of the applicant, it is also often the least understood. The admissions committee is looking not necessarily to judge the nature of the dilemma but rather the candidate's ability to articulate an often personal and complex decision-making process. The key to an effective Essay #4 is in dissecting the terms *ethical* and *dilemma*. Too often, themes reflected in this essay are of a legal nature: Should I disagree with my boss? Should I turn a co-worker in who's stealing office supplies? Should I break the law? And many situations do not accurately present a true dilemma in which there is no clear right or wrong answer but two or more possible solutions, none of which are necessarily better than another.

The essay above serves as an outstanding example by setting the scene, explaining clearly the nature of the dilemma and summing up the candidate's experience in a concise and well-written essay. The admissions committee was particularly impressed by the author's honest approach and engaging writing style. The firm does not have to be well-known, in this case BCCI, nor must the dilemma involve large sums of money or shady characters. Rather, the essay should reflect the candidate's personal and professional commitment to ethics, a commitment that also underlies the foundation of the Darden School.

CHAPTER EIGHT

Schools Rated by Category

About These "Rankings"

Now before you say, "Hey, wait a minute! I thought this book wasn't going to rank schools," let us explain. Surveying 15,500 business school students is no easy task. In fact, it practically killed several staff members. But among the fruits of our labors—a reward that made our task seem worthwhile — was the fascinating numbers we came up with. We wanted to present those numbers to you in an informative and slightly less-than-serious way. The following rankings cannot and must not be considered objective. These lists are based entirely upon student opinion. So when our list rates a campus location, for example, we didn't use any scientific formula based on cost of living, climate, crime rate, etc. We simply listed the schools at which students raved about the location most, or complained about it most. So focus on the categories that are important to you, and make of these opinions what you will.

And remember, every one of the schools profiled in this book is a top-notch institution.

ACADEMICS

STUDENTS DEVELOP STRONG GENERAL MANAGEMENT SKILLS
Dartmouth College
University of Virginia
Georgetown University
Yale University
Harvard University
Wake Forest University
University of North Carolina/Chapel Hill
Stanford University
Duke University
University of Southern California

WEAK GENERAL MANAGEMENT SKILLS
Pennsylvania State University
City University of New York/Baruch College
University of Kentucky
University of Rochester
Georgia Institute of Technology
University of Rochester
Hofstra University
University of Texas/Arlington
University of Massachusetts/Amherst
University of Kansas

QUANT JOCKS
(students develop strong quantitative skills)
Carnegie Mellon University
University of Chicago
Purdue University
Massachusetts Institute of Technology
University of Rochester
Yale University
University of Maryland
University of Pennsylvania
Columbia University
Rice University

POETS
(weak quantitative skills)
Harvard University
Syracuse University
Northwestern University
Boston University
Cornell University
Claremont Graduate School
Hofstra University
City University of New York/Baruch College
Brigham Young University
Pennsylvania State University

STUDENTS DEVELOP STRONG INTERPERSONAL SKILLS
Georgetown University
University of Tennessee
University of Virginia
University of Southern California
Dartmouth College
Texas Christian University
Yale University
Southern Methodist University
Stanford University
Duke University

WEAK INTERPERSONAL SKILLS
University of Kentucky
City University of New York/Baruch College
Syracuse University
University of Washington
Georgia Institute of Technology
Loyola University/Chicago
Texas A&M University
University of Wyoming
University of Texas/Arlington
Claremont Graduate School

STUDENTS DEVELOP STRONG COMMUNICATION SKILLS
Texas Christian University
University of Tennessee
Southern Methodist University
Tulane University
Georgetown University
Duke University
Dartmouth College
College of William and Mary
Purdue University
Wake Forest University

WEAK COMMUNICATION SKILLS
University of Kentucky
Syracuse University
Loyola University/Chicago
University of Washington
Harvard University
University of Massachusetts/Amherst
Cornell University
University of Texas/Arlington
Claremont Graduate School
Hofstra University

STUDENTS DEVELOP STRONG TEAMWORK SKILLS
Dartmouth College
Georgetown University
University of Tennessee
Duke University
Yale University
Northwestern University
University of North Carolina/Chapel Hill
University of Virginia
Texas Christian University
Wake Forest University

NOT MUCH TEAMWORK
Harvard University
University of Kentucky
City University of New York/Baruch College
Loyola University/Chicago
University of Texas/Arlington
University of Wyoming
Syracuse University
Pennsylvania State University
Hofstra University
University of Massachusetts/Amherst

STUDENTS DEVELOP STRONG OPERATIONS SKILLS
Carnegie Mellon University
Georgetown University
Washington University
Massachusetts Institute of Technology
University of Virginia
Purdue University
University of Southern California
Southern Methodist University
Ohio State University
Tulane University

OPERATIONS NOT A STRONG POINT
Cornell University
University of Kentucky
Syracuse University
University of Massachusetts/Amherst
Rice University
University of Michigan
Hofstra University
University of Texas/Arlington
Claremont Graduate School
City University of New York/Baruch College

STUDENTS DEVELOP STRONG ACCOUNTING SKILLS
University of Chicago
University of Southern California
University of Maryland
Washington University
Yale University
University of Pennsylvania
University of Texas/Austin
Dartmouth College
University of Washington
University of Colorado/Boulder

WHAT'S A SPREAD SHEET?
Pennsylvania State University
Ohio State University
University of Tennessee
Hofstra University
Syracuse University
Babson College
University of Kentucky
Harvard University
University of Arizona
Brigham Young University

FINANCE WHIZZES
(students develop strong finance skills)
University of Chicago
University of Pennsylvania
Yale University
Columbia University
New York University
University of Rochester
University of Southern California
University of Virginia
Rice University
Massachusetts Institute of Technology

HAVE TROUBLE MAKING CORRECT CHANGE
(weak finance skills)
University of Kentucky
Pennsylvania State University
University of Tennessee
College of William and Mary
Syracuse University
Texas A&M University
University of Massachusetts/Amherst
Emory University
Hofstra University
University of Wyoming

STUDENTS DEVELOP STRONG MARKETING SKILLS
Northwestern University
Georgetown University
University of Maryland
University of Tennessee
Dartmouth College
Wake Forest University
Rice University
University of Southern California
University of Virginia
University of California/Berkeley

WEAK MARKETING SKILLS
Syracuse University
University of Rochester
Brigham Young University
Boston University
Northeastern University
City University of New York/Baruch College
University of Washington
Rensselaer Polytechnic Institute
University of Kentucky
University of Texas/Arlington

COMPUTER GENIUSES
(students comfortable with computers and managing data)
Carnegie Mellon University
Wake Forest University
Massachusetts Institute of Technology
Duke University
Southern Methodist University
Purdue University
University of Illinois/Champaign-Urbana
Texas Christian University
Georgia Institute of Technology
Stanford University

HOW DO I TURN THIS THING ON?
(students uncomfortable with computers)
Harvard University
University of Kentucky
Boston University
Claremont Graduate School
Loyola University of Chicago
Hofstra University
Cornell University
Syracuse University
Pennsylvania State University
City University of New York/Baruch College

BEST OVERALL SKILLS
(in the functional areas)
Georgetown University
Wake Forest University
Southern Methodist University
University of Southern California
Dartmouth College
University of Virginia
Carnegie Mellon University
Yale University
Purdue University
University of Maryland

WEAKEST OVERALL SKILLS
(in the functional areas)
University of Kentucky
Syracuse University
City University of New York/Baruch College
Pennsylvania State University
Harvard University
Hofstra University
Loyola University/Chicago
University of Texas/Arlington
Boston University
Claremont Graduate School

PRESSURE

OVERALL MELLOW
Emory University
University of Wyoming
Stanford University
University of California/Berkeley
University of Kentucky
Loyola University of Chicago
Cornell University
Ohio State University
Wake Forest University
University of Massachusetts/Amherst

OVERALL TENSE
Northwestern University
Carnegie Mellon University
University of Southern California
College of William and Mary
University of Virginia
Rensselaer Polytechnic Institute
Purdue University
Massachusetts Institute of Technology
Rice University
University of Pittsburgh

GOOD SAMARITANS
(non-competitive students)
Yale University
Stanford University
University of California/Berkeley
University of Washington
Northwestern University
Georgetown University
Case Western Reserve University
Emory University
Duke University
University of Wyoming

BACK-STABBERS
(competitive students)
University of Alabama/Tuscaloosa
New York University
Northeastern University
Arizona State U
Purdue University
Rice University
Rensselaer Polytechnic Institute
University of Texas/Austin
University of Connecticut
Texas Christian University

UP ALL NIGHT
(heavy work load)
Carnegie Mellon University
University of Virginia
University of Southern California
Massachusetts Institute of Technology
Georgetown University
Purdue University
Dartmouth College
Rice University
Indiana University/Bloomington
Rensselaer Polytechnic Institute

LIGHT WORK LOAD
Emory University
University of Kentucky
Loyola University/Chicago
University of Wyoming
University of Florida
Stanford University
University of California/Berkeley
University of California/Los Angeles
Texas Christian University
Boston University

SOCIAL LIFE & FELLOW STUDENTS

"SHINY, HAPPY MBAs"
(best quality of life)
Dartmouth College
Georgetown University
Stanford University
Northwestern University
University of Colorado/Boulder
Yale University
University of California/Berkley
University of Virginia
Washington University
Duke University

SCHOOL OF THE LIVING DEAD
(worst quality of life)
Syracuse University
City University of New York/Barch College
Hofstra University
University of Kentucky
Pennsylvania State University
Texas A&M University
University of Kansas
Georgia Institute of Technology
University of Rochester
Boston University

YOUR BROKERAGE OR MINE?
(students date often)
Northwestern University
University of Denver
Southern Methodist University
University of North Carolina/Chapel Hill
Brigham Young University
Wake Forest University
Tulane University
University of California/Berkeley
University of Florida
Ohio State University

WELCOME TO THE MONASTERY
(students don't date)
University of Arizona
University of Rochester
Babson College
City University of New York/Baruch College
Cornell University
University of Michigan
University of Washington
Carnegie Mellon University
University of Notre Dame
University of Minnesota/T.C.

TOP OF THE MORNING TO YOU
(students are very friendly)
University of Maryland
Dartmouth College
University of Southern California
University of Colorado/Boulder
Yale University
Georgetown University
Northwestern University
Stanford University
University of Wisconsin/Madison
Indiana University/Bloomington

DON'T BOTHER ME
(students aren't very friendly)
University of Kentucky
Hofstra University
Pennsylvania State University
Syracuse University
University of Texas/Arlington
Texas A&M University
University of Rochester
City University of New York/Baruch College
University of Illinois/Champaign-Urbana
New York University

SOCIAL BUTTERFLIES
(active social lives)
Stanford University
Dartmouth College
Georgetown University
Wake Forest University
University of California/Berkeley
Southern Methodist University
University of North Carolina/Chapel Hill
Duke University
University of Colorado/Boulder
Tulane University

HERE'S MY CARD
(students will keep in touch)
Georgetown University
Dartmouth College
University of Virginia
Stanford University
Yale University
Northwestern University
Southern Methodist University
University of Southern California
University of California/Berkeley
Columbia University

MULTICULTURAL SMORGASBORD
(ethnic & racial diversity)
University of Michigan
Columbia University
Tulane University
University of Pennsylvania
University of California/Berkeley
Massachusetts Institute of Technology
University of Pittsburgh
Rensselaer Polytechnic Institute
City University of New York/Baruch College
Northeastern University

THE HEART IS A LONELY BROKER
(moribund social lives)
University of Texas/Arlington
City University of New York/Baruch College
University of Arizona
University of Rochester
Rensselaer Polytechnic Institute
University of Kentucky
Babson College
Syracuse University
Northwestern University
College of William and Mary

WHAT'S NETWORKING?
(students won't stay in touch)
University of Kentucky
Pennsylvania State University
Hofstra University
University of Texas/Arlington
Syracuse University
University of Wyoming
Texas A&M University
City University of New York/Baruch College
Boston University
Loyola University/Chicago

WHITE BREAD
(ethnic & racial homogeneity)
Brigham Young University
Southern Methodist University
College of William and Mary
University of Alabama/Tuscaloosa
Dartmouth College
Texas A&M University
Rice University
University of Notre Dame
University of Washington
Arizona State University

STUDENTS ARE EAGER TO HELP OTHERS
Dartmouth College
Yale University
Georgetown University
University of Virginia
Stanford University
Southern Methodist University
Northwestern University
University of California/Berkeley
Duke University
University of Maryland

(students say classmates are smart)
Yale University
Stanford University
Dartmouth College
Massachusetts Institute of Technology
Georgetown University
Duke University
University of Virginia
Northwestern University
University of Maryland
University of Chicago

"BEEN THERE, DONE THAT"
(students have diverse work experience)
Yale University
University of California/Berkeley
Columbia University
University of Virginia
Northwestern University
University of Pennsylvania
Georgetown University
Cornell University
Massachusetts Institute of Technology
University of Michigan

ONLY IF YOU ASK
Pennsylvania State University
Hofstra University
University of Kentucky
City University of New York/Baruch College
Loyola University/Chicago
University of Rochester
University of Texas/Arlington
Georgia Institute of Technology
University of Illinois/Champaign-Urbana
Boston University

GENIUS FOLK

NOT SO BRIGHT
(students say classmates are not smart)
Syracuse University
Pennsylvania State University
City University of New York/Baruch College
University of Kentucky
University of Illinois/Champaign-Urbana
Hofstra University
University of Denver
Boston University
University of Texas/Arlington
Loyola University/Chicago

DO YOU WANT FRIES WITH THAT?
(students' work experience NOT diverse)
Texas A&M University
University of Illinois/Champaign-Urbana
University of Wyoming
Brigham Young University
University of Kentucky
Pennsylvania State University
University of Kansas
Syracuse University
University of Denver
University of Iowa

FACILITIES

ON-CAMPUS HOUSING GOOD
Dartmouth College
Wake Forest University
Babson College
Southern Methodist University
University of Notre Dame
Stanford University
University of Virginia
Purdue University
University of Iowa
University of Texas/Austin

LOUSY
University of Chicago
University of California/Berkeley
University of Pennsylvania
Georgia Institute of Technology
Yale University
University of Pittsburgh
University of Rochester
University of Southern California
Syracuse University
Case Western Reserve University

MAXIMUM PUMPITUDE
(gym facilities excellent)
Harvard University
Vanderbilt University
Tulane University
University of Alabama/Tuscaloosa
Arizona State University
University of Colorado/Boulder
Purdue University
University of Virginia
University of Texas/Austin
Northwestern University

"WIMPY, WIMPY, WIMPY"
(like maybe a jump rope or something)
City University of New York/Baruch College
Massachusetts Institute of Technology
Columbia University
Carnegie Mellon University
Duke University
Claremont Graduate School
Cornell University
University of Pennsylvania
Boston University
Loyola University/Chicago

SCHOOL TOWN IS PARADISE
University of Colorado/Boulder
University of Texas/Austin
University of Washington
Emory University
University of North Carolina/Chapel Hill
Southern Methodist University
Georgetown University
Columbia University
University of Virginia
University of Wisconsin/Madison

SCHOOL TOWN A PIT
Hofstra University
Rensselaer Polytechnic Institute
University of Pennsylvania
University of Rochester
University of Connecticut
University of Notre Dame
Yale University
Syracuse University
Texas A&M University
Purdue University

SO MUCH TO DO
(lots of school clubs & activities)
Northwestern University
Harvard University
Stanford University
Columbia University
University of Virginia
Indiana University/Bloomington
University of Texas/Austin
Georgetown University
University of Pennsylvania
University of Colorado/Boulder

A FIVE-STAR LIBRARY
University of Michigan
Stanford University
Dartmouth College
Harvard University
University of Illinois/Champaign-Urbana
Washington University
University of Maryland
Vanderbilt University
University of Texas/Austin
Arizona State University

BOOOOOORING
(not many school activities)
City University of New York/Baruch College
Loyola University/Chicago
University of Kentucky
Claremont Graduate School
Babson College
Northeastern University
University of Massachusetts/Amherst
Hofstra University
University of Texas/Arlington
Boston University

SOMEONE LOST THE BOOK
Georgia Institute of Technology
Case Western Reserve University
Texas A&M University
University of Southern California
University of Kentucky
City University of New York/Baruch College
College of William and Mary
Ohio State University
University of Washington
New York University

PLACEMENT & RECRUITING

RECRUITING
(quality, range, & number of companies recruiting on-campus)

University of Pennsylvania
Northwestern University
Stanford University
University of Chicago
University of Virginia
University of Maryland
Columbia University
Duke University
University of California/Los Angeles
University of Michigan

RECRUITING
(not satisfactory)

University of Wyoming
University of Massachusetts/Amherst
University of Arizona
City University of New York/Baruch College
Claremont Graduate School
Emory University
University of Kentucky
Hofstra University
Cornell University
Case Western University

WE GOT JOBS
(placement office very effective)

Stanford University
University of Maryland
University of Pennsylvania
Northwestern University
University of Chicago
Harvard University
Dartmouth College
Indiana University/Bloomington
Rice University
Washington University

ARE YOU HIRING?
(placement office not so great)

City University of New York/Baruch College
University of Illinois/Champaign-Urbana
University of Wyoming
Cornell University
University of Massachusetts/Amherst
Texas A&M University
University of Tennessee
University of Arizona
University of Kentucky
Emory University

CHAPTER NINE

Profiles of the Best Business Schools

UNIVERSITY OF ALABAMA: MANDERSON GRADUATE SCHOOL OF BUSINESS

ADMISSIONS FACTS

Type of school	Public

Demographics

No. of men	129
No. of women	43
No. of minorities	6
No. of int'l students	11

EQUAL TREATMENT GRAPH

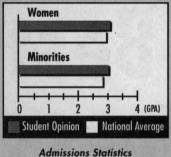

Admissions Statistics

Avg. GMAT	585
Avg. undergraduate GPA	3.18
Avg. age at entry	24
No. of applicants	242
No. accepted	127
No. enrolled	58

Deadlines and Notifications

Regular application	7/1
Regular notification	within 4 weeks

Focus of Curriculum

Specialized

Academic Specialties

Finance, Accounting

Joint Degrees

MBA/JD, The Three/Two Program, Executive MBA Program

Special Programs

The Three/Two Program, Executive MBA Program

FINANCIAL FACTS

In-state tuition	$2,172
Out-of-state tuition	$5,424
On-campus housing	$3,600

ACADEMICS

If you've postponed or avoided getting an MBA because of the high tuition, the University of Alabama offers one of the most low-cost, sought-after MBAs.

But this doesn't come at the cost of academics. One student raved, "The standards are very high." Enthused another, "The program is insightful and targeted towards today's business needs." First-year students take core courses in a "lockstep" sequence. Translation: Courses are in a preset order and the sixty-five entering students take them all together. Praised one MBA " The school is very flexible in what electives you can take. I could take an advertising class in the Communications School to go with my marketing concentration." Second-year students select a concentration in either finance/accounting, international business, human resources management, marketing, or production/operations management. Wrote one student, "I've found the Strategic Management and Human Resources programs very strong." Beyond the basic curriculum, students are enrolled in a yearlong professional development program that could easily pass for a finishing school.

Students we surveyed gave their professors above-average marks for their teaching and after-class accessibility. Wrote one, "Professors are helpful and friendly. They don't act superior or intimidating." Students are equally pleased with the administration. Indeed, Alabama is among only a dozen or so schools where students are satisfied with the way the school is run. Alabama has tried hard to win its students' respect. Chief among their efforts is the new, high-tech B-school building. They've also integrated more computer and team assignments into the curriculum. And they score well on the basics, too: It's a cinch to get into popular courses.

As one might expect, with a $5,000 price tag for out-of-state residents and $2,000 for natives, the overwhelming majority of students say this program is well worth the investment. Adds one MBA, "Alabama offers over a century of tradition and a very strong alumni network and support."

PLACEMENT AND RECRUITING

The Alabama Placement Office shares services and staff with the undergraduate program. One student told us, "The placement office needs to operate as a separate entity from the college. This would enhance our ability to achieve top tier status." Sensing student resentment with this "sharing" arrangement, the administration has added a part-time staff person to focus on MBA placement. Alabama has also joined several other schools in participating in the Southeastern MBA Consortium, a shared recruiting day. MBAs are still disappointed with the overall capabilities of the placement office. In particular, they'd like a broader and deeper range of companies to visit campus. Sixty-three percent of 1993 MBAs had been placed within three months of graduating.

UNIVERSITY OF ALABAMA: MANDERSON GRADUATE SCHOOL OF BUSINESS

STUDENT LIFE/CAMPUS

The workload at Alabama is at its heaviest during the first year. The majority of students report spending an average of fifteen to twenty-five hours a week preparing for class, although this is light by top B-school standards. Almost everyone works in a study group. By the second year, students know the shortcuts and relax a bit.

Students are very competitive, but not into backstabbing. In such a small program, the emphasis is on cooperation and mutual support. Most students claim their closest friends are found within the B-school. Judging by the responses to our survey, they expect these relationships to continue long after the program has ended. Students are impressed by the depth and range of professional experiences that their peers bring to the program. They're even more impressed by their smarts, which they describe as "sharp."

The majority of students live off-campus in nearby apartments. Parking isn't great. Consider living within walking distance. Or bring a bike. Back on campus, students work out in a fully equipped, high-tech gym. They also enjoy Alabama's top-ranked athletic teams. Wrote one MBA, "We have a kick-ass football team." For those who want to do more than watch football, the MBA Association sponsors a wide range of professional and social events, including MBA Week, which features a golf tournament with both MBAs and local entertainers as players.

ADMISSIONS

The admissions office considers your college GPA to be most important; after that, in descending order, they consider your GMAT scores, work experience, essays, letters of recommendation, extracurricular activities, and interview.

According to the school, "The undergraduate record, from a good school, is the first step to successful admission, since it demonstrates motivation. GPAs of less than 3.0 (out of a 4.0) should be explained in depth. The GMAT score should be at least 500, although no cutoff is used. Work experience is always a plus. You should take the short essay very seriously. This reflects upon your writing skills and ability to proof your materials." Decisions are made on a rolling admissions basis. Applicants are notified of a decision within approximately one month after the application has been received. Waitlisted applicants are notified of a spot by April 15th. Admitted applicants may defer admission for up to one year.

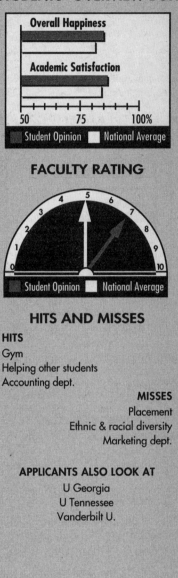

STUDENTS' OVERVIEW BOX

Overall Happiness

Academic Satisfaction

50   75   100%

■ Student Opinion □ National Average

FACULTY RATING

■ Student Opinion □ National Average

HITS AND MISSES

HITS
Gym
Helping other students
Accounting dept.

MISSES
Placement
Ethnic & racial diversity
Marketing dept.

APPLICANTS ALSO LOOK AT
U Georgia
U Tennessee
Vanderbilt U.

FOR MORE INFORMATION, CONTACT:
Manderson School of Business
P.O. Box 870223
Tuscaloosa, AL 35487
(800) 365-8583

UNIVERSITY OF ARIZONA: KARL ELLER GRADUATE SCHOOL OF MANAGEMENT

ADMISSIONS FACTS

Type of school   Public

Demographics

No. of men	148
No. of women	66
No. of minorities	33
No. of int'l students	23

EQUAL TREATMENT GRAPH

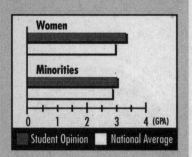

Admissions Statistics

Avg. GMAT	599
Avg. undergraduate GPA	3.2
Avg. age at entry	27
No. of applicants	542
No. accepted	199
No. enrolled	70

Deadlines and Notifications

Regular application	3/15
Regular notification	rolling
Special dates	12/01 (transfers)

Focus of Curriculum

General Management

Academic Specialties

Marketing, MIS, Entrepreneurship, Finance

Joint Degrees

JD/MBA, MBA/Masters in International Management, MBA/MIM, MS MIS/MIM

Special Programs

Accelerated Three/Two program with the College of Arts and Sciences

FINANCIAL FACTS

In-state tuition	$922
Out-of-state tuition	$3,675
On-campus housing	$2,700

ACADEMICS

Where can you find a first-rate Management Information Systems Department, a resort like campus, gorgeous weather, and bargain-basement tuition? At the University of Arizona (U of A), which not only boasts a nationally renowned information technology department but also a technological environment consistently supported by large grants from some of America's premier technology companies: IBM, Apple Computer, and Hewlett-Packard. Interested in the development of new business ventures? Then U of A is also a natural choice. Students can study in the Berger Entrepreneurship Program in the Eller Center for the Study of the Private Market Economy, which was cited as a model program by the U.S. Association for Small Business in 1989. Here students get hands-on experience in workshops and two-person projects presented in a Business Plans Competition judged by local Arizonians. Other strong departments include marketing, finance, and operations.

The U of A offers a basic, meat-and-potatoes MBA, but with a heavy quantitative slant. During the first year, a broad management education is emphasized with ten core courses. Four of these are "integrative" to introduce students to multidisciplinary approaches. All first-years participate in a competitive business simulation game. To balance out the emphasis on quantitative analysis, students also receive special training in communication and presentation skills. New at Eller is the *Management Experience*, a computer simulation game which student teams begin in the third week if their first semester. According to the school, "Students make weekly decisions regarding market opportunities, product development, production planning, and strategic positioning. They receive weekly feedback in the form of sales results, market-share data and bottom-line profits." Even in the virtual world of bits and bytes, the takeover spirit runs high. Second-years recruit their own teams to take-over the first year's companies Unsurprisingly, students in our survey reported feeling well prepared by their training in presentation and communication skills. They also felt confident of their finance and general management skills. Overall, students are unanimous—the U of A MBA is worth the investment of time and money. But not everyone agrees that it's meeting their academic expectations.

PLACEMENT AND RECRUITING

Previously, Eller MBAs said they were unhappy with the range of companies recruiting and a less-than-aggressive-placement office. In response, a new dedicated-MBA director was hired in 1994. Writes the school, "This individual is a grad of the Eller School. In the director's first year, an alumni network was established, videotaped mock interviews were conducted by business executives, and interviews via video conference were made available to national employers." In 1994, 90% of Eller grads had jobs within 3 months of graduation. The average starting salary was $43,000. 25% of students went into finance; 22% each into strategic planning and marketing. Top employers: Hewlett Packard, Tektronix, Ford Motor Company, American Management Systems, Andersen Consulting, IBM, Dial Intet, Ernst and Young, General Motors.

UNIVERSITY OF ARIZONA: KARL ELLER GRADUATE SCHOOL OF MANAGEMENT

STUDENT LIFE/CAMPUS

Students here study an average of twenty-five to thirty-five hours a week, and report an intense first-year workload. By the second year, both the workload and pressure lighten up. There is an emphasis on team and group work. Still, like other B-school students, many U of A MBAs say they do assignments selectively—skimming and skipping—to lighten the load. They also collaborate on assignments in study groups. Bonus points go to the school for actively preparing students for the demands of the program in two ways: quantexcel learning sessions and a four-week summer prep session offered to all first-years. Class discussions tend to be lively as class participation counts heavily towards the grade. Classes are small and held Monday through Thursday. Classless Fridays are reserved for activities such as on-site business visits and the quantexcel workshops.

Most U of A students agree classmates are professionally diverse. But one MBA moaned, "Students lack business perspective, are too grade oriented. "As for their competitiveness, it depends on whom you ask. While the majority of students say U of A MBAs are very competitive, a not insignificant number say they're laid back. Perhaps because many students choose the U of A because it's close to home, the on-campus social scene is not as happening as it is at other B-schools. But one MBA wrote, "I've made friendships that will last a lifetime; people are smart and hardworking, but also friendly and root for each other!" Social and professional activities are organized by the student-run Master of Business Administration Student Association.

The U of A campus is beautiful, and everyone seems to like the town of Tucson, although it's hardly a hopping metropolis. A few hours' drive away is Phoenix, the Grand Canyon, or even a Mexican beach. Students get most pumped about the gym, which is reportedly amazing. The majority of students live off-campus in surrounding neighborhoods. As for housing, this MBA says, "It is more and more difficult to find apartments at reasonable prices," although students said there's no shortage of housing, even if it is expensive. A final note: Sit on your cash, you don't need to purchase a PC to go here.

ADMISSIONS

The admissions department considers work experience most important, followed by undergraduate course work, undergraduate GPA, GMAT scores, essays, and recommendations. The admissions office notes, "In general, we look at the "whole person" and not just isolated components of individual performance such as GMAT or GPA."

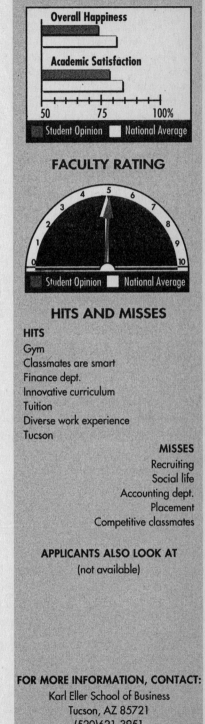

STUDENTS' OVERVIEW BOX

Overall Happiness

Academic Satisfaction

50   75   100%

Student Opinion ■ National Average

FACULTY RATING

Student Opinion ■ National Average

HITS AND MISSES

HITS
Gym
Classmates are smart
Finance dept.
Innovative curriculum
Tuition
Diverse work experience
Tucson

MISSES
Recruiting
Social life
Accounting dept.
Placement
Competitive classmates

APPLICANTS ALSO LOOK AT
(not available)

FOR MORE INFORMATION, CONTACT:
Karl Eller School of Business
Tucson, AZ 85721
(520)621-3951
eMail: dvidal@bpa.arizona.edu

ARIZONA STATE UNIVERSITY COLLEGE OF BUSINESS

ADMISSIONS FACTS

Type of school   Public

Demographics

No. of men	145
No. of women	90
No. of minorities	58
No. of int'l students	28

EQUAL TREATMENT GRAPH

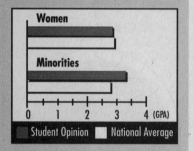

Admissions Statistics

Avg. GMAT	605
Avg. undergraduate GPA	3.3
Avg. age at entry	27
No. of applicants	846
No. accepted	226
No. enrolled	127

Deadlines and Notifications

Regular application   5/1
Regular notification maximum 6 weeks
Special dates   2/15 (early decision)

Focus of Curriculum

General Management

Academic Specialties

Marketing, Accounting, Finance,
Purchasing and Logistics

Special Programs

PepsiCo Minority Scholarship Program

FINANCIAL FACTS

In-state tuition	$1,828
Out-of-state tuition	$7,434
On-campus housing	$3,200

ACADEMICS

The Arizona State University (ASU) B-school does a good job of living up to the reputation it has created. Students say it offers first-rate academics, an innovative learning environment, and one of the least expensive MBAs in the nation. One told us, "ASU is an up-and-coming school that is extremely student oriented and aggressive in its pursuit of a quality education." Thoroughness is the operative game plan here. ASU's program builds strength in every conceivable area: 1) core knowledge—technical and analytical skills in the major business disciplines of business; 2) basic skills—computing, writing, speaking, time management, and teamwork; and 3) managerial abilities—ethics, diversity issues, global business, and quality in service and products. But the program doesn't stop here. To aid team formation, students are given psychological tests during orientation. As part of the emphasis on cooperative learning, students with previous course work no longer "opt out" of core courses; they take the class and serve as discussion leaders. During the first semester, students are expected to participate in a one-time volunteer activity such as renovating a shelter. The academic program focuses on theoretical foundations and essential skills such as communication and information technology. One MBA exhorted, "There is outstanding flexibility in the studies and exceptional opportunities for assistantships." Students may specialize or take a cross-functional sequence of electives.

To judge by the responses to our survey, the administration is customer oriented and responsive to student needs. Reported one MBA, "They restructured the core course offerings to limit the days we are in class—at the students' request!" A significant number feel there are still major kinks in the system. Explained one MBA, "A lot of new ideas are being implemented, which will be fine once the details are ironed out." However, students feel the school is "well run." Professors receive high marks for their after-class accessibility and "desire to help." Overall, students report that taking time off to get an ASU MBA is well worth it. Summed up one: "I couldn't have picked a better school to attend."

PLACEMENT AND RECRUITING

The B-school has hired a Director of Career Management for MBAs, but still shares a Career Center with the University. In 1994, 55 companies recruited on campus for MBAs. 75 companies are line up for recruiting in the 1995-96 academic year. Hiring stats are only available from 1994: ninety-one % of grads had a job within three months of graduation. The average starting salary was $45, 521. Top employers: INTEL, Motorola, US West, Hewlett Packard, Dial Andersen Consulting, Coopers and Lybrand, Dow Chemical Johnson and Johnson, Sara Lee, 3m, KPMG Peat Marwick. Still, MBA appetites are huge. Students told us they want to see even more companies recruiting.

ARIZONA STATE UNIVERSITY COLLEGE OF BUSINESS

STUDENT LIFE/CAMPUS

The first-year workload is heavy and demanding. Students spend roughly thirty to forty hours a week chugging through it. Explained one weary MBA, "The new trimester system makes this program difficult. It's hard to cover all the material in ten short weeks." Added another, "If you're looking for an MBA boot camp for two years, this is it. " Classes are small and feature group assignments. To bolster communication skills, many of these involve oral presentations to an audience of peers and faculty. Observes one MBA, "Diversity of student background and required group interactions are key ingredients of our learning." Outside of teamwork, students here are competitive, but not cutthroat. Remarks one MBA, " Students help each other, because grading is generally not based on a curve." But grading, according to one student, can be erratic: "In some courses, everyone gets an A." A majority of students report they like each other and expect to continue their friendships after school. Students also agree the student body is professionally diverse and "bright." All full-time MBA students are members of a newly formed MBA Association, which sponsors numerous educational events. Other organizations include Graduate Women in Business and the MBA Consulting Group. A point worth noting: Social responsibility is not left to classroom lessons alone. All MBA students must complete at least one community service project.

ASU boasts great libraries and state-of-the-art facilities. It's also located in Tempe, rated "one of the top ten college towns in America." The climate and dramatic desert setting make it a great place to go to school. Several students told us they weren't sure if they came here for the sun or the MBA. Perhaps they came for ASU's own eighteen-hole, 160-acre golf course. Maybe they came for the gym, which students said was as good as you'll find at any five-star resort. As for student life, popular extracurriculars involve any activity in the great outdoors. Students annually organize a trip to one of Arizona's scenic destinations, such as the Grand Canyon. Raved an ASU MBA, "Quality of life is tremendous. One of the 'coolest' schools in the country." In addition to the sun and fun, students say, "Tempe is a haven for retirees. We have access to former CEO's and presidents, a great pool from which we draw mentors and career support."

ADMISSIONS

According to the admissions department, your work experience/resume and GMAT score are weighted most heavily. Then, in descending order, your college GPA, "a personal statement reflecting on maturity, strength of purpose, academic potential and ability to communicate clearly," letters of recommendation, extracurricular activities, and the interview. Applications are reviewed in rounds. The deadlines for each round are December 15, March 1, and May 1. It is advisable to apply in round one or two. Joint degree programs include: MBA/MIM with Thunderbird and MBA/JD. Scholarships and assistantships are available, including the PepsiCo Minority Scholarship Program.

STUDENT'S OVERVIEW BOX

Overall Happiness

Academic Satisfaction

50   75   100%

Student Opinion   National Average

FACULTY RATING

Student Opinion   National Average

HITS AND MISSES

HITS
Gym
Marketing dept.
Tempe

MISSES
Off-campus housing

APPLICANTS ALSO LOOK AT
Thunderbird
U Arizona

FOR MORE INFORMATION, CONTACT:
MBA Program Office
College of Business
Tempe, AZ 85287-4906
(602) 965-3332
eMail: iackjkh@asuvm inre.asu.edu

BABSON COLLEGE GRADUATE SCHOOL OF BUSINESS

ADMISSIONS FACTS

Type of school	Private

Demographics

No. of men	220
No. of women	115
No. of minorities	15
No. of int'l students	104

EQUAL TREATMENT GRAPH

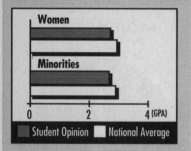

Admissions Statistics

Avg. GMAT	580
Avg. undergraduate GPA	3.0
Avg. age at entry	26
No. of applicants	627
No. accepted	N/A
No. enrolled	120

Deadlines and Notifications

Regular application	5/1
Regular notification	1 month
Special dates	N/A

Focus of Curriculum

General Management, option to specialize

Academic Specialties

Entrepreneurial Management, International Business

Joint Degrees

Two-year MBA, One-Year MBA for Business graduates, Evening MBA

Special Programs

International Management Program (IMP), Management Consulting Field Experience (MCFE), International Study Programs

FINANCIAL FACTS

In-state tuition	$9,250
Out-of-state tuition	$9,250
On-campus housing	$4,975

ACADEMICS

Babson has retooled its curriculum to reflect the latest trends in business education today. Individual courses specific to each of the functional areas have been scrapped in favor of cross-functional, holistic "modules," which are taken during the first year. Sub-themes of each module are "values and ethics, innovation, quality, entrepreneurship, global thinking, and leadership." This teaching concept is a big draw for students; several wrote they picked Babson because of the "new curriculum." The majority agreed this program is earning its stripes: "This innovative program is working very well. It's making learning more symbiotic with the business world." One went so far as to boast "Harvard B-school is benchmarking us." Still, a number of students echoed this sentiment: "It will be a few years before all the kinks are worked out "

Babson offers two options for full-time study: a two-year MBA and an accelerated one-year MBA, although it's probably best known for its entrepreneurial studies and international programs. Considered one of the top two B-schools in the nation in entrepreneurship studies, Babson offers more learning and networking opportunities for would-be entrepreneurs than almost any other program. In addition to extensive courses on the subject, such as managing business growth, there's entrepreneurial fieldwork. Students learn how to write a comprehensive business plan, obtain capital, and manage a growing business. Many students agreed with the one who wrote: "I chose this school because of its global and international perspective." Cross-cultural experiences are strongly encouraged, and a formal concentration in International Business is available. All Babson students must complete a rigorous cross-cultural requirement, which may be met taking a summer-long international internship, spending a semester abroad, or taking an intensive three-week international course. The Center for Language and Culture conducts orientation programs for students heading off to foreign lands, which includes pre-departure language training. In terms of academic preparedness, Babson MBAs judged their marketing, general management and interpersonal skills to be particularly strong. In the weak department: accounting and operations, due in part to the school's academic emphasis.

PLACEMENT AND RECRUITING

All students are required to participate in the Career Management Program, which takes a marketing-oriented approach to job seeking and helps students plan one-of-a-kind job searches. Particularly noteworthy is Career Search, "an automated data base of more than 183,000 employers around the U.S." In 1993, sixty-five percent of all students had accepted positions by commencement. Over 102 companies recruited Babson MBAs. Leading the pack were recruiters Johnson & Johnson, Proctor & Gamble, State Street Bank, and Bay Bank. Nonetheless, students gave a thumbs down to the placement office. Babson MBA's would like to see a wider range of companies recruiting there.

BABSON COLLEGE GRADUATE SCHOOL OF BUSINESS

STUDENT LIFE/CAMPUS

An attractive aspect of life at Babson is the sense of community, fostered by its size and location. Wrote one student: "Very small, very personal, very far from Boston!" Located on a secluded, 450-acre wooded site in Wellesley, Massachusetts, the Babson Campus offers students an idyllic, country-inn atmosphere. Most students enjoy the tranquillity of the campus; however, it can feel isolated. Popular events include the Spring Cruise, the Fall and Spring Formals, and "The Buffoonery"—the annual spring talent show in which students spoof their profs (who serve as judges for the event). Because many students live on campus, dorm parties are common. One-third of the student body is foreign, so many of these have international themes. Trips are organized to Martha's Vineyard, Montreal (for skiing), and Boston (for sports events). Despite all the opportunities for socializing, the majority of Babson MBAs judged themselves to have a ho-hum social life. Griped one, "General track students are apathetic towards extracurricular activities and social events."

Babson offers a small and intimate program with plenty of up-close and personal contact with both faculty and students. One student wrote that the program is "small enough to encourage participation by all." Agreed another, "The school has an attitude of intimacy and is team-oriented." Class size is limited to a maximum of forty-two students. All students are assigned to study sections with a group of thirty-five to forty other students. Advises one MBA, "No one gets below a B who shows up for class." Students are competitive, but they also rated themselves as very friendly. How friendly? One MBA tells us, "My class is called HAPPY CLASS." Students obviously enjoy each other and the laid-back atmosphere. Wrote one enthusiastic student, "I love it! Students are REALISTIC, so are the profs. No Harvard-type weenies here."

ADMISSIONS

The Babson admissions office ranks your work experience as most important, and then, in descending order, the interview (required), GMAT scores, college GPA, essays, letters of recommendation, and extracurricular activities. According to the school, though, "The ranking of these criteria will vary by candidate."

Wrote the school: "At Babson, we consider each candidate as an individual, and look at the entire package, not simply at test scores and GPAs. Accordingly, we require an interview. This personal approach provides both Babson and our candidates an opportunity to determine whether there is a 'fit' within the Babson community. We look for goal-oriented individuals with an entrepreneurial spirit, a global mindset, and an ability to grapple with the ambiguities of managing change in a dynamic business world. For the one-year program, applicants must have an undergraduate degree in business administration. Babson batches applications by rounds. There are three rounds for the two-year program and two rounds for the one-year program. Students may defer admission for up to one year."

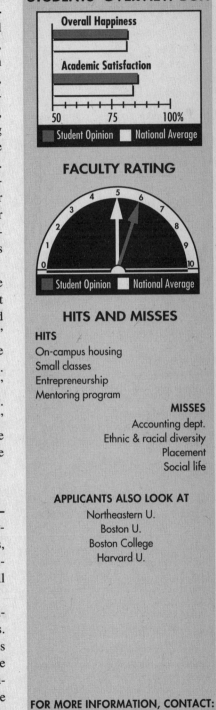

STUDENTS' OVERVIEW BOX

Overall Happiness

Academic Satisfaction

50   75   100%

■ Student Opinion □ National Average

FACULTY RATING

0 1 2 3 4 5 6 7 8 9 10

■ Student Opinion □ National Average

HITS AND MISSES

HITS
On-campus housing
Small classes
Entrepreneurship
Mentoring program

MISSES
Accounting dept.
Ethnic & racial diversity
Placement
Social life

APPLICANTS ALSO LOOK AT
Northeastern U.
Boston U.
Boston College
Harvard U.

FOR MORE INFORMATION, CONTACT:
Graduate Admissions
Babson Park, MA 02157
(617) 239-4317

BOSTON UNIVERSITY SCHOOL OF MANAGEMENT

ADMISSIONS FACTS

Type of school	Private

Demographics

No. of men	807
No. of women	661
No. of minorities	132
No. of int'l students	266

EQUAL TREATMENT GRAPH

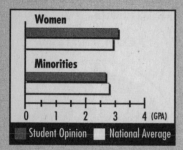

Women

Minorities

0 1 2 3 4 (GPA)

■ Student Opinion □ National Average

Admissions Statistics

Avg. GMAT	580
Avg. undergraduate GPA	3.1
Avg. age at entry	26
No. of applicants	1,531
No. accepted	735
No. enrolled	496

Deadlines and Notifications

Regular application	5/1
Regular notification	rolling
Special dates	N/A

Focus of Curriculum

Specialized

Academic Specialties

Operations, MIS, Non-profit Management

Joint Degrees

MBA/JD; MBA/JD with concentration in Health Care Management; MBA/MA in Economics, International Relations, and Medical Sciences; MBA/MS in Management Information Systems, Manufacturing Engineering, and Broadcast Administration

Special Programs

Leadership, Careers, and Self-Assessment Program; Kobe, Japan Program; The Asian Management Field Seminar; International Study in England.

FINANCIAL FACTS

In-state tuition	$19,420
Out-of-state tuition	$19,420
On-campus housing	$4,110

ACADEMICS

The Boston University School of Management is best known for its 'niche' programs and specialized concentrations such as public management, MIS, accounting, health care management and real estate. A sizable number of students come to study in one of the school's many dual-degree programs. Other concentrations include finance and economics, marketing, management policy, operations, and organizational behavior. Wrote one student, "The choice of electives in most departments is outstanding." Praised another MBA, "The MIS department is exceptionally strong." Other standout concentrations are Information Systems Management and Public and Not-for-Profit Management. Each of these involves unique course work and field experiences. Overall, students told us they feel well prepared by their training in finance, accounting, operations, and general management. The vast majority of students feel less confident about their quantitative and computer skills.

Professors received better grades for their accessibility than their teaching. Some students complained that the quality of instruction is uneven. Wrote one disgruntled MBA, "Fifty percent of faculty are excellent, fifty percent are average." An apparent exception : "The finance faculty are unbelievably good."

Complaints also extended to BU's administration. Griped one student, "The program is well designed and specialized programs are great, but the MBA program as a whole gets bogged down in the red tape typical of a large university. But help may be on the way. Spearheaded by Dean Laitaif, "The school is undertaking a Total Quality Management approach and is going to improve much in the near future." Students credit the Dean with priming the school for change with his "contagious enthusiasm" and "renewed vigor for the program." Thus far a new curriculum features team-teaching and team learning, as well as terrific flexibility in what courses students can take. The latter allows MBA's to draw on "cross-departmental" expertise. Students overwhelmingly cited prestige as the most important factor in choosing BU's program. And they're in good company. Prominent Boston alumni include: Millard Dexler, CEO, The GAP; Jack Smith, President/CEO, General Motors; Howard Clark, Vice Chairman, Lehman Brothers; and here's a fun job, Kenneth Fled, President/Producer of Ringling Brothers Barnum & Bailey.

PLACEMENT AND RECRUITING

An exciting new service at BU is Career Search. According to the school, this "state-of-the-art database covers nearly 180,000 companies with customized retrieval capabilities and allows users to swiftly identify companies that match their interests and experience." Forty companies recruited on campus in 1994. By graduation, sixty -seven percent of the class had accepted a position., eighty percent, three months later. The companies many went to: AT & T, American Management Systems, Brown Brothers Harriman, Johnson and Johnson International, GE, and Andersen Consulting. Average starting salaries here are $52, 700.

BOSTON UNIVERSITY SCHOOL OF MANAGEMENT

STUDENT LIFE/CAMPUS

Entering full-time students are divided into sections of roughly fifty students each and take first-semester courses together. The sections foster the formation of study groups and help develop camaraderie. The mood here is noncompetitive, relaxed, and cooperative. This may be due in part to the moderate workload. The vast majority of students report they spend roughly twenty hours a week studying/preparing for class, a light schedule by most B-school standards. Observed one student, "A high percent do not prepare for class at all. " Obviously, this leaves plenty of time for extracurriculars, such as Thursday bar nights at the B.U. Pub. Faculty tend to congregate there, too. Favorite activities include student government, ski trips, outings to Boston events, and golf and tennis tournaments. A big crowd turns out for the volleyball matches against Wharton and MIT. One-third of the student body is foreign, which leads to many international social events and "dining" nights. A popular on-campus spot is The Lounge, a newly built area for MBAs to study and relax. The Lounge contains wall-size U.S. and world maps with pins designating each student's hometown. Big news: the Computer Club is setting up a BU on-line network so that students and professors can e-mail each other.

Student relations at BU seem most affected by the mix of full- and part-time students in the same program. Although one MBA raved, "The range and quality of people is exceptional," another moaned, "This isn't a place where students hang out with each other." Advised one disgruntled MBA, "The school needs more daytime classes, full-time students, and clubs and activities." Despite the high global/international feel to this program, the school also needs better domestic minority representation, according to some BU MBAs. But as for women, this school has managed what most others haven't, 45% of the student body are women!

Other complaints centered around the poor condition of the school's physical structures and equipment. Wrote one MBA, "Horrible physical facilities. Classrooms have windows that don't close, falling ceilings. Because the building is on a busy street, classrooms are extremely noisy when windows are open (and there's no A/C)." Reported another, "No business school library." Of BU's home city, however, students are not only complaint-free, but uncharacteristically positive. Raved one, "It combines the best aspects of a college town with a modern urban area. There's tons to do."

ADMISSIONS

The admissions selection process places equal importance on all credentials: essays, college GPA, GMAT score, work experience, letters of recommendation. Interviews are *not* part of the process. Advises the school, "Work experience is strongly preferred. BU is interested in attracting a high level of diversity in the classroom in work experience, ethnicity, nationality, and gender." Decisions are made on a rolling basis in four "cycles," beginning in February for the September cycle (full- and part-time). Applicants are advised to apply early and are notified of a decision within three to four weeks of receipt of the completed application. Students may defer admission up to one year.

STUDENTS' OVERVIEW BOX

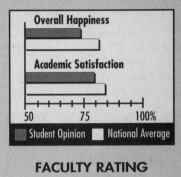

Overall Happiness

Academic Satisfaction

50   75   100%

Student Opinion   National Average

FACULTY RATING

Student Opinion   National Average

HITS AND MISSES

HITS
Ethnic & racial diversity
Boston

MISSES
Marketing dept.
Don't like classmates
Gym
Quantitative skills

APPLICANTS ALSO LOOK AT

Boston College
Babson College
New York University
U Rochester
U Pittsburgh

FOR MORE INFORMATION, CONTACT:

School of Management
685 Commonwealth Ave.
Boston, MA 02215
(617) 353-2670
eMail: MBA@bu.edu

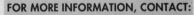

Brigham Young University: Marriott School of Management

ADMISSIONS FACTS

Type of school	Private

Demographics

No. of men	102
No. of women	20
No. of minorities	N/A
No. of int'l students	34

EQUAL TREATMENT GRAPH

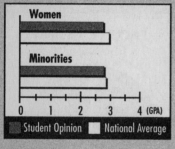

Women

Minorities

0 1 2 3 4 (GPA)

■ Student Opinion □ National Average

Admissions Statistics

Avg. GMAT	587
Avg. undergraduate GPA	3.5
Avg. age at entry	26
No. of applicants	311
No. accepted	180
No. enrolled	122

Deadlines and Notifications

Regular application	5/15
Regular notification	2 weeks after committee decision
Special dates	N/A

Focus of Curriculum

General Management

Joint Degrees

General Management, Accounting, Finance

Special Programs

The Executive Lecture Series, Entrepreneurship Lecture Series, International Business Series, Computer Summer Prep

FINANCIAL FACTS

In-state tuition	$4,400
Out-of-state tuition	$13,200
On-campus housing	$3,580

ACADEMICS

Brigham Young University is the official school of the Church of Latter-Day Saints (Mormons). According to the school, two slogans greet BYU visitors as they enter the campus: "Enter to Learn; Go Forth to Serve" and "The World Is Our Campus." This sets the tone for what is easily one of the most ethics-oriented and spiritual B-schools in the nation. There's a dress code. Students are expected to abstain from drugs, alcohol, and tobacco. In the classroom, ethics and the moral responsibilities of leadership are emphasized. Says one MBA, "The university and B-School are remarkably strong in moral responsibility and honor code. This is where the competitive advantage of the school is." A by-product of the Mormon affiliation, which requires service in a foreign country, is that over eighty percent of the student body has had one to two years of foreign work experience; eighty-five percent speak a second language, thirty percent a third. The high level of cross-cultural knowledge enhances the study of international business.

BYU features a progressive curriculum. In almost all of the core courses, several professors share the podium, team-teaching cases from a cross-functional perspective. This approach doesn't please everyone, however, as one student griped, "Overemphasis on case method. I feel I'm not getting the practical skills that will be valuable in the short-term."

There are only 120 or so students in each entering MBA class, and during the first year, students take roughly ten core courses in the functional areas. But here's where things get strange: MBA students share the core courses with students from the Master of Organizational Behavior, Master of Accountancy, and Master of Administration programs. The school lumps *all* the first-year business masters students together and then divides them into more manageable sections of seventy-five students each.

In the second year, there are only two required courses: Ethics and Business Policy. After that, students have twelve electives, enabling them to specialize in an area. A popular offering is Management Consulting and Projects, where Utah businesses pay students to consult in their organization.

Overall, students say BYU is meeting their academic expectations. Students judged their teamwork, presentation, general management, and finance skills as strong. But students felt they had weak spots in marketing, operations, quantitative methods, accounting and computers The most common criticism is that the range of students goes from "very prepared" to "what are they doing here." Also, in the complaint box, "there are too many free-riders."

PLACEMENT AND RECRUITING

The B-school uses both its own placement personnel and that of the university placement center to assist students in their job search. Students are entered in a database from which recruiters select candidates for positions. In addition the school compiles a resume book and intern resume packets for employers. Like many B-school students, BYU MBAs told us they were not entirely satisfied with the efforts of the placement office. They felt a whole lot better about the school's alumni, with whom the school has close ties.

BRIGHAM YOUNG UNIVERSITY: MARRIOTT SCHOOL OF MANAGEMENT

STUDENT LIFE/CAMPUS

Students report a heavy workload. They crack the books an average of twenty to thirty hours a week. Not surprisingly, they say it's important to do all the required reading. Teamwork is heavily promoted, which results in what students report as "a strong camaraderie among the MBA students." Students say they're competitive, but—you know the answer here—most eager to help a fellow classmate out. They do draw a line with camaraderie. In particular, they dislike "competing with undergrads for computer lab time and printing facilities."

Life at a Mormon school can be interesting for a single person. At what is known as "Breed-em Young" University, dating (especially among undergrads) is geared toward finding a mate. Indeed, several B-school students told us they chose BYU to do just this. (Not that we want to get in the personals business, but each was looking for a wife.) Further hindering the social scene is the school honor code, which doesn't permit drinking or smoking on campus. Extracurriculars here are devoted to church, family life, informal get-togethers, and outdoor activities in the nearby mountains. The MBA Association sponsors many events, including community service projects such as reading to the blind and helping foreign students with English. There's even a vice-president for Community Service.

The Mormon community is divided into "wards" of 100 or so families who plan social activities. Non-Mormons are welcome to attend. There's also an active "Spouse Association" that organizes dinners and outings. According to one student, "Single housing is great. Married housing is terrible (old apartments that are expensive)." The majority of students opt to live in suburban-style garden apartments off-campus in the foothills of the Wasatch Mountains.

As for diversity: forget it. The majority of students here are Mormons. They're conservative. They're white. Of the student body, seventy percent are married and many of them have two or more children. Non-Mormons do attend school here. But the only part of the honor code they're exempted from is mandatory church attendance.

ADMISSIONS

According to the admissions office, your GMAT score is considered most important. After that, in descending order, your college GPA, letter of intent, letters of recommendation, language spoken, work experience, and leadership activities are considered. Writes the school, "Though we look carefully at GMAT and GPA qualifications, we also look at the person behind the numbers. The letter of intent and letters of recommendation are valuable resources in getting acquainted with the person. We strongly suggest prerequisites in Accounting, Economics, and Statistics, as well as computer skills. Because of the international emphasis in our MBA program we look favorably at applicants who speak a second and third language. As a result we encourage any undergraduate major except business, and we also encourage some work experience." Students may defer admission for up to one year for either a mission or specialized work.

STUDENTS' OVERVIEW BOX

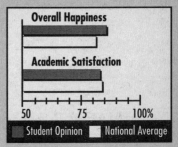

FACULTY RATING

HITS AND MISSES

HITS
Finance dept.
Classmates are smart
On-campus housing
Family

MISSES
Marketing dept.
Ethnic & racial diversity
Recruiting

APPLICANTS ALSO LOOK AT
(not available)

FOR MORE INFORMATION, CONTACT:
MBA Program
640 N. Eldon Tanner Building
Provo, UT 84602
(801) 378-3500

UNIVERSITY OF CALIFORNIA–BERKELEY: WALTER A. HAAS SCHOOL OF BUSINESS

ADMISSIONS FACTS

Type of school	Public

Demographics

No. of men	133
No. of women	85
No. of minorities	45
No. of int'l students	58

EQUAL TREATMENT GRAPH

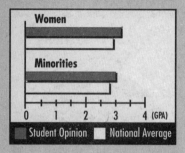

Admissions Statistics

Avg. GMAT	N/A
Avg. undergraduate GPA	N/A
Avg. age at entry	27.5
No. of applicants	1,977
No. accepted	454
No. enrolled	218

Deadlines and Notifications

Regular application	3/15
Regular notification	within 6–8 weeks
Special dates	11/18 (early decision)

Focus of Curriculum

General Management

Academic Specialties

International Business, Management of Technology, Innovation and Entrepreneurship, Real Estate

Joint Degrees

JD/MBA, MBA/MA in Asian Studies, MBA/MPH

Special Programs

International summer internships, Language workshops, Partners in Entrepreneurial Leadership (PEL)

FINANCIAL FACTS

In-state tuition	$2,526.25
Out-of-state tuition	$6,375.75
On-campus housing	$5,245

ACADEMICS

By any yardstick, Berkeley is one of the nation's best public B-schools. First-years take a minimum of seven out of ten required courses. Second-years choose from over 195 electives offered both within and outside the B-school. Haas offers several joint curriculum programs and among them, the one in Real Estate Development, with both the Department of City and Regional Planning and the Center for Real Estate and Urban Economics, is among the country's most respected.

Of equal renown is the school's international focus. Faculty have integrated international content into virtually every MBA course. Students wrote, "Berkeley is a great place for an international perspective" and "Berkeley has a large percentage of the student population from overseas or with foreign job experience." I Several students told us they selected Berkeley because of its entrepreneurship studies. Commented one would-be entrepreneur, "Outstanding training—enough to get anyone launched." Partners in Entrepreneurial Leadership (PEL) offers training programs for aspiring entrepreneurs. Students complete a "residency" with a high-growth company for seven months and attend biweekly classes on entrepreneurial management. Hass' intense focus on technology is also a draw.

Overall, students said they chose Haas because of its value, prestige, geographic location, and access to the biotech industry and firms in Silicon Valley. One students summed it up by saying, "When one looks at the whole Berkeley package of value relative to costs for a B-school, Haas comes out at the very top." Of the first-rate faculty, students said forty to sixty percent of their professors are recognized leaders in their field. They also gave them high marks for their teaching abilities. Reported one, "No rookies teaching the core." According to our survey, high marks also go to the administration for it's responsiveness to students needs.

PLACEMENT AND RECRUITING

Berkeley's Career Center helps students secure international summer internships (many of which are underwritten by corporations) and offer language workshops. Berkeley is also a member of the MBA Enterprise Corps, which matches recent grads to Eastern European companies.

The Career Center brings in over 250 employers for on-campus interviews. With these efforts, students agree, career services have improved over the last two years. The most popular destinations re finance (22%) and marketing (18%). The class has a starting average salary of $62,000. "tight network with San Francisco firms and Silicon Valley," reported one MBA. Ninety-five percent of the Haas MBA class of '94 had been placed within three months after graduation. The big recruiters: Hewlett-Packard, Intel, McKinsey, Clorox, Coopers & Lybrand, Wells Fargo Bank, American Airlines, and Silicon Graphics.

UNIVERSITY OF CALIFORNIA–BERKELEY: WALTER A. HAAS SCHOOL OF BUSINESS

STUDENT LIFE/CAMPUS

Haas has addressed it's number one student complaint - the physical plant. In January 1995, the Haas school moved into its "stunning" new home on the Berkeley campus. The new Haas mini-campus consists of three buildings set around a central courtyard and features three floors of classrooms, state-of-the-art facilities for the computer and career centers, and a business and economics library. The facilities were made possible by a $24 million donation from the Haas family of Levi Strauss & Co. Described as "awesome", one Haas MBA declares "We just moved from a Volkswagen bus to a Rolls Royce." A majority of students live off-campus in apartments in the Berkeley/Oakland area. Students wrote they love the college-town atmosphere of Berkeley. According to one student, you'll find that the "rock-climbing, skiing, mountain biking, the ocean, San Francisco, the attitudes...are all the best."

Students at Berkeley like each other. They describe a "splendid social life." Extracurriculars include intramural sports, and—no surprise here—student government. This may be because Berkeley encourages students to have a say in just about everything—classes, administration, and policy. A huge number of programs, such as the annual Serv-A-Thon (a weekend of volunteer work), are student initiated and run. In the diversity department, students also give this school a thumbs up, adding that the school has few "business-school types" and is team-oriented.

The Haas School is a small program of 441 MBA students, seventy-five full-time faculty, and fifty visiting professors/lecturers in the midst of a huge (31,000 students) university. MBA students share a sense of community fostered by the small size of the program. Students are competitive, but not sharks. The pressure, relative to other top B-Schools is relatively light. Among all this relative peace, one student did complain that his fellow "Students could be a bit more aggressive." Classmates rated each other as smart. Raved one, "The people at Berkeley really make this program stand out!"

ADMISSIONS

The admissions office reports that it accepts applications during one long "continuous cycle" which goes from November to March. Students are notified of a decision generally within six weeks of a file's completion, except for the final deadline. One-year deferments are granted on a case-by-case basis. According to Berkeley, "The admissions committee reviews files and makes decisions continuously. Applicants who apply prior to the final deadline have a stronger chance of being admitted." The Haas School is also a member of the Consortium for Graduate Study in Management, which offers scholarships to talented minority students.

The following criteria are considered in descending order of importance: the essays, college GPA or academic record, GMAT score, work experience, letters of recommendation, extracurricular activities, and the interview. Students are required to complete one course in calculus before enrollment.

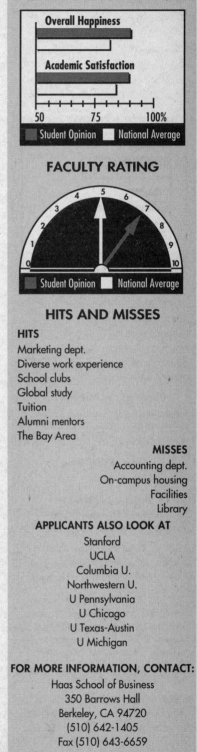

STUDENTS' OVERVIEW BOX

Overall Happiness

Academic Satisfaction

50   75   100%

■ Student Opinion   □ National Average

FACULTY RATING

■ Student Opinion   □ National Average

HITS AND MISSES

HITS
Marketing dept.
Diverse work experience
School clubs
Global study
Tuition
Alumni mentors
The Bay Area

MISSES
Accounting dept.
On-campus housing
Facilities
Library

APPLICANTS ALSO LOOK AT
Stanford
UCLA
Columbia U.
Northwestern U.
U Pennsylvania
U Chicago
U Texas-Austin
U Michigan

FOR MORE INFORMATION, CONTACT:
Haas School of Business
350 Barrows Hall
Berkeley, CA 94720
(510) 642-1405
Fax (510) 643-6659

University of California–Los Angeles: John E. Anderson Graduate School of Management

ADMISSIONS FACTS

Type of school	Public

Demographics
No. of men	466
No. of women	207
No. of minorities	110
No. of int'l students	140

EQUAL TREATMENT GRAPH

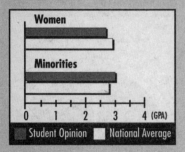

Women

Minorities

0   1   2   3   4 (GPA)

Student Opinion — National Average

Admissions Statistics
Avg. GMAT	640
Avg. undergraduate GPA	3.5
Avg. age at entry	27.6
No. of applicants	2,670
No. accepted	623
No. enrolled	302

Deadlines and Notifications
Regular application	4/1
Regular notification	6/20
Special dates	N/A

Focus of Curriculum
General Management

Academic Specialties
Entrepreneurial Studies, Finance, Marketing, MIS, Arts Management

Joint Degrees
JD/MBA, MBA/MA in Latin American Studies, MBA/MA in Urban Planning

Special Programs
The Center for International Business, Education & Research, The Center for Finance & Real Estate, The Center for Technology Management

FINANCIAL FACTS
In-state tuition	$7,222
Out-of-state tuition	$14,000
On-campus housing	$5,580

ACADEMICS

As a top business school, Anderson places great emphasis on the balance between theory and practice. Classroom learning favors the case study method and is supplemented with internships, consulting projects, and other off-campus programs in what the school calls the "laboratory of Los Angeles." There are three main components to the curriculum: the management core, advanced electives, and field study. Students can take electives in other departments at the university to build an interdisciplinary area of strength. Two of the most popular areas are arts management and entertainment management. Students run to take electives in the graduate school of film, where they get a taste of Hollywood in Peter Guber's "The Development Process in Feature Film Productions" course. One happy student wrote, "Anderson's program caters to individual needs." Anderson's "capstone" experience, the management field study, offers teams of students experiential instruction in companies such as Disney, the L.A. Dodgers, and Bugle Boy.

The hottest area of study at Anderson is Entrepreneurship. In 1991, the Association of Collegiate Entrepreneurs acclaimed Anderson's entrepreneurial program the best in the U.S. It offers an incomparable array of experiences: mentoring, small-business consulting, a venture proposal competition, visiting entrepreneur series, and assistance with placement in venture capital and portfolio companies. Indeed, the Entrepreneurial Association is the largest student club on campus. An equally exciting program is the International Management Fellows (IMF) Program, which offers an immersion in international business, culture, and language. It runs concurrently with the regular MBA program, takes twenty-four months to complete, and involves a total of nine months outside the United States, as well as intensive language/cultural instruction. Japanese, French, German, and Spanish tracks are available. In addition to the newcomer specialties of international business and entrepreneurship, UCLA is well known for its outstanding finance department.

All in all, the majority of students say that taking time off to pursue an Anderson MBA is well worth it. Claimed one, "Best value for the education. The new Dean is moving this school forward." Students we surveyed rated their general management skills as very strong. Students also doled out high marks for their marketing, finance, and accounting finesse. They judged themselves to be weaker in operations, quantitative methods, and computer skills. Another disappointment: the faculty. The school has brilliant, though not necessarily eloquent teachers. Problems with teaching quality are most evident in the core courses. Electives profs are among students' favorites.

PLACEMENT AND RECRUITING

Approximately 250 companies recruit for permanent positions on-campus annually. In 1993, eighty percent of the class had accepted an offer by the end of the academic year. With these figures, students told us they were moderately satisfied with the efforts of the placement office. Students were much more pleased with the school's alumni, whom they contacted in their job search and found very helpful.

UNIVERSITY OF CALIFORNIA–LOS ANGELES: JOHN E. ANDERSON GRADUATE SCHOOL OF MANAGEMENT

STUDENT LIFE/CAMPUS

Students report a manageable workload: they spend roughly twenty to thirty hours a week studying. To encourage student bonding, the entering class of 360 is divided into sections of approximately sixty each. Each semester, students are rotated into a new cohort; by the end of the year, you've been shuffled in the deck so much, you've met everyone in your class.

The B-school is housed in one high-rise building in which undergrads also take classes. A new seven-building B-school complex is in the process of being built and should go a long way toward enhancing student life and fostering a strong school identity. UCLA is located in West L.A., adjacent to Westwood Village, a trendy neighborhood of shops and restaurants catering to the college crowd. Roughly eighty percent of students opt to live off-campus in nearby Brentwood and Santa Monica, or further out in the Hermosa and Long Beach communities.

Along with their sunglasses and tans, Anderson students sport a laid-back attitude. They're competitive, but not out to demolish each other. Classroom dynamics don't require it. Unlike case study classes at Harvard and Darden, classes here rarely place students in the hot seat. Professors are more likely to open a case with a "softball" (a question that guides the student to the answer) than a hard cold call. Students also report, "There is incredible camaraderie. Everyone helps each other with academics, the job search, and social life." It doesn't hurt that the school has a somewhat loose grading policy. Griped one MBA, "Anyone with a pulse gets no lower than a B." Much of student life revolves around the activities of the student-run clubs such as the Anderson Golf and Country Club and MBA Students for the Environment. Every Thursday a "Beer Bust" is held on the outdoor patio, of course, after which everyone heads to the bar of the week. Intramural sports and volleyball on the beach are especially popular sports. Student involvement is also important. After the L.A. riots in the spring of 1992, students went out in the community to pitch in and clean up. Several work in a mentor program with ex-gang members.

One student paid this compliment to fellow classmates: "Anderson has quality students with quality backgrounds (career and education)." Added another, "We also have the best-looking undergrads." To sum it up, "Unbeatable lifestyle."

ADMISSIONS

Writes the admissions office, "In evaluating applications for admission, the school looks for evidence of exceptional academic ability and managerial potential. An applicant's leadership qualities, interpersonal skills, personal values and unique character are especially important to us. A special effort is made to recruit minority students." Notes the school, "Our minority graduate advisors (Black, Latino, and Asian MBA students at Anderson) play an important role in providing information and counseling for prospective minority applicants. Advisors organize an MBA Information Day for minority applicants." Decisions are made on a rolling admissions basis, although applications are batched in rounds. Early application is strongly advised.

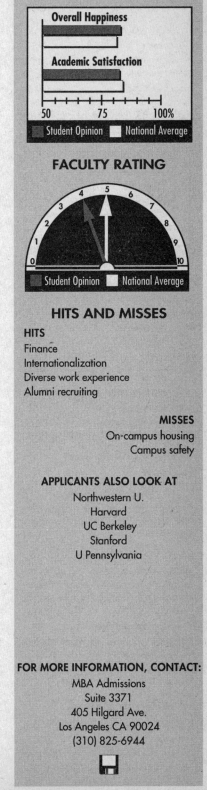

STUDENTS' OVERVIEW BOX

Overall Happiness
Academic Satisfaction
50 75 100%
Student Opinion National Average

FACULTY RATING
Student Opinion National Average

HITS AND MISSES

HITS
Finance
Internationalization
Diverse work experience
Alumni recruiting

MISSES
On-campus housing
Campus safety

APPLICANTS ALSO LOOK AT
Northwestern U.
Harvard
UC Berkeley
Stanford
U Pennsylvania

FOR MORE INFORMATION, CONTACT:
MBA Admissions
Suite 3371
405 Hilgard Ave.
Los Angeles CA 90024
(310) 825-6944

CARNEGIE MELLON UNIVERSITY GRADUATE SCHOOL OF INDUSTRIAL ADMINISTRATION

ADMISSIONS FACTS

Type of school   Private

Demographics

No. of men   N/A
No. of women   N/A
No. of minorities   N/A
No. of int'l students   N/A

EQUAL TREATMENT GRAPH

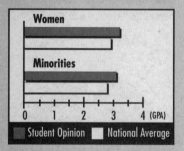

Admissions Statistics

Avg. GMAT   N/A
Avg. undergraduate GPA   N/A
Avg. age at entry   N/A
No. of applicants   N/A
No. accepted   N/A
No. enrolled   N/A

Deadlines and Notifications

Regular application   N/A
Regular notification   N/A
Special Dates   N/A

Focus of Curriculum

Specialized

Academic Specialties

Management Information Systems, Entrepreneurship, Production/Operations Management

Joint Degrees

MS in Information Networking, JD/MSIA, Joint Master's Program with the Engineering College, Collaborative program with the School of Urban and Public Affairs

Special Programs

Exchange programs in Europe, Japan & Mexico, Total Quality Management University Challenge, Program in Financial Analysis and Security Training

FINANCIAL FACTS

In-state tuition $20,500
Out-of-state tuition $20,500
On-campus housing   N/A

ACADEMICS

Carnegie Mellon offers the Master of Science in Industrial Administration (MSIA), which is similar to an MBA. Don't worry, the program is accredited as a graduate B-school by the American Association of Collegiate Schools of Business. Carnegie Mellon is particularly renowned for its innovations in both education and research. In fact, there are too many to list here. Let's just say if you attend Carnegie Mellon, you'll study among Nobel Prize-winning faculty who are expanding the frontiers of business. True to their emphasis on innovation, the Graduate School of Industrial Administration (GSIA) has scrapped the traditional fall/spring semester. In its place, four seven-and-a-half-week-long mini-semesters make up the school year. Students appreciate the school's trailblazing. Wrote one, "When I talk with friends at other B-schools, I always find GSIA is in the forefront of teaching techniques." Raved another, "The school is a leader; take a look at the research that comes out of here."

Particularly noteworthy is the "Management Game," a computer simulation of a consumer products company, which students are required to take in the final semester. "Game" teams meet with a board of directors (four of whom are corporate executives), negotiate mock contracts with actual representatives from unions, secure "financing" through Pittsburgh banks, and obtain legal advice from third-year law students.

GSIA has a reputation as a quantitative, technical school. But one student wrote, "GSIA's curriculum is frequently misunderstood by applicants. The school is technical, but this doesn't mean you won't become a strong generalist. GSIA emphasizes a generalist education while exposing you to the technical and theoretical business functions." But one student complained, "The school needs to tone down on the quant stuff. If you're not comfortable with numbers don't come here." Happily, students said the school is also strong in other areas. For example, thirty to forty percent of all graduates are entrepreneurs. Students rate the entrepreneurial classes as excellent. And a recent one-million-dollar gift from Pittsburgh entrepreneur Donald H. Jones will go a long ways toward further establishing an entrepreneurship center at the school. Students also give high marks to the finance department. Wrote one, "GSIA is the best-kept finance secret of the top twenty B-schools." Other areas in which students report standout skills: operations, computers, general management, and a surprise at this rigorous, techie school: teamwork.

PLACEMENT AND RECRUITING

According to the school, in 1992 the Career Opportunities Center (C.O.C.) handled 2,815 on-campus interviews. Despite all this, students were only moderately satisfied with the C.O.C. Wrote one, "My primary complaint: C.O.C. isn't too swift. Companies are attracted to the quality of the school; they're not here because of C.O.C.'s efforts." Said another, "Recruiting could be better." Alumni, whom the majority of students contacted in their job search, were considered very helpful.

CARNEGIE MELLON UNIVERSITY GRADUATE SCHOOL OF INDUSTRIAL ADMINISTRATION

STUDENT LIFE/CAMPUS

First-year students report a killer, barely survivable workload. This is compounded by the acceleration of the mini-semester schedule and up-all-night number-crunching assignments. According to our survey, this is a source of great stress, and the pressure is formidable. Fortunately, many courses are structured around team projects. Most students rely on help from their study groups. MBAs at GSIA get to know each other quickly. A total student body of 400 fosters a "close-knit group of people." Students rated their classmates as very smart, interested in helping each other—but with a healthy degree of competitiveness. Wrote one, "Students are high caliber and hard working." But one student reported, "There's a wide variance in student abilities." Still, this is not an unhappy bunch. The majority report a high quality of life and say taking the time off to pursue a Carnegie Mellon MBA is well worth it.

Again and again students told us the "new building and facilities are great." Indeed, new additions recently doubled the physical size of the B-school, although, according to students, the library is still sub-par. The campus is located in the Oakland section of Pittsburgh, a relaxed, safe, "college town" area. The immediate neighborhood is tree-lined and residential. Because on-campus housing is not available, many students live in the nearby communities of Shadyside, Oakland, and Squirrel Hill, which are among Pittsburgh's trendiest. As for the city of Pittsburgh, well, your ideas about it are probably wrong. Consistently rated one of America's most livable cities, it's clean, modern, and teeming with cultural events.

Back on campus, the volunteer GSIA social committee organizes many school events: picnics, holiday parties, boat cruises, and talent shows are all regular events. Weekends are often spent at informal get-togethers in students' homes. But students say their social lives are hindered by the ultra-heavy workload. Of the student body, students agree that their classmates are ethnically and racially diverse. As for types, one student told us there are "a lot of conservative geeks." But you know the saying—it takes one to know one.

ADMISSIONS

According to the admissions office, the following criteria are weighted equally: essays, college GPA, letters of recommendation, extracurricular activities, work experience, interview (required), and GMAT score. Notes the school, "When we evaluate an application, we try to understand that person as an individual. For example, we examine the entire academic record: grade trends, the major, the school extracurriculars, and part-time work, if any." Applications are batched in rounds. The admissions office suggests applying in round two.

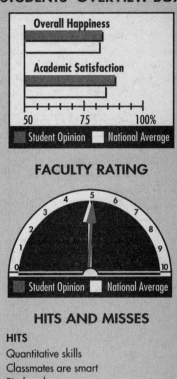

STUDENTS' OVERVIEW BOX

Overall Happiness

Academic Satisfaction

50   75   100%

■ Student Opinion □ National Average

FACULTY RATING

■ Student Opinion □ National Average

HITS AND MISSES

HITS
Quantitative skills
Classmates are smart
Pittsburgh
Innovative curriculum
Consulting projects

MISSES
Accounting dept.
Administration
Social life
Gym

APPLICANTS ALSO LOOK AT
Cornell U.
Mass. Inst. of Tech.
UNC Charlotte
U Chicago
U Michigan
U Rochester
New York University
Boston College

FOR MORE INFORMATION, CONTACT:
Graduate School of
Industrial Administration
Schenley Park
Pittsburgh, PA 15213-3890
(412) 268-2272

CASE WESTERN RESERVE: WEATHERHEAD SCHOOL OF MANAGEMENT

ADMISSIONS FACTS

Type of school   Private

Demographics

No. of men	172
No. of women	81
No. of minorities	21
No. of int'l students	56

EQUAL TREATMENT GRAPH

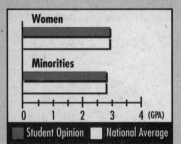

Women

Minorities

0   1   2   3   4 (GPA)

■ Student Opinion   □ National Average

Admissions Statistics

Avg. GMAT	590
Avg. undergraduate GPA	3.26
Avg. age at entry	27
No. of applicants	573
No. accepted	331
No. enrolled	129

Deadlines and Notifications

Regular application	4/15
Regular notification	rolling
Special dates	N/A

Focus of Curriculum

General Management

Academic Specialties

Industrial Marketing, Commercial Banking, MIS, Health Systems Management, Entrepreneurship, Operations Management

Joint Degrees

JD/MBA, MBA/MS in Management Science, MSMS/MBA, MSN(Master in Science and Nursing)/MBA, MNO/JD, MNO/MS in Social Work, Master in Int'l Mgmt./MBA (with Thunderbird), MNO/MA in Music History

Special Programs

The Weatherhead Mentor Program, Internat'l Exchange Programs, the 42 Credit-Hour Accelerated Curriculum, 11-month program for students with undergrad business degrees

FINANCIAL FACTS

In-state tuition	$18,400
Out-of-state tuition	$18,400
On-campus housing	$3,550

ACADEMICS

The Weatherhead School of Management (WSOM) takes an almost liberal-arts approach to business education. Entering students participate in a Management Assessment and Development course to diagnose strengths and weaknesses and develop a competency-based learning plan. At the close of the course, students list the academic and extracurricular activities—courses, internships, mentorships—they'll need to complete their learning plan. Faculty advisors check that it meets degree requirements, and their self-styled MBA program is launched. Of course, MBAs still take the pre-scribed set of core courses. In addition, they take two team-taught, interdisciplinary Perspectives Courses, which focus on global management, industrial development, or technology management. According to one student, these courses "bring students in touch with how they and others think." Particularly impressive are all the opportunities outside the classroom. Notes the school, "Approximately twenty-five percent of courses require field projects in which students work with local companies and nonprofit organizations for their research." Thirty percent of all classes have a team-work requirement. During the second year, students take six electives to complete their learning plan and specialize. Grading goes by an old-fashioned A, B, C, D—there's no forced curve. But this doesn't mean that the academic environment isn't challenging or demanding. According to students, there have been expensive trade-off's associated with the eclectic, participatory model of learning. Wrote one student, "The school's intense focus on the qualitative approach has led to quantitative disciplines being almost completely ignored. I feel sorry for any students coming from a liberal arts background. Should these students enter positions requiring quantitative skills, I suspect the learning curve will resemble the North Face of the Eiger—very steep and very difficult to climb."

PLACEMENT AND RECRUITING

The school offers a Mentor Program (the first in the United States), which matches each first-year student with a senior-level manager in the student's area of career interest. The school's Office of Career Planning and Placement also hosts networking receptions and career forums, as well as on-campus recruiting programs and career planning workshops. Students link up with off-campus recruiters via the distribution of resume books and postings for permanent and summer jobs.

In 1994, 70 companies recruited Weatherhead MBAs. Ninety percent of the class of 1994 had jobs within three months of graduation where 28% went in to finance and another 28% headed into general management. The major recruiters: Deloitte and Touche LLP, Avery Dennison, G.E., Ernst & Young, FHP Inc., KeyCorp, McKinsey, A.T. Kearney, and Andersen Consulting. The average starting salary was $46, 900. Students were extremely happy with the role alumni played in their career search. The majority of students surveyed contacted alumni and found their counsel useful.

CASE WESTERN RESERVE: WEATHERHEAD SCHOOL OF MANAGEMENT

STUDENT LIFE/CAMPUS

A full-time student body of 250, small classes, lots of student/faculty inter-action—as one student put it, "One of the best advantages of WSOM is its size." Students here are among the least competitive of all the B-schools we surveyed. There's pressure to succeed, and under the new curriculum students report a moderately heavy workload. Students spend about thirty-five to forty-five hours a week studying and completing group assignments.

Case Western's hometown is Cleveland—a livable city that boasts the third-largest number of Fortune 500 industrial corporate headquarters in America. For an urban school, Case Western is surprisingly campus-like, with wide open spaces and plenty of greenery. The school's management computer laboratory was the first to provide a fully integrated network of PCs for MBAs. But as modern as the computer center is, the library is a dinosaur. Griped one MBA, "Business info is either difficult to obtain or unavailable." However, the school will be building a new library in the next two years.

According to students, both on- and off-campus housing are terrific. Most students prefer apartment living in homes on the tree-lined streets of Cleveland Heights or Shaker Heights, both a short distance from campus. The social scene is dominated by the Graduate Student Association, which organizes activities like intramural sports, parties, and the survival series happy hour. Thursday nights, everyone heads to the designated bar of the week. Favorites are the Euclid Tavern and Knotty Pine. Popular student clubs include: Human Resources Club, Investment Operations Group, and the Multi-Cultural Task Force.

Almost forty percent of the students are from the Midwest. Otherwise, this school seriously values diversity. Thirty-four percent of the student population is international. An above-average number of women are enrolled: forty-one percent. Although only ten percent of the students are minorities, the general atmosphere is one of acceptance. It wouldn't be a stretch to call WSOM a progressive institution.

ADMISSIONS

According to the admissions office, your work experience is most important and then, in descending order, College GPA, the interview, GMAT scores, essays, letters of recommendation, and extracurricular activities. Personal interviews are recommended for admission. Students are notified of a decision four weeks after filing an application. Decisions are made on a rolling admissions basis. Students may defer admission for up to one year.

STUDENTS' OVERVIEW BOX

Overall Happiness

Academic Satisfaction

50 75 100%

Student Opinion National Average

FACULTY RATING

Student Opinion National Average

HITS AND MISSES

HITS
Accounting dept.
Diverse work experience
Ethnic & racial diversity
School clubs

MISSES
Quantitative skills
Library

APPLICANTS ALSO LOOK AT

U Iowa
Indiana U.-Bloom.
Ohio State U.
U Chicago
Washington U.
Carnegie Mellon U.
U Michigan
U Pittsburgh

FOR MORE INFORMATION, CONTACT:
MBA Admissions
10900 Euclid Ave.
Enterprise Hall RM 310
Cleveland, OH 44106
(800) 368-2030
eMail: lxg10@po.cwru.edu

University of Chicago Graduate School of Business

ADMISSIONS FACTS

Type of school	Private

Demographics

No. of men	2017
No. of women	686
No. of minorities	427
No. of int'l students	302

EQUAL TREATMENT GRAPH

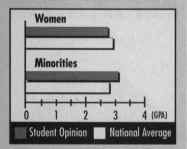

Admissions Statistics

Avg. GMAT	650
Avg. undergraduate GPA	3.4
Avg. age at entry	27.1
No. of applicants	3,255
No. accepted	1,072
No. enrolled	515

Deadlines and Notifications

Regular application	3/12
Regular notification	within 6 weeks
Special dates	N/A

Focus of Curriculum

General Management

Academic Specialties

Accounting, Economics, Finance, Total Quality Management

Joint Degrees

JD/MBA, AM/MBA, MD/MBA, SM/MBA

FINANCIAL FACTS

In-state tuition	$22,350
Out-of-state tuition	$22,350
On-campus housing	$6,000

Academics

The University of Chicago has a lot to boast about. For starters, it's the first B-school to boast four Nobel laureates on it's faculty, most recently Merton Miller, winner of the 1990 Nobel Prize in Economics, and Robert Fogel, winner of the same in 1993. It's also the first to publish a scholarly business journal and initiate a Ph.D. program. But the nation's second oldest B-School hasn't chosen to rest on its laurels. As one student put it, "This school is continuously trying to improve itself. There are so many innovative opportunities here. Chief among them is LEAD, a mandatory leadership program that students—not faculty—design each year." Another first for Chicago: among B-Schools, LEAD pioneered the emphasis on leadership, interpersonal and multi-cultural programs, and learning by doing. Unsurprisingly, Chicago students give themselves high marks for their interpersonal skills, (unique to a "quant" school) and tell us minorities and women are more than comfortable here. For more innovation, students can participate in Chicago's New Product Laboratory, acting as consultants to major corporations. Summed up one enthusiastic student, "Chicago is brilliant theoretically, and more applications-oriented than ever."

As for the curriculum, students declare it's "the single most flexible around." Other than the non-credit, year-long LEAD program, there are only two required core courses. Another curriculum plus: students aren't required to repeat work they have mastered elsewhere. Specializations are created by bundling four courses in one discipline. A unique area of study is Total Quality Management; the school has designated this up-and-coming field a true concentration. The newest addition to Chicago is the International MBA, which according to the school, "builds truly global management skills." Explains Dean Robert S. Hamada, "Our market research indicates that employers who hire our graduates for careers in international business want people with substantial knowledge of the culture, society, and language of a foreign country."

Chicago is best known for its economics and finance departments and is considered "numbers-heavy." But a majority of Chicago MBAs told us "It isn't a quant school as much as people think. We're not all quant-jocks and nerds." Added another, "There's more to academic life here than finance." There's truth to this. Chicago offers more courses in marketing than they do in finance. Unfortunately, according to our survey, students don't feel nearly as competent about their marketing skills as they do about their quant and finance skills, which they rate excellent. They do feel terrific about Chicago's faculty whom they consider terrific teachers. Said one student, "Even in the boring classes, they're good." But there are a few flaws in this academic Eden: an over—emphasis on the job search which students tell us begins on "Day 1," an inefficient bidding process for classes, (students say it should be on-line), and the Hyde park neighborhood in which the school is located (more on that later).

Placement and Recruiting

Chicago MBAs say they're satisfied with their career placement office. We're not surprised. In 1994, 248 companies recruited on campus for both summer internships and full-time positions. Eighty-seven percent of the second-year class had a job by graduation and ninety-seven percent shortly thereafter. Top employers of Chicago MBAs are Booz Allen & Hamilton, Goldman Sachs, Boston Consulting Group, Coopers and Lybrand, and Deloitte & Touche. The average starting salary of graduates is $60,000.

UNIVERSITY OF CHICAGO GRADUATE SCHOOL OF BUSINESS

STUDENT LIFE/CAMPUS

As one student put it, "The pressure here is subjective, although certainly the workload is substantial." There is an emphasis on grades, but the most pressure seems to come from trying to juggle a job search with academics. Complained one MBA, "This place would deliver a better business education if there were less conflict with full-time job searching. Ask people how many pass/fail classes they take." The majority of students work in study groups. Classes tend to be large. As for class structure, one student wrote, "Some are mostly problem sets and exams, some are mostly papers and presentations, and some are both."

Over and over, students told us they were "pleasantly surprised" by the "attitudes of the other students." Explained one student, "Classmates are more inclined to help each other out, rather than stab each other in the back." Reported another, "Students are competitive, but collegial, too." Of the professionally diverse student body, most are "extremely bright, intense, and ambitious. Still, there were a few complaints. One MBA wrote, "Students here are too narrow and dull—they need some liberal humanities education."

The school sits on a beautiful campus in the Hyde Park section of Chicago. Known as the "South Side", it's not centrally located. Translation: it's miles away from the city proper and all is has to offer. Suggestion: live on the North Side and commute as many students do. As for safety, Hyde Park is rumored to have problems. But it has a better crime rate (per capita) than Cambridge, Mass and the campus is heavily patrolled. As for the social scene, it's teeming with activity. There are plenty of planned activities, both professional and social. Wrote one student, "For those of us who like to party, there are plenty of events at least three nights a week. I really feel like I'm back in college." Although students report active social lives, this doesn't include dating. But the group thing works. Chicago MBA's say they'll be buddies with their classmates long after they graduate.

ADMISSIONS

According to the admissions office, your GMAT scores, work experience, essays, college GPA, letters of recommendation, and extracurricular activities are all considered equally. The interview is strongly recommended, but not required. Notes the school, "All of the above are considered equally. We have no cutoffs on GPA or GMAT scores." Decisions are made on a rolling admissions basis, but are batched in rounds. Applicants are notified of a decision following each of four rounds: October 22, November 28, January 2, February 10, March 12.

STUDENTS' OVERVIEW BOX

Overall Happiness

Academic Satisfaction

50   75   100%

Student Opinion   National Average

FACULTY RATING

Student Opinion   National Average

HITS AND MISSES

HITS
Quantitative skills
Accounting dept.
Finance dept.
Diverse work experience
Placement & recruiting
Classmates are smart

MISSES
Marketing dept.
On-campus housing
Hyde Park

APPLICANTS ALSO LOOK AT
Stanford U.
U Pennsylvania
Northwestern U.
Cornell U.
Harvard
Dartmouth College
Massachusetts Institute of Tech.
Columbia U.
UC Los Angeles
U Virginia

FOR MORE INFORMATION, CONTACT:
Graduate School of Business
1101 East 58 St.
Chicago, IL 60637
(312) 702-7369

CLAREMONT GRADUATE SCHOOL: THE PETER F. DRUCKER GRADUATE MANAGEMENT CENTER

ADMISSIONS FACTS

Type of school   Private

Demographics

No. of men   139
No. of women   88
No. of minorities   52
No. of int'l students   45

EQUAL TREATMENT GRAPH

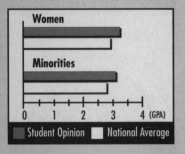

Women

Minorities

0   1   2   3   4 (GPA)

■ Student Opinion   ■ National Average

Admissions Statistics

Avg. GMAT   547
Avg. undergraduate GPA   3.3
Avg. age at entry   28
No. of applicants   283
No. accepted   156
No. enrolled   54

Deadlines and Notifications

Regular application   6/1
Regular notification   within 4–6 weeks
Special dates   N/A

Focus of Curriculum

General Management

Academic Specialties

Strategic Management, Managing
People

Special Programs

Strategic Management

FINANCIAL FACTS

In-state tuition $18,120
Out-of-state tuition $18,120
On-campus housing   N/A

ACADEMICS

The Claremont Graduate School has "brand recognition" due to Peter F. Drucker, a professor at the school since 1971, and the world's most widely read author on the subject of management. Probably because of his influence, the school is renowned for the relevance of the faculty's research into managerial practices. But the talent pool isn't limited to Drucker. As one student put it, "The faculty has become increasingly top tier with the addition of highly recognized leaders in their respective fields." You can study here with former Harvard professors Dick Ellsworth, Vijay Sathe, Christine Ries, and Robin Cooper, the latter of whom is one of the originators of activity-based accounting and was among Harvard's most popular teachers. But these are obviously some of the best. The majority of MBAs polled felt teaching was uneven. One student summed up the sentiments of his classmates by saying,, "It's hit or miss with the quality of teaching. Profs are either great or disappointing. No in-between."

According to the school, "The Drucker Center's educational philosophy emphasizes an understanding of global forces affecting markets, recognizes the growing importance of information technology, and focuses on individual leadership skills." Students attend Claremont to study general management and to pursue careers in product management, corporate finance, management consulting, and banking. The integrated curriculum "stresses an interplay between the real world and the classroom." One of the most popular courses is "The Human Component," in which student teams perform an analysis of an industry and then present conclusions to real-life players. Most recently, Bob Kohler, head of a TRW subsidiary, made a guest appearance and provided feedback to students on their analyses. What do students say about what they're learning at Claremont? They give themselves high marks first for their general management skills, and then for their marketing acumen. The only academic weak spot is operations.

One standout feature at Claremont is the mentor program, which places full/part-time MBA students in mentoring relationships with senior managers in the Executive Education Program. As for the way this school is run, students rave about the personal attention: "Each and every person employed here—faculty, administration—goes out of their way to make sure the students are happy." Overall, the majority of Claremont MBAs agree and say this program is exceeding their academic expectations.

PLACEMENT AND RECRUITING

It's hard to run a placement office when fifty percent of your students already have jobs. Moreover, companies like to recruit at schools that can yield the greatest number of hires. Claremont is too small to reel in large numbers of major on-campus recruiters. Nonetheless, 1994 stats are strong. Ninety-two percent of those seeking a new position were placed by July. The average starting salary was $50,000. The big recruiters were: Avery Dennison, FHP, Andersen Consulting, Deloitte & Touche and PepsiCo. More specifically, 33% of grads went into general management, 20% into banking or investment banking, 15% into operations, and nd 15% into marketing.

CLAREMONT GRADUATE SCHOOL: THE PETER F. DRUCKER GRADUATE MANAGEMENT CENTER

STUDENT LIFE/CAMPUS

According to our survey, students have a moderate workload. Of the one hundred students in each entering class, approximately fifty are part-timers. These two groups take courses together. The average class size is twenty-six students. Class participation counts heavily towards the grade. Similar to prospective MBAs across the country, Claremont students work in study groups. However, unlike MBAs at full-time programs, Claremont students find it difficult to build social networks. Others agreed "Students here are not as socially outgoing as they are at other schools." On the plus side: Claremont MBAs are noncompetitive and interested in helping each other out. There is a strong teamwork ethic. Several students raved, "A great place for international students!"

Claremont is located in southern California, about a forty-minute drive away from L.A. and the beach. But the setting is all California: palm trees, red-tiled roofs, and the San Gabriel Mountains as a backdrop. Half of all full-timers live on campus, the other half rent apartments off-campus in Claremont, Upland, and Montclair. Housing is plentiful and affordable. Everyone joins the Graduate Management Association, which sponsors everything from corporate speaker series to social events like the annual spring formal and barbecues. Other clubs to join: International Business Association, American Marketing Association and the Finance Club.

ADMISSIONS

According to the admissions office, college GPA and work experience are considered most important. Then, in descending order of importance, GMAT score, letters of recommendation and essays, interview, and extracurricular activities. Adds the school, "Extracurriculars and work experience are not required, but are considered. Interviews are recommended." Admissions decisions are made on a rolling basis. Students may defer admission for up to one year.

STUDENTS' OVERVIEW BOX

Overall Happiness

Academic Satisfaction

50   75   100%

■ Student Opinion □ National Average

FACULTY RATING

■ Student Opinion □ National Average

HITS AND MISSES

HITS
Accounting dept.
Finance dept.
Diverse work experience
Placement & recruiting
Classmates are smart

MISSES
Marketing dept.
On-campus housing

APPLICANTS ALSO LOOK AT
UC Los Angeles
U Southern CA
Wharton
Pepperdine
Thunderbird
UC Irvine
New York University

FOR MORE INFORMATION CONTACT:
Michael A. Kraft
925 North Dartmouth Ave.
Claremont, CA 91711
(909) 621-8073

UNIVERSITY OF COLORADO AT BOULDER GRADUATE SCHOOL OF BUSINESS ADMINISTRATION

ADMISSIONS FACTS

Type of school	Public

Demographics

No. of men	N/A
No. of women	N/A
No. of minorities	N/A
No. of int'l students	N/A

EQUAL TREATMENT GRAPH

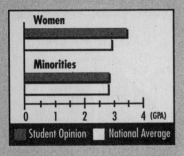

Women

Minorities

0 1 2 3 4 (GPA)

■ Student Opinion □ National Average

Admissions Statistics

Avg. GMAT	570
Avg. undergraduate GPA	3.0
Avg. age at entry	27
No. of applicants	405
No. accepted	141
No. enrolled	64

Deadlines and Notifications

Regular application	4/1
Regular notification	rolling
Special dates	N/A

Focus of Curriculum

Specialized

Academic Specialties

Technology and Innovation, Finance, Marketing

FINANCIAL FACTS

In-state tuition	$3,308
Out-of-state tuition	$11,844
On-campus housing	$4,131

ACADEMICS

There are plenty of students whose primary reason for attending the University of Colorado (UC) is summed up by the one who wrote, "I'm here for the Boulder experience." Plenty wrote, "I wanted to get my MBA in a state where I would live." Of course, many students also mentioned academic reputation as a strong drawing card. But it's really the best of both worlds—students agree a top-notch education and skiing come in an unbeatable package at UC. That education includes a newly created full-time "lock-step" program whereby one hundred entering students are divided into two cohorts of fifty students and take core courses together. Explained one MBA, "This is a new program. Although the kinks need to be worked out, the potential for real-world management training is excellent. Teamwork and communication are main themes." Wrote another, "There is a reliance on the case study method and an emphasis on interactive learning." The first year is filled with courses in the functional areas and features a quantitative slant. It also integrates global themes, which are enhanced by a student body that is one-quarter international. Second-year students major in finance, marketing, organization management, or technology and innovation management. The accounting department is considered tops. Several other MBAs echoed this sentiment: "Excellent place to be for innovation and entrepreneurial studies. Alumni participation is great for small business majors." Unique to UC is the option to pursue a self-designed major. For example, a student with an engineering background might design an interdisciplinary telecommunications major and take classes in the engineering school.

As for teaching, there is a high degree of variability. Wrote one student, "Some professors are fantastic. Others are barely tolerable." Professors receive better grades for their after-class accessibility, which is considered above average. All in all, the majority of students say this program offers very high value and low cost, especially with the low in-state tuition factored in. The new program may still be in its infancy, but satisfied MBAs say Colorado is well poised to "vault into the top 20 in the next few years."

PLACEMENT AND RECRUITING

No matter where you go, students are unhappy with their career development office. UC students are not the exception. One MBA sounded off: "The placement center is hopelessly bogged down in red tape." The schools counters by saying: "The Graduate School of Business relied on Career Services serving the main university to place MBA students. As of March 1, 1995 a Director for MBA Career Development and Placement Services is available to assist MBA students with job placement. As such, statistical information will (soon) be available on a consistent basis." Here's what they do have: In 1994 thirty-five companies recruited on-campus and 30% of the graduating class went into finance, 30% into marketing, the remainder into accounting, MIS, human resources and Transportation Management. The average starting salary—$45,003.

UNIVERSITY OF COLORADO AT BOULDER GRADUATE SCHOOL OF BUSINESS ADMINISTRATION

STUDENT LIFE/CAMPUS

As a function of the new lock-step system, students are assigned to study groups organized around student members' strengths and weaknesses. During the first year, the workload is especially heavy. Wrote one student, "It's tough, but good." Students spend an average of twenty-five to thirty-five hours a week in study group and/or preparing for class. Partly because of the competitive grading system, students feel a lot of pressure. There is a targeted grade distribution—thirty percent of the class get A's, sixty percent B's, ten percent C's. UC MBAs need a solid B average to graduate, and B minus doesn't cut it. In most courses, class participation, grades, and papers count equally toward the grade.

As one might expect, students are fairly competitive. But this is kept in check by the cohort system and small class size, which tend to foster cooperation. Explained one team player, "Fantastic program where students work together. The attitude is not cutthroat and deceptive." UC MBAs say classmates are smart and of "high quality," but not as professionally diverse as they'd like them to be. Groused one, "Four years' work experience was suggested, but not mandatory; it should have been." On a positive note, students are unanimous: they've benefited from the strong international student body—over 25 countries are represented.

Students here are thrilled about the high quality of life. One MBA's comments seemed to say it all: "I love to ski. There is no better place in which to live and go to school." Boulder is beautiful, but expensive. Students who opt to live off-campus (most do) find inexpensive housing outside of town. Public transportation is great—students get free metro bus passes. Social and professional activities are sponsored by the Graduate Students Business Association (GSBA) and include weekly Thursday night get-togethers (no class on Friday), a faculty/student softball game, and what you'd expect—plenty of ski trips. Raved one MBA, "Without the GSBA, this would be like any other school." Added another, "The Boulder business community is very involved with the school—networking opportunities, internships."

A final note: There are a variety of student-run, specialized clubs for female and minority students, including the Black Business Students Coalition and the Hispanic Business Students Association. Unfortunately, there are few minority students to join them.

ADMISSIONS

According to the admissions office, your work experience is considered most important. After that, in descending order, your GMAT score, college GPA, interview, essays, letters of recommendation, and extracurricular activities. Domestic ethnic minorities receive special consideration. Decisions are made on a rolling basis. Applicants are notified of a decision six to eight weeks after a completed application has been received.

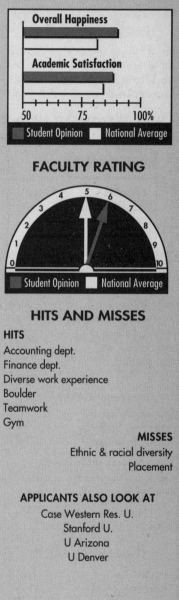

STUDENTS' OVERVIEW BOX

Overall Happiness

Academic Satisfaction

50   75   100%

Student Opinion   National Average

FACULTY RATING

Student Opinion   National Average

HITS AND MISSES

HITS
Accounting dept.
Finance dept.
Diverse work experience
Boulder
Teamwork
Gym

MISSES
Ethnic & racial diversity
Placement

APPLICANTS ALSO LOOK AT
Case Western Res. U.
Stanford U.
U Arizona
U Denver

FOR MORE INFORMATION, CONTACT:
Graduate School of Business
Administration Box 419
Boulder, CO 80309-0419
(303) 492-1831
eMail: langein@spot.colorado.edu

COLUMBIA UNIVERSITY: COLUMBIA GRADUATE SCHOOL OF BUSINESS

ADMISSIONS FACTS

Type of school	Private

Demographics

No. of men	901
No. of women	390
No. of minorities	147
No. of int'l students	340

EQUAL TREATMENT GRAPH

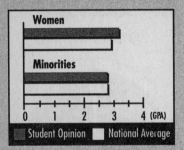

Admissions Statistics

Avg. GMAT	N/A
Avg. undergraduate GPA	N/A
Avg. age at entry	N/A
No. of applicants	N/A
No. accepted	N/A
No. enrolled	N/A

Deadlines and Notifications

Regular application	N/A
Regular notification	N/A
Special dates	N/A

Focus of Curriculum

General Management, specialization required

Academic Specialties

Finance, International Business

FINANCIAL FACTS

In-state tuition	$21,000
Out-of-state tuition	$21,000
On-campus housing	$4,500–$9,000

ACADEMICS

The Columbia Business School (CBS) is considered one of the finest MBA programs in the nation. Like many B-schools, CBS has recently introduced a new curriculum and is continuing to refine its program. Wrote one student, "The school recently implemented a required core based on globalization, ethics, total quality management, and human resources management." These themes are now integrated across the traditional disciplines of business. Students may choose from among twelve concentrations. The newest one is the Management of Information, Communications, and Media. Students agree, "Finance is an outstanding department here." But some complained that because Finance is so much better than the other dept's, "most of the students want to do finance." Still others told us, "Resources and programs at the school are very strong for those interested in international careers." Columbia has a math requirement that can be satisfied by previous coursework, passing an exemption exam, or by attending the popular summer "math camp." To bolster skills in school, review sessions are held for all quantitative core courses and some upper-level electives on class-free Fridays. Students who need extra help can work one-on-one with a peer tutor. According to our survey, Columbia MBAs are "Exceptionally compouter literate due to the computer initiative requiring each person to own a laptop and use course material provided on the computer network." Unique to Columbia's program is the fact that students can begin school in any one of three terms starting in September, January, or May. If they choose to, students can go straight through and graduate in sixteen months.

According to the students in our survey, Columbia is a school whose candle continues to burn brighter and brighter. One student's praise was typical of his classmates: "The school Dean is outstanding, involved, and informed. Students, faculty, and administration are committed to making Columbia the number one business school." In order to promote camaraderie, Columbia's administration implemented "clusters" which section first-year students into "homeroom" groups of roughly fifty-five each. Students take all 10 first year core classes with their cluster. As you would expect given Columbia's reputation, students rate their finance skills as tops. They also award themselves strong scores for their skills in accounting and genenral management. They were less positive about their marketing and operations skills. Nonetheless, MBAs say this school is sizzling. Get your application in early. A surge in applications has made Columbia tough to get into, a remarkable change from just several years ago.

PLACEMENT AND RECRUITING

The Office of Career Services offers the standard fare: counseling sessions, résumé writing workshops, and seminars on job search strategies. But what puts Columbia on top is its New York location. Over 10,000 Columbia alumni live or work in New York. Chided one MBA, "You are nuts to go outside of NYC for your MBA. You have to be here to make contacts. It's that simple."

In 1994 Columbia boasted a ninety percent placement rate. One student's comment typified the state of affairs here, "The school is very oriented towards two occupations - investment banking, Wall Street and consulting. In 1993, about fifty percent of graduating students went in to financial services. Of that fifty percent, thirty percent went into investment banking and investment management—numbers that parallel the former all-time high in 1986 for this school. Wrote one MBA,"You are so close to Wall Street and many corporate HQs. Alums are usuallly very receptive to setting up interviews or a at least speaking with you over the phone to give you advice." Said another "You're constantly networking and meeting potential employers."

COLUMBIA UNIVERSITY: COLUMBIA GRADUATE SCHOOL OF BUSINESS

STUDENT LIFE/CAMPUS

The majority of first-year students describe an up-all-night workload and hit the books an average of thirty-five to forty hours a week. One student explained it this way: "Because we have a shorter academic year (by about six weeks compared to other B-schools), yet cover the same amount of material, our courseload is intense." Shorter year or not, academics are rigorous and demanding. Unsurprisingly, students say it's important to do all or most of the work. The wise ones form study groups to get through it. Explained one MBA, "The first semester is by far the most competitive and difficult. Later, students relax a bit more, become more sociable, and take more time to get invovled in activities."

Has Columbia changed from a cutthroat to team-oriented school? It's heading in that direction. Wrote one MBA, "The redesigned courses at Columbia had a positive effect on stressing effective group work (while still being able to differentiate yourself through exams.)"Agreed another, "Students are more firendly and intereted in helping other students than Columbia Businesss School is usually credited with." Students seem to enjoy each other's company, too. They also said they'll continue their friendships postgraduation. Even so, some sharp elbows remain. Several students said, "Columbia can be very competitive" and "Lots of students go their own way." Summed up one MBA, "Columbia is in many ways a microcosm of New York City. The energy and motivation required to succeed in NYC are also necessary to succeed here." A few students feel there is a need to improve racial sensitivity: "There is absolutely no sensitivity training to people of different cultures, backgrounds, and sexual orientations."

Columbia students all agree that being located in what one student terms "the financial and media mecca of the world" is a quite an advantage. Columbia's location allows the school to get a lion's share of visiting business luminaries, from Henry Kravis to Warren Buffett. Confirmed one student, "Through the Distinguished Leader Lecture Series, power-hitters are constantly on campus." Another plus: Over and over, students told us about an impressive line-up of speakers. "In a 2-week period Jimmy Rogers, Warren Buffet, Dennis Weatherstone, and Mike Milken all came to speak—need I say more?" Columbia brings in NYC business professionals as adjunct professors. The bad points have to do with what one student calls the "tight New York space factor." Simply put, Columbia's one-building schoolhouse doesn't offer enough room or ambiance. The immediate neighborhood isn't Camelot, but is fairly yuppified, due to the presence of Columbia/Barnard. The majority of students live off-campus in apartments around the campus or further downtown. For extracurricular activities, students choose from more than 80 student-run clubs. Thursday nights, they kick off their weekend with a happy hour in the school's eatery.

ADMISSIONS

According to the admissions department, your work experience and professional goals are considered most important. After that, your extracurricular activities, college GPA, essays, interview/letters of recommendation, and GMAT score are equally important. Notes the school, "Applicants are evaluated in three categories, listed in order of importance: professional promise, personal characteristics, and academic credentials." Alumni children/spouses receive special consideration. Decisions are made on a rolling basis.

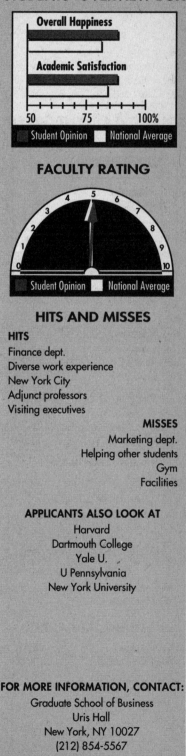

STUDENTS' OVERVIEW BOX

Overall Happiness

Academic Satisfaction

50   75   100%

Student Opinion   National Average

FACULTY RATING

Student Opinion   National Average

HITS AND MISSES

HITS
Finance dept.
Diverse work experience
New York City
Adjunct professors
Visiting executives

MISSES
Marketing dept.
Helping other students
Gym
Facilities

APPLICANTS ALSO LOOK AT
Harvard
Dartmouth College
Yale U.
U Pennsylvania
New York University

FOR MORE INFORMATION, CONTACT:
Graduate School of Business
Uris Hall
New York, NY 10027
(212) 854-5567

UNIVERSITY OF CONNECTICUT SCHOOL OF BUSINESS ADMINISTRATION

ADMISSIONS FACTS

Type of school	Public

Demographics

No. of men	137
No. of women	87
No. of minorities	23
No. of int'l students	66

EQUAL TREATMENT GRAPH

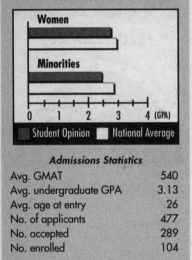

Admissions Statistics

Avg. GMAT	540
Avg. undergraduate GPA	3.13
Avg. age at entry	26
No. of applicants	477
No. accepted	289
No. enrolled	104

Deadlines and Notifications

Regular application	rolling
Regular notification	rolling (4 weeks)
Special dates	N/A

Focus of Curriculum

Specialized

Academic Specialties

Accounting, Finance, Real Estate

Joint Degrees

MBA/JD, MBA/MA, MBA/MIM

Special Programs

Foreign Study in France, Germany, and the Netherlands.

FINANCIAL FACTS

In-state tuition	$5,516
Out-of-state tuition	$13,190
On-campus housing	$2,888

ACADEMICS

As several students told us, the best things about the University of Connecticut (UConn) are the low-cost/high-value education, the accounting and finance department, and the Center for Real Estate Studies. An added benefit is that the school maintains strong ties with the local business community. Students have frequent contact with visiting business professionals from the region. Students say academics at UConn are both challenging and rigorous. "The majority of course work deals with applying business theory to real-life situations," said one student. MBAs take six electives to concentrate in one of nine areas. Noted one, "The quality of the courses (i.e., content, professors) increases as you get into your concentration." The program has a definite international flavor. Reported one student, "About twenty percent of the students are from foreign countries, which truly gives an international flair to class discussions, as well as enhances social tolerance outside the classroom." In addition, all students must take an international studies course.

Over and over, students told us that collaboration is heavily emphasized. Wrote one student, "There is a strong focus on teamwork and presentations, but with individual accountability. Good combination." Other students told us it's too much. Griped one unhappy teammate, "UConn enforces group projects. It's overdone and takes time away from studying. "As for the professors, one student's comments typified the prevalent feeling here: "Overall, faculty are a little inconsistent. But we have some outstanding teachers." The majority agreed with this UConn MBA: "Most professors are genuinely concerned and very accessible." Although the administration is considered "helpful and responsive," more than fifty percent of the students surveyed said the school needs some fine-tuning. Problems and complaints: "We are not financially supported by the state of Connecticut—the physical plant is deteriorating, electives are being reduced" and "the future of the program is uncertain." All in all, students say this program is well worth the investment of time and money. For the majority, it has exceeded academic expectations. Summed up one satisfied student, "I have learned more in my first semester here than in four years of undergraduate education. Despite UConn's inferiority complex, I anticipate a high return on my investment."

PLACEMENT AND RECRUITING

Wrote one pleased customer about the career center, "I've received three job offers at top public accounting firms after interviewing with eleven companies." Granted, UConn does tend to do well with placement in its star academic areas. But the majority of the students surveyed told us they're disappointed with the "lack of national corporation recruiting on campus." Still, the placement rate is strong. In 1994, 50 companies recruited on-campus. Eighty-four percent of UConn MBAs had been placed by the August after graduation, 100%, within one year of graduation. Twenty-six percent go into finance. Employers grabbing the most MBAs: G.E., "Big - 6" Accounting Firms, CIGNA, AEINA, IBM, United Technologies Corp., Andersen Consulting, American Management Systems. The average starting salaries of grads were $41, 200.

UNIVERSITY OF CONNECTICUT SCHOOL OF BUSINESS ADMINISTRATION

STUDENT LIFE/CAMPUS

As one student put it, "Many activities go on on-campus, but the workload is so heavy, you don't usually have time to participate and enjoy yourself." Observed another, "The workload is intense with quantity, not necessarily in-depth study."

Students are bogged down in schoolwork an average of twenty-five to thirty-five hours a week. The vast majority report it's important to do all or most of the assigned reading. Study groups help students synthesize their ideas, but MBAs report there's still a lot of pressure. This may be caused by school policy: first-year students must maintain a 3.0 GPA to continue in the program. But don't break out in a sweat yet. Students told us, "Unless you're a complete idiot, everyone gets a 3.0." As one student put it, "This is a good combination of a large university campus with the small, intimate environment of only 260 students. The small size gives UConn a sense of 'family.' " Raved another, "Very strong *esprit de corps*." Students are competitive, but not into one-upmanship. They help each other academically, and also enjoy hanging out together. Students feel classmates "are not only smart, but have great character." The majority reported that the student body is both ethnically and professionally diverse. One complaint: "Too many cocky students straight out of undergraduate school." Over and over, we heard "getting involved is the key." Advised one UConn MBA, "Anyone who comes here and sits back will not gain much." Reported another, "There are many opportunities for the ambitious student to stand out." The be-all and end-all extracurricular group is the student-run Graduate Business Association, which UConn MBAs rave about. As one student put it, "It supplements the MBA office and placement with professional development exercises, networking, recruiting, etc. A lot of the gaps in the program are filled in by the Graduate Business Association." It also organizes social activities at favorite watering holes such as Ted's and Husky's. Of the students, sixty percent live off-campus, but housing can be pricey. Also, you'll need a car. On-campus housing is a decent bet for a single student. UConn is located in Storrs, a rural area about a one-and-a-half-hour train ride from New York City and forty-five minutes from Hartford.

ADMISSIONS

According to the admissions office, the following three criteria are considered most important and are weighted equally: your GMAT score, work experience, and college GPA. Then come your essays, letters of recommendation, and extracurriculars. Writes the school, "We do not use cutoffs for GMAT scores or GPA. Evidence of high promise in one area can offset average accomplishment in another." Admissions decisions are made on a rolling basis throughout the year. There are no deadlines until the class has filled up. Students typically receive a decision within one month of completion of their file. They may defer admission for up to one year, depending on the circumstances.

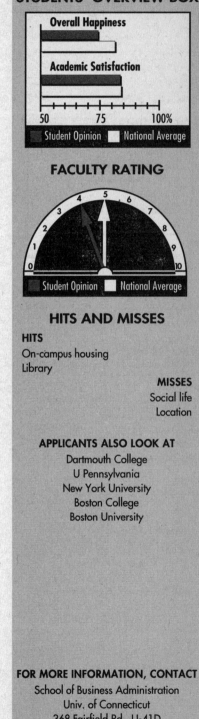

STUDENTS' OVERVIEW BOX

Overall Happiness

Academic Satisfaction

50   75   100%

■ Student Opinion □ National Average

FACULTY RATING

■ Student Opinion □ National Average

HITS AND MISSES

HITS
On-campus housing
Library

MISSES
Social life
Location

APPLICANTS ALSO LOOK AT
Dartmouth College
U Pennsylvania
New York University
Boston College
Boston University

FOR MORE INFORMATION, CONTACT
School of Business Administration
Univ. of Connecticut
368 Fairfield Rd., U-41D
Storrs, CT 06269-2041
(203) 486-2872
eMail:
DPalmer@UCONNVM.UCONN.EDU

CORNELL UNIVERSITY: JOHNSON GRADUATE SCHOOL OF MANAGEMENT

ADMISSIONS FACTS

Type of school	Private

Demographics

No. of men	375
No. of women	125
No. of minorities	20
No. of int'l students	170

EQUAL TREATMENT GRAPH

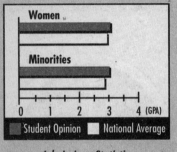

Women

Minorities

0   1   2   3   4 (GPA)

■ Student Opinion   □ National Average

Admissions Statistics

Avg. GMAT	636
Avg. undergraduate GPA	3.3
Avg. age at entry	27
No. of applicants	1,820
No. accepted	620
No. enrolled	270

Deadlines and Notifications

Regular application	3/15
Regular notification	rolling (8 weeks)
Special dates	EDP 1/15
EDP notification	3/15

Focus of Curriculum

General Management, specializations

Academic Specialties

International Business, Asian and European Business Studies, Finance

Special Programs

International Business, Asian and European Business Studies, Finance

FINANCIAL FACTS

In-state tuition	$20,400
Out-of-state tuition	$20,400
On-campus housing	$7,000

ACADEMICS

International electives and foreign study options overflow the Cornell course catalog. The students we spoke to repeatedly emphasized three innovative programs: FALCON (Full-year Asian Language Concentration), designed for students who have never spoken a word of Japanese; the MBA concentration in Japanese business; and the joint MBA/MA in Asian studies. In the past, students have interned with the Industrial Bank of Japan and Nippon Telegraph and Telephone. Beyond the study of Japanese business, concentrations are available in international economics and trade, international public policies, and international management. Seven first-years have the opportunity to work in the summer in developing countries in Central and Eastern Europe.

As for the MBA program itself, Cornell is not very different from others included in this book. The first year is filled with core courses. During the second year, students use electives that are organized into "maps" to pursue a broad or specialized course of study. What distinguishes Cornell is the flexibility students have in taking electives in other university schools (like the Cornell School of Hotel Management; the College of Art, Architecture, and Planning; and the School of Industrial and Labor Relations). One student reported, "The Johnson school relies heavily on other parts of Cornell to provide a full range of classes. But this is both a weakness and a strength." Cornell has also been known to turn out an entrepreneur or two. Most of these are students who have taken Entrepreneurship and Enterprise, one of the most popular electives.

As for the professors at Cornell, the majority of students give their instructors solid marks for both their teaching and accessibility. Claimed one booster, "The professors open door policy is a big plus for the school. Most of the time one hardly has to wait to see a prof. "It's not uncommon for professors to give out their home phone number, take students on a field trip, or have them over for dinner. A few flaws in this academic utopia are large classes and facilities that are in need renovation (a new B-school is being built). Nonetheless, the majority agreed that "Cornell is more than I expected and all that I needed." A sizable minority felt less certain.

PLACEMENT AND RECRUITING

Advised one MBA, "The remote location and small size make independent job searches more important." Reported one Cornell fan, " I have fourteen interviews from summer internships. The number of company's recruiting has increased 30% per year over the last couple of years. Most students in our survey sought out alumni for career advice. Reported one job seeker, "Alumni (not limited to the Johnson School) are generally very loyal and supportive in job search efforts." In 1994, eighty-five percent of the class had offers by graduation.

CORNELL UNIVERSITY: JOHNSON GRADUATE SCHOOL OF MANAGEMENT

STUDENT LIFE/CAMPUS

The Cornell program stresses teamwork and oral and written communications skills. Reported one MBA, "There are many learning opportunities through frequent guest speakers." There are also a large number of out-of-class experiences: a Community Weekend in September, a retreat for first-years led by second-years, winter-break trips to Japan and Russia, and week-long Outward Bound-like summer leadership programs in rugged locales like the Hurricane Islands, Adirondacks, and the Rockies. Students report only a moderately heavy workload. The pressure is manageable. Students hit the books an average of twenty-five to thirty-five hours a week, hardly a killer by top B-school standards.

The defining characteristic of life here seems to be the tight-knit community of students. Wrote one student, "The best selling point about Johnson are the students. They all work together to get things done. We are each other's support networks and it's wonderful." We also heard insightful comments like "It rules" and "It's awesome," but what is apparent is the student body's enthusiasm for one another. Students are congenial and not back-stabbingly competitive. Students also report classmates are smart and professionally diverse. As for the campus itself, it's beautiful. Students agreed, "Ithaca is a great place to live in," although the weather is often incredibly dreary. According to our survey, both on- and off-campus housing is considered excellent. Because of its remote location, most extracurricular activities occur on campus. One of the most unusual is the Frozen Assets Hockey Team, a group of all female MBAs who compete against Dartmouth's Tuck school in an annual tournament.

ADMISSIONS

According to the admissions office, your interview is considered *most important,* and then, in descending order, the type of undergrad institution attended, your GMAT scores, work experience, essays, college GPA, letters of recommendation, and extracurricular activities. Adds the school, "We prefer liberal arts majors." They also write, "We work to attract minority and women applicants, as well as disabled applicants." It pays to be a child or relative of an alum. "All things being equal," notes the admissions office, "sometimes" these applicants receive extra consideration. Decisions are made on a rolling basis. Students are notified of a decision within one month of receipt of the completed file. Some advice from the school: "The earlier you apply, the better your chances. Send in part one of the application ASAP so we can arrange an alumni interview for competitive applicants." Deferrals are granted to students on a case-by-case basis.

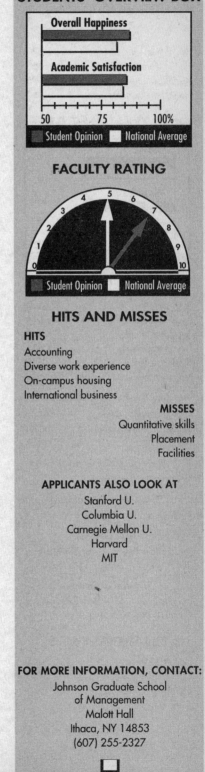

STUDENTS' OVERVIEW BOX

Overall Happiness

Academic Satisfaction

50   75   100%

■ Student Opinion   ■ National Average

FACULTY RATING

■ Student Opinion   ■ National Average

HITS AND MISSES

HITS
Accounting
Diverse work experience
On-campus housing
International business

MISSES
Quantitative skills
Placement
Facilities

APPLICANTS ALSO LOOK AT
Stanford U.
Columbia U.
Carnegie Mellon U.
Harvard
MIT

FOR MORE INFORMATION, CONTACT:
Johnson Graduate School
of Management
Malott Hall
Ithaca, NY 14853
(607) 255-2327

CUNY BARUCH COLLEGE SCHOOL OF BUSINESS AND PUBLIC ADMINISTRATION

ADMISSIONS FACTS

Type of school	Public

Demographics

No. of men	1,040
No. of women	668
No. of minorities	596
No. of int'l students	457

EQUAL TREATMENT GRAPH

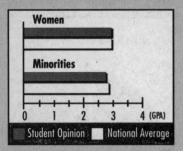

Women

Minorities

0   1   2   3   4 (GPA)

■ Student Opinion □ National Average

Admissions Statistics

Avg. GMAT	554
Avg. undergraduate GPA	3.16
Avg. age at entry	30.8
No. of applicants	1,634
No. accepted	877
No. enrolled	547

Deadlines and Notifications

Regular application	rolling
Regular notification	rolling
Special dates	N/A

Focus of Curriculum

Finance, Accounting

Academic Specialties

Accounting, Taxation

Joint Degrees

MBA/HC (with Mt. Sinai), JD/MBA (Brooklyn Law), JD/MBA (NY Law)

Special Programs

Executive MBA, MPA, MS-Tax, National Urban/Rural Fellowship

FINANCIAL FACTS

In-state tuition	$3,350
Out-of-state tuition	$5,850
On-campus housing	N/A

ACADEMICS

Most students would agree with the individual who wrote, "For the money, you get a quality education and star faculty." The "star" is a reference to a Nobel Prize-winning finance professor, several others in the same department, June O'Neill, Director of the Congressional Budget Office, and Professor Yoshiro Tsurumi, a Harvard Ph.D. who is a top scholar on U.S./Japanese relations. It was Tsurumi who the national media turned to for his in-depth analysis of former President Bush's notorious trip to Japan. Other standout faculty include the school's accounting professors. Indeed, Baruch boasts it is "rated first in the nation for the number of candidates with advanced degrees who successfully take the CPA exam." Several students had high praise for the International Marketing program. Baruch is also home to several power alum: Jules Winter, COO of the American Stock Exchange; Bert Wasserman, Exec V.P. at Time Warner; and Laura Altschuler, President of the New York City League of Women Voters.

Baruch is basically a part-time, go-at-your-own-pace program. The majority of students take only a small number of courses per semester and create their own academic schedule while working full time. It can take up to four years to complete the program. The first half of the program is devoted to the standard core curriculum; the latter half covers an area of specialization. Recently, a winter session was introduced during which students take one or more core courses.

Students reported feeling well prepared by their studies in the school's power subjects—accounting and finance. As one might expect, Baruch boasts strong quantitative skills. A surprise finding, students report above average skills in the area of presentation and communications. Students felt less confident of their skills in general management, marketing, and operations. Also in the complaint department: Getting into any course, even a required class, is a nightmare. Planning a course of study is equally frustrating. Moaned one MBA, "First, figuring out what you need to take to graduate is impossible. Everything must be done with consultation with an advisor. Then getting an appointment to set up a program is *impossible*." Other trouble spots: the library, class facilities, and the placement office. On the upside, Baruch offers students access to databases such as LEXIS and NEXIS for free, making research and the job search less painful. Although several students described faculty as "excellent" and "very knowledgeable in their field of study," the majority rated them as mediocre and inaccessible. Not surprisingly, many Baruch MBAs feel the academic program is not meeting their academic expectations. Not to worry, the majority say the long-term benefits of the degree will positively offset this short-term dissatisfaction.

PLACEMENT AND RECRUITING

The Office of Career Services serves the entire school of business, which encompasses an undergraduate population of 13,000 students. In 1994, 240 companies recruited on-campus. Despite the job hunting competition, 94% of grad had a job within three months of graduation. The average starting salary of would-be tycoons, $39, 747. The top employers of Baruch MBAs: Deloitte and Touche, Andersen Consulting, Cooper and Lybrand, NYNEX, Pepsi Cola, Republic National Bank, and U.S., NS, and NYC government.

CUNY BARUCH COLLEGE SCHOOL OF BUSINESS AND PUBLIC ADMINISTRATION

STUDENT LIFE/CAMPUS

Baruch is one of the largest B-schools in the nation, packing in upward of 2,500 students into its two-year program. Surprisingly, this doesn't affect class size, which is kept to an average of thirty-five to forty-five in the core courses, half that in the electives. In almost all classes, exams count most heavily toward the grade, then papers. The workload is manageable, the pressure moderate to light. Students report they only study an average of fifteen to twenty-five hours a week, a cakewalk by most B-schools' standards.

Students rate themselves only moderately competitive, but this isn't the result of a cozy, all-for-one student community. The student community is basically nonexistent. Baruch's large size and "commuter" characteristics make bonding difficult. Social relationships and on-campus reverie are bound to suffer. But they're hardly solo flyers. The overwhelming majority belong to a study group. Although a unified student body might be hard to find under these circumstances, Baruch is considered one of the best commuter schools in the nation. To bring students back on campus and foster strong school relationships, the administration plans on introducing a cohort system and more planned activities. As for the student body, Baruch MBAs agree, classmates are both professionally and racially diverse. There's a large contingent of foreign and minority students.

Baruch is located in the Gramercy Park section of midtown Manhattan, in what students term the "heart of New York City." The campus is safe, public transportation extremely accessible. Students live all around the city and its neighboring areas.

ADMISSIONS

According to the admissions board, your college GPA and GMAT scores are considered most important. After that the board considers, in descending order, your essays, letters of recommendation, and work experience. TOEFL and TWE is required for students with degrees from non-English speaking countries. Students may defer admission for up to two years.

STUDENTS' OVERVIEW BOX

Overall Happiness

Academic Satisfaction

50   75   100%

■ Student Opinion   □ National Average

FACULTY RATING

■ Student Opinion   □ National Average

HITS AND MISSES

HITS
Accounting dept.
New York City
Tuition
Diversity

MISSES
Marketing dept.
Gym
Off-campus housing
Social life

APPLICANTS ALSO LOOK AT
St. John's U.
New York University
Fordham U.
Columbia U.

FOR MORE INFORMATION, CONTACT:
Office of Graduate Admissions
17 Lexington Ave. Box 276
Baruch College/CUNY
New York, NY 10010
(212) 802-2331

DARTMOUTH COLLEGE: THE AMOS TUCK SCHOOL OF BUSINESS ADMINISTRATION

ADMISSIONS FACTS

Type of school	Private

Demographics

No. of men	130
No. of women	50
No. of minorities	8
No. of int'l students	23

EQUAL TREATMENT GRAPH

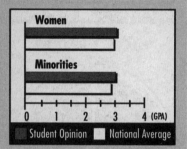

Admissions Statistics

Avg. GMAT	660
Avg. undergraduate GPA	3.40
Avg. age at entry	27.1
No. of applicants	2,238
No. accepted	382
No. enrolled	185

Deadlines and Notifications

Regular application	4/11
Regular notification	5/22
Special dates	N/A

Focus of Curriculum

General Management

Academic Specialties

General Management

Joint Degrees

MBA/MALD in International Affairs, MBA/MS in Engineering, MBA/MD, MBA/MS (with Tufts), MBA/MS (with Thayer School of Engineering), MBA/MO (with Dartmouth Med School)

Special Programs

Executive-in-Residence Program (EIR)

FINANCIAL FACTS

In-state tuition	$22,500
Out-of-state tuition	$22,500
On-campus housing	$3,900

ACADEMICS

Founded in 1900, Tuck was the first graduate school of management in the world and the only top U.S. business school that offers only the MBA degree. This means Tuck focuses *all* of its resources on its MBA students. Tuck has a reputation for developing talented general managers through rigorous, quantitatively demanding academics. By any standards, the workload is heavy and the curriculum very structured. Reports one student, "Tuck's workload is much heavier than at any other school -except maybe Darden."

Tuckies experience an Outward Bound-type of orientation similar to that offered at other B-schools. But here's the difference: Tuckies live and die by teamwork. Well into the second year, group projects continue to dominate class work. In terms of the basics, first-years take thirteen required core courses. Second-years choose from over fifty electives to specialize or build breadth. The emphasis here is on a general management education. The curriculum at Tuck stresses a "theory into practice" understanding of business. Several enthusiastic students told us about Tuck's first-year, three-day business simulation game, TYCOON. Student teams start with assets of $25 million with which to purchase and then manage a company. Professors impose "surprise" conditions and disasters upon different companies—from floods to labor strikes—to test students' managerial abilities. The result is best summarized by this student: "During my summer internship I saw that I was much more adept at blending strategy work with accounting, and operations with organizational behavior, than my colleagues from other schools." Students also raved about the Executive-in-Residence Program. More than 100 senior executives visited the campus last year.

Tuck features a learning environment that is personal and intimate. An unusually low student/faculty ratio of ten to one means Tuck professors are accessible to students. Moreover, the emphasis is on teaching, not research: "The school does not operate as a think tank." According to students, they're also off-the-Richter-scale terrific teachers. More cooperative than competitive, Tuckies are an all-for-one and one-for-all bunch. Wrote a typical booster, "Tuck is nothing like other B-schools. The peer pressure is completely against backstabbing." But one realist wrote, "For fear of making Tuck sound like a summer camp—I'll be honest. I worked harder than I've ever worked in my life."

PLACEMENT AND RECRUITING

One hundred companies interview on-campus. By graduation in June of 1994, eighty-nine percent of the class was placed. Three months after graduation, ninety-four percent was placed. Grabbing the most MBAs were: Coopers & Lybrand, J. P. Morgan, McKinsey, Andersen Consulting, General Mills, Goldman Sachs, Citicorp and Merrill Lynch. An impressive 42% of grads went in to finance with starting salaries of $55,000 and 33% went in to consulting where the pay - not including $20,000 sign-on bonuses was much higher - $80,000. "Everyone goes into Wall St. or consulting," reported one MBA, "But that's why people come here - to get those jobs."

DARTMOUTH COLLEGE: THE AMOS TUCK SCHOOL OF BUSINESS ADMINISTRATION

STUDENT LIFE/CAMPUS

Tuckies, as they like to call themselves, gave their school the highest quality of life ratings. Whether they were married with children or single, in their mid-thirties or a few years out of college, dozens of students wrote, "I LOVE TUCK!" In fact, the survey results suggest a veritable lovefest! Tuckies are extremely happy. Many raved, "Best two years of my life" and "I've made friends that will last a lifetime." Almost all first-year students live in Tuck dorms, making it a very cozy, residential experience. (Married students and their spouses can live in nearby Sachem Village.) One Tuckie warns, "Tuck is too involved a place if you're simply looking to get your MBA stamp."

Many describe the campus as "beautiful" and the rural, outdoorsy setting as "perfect." Tuck is located in the quaint town of Hanover, right next to the Connecticut River, Vermont, and the Appalachian Trail, so students have access to many outdoor activities. Wrote one enthusiast, "There's skiing, cross-country, canoeing, hiking and biking!" Added the school, "Most students look forward to winter; the biggest sports here are ice hockey and skiing." Skiing is available at Killington, Stowe, and Dartmouth's Skiway. And each year Tuck hosts Winter Carnival, an invitational slalom race, complete with serious apres-ski partying. Tuckies also enjoy an active social life in which spouses/partners are merrily included. "Partying, dancing, and late nights" are common. So are intramural sporting events, talent nights and student club activities. But Tuck is also family oriented; the campus is crawling with babies and puppies. Declared one student dramatically, "Tuck is a true American MBA experience." But they agree theirs is not a diverse community; a meager eight percent are minority. About seventy-two students are foreign. A final note: Whereas most alumni fund agents at most schools are happy to achieve twenty percent participation in annual giving from recent grads, Tuck alumni have an astounding ninety percent participation rate, proving that this tight-knit group stays that way long after their school days.

ADMISSIONS

The admissions office reports that "although the GMAT, GPA, and work experience are very important, we look for well-roundedness in our candidates; a formula is not used to determine admission. Tuck looks for applicants who exhibit leadership, creativity, and a strong foundation of business skills." Strong letters of recommendation are important.

An interview is strongly recommended. Tuck goes by "rounds". It is advisable to apply "within the first three." Only 16% of applicants are accepted.

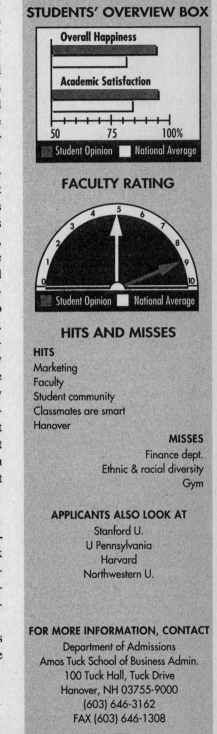

STUDENTS' OVERVIEW BOX

Overall Happiness

Academic Satisfaction

50   75   100%

Student Opinion   National Average

FACULTY RATING

0 1 2 3 4 5 6 7 8 9 10

Student Opinion   National Average

HITS AND MISSES

HITS
Marketing
Faculty
Student community
Classmates are smart
Hanover

MISSES
Finance dept.
Ethnic & racial diversity
Gym

APPLICANTS ALSO LOOK AT
Stanford U.
U Pennsylvania
Harvard
Northwestern U.

FOR MORE INFORMATION, CONTACT
Department of Admissions
Amos Tuck School of Business Admin.
100 Tuck Hall, Tuck Drive
Hanover, NH 03755-9000
(603) 646-3162
FAX (603) 646-1308

UNIVERSITY OF DENVER GRADUATE SCHOOL OF BUSINESS

ADMISSIONS FACTS

Type of school	Private

Demographics

No. of men	377
No. of women	279
No. of minorities	58
No. of int'l students	126

EQUAL TREATMENT GRAPH

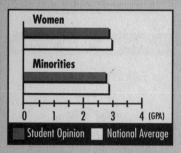

Admissions Statistics

Avg. GMAT	N/A
Avg. GPA	N/A
Avg. age at entry	N/A
No. of applicants	435
No. accepted	356
No. enrolled	208

Deadlines and Notifications

Regular application	6/1
Regular notification	rolling (2 weeks)
Special dates	N/A

Focus of Curriculum

Generalized

Joint Degrees

Masters in International Management, Masters in Domestic and International Tourism, JD/MBA

FINANCIAL FACTS

In-state tuition	$15,300
Out-of-state tuition	$15,300
On-campus housing	$3,936

ACADEMICS

Students looking for a progressive academic curriculum and an outdoorsy lifestyle, look no further; the University of Denver (U of D) offers both. This generalist program provides MBAs traditional nuts-and-bolts skills, as well as exposure to critical '90s issues: leadership, team-building, negotiation and communication, gender and cultural diversity. The program also features many experiential components—Outward Bound leadership and team building training, a community service project, and an "integrative challenge which brings all the program elements together in a practical business application." Wrote one MBA, "The recently revised MBA curriculum offers a variety of courses and electives that are very pertinent to today's business issues." The newly opened Center for Managerial Communication provides students the facilities and resources to work on presentation, communication and group dynamics skills. In addition to the MBA, the U of D also offers a Masters in International Management (MIM), Master of Real Estate and Construction Management, and Master of Science in Tourism. MBA and MIM specializations are available in accounting, finance, MIS, marketing, real estate finance, and real estate and construction management.

Overall, U of D students report they feel well prepared by their studies in finance, accounting, and general management. Due to the emphasis on soft skills, they report a high level of confidence in their teamwork, interpersonal, and presentation abilities. But students say their skills need bolstering in marketing and computers. Although the vast majority of students told us taking time off to pursue a U of D MBA is worth it, they disagreed on the value of their education relative to its cost. Students were unanimous—U of D's low tuition is a draw. But several students agreed with the one who wrote, "Value of education received in terms of dollars is a little low." Complained another, "The tuition is high, given that the school facilities are below average." Students also complained about the difficulty of getting into popular courses.

PLACEMENT AND RECRUITING

Wrote one student, "There are good job opportunities and networking here." But the majority said their job placement office needs to work harder. They also complained about the range and number of companies recruiting on campus. Nevertheless, over eighty-eight percent were placed within three months after graduation. Seventy percent of MBAs were placed within three weeks of graduation in 1993. Approximately eighty companies recruited on campus.

UNIVERSITY OF DENVER GRADUATE SCHOOL OF BUSINESS

STUDENT LIFE/CAMPUS

According to one MBA, "Course workloads usually include a good mixture of exams, research projects (individual and group), and class participation."

Classes are small, many with twenty to twenty-five students in each. The workload is average, although it's heavier during the first year. The majority of students study an average of fifteen to twenty-five hours a week; several diehards report they hit the books thirty to forty hours a week. As for the academic pressure, students are split. Half say it's intense, the other half say it's barely there.

U of D MBAs aren't killer-competitive. They're more oriented towards cooperation. One student's comments typified the prevalent feeling here that "people are very helpful and friendly." Because the school is so small, the tight-knit student body tends to hang out with and enjoy each other. Unsurprisingly, they also report an active social life. Three hundred days of sunshine a year and the nearby mountains provide students unsurpassed recreational opportunities. Favorite extracurriculars include anything to do with the great outdoors: whitewater rafting, rock climbing, mountain biking, fishing. The B-school organizes frequent skiing trips. Also popular are trips to Central City for Vegas-style gambling. As for the city of Denver, students think it's great. The majority of MBAs opt to live off-campus in apartments within walking distance of school.

ADMISSIONS

According to the admissions office, your college GPA is considered most important. After that, in descending order, your GMAT score, essays, work experience (not required), and letters of recommendation. Notes the school, "U of D is the eighth oldest school of business in the nation, and has been AACSB accredited since 1923. We offer the following degrees: Masters of Business in administration, international management, real estate and construction management, taxation, a Masters of Science in domestic and international tourism, and accountancy." Decisions are made on a rolling basis. Students are notified of a decision three weeks after the completed application has been submitted. The final application deadline is June 1. Waitlisted students are notified of a spot by August 1.

STUDENTS' OVERVIEW BOX

Overall Happiness

Academic Satisfaction

50   75   100%

■ Student Opinion   □ National Average

FACULTY RATING

■ Student Opinion   □ National Average

HITS AND MISSES

HITS
Safety
Social life
Denver

MISSES
Marketing
Ethnic & racial diversity
On-campus housing

APPLICANTS ALSO LOOK AT
U Colorado-Boulder
U Colorado-Denver

FOR MORE INFORMATION, CONTACT:
Graduate Business School
Admission Office
2020 S. Race St. BA 122
Denver, CO 80208
(303) 871-3416

DUKE UNIVERSITY: FUQUA SCHOOL OF BUSINESS

ADMISSIONS FACTS

Type of school	Private

Demographics

No. of men	N/A
No. of women	N/A
No. of minorities	N/A
No. of int'l students	N/A

EQUAL TREATMENT GRAPH

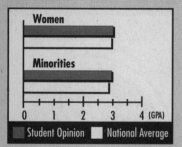

Admissions Statistics

Avg. GMAT	N/A
Avg. undergraduate GPA	N/A
Avg. age at entry	N/A
No. of applicants	N/A
No. accepted	N/A
No. enrolled	N/A

Deadlines and Notifications

Regular application	N/A
Regular notification	N/A
Special dates	N/A

Focus of Curriculum

General Management

Academic Specialties

General Management, Accounting, Finance, Marketing

Joint Degrees

MBA-AM in Public Policy Studies, MBA/JD, MBA/MF in Forestry or Environmental Management, MBA/MS in Engineering

Special Programs

International Study Opportunities, The MBA Enterprise Corps

FINANCIAL FACTS

In-state tuition	$19,800
Out-of-state tuition	$19,800
On-campus housing	N/A

ACADEMICS

From marketing to finance, from quant skills to teamwork, Fuqua's departments are solid across the board. Distinct to the school is a hot, new experiential program called Integrative Learning Experience (ILE). Four one-week-long seminars embrace the trendy topics of the '90s in diversity, internationalization, etc., and provide students an opportunity to learn by doing. Each ILE precedes a semester of traditional classroom instruction. Over the two-year program, students take four ILEs: Team Building and Leadership; Managing Quality and Diversity; Competitive Business Strategy, and Complex Management Programs. The last two are the "capstone" experiences in that they involve business-emulation games and team competitions. Wrote one student, "Fuqua's addition of the Integrative Learning Experiences has been very successful." Raved another, "Fuqua's updated curriculum is on top of market trends."

First-years squeeze in a whopping fourteen core courses and have room for two electives. As one student put it, "It moves so fast, there's no time to fall behind. Good time management skills are essential." A prereq for the program is a working knowledge of calculus. Advised one student, "Liberal arts majors with no experience in business courses should be prepared to hit the ground running." Second-year students take only one required course, the International Environment, and have up to eleven electives to pursue more individualized study. Four of these may be taken in other schools or departments at Duke University. As for the faculty, one student wrote, "Profs all have open-door policies. They know your name." Although students say professors are good teachers, overall they don't compare favorably with the teachers at other competitive schools. We kept hearing that "Core courses tend to be taught by relatively inexperienced profs." Some of the problem seems to be that Fuqua's profs who teach core courses are young and inexperienced.

From the dean of the school to the maintenance department, staff members are trained in the techniques of TQM (Total Quality Management) and aim to provide customer satisfaction. It must be working. As one student put it, "More than any other school, Fuqua treats its students like customersÑwe're paying a lot and getting our money's worth." Agreed another, "Excellent school. I'm very satisfied, even at $20,000 a year."

PLACEMENT AND RECRUITING

In 1993, 140 companies interviewed on-campus, and there were 3,063 interviews scheduled. Over ninety percent of the graduating class had jobs by commencement. According to the respondents in our survey, the placement office is doing a decent job, but could stand improvement. One student explains, "Fuqua offers a terrific education in great surroundings, but it's not New York or Chicago. " The placement office should be working twice as hard to bring companies to campus." Students were also critical about the lack of international company recruiting on campus. One international student claimed, "People are totally domestic and uninterested in international business overall. Consequently, companies hiring Fuqua students are not international." Students were most satisfied with the *number* of companies recruiting on campus.

DUKE UNIVERSITY: FUQUA SCHOOL OF BUSINESS

STUDENT LIFE/CAMPUS

Students reported that "Fuqua is seriously outgrowing its facilities." This is because the program continues to fill every spot; at 330 students per entering class, Fuqua is at its max and students feel the pinch. But don't expect them to expand facilities soon. The modern B-school building was just completed in 1983 and boasts state-of-the-art facilities.

As for the campus itself, Duke's is one of the nation's most beautifulÑcomplete with Gothic architecture and sweeping lawns. A mile of woodlands divides the campus in two. Fuqua is perched on the edge of Duke Forest on Duke's West Campus. Most students opt to live off-campus in small groups in apartment complexes nearby. One student advised "The triangle area is a goo dplace to live in." Housing, both on- and off-campus, is good and very affordable, about $500-$750 for a two-bedroom apartment. Most students bring a car, but parking is a nightmare at peak times.

Although students report an above-average social life, dating, for some reason, barely figures into the picture. As for extracurriculars, there are plenty. Reported one MBA, "Students work hard, but like to have fun tooÑkegs every Friday at 5:30." There's a Fuquavisions show every other month (like a "Saturday Night Live" video), and a Winter Gala Black Tie party. Intramural sports are big. And if you like to golf, students say the course is terrific. Student clubs play a big part in campus life as well. The Black MBA Organization hosts a Wall Street panel. The Entrepreneurship Club hosts a two-day seminar.

One student's remarks typified the prevalent feeling here: "I have never been involved with a more outstanding and bright group of people! The term *teamwork* does not do justice to the genuine concern the students have for one another's performanceÑhelp is always available." However, contradicting this, one student wrote "Students are a lot more concerned about grades than they should be."

ADMISSIONS

According to the admissions office, "We encourage, but do not require, evaluative interviews. We feel that the interview is an important component of the application process." Other components include the GMAT score, college GPA, essays, work experience, letters of recommendation, and extracurricular activities. Decisions are made on a rolling admissions basis. Applicants are notified of a decision six to eight weeks after the admissions office has received a completed application. Accepted applicants may defer admission for up to two years for health issues or special job opportunities. Fuqua may also offer college seniors a two-year deferred admission with the expectation that there will be appropriate work experience in the interim.

STUDENTS' OVERVIEW BOX

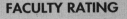

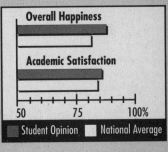

FACULTY RATING

HITS AND MISSES

HITS
Finance dept.
Classmates are smart
School community
Facilities
Placement

MISSES
Ethnic & racial diversity
Gym
Crowd control

APPLICANTS ALSO LOOK AT
Northwestern U.
U Pennsylvania
U Virginia
Dartmouth College
Harvard

FOR MORE INFORMATION, CONTACT:
Fuqua School of Business
Towerview Dr.
Durham, NC 27706
(919) 660-7705

EMORY BUSINESS SCHOOL

ADMISSIONS FACTS

Type of school	Private

Demographics

No. of men	179
No. of women	91
No. of minorities	34
No. of int'l students	46

EQUAL TREATMENT GRAPH

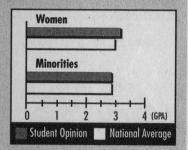

Student Opinion   National Average

Admissions Statistics

Avg. GMAT	625
Avg. undergraduate GPA	3.2
Avg. age at entry	26
No. of applicants	764
No. accepted	274
No. enrolled	126

Deadlines and Notifications

Regular application	3/15
Regular notification	rolling
Special dates	12/31

Focus of Curriculum

General Management

Academic Specialties

International Finance, International Business, General Management

Joint Degrees

JD/MBA, MBA/DIV, MBA/MPH, MBA/MN

Special Programs

Emory's Customer Development Track (CDBT), Student Exchange Programs, The Center for Leadership and Career Studies

FINANCIAL FACTS

In-state tuition	$19,950
Out-of-state tuition	$19,950
On-campus housing	$6,000

ACADEMICS

Emory is highly regarded for its progressive curriculum, international studies program, and dedicated faculty. The latest teaching methodologies, such as field projects and computer simulations, are used in all areas of the program. One of its greatest strengths is that it provides unique opportunities for individualized study which make Emory "excellent for self-starters." It's also excellent for non-quant types. According to the school, "There is a balanced emphasis on quantitative and qualitative approaches." For those who need a little help, the school runs an optional three-day course in computer applications prior to orientation.

The first-year curriculum is prescribed. Students take eleven core courses (a few are minis) in the functional areas of business. A unique requirement is the Communication Skills Workshop, in which students participate in a communications lab.

The second year, as one student put it, "is flexible to individual student needs." Students take up to nine electives, and may take classes in other university departments such as Law, Political Science and Foreign Language. A particularly noteworthy opportunity is the Directed Study Elective, which allows students basically to do their own thing, design their own field of study (under the direction of a faculty member, of course). Also available are unique "fieldwork" courses, which involve students in the community or place them in top national and international firms, and standout programs like the Latin American and Eastern European Studies Concentrations and the Center for Relationship Marketing.

Overall, students say taking the time off to pursue an Emory MBA is worth it, although several students told us "It's too expensive." Emory MBAs judged their skills in marketing, accounting, teamwork, presentation/communications, and especially general management to be strong. Weaker areas were finance, computers, and quantitative skills. The development of this uneven skill set may be why a significant minority of MBAs say Emory is not meeting their academic needs. Nonetheless, the majority are happy here.

PLACEMENT AND RECRUITING

Over seventy-six companies came to recruit on campus in 1993. Eighty-one percent of the graduating class had a position by September with companies such as Bell South, Ernst & Young, Pizza Hut and Proctor & Gamble. But this didn't seem to impress students very much. Students uniformly agree, the job placement office is not one of Emory's strong suits. "I thought I would get some more help in my job search than I am getting" seems to be the common refrain among students. Still, many others feel, "It's poor now, but very much improving." Students are enthusiastic about the alumni. The majority of students surveyed told us they contacted alumni in their job search and found them helpful. Many relationships are developed in the Emory Mentor Program, which matches current students with local alumni.

EMORY BUSINESS SCHOOL

STUDENT LIFE/CAMPUS

Emory provides its students with the best of both worlds: an expansive, beautiful campus, and the city of Atlanta, a thriving southern metropolis. Students told us, "The quality of life can't be beat." Over 450 Fortune 500 companies are either headquartered or have an office in Atlanta. Students also told us, "The B-school is actively involved with the business community in Atlanta. This gives students the opportunity to expand upon the knowledge gained in the classroom."

Students note they "need a new B-school library." A new state-of-the-art structure should go a long way to restoring on-campus spirit and providing the necessary facilities. Many students spend their time outside the classroom doing community service projects, although they also find plenty of time to hit the town—together. Popular student clubs include the International Business Association, Emory Outreach Program, Marketing Club, New Venture Club, and the Black MBA Association.

The students at Emory really like each other and made a point of telling us that their classmates are a great, smart group of people: "The student body is strong, aware, and very versatile." With only 115 students in each entering class, and an average of thirty-five in the classroom, students describe "a warm, congenial environment" and a high level of faculty accessibility. Emory's student body is pretty homogeneous. However, most students share this second-year student's opinion: "Emory is an excellent choice if you like an intimate atmosphere where both students and professors are supportive and interested in seeing that you get the most out of the program."

Students often skip readings (a shortcut almost universally applied by B-school students). Still, Emory MBAs hit the books an average of twenty to thirty hours per week. The majority say the academic pressure can be intense, but it depends on whom you ask. Several indicated pressure is self-imposed. Competition is against the grade, not fellow students.

ADMISSIONS

According to the admissions office, your work experience is considered most important. After that, in descending order, your GMAT scores, interview, essays, college GPA, extracurricular activities and letters of recommendation are considered. Notes the school, "Interviews are strongly encouraged. Candidates are also encouraged to visit a class with one of our current students."

Emory recommends that applicants have completed one semester of college calculus and be computer literate. Decisions are made on a rolling admissions basis. The school may allow applicants to defer admission for up to two years; this is decided on a case-by-case basis.

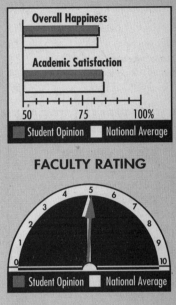

STUDENTS' OVERVIEW BOX

Overall Happiness

Academic Satisfaction

50   75   100%

■ Student Opinion   □ National Average

FACULTY RATING

0 1 2 3 4 5 6 7 8 9 10

■ Student Opinion   □ National Average

HITS AND MISSES

HITS
Marketing dept.
Diverse work experience
Atlanta

MISSES
Quantitative skills
Don't like classmates
Recruiting

APPLICANTS ALSO LOOK AT
Duke U.
UNC-Chapel Hill
Vanderbilt U.
Washington U.

FOR MORE INFORMATION, CONTACT:
Office of Admissions
Goizueta Business School
Emory Univ.
1602 Mizell Dr.
Atlanta, GA 30322
(404) 727-6311
eMail: Admissions@bus.emory.edu

UNIVERSITY OF FLORIDA BUSINESS SCHOOL

ADMISSIONS FACTS

Type of school	Public

Demographics

No. of men	178
No. of women	88
No. of minorities	34
No. of int'l students	59

EQUAL TREATMENT GRAPH

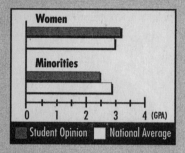

Admissions Statistics

Avg. GMAT	612
Avg. undergraduate GPA	3.28
Avg. age at entry	25.5
No. of applicants	886
No. accepted	197
No. enrolled	126

Deadlines and Notifications

Regular application	3/31
Regular notification	rolling
Special dates	N/A

Focus of Curriculum

Specialized

Academic Specialties

Agribusiness, Sports administration, Health care management

Joint Degrees

JD/MBA, MBA/Masters of Health Sciences, 11-month Accelerated MBA

Special Programs

Entrepreneurship program

FINANCIAL FACTS

In-state tuition	$2,600
Out-of-state tuition	$8,600
On-campus housing	$3,600

ACADEMICS

According to our survey, there are many reasons to choose the University of Florida. Chief among them are prestige, small class size, numerous joint degree programs, strong state contacts and alumni relationships, the bang-for-buck, and unsurprisingly, Florida's tropical lifestyle. A huge drawing card is U of F's innovative Entrepreneurship Program which students say is one-of-a-kind and attracts MBAs who plan on careers as venture capitalists or entrepreneurs in their own start-ups. In 1992, in fact, five new companies were started by Florida entrepreneurs.

Other strong specializations that provide Florida MBAs' unique career choices are Agribusiness, Arts Administration, Global Management, Real Estate, Human Resources, Entrpreneurship, and Sports Administration. Equally strong is Florida's Health Care Program, which is one of only three in the nation to be accredited by both the AACSB and the Accrediting Commission on Education for Health Services Administration (ACEHSA). Students are mildly disappointed that Florida does not offer a concentration in Operations and Accounting. One complained, "The number of elective courses are few and far between. For those MBAs who are not concentrating in DIS, Marketing, or Finance, there is too little to choose from." As for the faculty, most students would agree with this remark: "Our faculty care about the students and their performance, are incredibly helpful, and share amazing anecdotes and expertise." Added another, "The administration and faculty have a wonderful open door policy." But when it comes to their teaching abilities, it depends on whom you ask. Most students agree eloquent teaching occurs in the areas of specialization. Noted one MBA, "Many instructors bring significant, practical experience to the classroom." However, another countered, "There are no 'MBA Faculty.' We rent profs from other departments."

Like many schools, Florida invites it's incoming students to a 4-day orientation that features team-building exercises such as a challenging ropes course. Hang-tight, when they get to the other side, there are numerous group projects throughout the two-year curriculum. Also notable about Florida is the student-run MBA Association is responsible for reading and evaluating all applicant essays and organizing an executive "Speaker Series." Overall, students say this program has got the right stuff: they expect to be leveraging their Florida MBAs long after their first job out of school. Summed up one satisfied student, "For a graduate program in a public university system, UF does an outstanding job of educating students. If the program had the private funding of other top schools, I'm sure it would be more recognized nationally than it already is."

PLACEMENT AND RECRUITING

While Florida's business school points out that 86% of its students are placed by the time they graduate, some of the students themselves were unimpressed. In particular, students think the office needs to work harder at attracting move diverse companies to the campus. One said, "The placement office needs work," and another went so far as to call it "miserable." This may be a bit harsh, for a regional school, considering the lack of recruiters they have immediately outside their door. According to the school, in 1994, 78 companies recruited on campus, while 53% of graduates went into finance, 19% into MIS, the remainder into marketing and general management. The four top employers of Florida MBAs are Andersen Consulting, Ernst and Young, Federal Express and CSX Transport.

UNIVERSITY OF FLORIDA BUSINESS SCHOOL

STUDENT LIFE/CAMPUS

With only 150 students in each class in the MBA program, students say Florida is very "personal, even though it is such a large school." Classes typically consist of ten to twelve students and group work comprises twenty-five to fifty percent of course work, which supports the small-school feeling. Wrote one MBA, "Such intimate settings (small classes) create the ideal and personalized learning environment." Another typical remark was "Student interaction is frequent and strong. Everyone is very friendly." Surprisingly, all this cozy camaraderie does not translate into an entirely stress-free environment. One student complained, "The quantity of busywork is excessive." And Florida MBAs describe a highly challenging and fairly competitive academic scene. Offsetting this is a strong study group system that stresses partnering. In addition, students are wildly enthusiastic over their new team-building orientation program run by second-years for incoming students. Over and over, they raved about this three-day welcome, which features seminars, ice-breaking activities and outdoorsy ropes courses, and sets the stage for lots of bonding. Students said fellow classmates are smart and professionally diverse, although a few complained Florida "needs to bet more experienced people." Added another, "The international exposure through classes, exchange opportunities (Italy, Holland, Hong Kong, France, Germany, Russia) and the large number of international students is excellent."

As for the facilities, Florida MBAs are quite happy with the school's new modern digs in Bryan Hall. They're especially fired up about Florida's computer facilities which they say are "outstanding!" Florida MBAs also consider the Student Rec Center, which houses their gym, "terrific, open late at night, and most important, free." The town of Gainesville, although quite attractive for campus life, is not the sunny mecca it's made out to be. Located in the northern part of the state, it gets more than its fair share of cold weather and is a long haul from resort hot-spots Miami and Fort Lauderdale. Gainesville does offer small college-town charm, however, and a great strip of shops and eateries. Most students opt to live off-campus in apartments and shared homes on the perimeter of campus.

ADMISSIONS

Florida's admissions office requires an interview, explaining that it "allows applicants to elaborate on strengths and weaknesses that may impact their applications." Other important factors, in descending order, are the applicant's work experience, essays, GMAT scores, extracurricular activities, letters of recommendation, and college GPA. The application deadline is April 1 and students are notified of the admissions office's decision within three weeks of the interview.

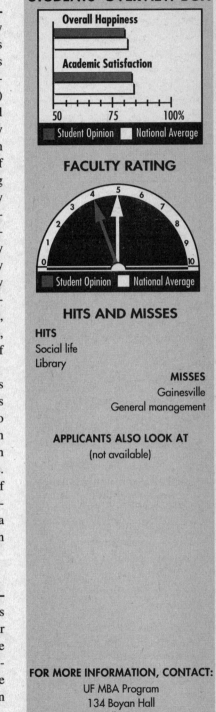

STUDENTS' OVERVIEW BOX

Overall Happiness

Academic Satisfaction

50   75   100%

☐ Student Opinion ☐ National Average

FACULTY RATING

☐ Student Opinion ☐ National Average

HITS AND MISSES

HITS
Social life
Library

MISSES
Gainesville
General management

APPLICANTS ALSO LOOK AT
(not available)

FOR MORE INFORMATION, CONTACT:
UF MBA Program
134 Boyan Hall
Gainesville, FL 32611
(904) 392-7992 ext. 200
eMail: barker11@wpgate.cba.ufl.edu

GEORGETOWN UNIVERSITY SCHOOL OF BUSINESS

ADMISSIONS FACTS

Type of school	Private

Demographics

No. of men	249
No. of women	141
No. of minorities	44
No. of int'l students	106

EQUAL TREATMENT GRAPH

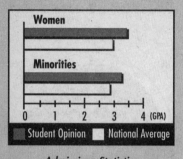

Women

Minorities

0 1 2 3 4 (GPA)

■ Student Opinion ■ National Average

Admissions Statistics

Avg. GMAT	520–690
Avg. undergraduate GPA	3.16
Avg. age at entry	27
No. of applicants	1,062
No. accepted	509
No. enrolled	208

Deadlines and Notifications

Regular application	5/1
Regular notification	4–6 weeks
Special dates	N/A

Focus of Curriculum

General Management, Option to specialize, International Business, Business and Government, Public Policy, Business Ethics, Management Communication

Academic Specialties

Int'l Business, Business and Government, Public Policy

Joint Degrees

JD/MBA, MBA/MSFS

Special Programs

The International Business Diplomacy Certificate, Summer Study Abroad Opportunities, International Exchange Opportunities, Summer Pre-Enrollment "Prep"

FINANCIAL FACTS

In-state tuition	$19,500
Out-of-state tuition	$19,500
On-campus housing	N/A

ACADEMICS

At Georgetown, academics are challenging, and coursework is relevant to what's going on in the real world. "What the University of Chicago talks about in its LEAD program," wrote one student, "we actually *do*." Particularly impressive is the focus on international business, which students praised: "The international flavor is highÑthirty percent international students and everyone else has lived or worked abroad and speaks a second language" and the "Opportuntites to study a foreign language on-campus are also exceptional."

In many classes, teamwork counts for up to twenty-five percent of the grade and class participation counts for another forty to sixty percent. The curriculum provides a general management orientation with a foundation in accounting, decision sciences, economics, finance, marketing, and management. The second year provides greater academic diversity and flexibility. There are four required courses: Ethics, Public Policy, Information Technology and Business Strategy, and Business Policy. One MBA points out that while, "Most B-Schools give lip service to ethics, Georgetown has two semesters of required ethics." Students may take electives in other graduate schools at Georgetown. And because Georgetown is part of the University Consortium System in the DC area, they can also take courses at consortium schools. Finally, to further pursue an interest in global business, students can get elective credit for courses taken in Area Studies Programs, and may also apply to receive an Area Studies Certificate. This involves choosing a geographic area of the world to study, taking all six electives in that area, and demonstrating proficiency in the native language. Area Studies options are African, Arab, Asian, Latin American, Russian, and German.

Across the board, students reported that Georgetown provided them excellent training in general management, marketing, accounting, operations management, and interpersonal/presentation skills. According to students, the school's only major weaknesses are due to its youth, which results in a lack of a national reputation, small library collection, limited alumni base, and lackluster placement services. However, the overwhelming majority of MBAs feel they're getting an incredible return on their investment. Fired-up Georgetown students say, "In ten years we will be tops!"

PLACEMENT AND RECRUITING

Georgetown's MBA Career Management office offers Career & Workplace Education Programs, videotaped mock interviews, a résumé referral program, and a résumé book, which is distributed upon request to employers. Both first- and second-year students are asked to submit résumés for Georgetown's résumé book. According to the school, "Many initial job contacts and invitations to interview, on- and off-campus, result from the résumé books." In 1993, fifty-seven companies recruited on-campus. Ninety percent of the graduating class of 1993 had offers by Sept. 1.

The hottest hirers: Ernst & Young, Coopers & Lybrand, Andersen Consulting, American Management Systems, OPIC, and Proctor & Gamble. Perhaps as a function of being only a thirteen-year-old program, Georgetown students said they were only moderately satisfied with the services of the Career Management Office. A note for international students: Job opportunities are limited by the type of visa that is held.

GEORGETOWN UNIVERSITY SCHOOL OF BUSINESS

STUDENT LIFE/CAMPUS

With only 320 students, Georgetown offers an intimate, cooperative learning environment students enjoy. Group work defines the learning experience—all courses require it. "Classes are small, and students develop close relationships with each other, the faculty, and administration." Almost everyone works in a study group. Not surprisingly, students are extremely friendly and supportive. In fact, students strongly advised, "This is not a school for cutthroats." Students say any competition at Georgetown is healthy, because underlying it is such a strong spirit of cooperation. Wrote one MBA "Georgetown has a fantastic, supportive environment. The only competition is with myself. My classmates are more than willing to help me and vice-versa." Not surprisingly, Georgetown MBAs rate their classmates as extremely smart, professionally diverse, and the type of people they expect to stay in touch with long after graduation. This atmosphere of camaraderie extends into an active social life. Students claimed, "MBAs go out together every weekend. Tight group." Student clubs that compete for their time: Graduate Women in Business, Alliance for Cultural Awareness, MBA Volunteers, and Students for Eastern European Development.

Located on the main campus, B-school students share an undergrad campus that comprises 104 acres and sixty buildings—many of them historic landmarks—and the athletic fields you'd expect of a sports powerhouse. For plenty of indoor *pumpitude*, students applaud their first-rate gym. On-campus housing, we were told, is also terrific. As for the semiurban setting, don't worry about it—students say the campus is ultrasafe. About the seat of government, one student wrote, "The Washington, D.C. location provides students access to government and business facilities," and most share this opinion. What really impressed us, however, was the students' high regard for their fellows: "The school attracts a special set of people who are genuinely interested in making a difference in the business world."

ADMISSIONS

According to the admissions office, your work experience, college GPA, and GMAT score are considered most important. Then in your essays, interview, letters of recommendation and extracurricular activities. Writes the school, "The admissions committee generally numbers twelve individuals, and includes both first- and second-year MBA students, faculty, and administrators. Each applicant's file is reviewed and discussed by the Committee. General considerations are professional experience, academic performance and potential, and personal interests, qualities, and skills. International experience and community involvement are of particular interest to the admissions committee, as are positions of leadership held in academic, professional, or community organizations." Decisions are made on a rolling admissions basis. Applicants are notified of a decision four to six weeks after the completed application has been received.

STUDENTS' OVERVIEW BOX

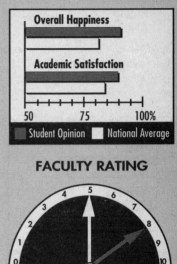

FACULTY RATING

HITS AND MISSES

HITS
Marketing dept.
Faculty
Student community
Washington, D.C.

MISSES
Quantitative skills
Ethnic & racial diversity
Job placement
Library

APPLICANTS ALSO LOOK AT
Duke U.
U Virginia
U Michigan
Northwestern U.
Columbia U.
Dartmouth College
U Penn
U Chicago
UNC-Chapel Hill

FOR MORE INFORMATION, CONTACT:
Graduate Admissions
105 Old North, Georgetown University
37 and O Streets
Washington, DC 20057-1008
(202) 687-4200
FAX (202) 687-7819

UNIVERSITY OF GEORGIA GRADUATE SCHOOL OF BUSINESS

ADMISSIONS FACTS

Type of school	Public

Demographics

No. of men	105
No. of women	48
No. of minorities	19
No. of int'l students	29

EQUAL TREATMENT GRAPH

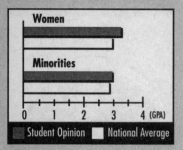

Admissions Statistics

Avg. GMAT	630
Avg. undergraduate GPA	3.17
Avg. age at entry	26
No. applicants	741
No. accepted	212
No. enrolled	102

Deadlines and Notifications

Regular application	3/15
Regular notification	rolling
Special dates	N/A

Focus of Curriculum

General Management

Academic Specialties

Accounting, Real Estate

FINANCIAL FACTS

In-state tuition	$2,250
Out-of-state tuition	$5,850
On-campus housing	$4,425

ACADEMICS

The University of Georgia in Athens (UGA) offers students either a one-year accelerated MBA or a two-year program. The one-year MBA is designed for students with an undergrad degree in business. Much of the required course work is based on individual weaknesses in the student's background. In the regular two-year program, students spend the first year studying the basics. During the second year, students choose two "sequences" from among twenty to develop a specialization. Sequences are unique to UGA—three pre-selected courses are packaged to guarantee expertise in an area. According to students, some of the best ones—pharmacy care management, media organization management, and textile management—involve study in other university departments. Within the school, standout sequences are found in the accounting and real estate departments. The most interesting component of the program is the yearlong professional development series, which focuses on teamwork, leadership, and presentation skills. Students take part in a range of activities—from a two-day, Outward bound-type exercise, to a cultural diversity workshop, to a wine education seminar conducted by *Wine and Spirits* magazine—in order to supplement their classroom instruction. A highlight of the series (besides the wine tasting) is Super Saturday, in which six corporate heavyweights conduct workshops on hot topics. As for the faculty, while profs are considered accessible and interested in students welfare, not all are stellar teachers. This may be because they have to do double-duty. Faculty serve *all* students on the College of Business, both undergrad and grad.

Despite all these innovations, many students feel there's a lot of window dressing at UGA. Wrote one student, "They offer a lot of hype and not enough substance." Almost fifty percent of the students surveyed said UGA is not meeting their academic expectations, suggesting that the school needs to revisit its academic strategy. One MBA said, "The program needs to be more academically challenging." Students also told us the school needs its own B-school library. According to one student, "The program is going through a transition and the administration is making improvements. Bugs will be worked out in due time."

PLACEMENT AND RECRUITING

UGA's Career Services Office offers the typical fare. One distinctive program is the Executive Breakfast Club, which invites senior management to breakfast with students. UGA has a new recruiting event, the Southeastern MBA Consortium, which was held for the first time in January 1994. The school already participates in the MBA Employment Conference and MBA Consortium in Chicago.

Like many B-school students, UGA MBAs report they're unhappy with career services and the range of companies recruiting. Wrote one MBA, "The school's main weakness is its inability to market the value of the program to future employers." UGA's placement office boasts a ninety percent placement rate (within 3 months of graduation) as of 1994. The average starting salary for UGA grads, $41,121. The majority of grads go into finance (14%), followed by marketing (19%), and MIS and Real Estate each, (14%). Among those grabbing the most UGA MBAs: Federal Express, Burlington Northern, Deloitte Touche.

UNIVERSITY OF GEORGIA GRADUATE SCHOOL OF BUSINESS

STUDENT LIFE/CAMPUS

First-year UGA students report a heavy workload and spend an average of twenty to thirty hours a week prepping for class. The pressure is intensified by the quarterly academic schedule, which causes courses to fly by. In particular, students told us there are many reading assignments during the first quarter—a mix of case studies, articles, and textbooks—and students say it's important to do all or most of them. The majority of UGA MBAs utilize study groups and divvy up the load. By the second year, things lighten up considerably.

UGA MBAs are competitive, but not overly so. Students are interested in lending a helping hand, a by-product of the emphasis on teamwork and small MBA class (only 106 per entering class). Although students rate their classmates as extremely smart, a sizable number indicate they don't intend to keep in touch with them after B-school.

UGA is located in Athens, a small city with a college-town feel. For road trips, Atlanta is just seventy miles away. According to students, housing is attractive/affordable either on- or off-campus. Students usually opt for off-campus living in apartments. The Graduate Business Association sponsors social, professional, and athletic activities. Especially popular are intramural sports teams of all types. Weekly happy hours provide relief from a diet of regression analysis.

ADMISSIONS

UGA weighs your GMAT score, work experience, and college GPA most heavily. After that, they weigh your letters of recommendation, extracurricular activities, and essays equally. Writes the school, "We try to treat each applicant as an individual customer. We make time for and are open to candidates questions. We respond in a timely manner to request for information. We are as interested in being as service oriented to our applicants as we are to those candidates we admit." The school recommends that students complete undergraduate course work in financial accounting, statistics, and microcomputers (spreadsheet applications) prior to applying. UGA utilizes a three-round admissions process and offers an early decision program. The school permits students to defer admission for up to one year.

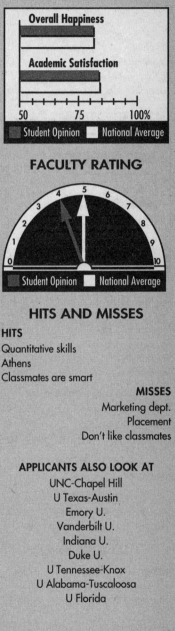

STUDENTS' OVERVIEW BOX

Overall Happiness

Academic Satisfaction

50   75   100%

■ Student Opinion □ National Average

FACULTY RATING

■ Student Opinion □ National Average

HITS AND MISSES

HITS
Quantitative skills
Athens
Classmates are smart

MISSES
Marketing dept.
Placement
Don't like classmates

APPLICANTS ALSO LOOK AT

UNC-Chapel Hill
U Texas-Austin
Emory U.
Vanderbilt U.
Indiana U.
Duke U.
U Tennessee-Knox
U Alabama-Tuscaloosa
U Florida

FOR MORE INFORMATION, CONTACT:
University of Georgia
Graduate School of Business
351 Brooks Hall
Athens, GA 30602-6264
(706) 542-5671
eMail: Dperry@cbacc.cba.uga.edu

GEORGIA INSTITUTE OF TECHNOLOGY SCHOOL OF MANAGEMENT

ADMISSIONS FACTS

Type of school	Public

Demographics

No. of men	140
No. of women	60
No. of minorities	30
No. of int'l students	50

EQUAL TREATMENT GRAPH

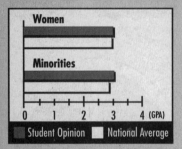

Women

Minorities

0   1   2   3   4 (GPA)

■ Student Opinion ■ National Average

Admissions Statistics

Avg. GMAT	620
Avg. undergraduate GPA	N/A
Avg. age at entry	26
No. of applicants	517
No. accepted	240
No. enrolled	105

Deadlines and Notifications

Regular application	7/1
Regular notification	rolling
Special dates	No EDP; 4/1 Ass'tships

Focus of Curriculum

Specialized

Academic Specialties

Finance, Accounting, Operations, Computers

FINANCIAL FACTS

In-state tuition	$2,277
Out-of-state tuition	$6,732
On-campus housing	N/A

ACADEMICS

Georgia Tech offers a Master of Science in Management (MSM) degree and is accredited by the American Assembly of Collegiate Schools of Business. Because of its technological orientation, the school focuses on and excels in providing students with strong technical, analytical, and computer skills. According to the students we surveyed, it also offers excellent training in accounting, finance, and operations. The first-year curriculum consists of traditional core course work. Two of the required courses—Quantitative Methods I and II—place a heavy emphasis on statistics. Two computer labs bolster Macintosh and IBM PC computing skills. During the second year, students design their own program of study through a specialization or through a combination of courses taken both in the B-school program and other university departments. Popular concentrations include: accounting, computer-integrated manufacturing systems, and management of technology. According to the school, "The MSM curriculum, both the core and many elective offerings, build on our strong technological roots and reflect the growth of the international business sector." Although one student told us, "The program is working hard to improve its international focus" another said this is just lip service: "There is a very low international orientation."

Indeed, it's unclear how satisfied students are with this school. While many say Georgia Tech is meeting their academic expectations, a not-insignificant number say they're dissatisfied. The most common gripe is about professors who "seem more interested in their own research than in teaching courses." Professors fare better when it comes to their accessibility. Unsurprisingly, students self-rate themselves as exceptionally strong in their quantitative, accounting, finance, and operations skills. A weak spot was the below average rating students gave their marketing skills.

As for interpersonal skills, the techie reputation sticks, because these skills aren't a strong suit. " Still, many concur with the student who said, "This school provides a stronger foundation than many top-twenty schools." And everyone agreed, "GT provides a great bang for the buck."

PLACEMENT AND RECRUITING

The Office of Management Career Services offers students all the typical services: a career seminar series, workshops on resume writing, and two resume books. According to the school, "The resume book is the principle means by which corporations learn about the current MSM class." GT is also a member of the MBA Consortium, which hosts a joint recruiting event with other B-schools..

Judging by the responses to our survey, students are not happy with the office of career services. Complained one student, "More emphasis is needed on bringing a wide range of employers to campus for recruiting." Ninety-five percent of 1994 Tech MBAs were placed within three months of graduation, a 10% increase over last years figures. Roughly 60% of all grads go into operations or MIS, while 16% went into general management. The average starting salary is $46, 580. Recruiters making the most offers Andersen, UPS, BellSouth, Ernst and Young, AMS, Coca-Cola, Federal Express, Intel, Nations Bank, ans AT & T.

GEORGIA INSTITUTE OF TECHNOLOGY SCHOOL OF MANAGEMENT

STUDENT LIFE/CAMPUS

GT boasts a rigorous and demanding curriculum. During the first year, this translates into a substantial workload. To keep up with it, students prepare for class an average of twenty to thirty hours a week. They also form study groups to divide and conquer assignments. The pressure, while not killer, can heat up quickly. Class participation counts heavily toward the grade. But students don't have to worry about facing a huge sea of faces: Classes average twenty-five to forty students.

There's some debate over how competitive students are here. The majority said "very." The remainder said "somewhat." One student's comments resolve the issue best: "While there's competition, we work together and support one another. It's not cutthroat here." Added another, "Very friendly and unstuffy atmosphere." Of the professionally diverse student body, students also said they're are extremely sharp.. Students are subject to an honor code and expected to sign a pledge on exams/individual assignments stating they have "neither given nor received help."

GT boasts modern classroom and computer facilities. A unique setup is found in "Classroom 2000," which is fully equipped with Macintosh II computers. Software allows the instructor to control any student's computer, as well as project individual screens for the entire class. Very cool. As for GT's hometown of Atlanta, it consistently rates as one of the most livable cities in the nation. As you might expect, the majority of students opt to live off-campus in apartments, and they say housing is great. On campus, they especially like the gym—a multipurpose athletic monument to sweat. Leisure time is spent on outdoor activities—barbecues, golf tournaments, and intramural sports.

ADMISSIONS

If you're thinking of applying to GT straight out of college, reconsider. The vast majority of Ivan Allen students have at least two years of work experience under their belts. Also of great concern to the admissions committee is your GMAT score: The average GMAT score of accepted applicants was a smashing 614—way up in the eighty-fifth percentile. Also considered are undergraduate GPA, essays, and letters of recommendation.

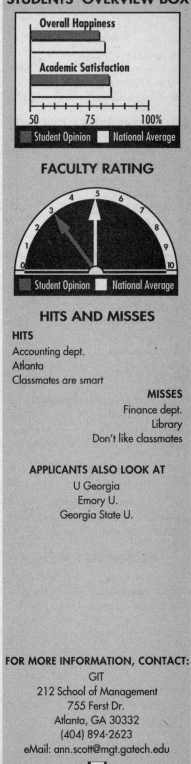

STUDENTS' OVERVIEW BOX

Overall Happiness

Academic Satisfaction

50   75   100%

Student Opinion   National Average

FACULTY RATING

Student Opinion   National Average

HITS AND MISSES

HITS
Accounting dept.
Atlanta
Classmates are smart

MISSES
Finance dept.
Library
Don't like classmates

APPLICANTS ALSO LOOK AT
U Georgia
Emory U.
Georgia State U.

FOR MORE INFORMATION, CONTACT:
GIT
212 School of Management
755 Ferst Dr.
Atlanta, GA 30332
(404) 894-2623
eMail: ann.scott@mgt.gatech.edu

Harvard University Graduate School of Business Administration

ADMISSIONS FACTS

Type of school	Private

Demographics

No. of men	33%
No. of women	28%
No. of minorities	14%
No. of int'l students	25%

EQUAL TREATMENT GRAPH

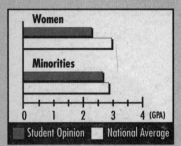

Admissions Statistics

Avg. GMAT	N/A
Avg. undergraduate GPA	3.5
Avg. age at entry	26.1
No. of applicants	N/A
No. accepted	N/A
No. enrolled	N/A

Deadlines and Notifications

Regular application	3/4
Regular notification	5/25
Special dates	N/A

Focus of Curriculum

General Management

Academic Specialties

General Management, Finance, Operations, Service Management

FINANCIAL FACTS

In-state tuition	$19,750
Out-of-state tuition	$19,750
On-campus housing	$6700

ACADEMICS

Harvard Business School (HBS) is indisputably the nation's most famous business school and it is also one of the most selective. In 1994 -95, a class of 800 students was admitted from among 6,000 applicants. With these numbers and a world-wide reputation as *the* B-School, HBS appears to be the envy of almost everybody in graduate business education. Further evidence of Harvard's unique standing is that it is the only B-school that doesn't require the GMAT. Unsurprisingly, the prevalent feeling here is summed up by one student's remarks: "If you're going to do an MBA, don't mess around. Come to the best B-school in the world." Those that are fortunate enough to be accepted, usually do. More than 90% of last year's "admits" chose to enroll.

How did Harvard come to occupy such an august position? First, as one of the oldest B-schools in the nation (it was founded in 1908), it got a head start on all the other programs. Second, as the biggest B-school—graduating roughly 800 MBAs per year—it's built a network of more than 58,000 alumni worldwide. And these are uncommonly loyal and generous alumni. Since 1980, the school's endowment has grown from $100 million to $600 million in 1995. HBS also boasts more CEO alums than any other program, a nationally renowned faculty, and authorship of ninety percent of the case materials used worldwide.

Harvard Business School (HBS) is renowned for how well it integrates all the aspects of general management and for its comprehensive coverage of the functional areas of business. General management is considered the cornerstone of the program, but, all of the departments are strong. In recent years, Harvard's programs have come under heavy criticsim. The complaints: HBS has not been responsive to changes in the marketplace. It's rigid program has featured little of the international perspectives, teamwork, student consulting, or innovative learning experiences now characteristic of B-School education in the U.S. Suprisingly, the venerable HBS has done what it considered unthinkable before and decided it's time for change. Under the guidance of outgoing Dean John H. McArthur, HBS has undertaken a stem-to-stern program overhaul called the Leadership Learning Initiative. It promises year round classes (students would enroll in September, January or June), sections of 80 instead of 90, and greater emphasis on skill building and field-based learning delivered in a much more cross-functional context.

PLACEMENT AND RECRUITING

HBS students get an average of 3.8 job offers each - the most of any B-school. Over eighty-five percent have a job by graduation. Twenty-six percent go into consulting, sixteen into investment banking, twenty-six into manufacturing, the remaining thirty-two percent into the nonmanufacturing sector. On average, Harvard students earn the highest starting salaries and also experience the greatest "differential factor"—the difference in salary between what they come in with and what they go out with. The big news: for the last few years, Harvard MBAs have been raking in six figure plus starting packages. That makes the tuition investment a little easier to handle now, doesn't it?

HARVARD UNIVERSITY GRADUATE SCHOOL OF BUSINESS ADMINISTRATION

STUDENT LIFE/CAMPUS

Harvard boasts one of the most beautiful, well-manicured campuses in the nation. It should. The school has plowed $200 million into it's buildings and grounds over the last 15 years. Over and over, students described its "country club" ambiance and told us about groundskeepers obsessed with sod and shrubbery. "A plant died here last week," one student told us. "They replaced it within three days. And they use a snowblower to clear leaves." Students rave about the ever-popular Shad Hall, Harvard's gym, which is a veritable temple to sweat: "Shad is worth the tuition alone."

Harvard MBAs enjoy an active social life, although one noted, "There is no such thing as dating at HBS. Local undergrads aren't bad if you hide the fact that you go to Harvard." Fifty-six student clubs keep students fully engaged. Many of the clubs sponsor black-tie affairs such as the well-known Predator's Ball. Favorite spots for section gatherings are The Border Cafe and The Boat House. On warm days, students can be found hanging out on the sun-drenched patios of Kresge, an on-campus eatery.

Harvard divides its 800 incoming students into sections of ninety; each section takes an entire year of prescribed courses together. Wrote one MBA, "Section life is a great experience. You develop great camaraderie with classmates from diverse cultural and professional backgrounds." Most of the first-year social life revolves around the section, which schedules dozens of section events to insure you get to know those ninety classmates well. The school highly recommends forming study groups. During orientation and the first week of class, students generally seek out classmates with whom to form a group. It's not uncommon for overanxious types to begin doing this in the summer, to lock in someone smart.

Harvard's reputation for intensity and competitiveness is well earned. The first four months are the most difficult. As one student explained, "It ramps up quickly. Students who know zero about accounting and stats get left behind." The pressure to succeed is formidable. A forced grading curve causes roughly ten percent of the students in each course to fail, which is known as "looping." In fact, about seventy percent of the first-year students loop at least one class. Too many loops, however, and the board evaluates whether you need to take a year or two off. Not to worry, though: the school reports that fewer that one percent of students are required to leave the program.

ADMISSIONS

The admissions board at Harvard considers the following criteria (not ranked in order of importance): college GPA/transcripts, essays, letters of recommendation, and extracurricular activities. Harvard does not consider the GMAT. The essays are considered extremely important. Applicants are interviewed at Harvard's discretion only to further evaluate the student's candidacy. Applications are batched in rounds. Applicants who apply as college seniors may be admitted with a mandatory deferral.

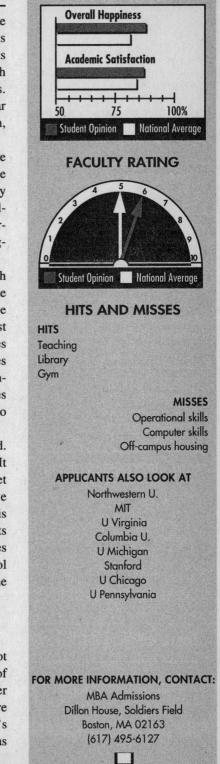

STUDENTS' OVERVIEW BOX

Overall Happiness

Academic Satisfaction

50   75   100%

☐ Student Opinion ☐ National Average

FACULTY RATING

0 1 2 3 4 5 6 7 8 9 10

■ Student Opinion ■ National Average

HITS AND MISSES

HITS
Teaching
Library
Gym

MISSES
Operational skills
Computer skills
Off-campus housing

APPLICANTS ALSO LOOK AT
Northwestern U.
MIT
U Virginia
Columbia U.
U Michigan
Stanford
U Chicago
U Pennsylvania

FOR MORE INFORMATION, CONTACT:
MBA Admissions
Dillon House, Soldiers Field
Boston, MA 02163
(617) 495-6127

HOFSTRA UNIVERSITY SCHOOL OF BUSINESS

ADMISSIONS FACTS

Type of school	Private

Demographics

No. of men	500
No. of women	320
No. of minorities	45
No. of int'l students	37

EQUAL TREATMENT GRAPH

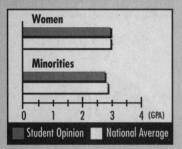

Admissions Statistics

Avg. GMAT	570
Avg. undergraduate GPA	3.2
Avg. age at entry	26.5
No. of applicants	1104
No. accepted	640
No. enrolled	175

Deadlines and Notifications

Regular application	5/1
Regular notification	rolling
Special dates	N/A

Focus of Curriculum

Specialized

Academic Specialties

Accounting, Finance, Information Systems

Joint Degrees

JD/MBA

Special Programs

The Hofstra Univ. Consulting Group, The Assoc. of Students of Economics and International Commerce (ASEIC), Beta Gamma Sigma, The Long Island Venture Group, The Retail Management Institute

FINANCIAL FACTS

In-state tuition	$11,500
Out-of-state tuition	$11,500
On-campus housing	$5,550

ACADEMICS

According to the B-School, a curriculum review has just been revised and completed. The phase-in is to begin in 1996. In the meantime, one of Hofstra's strengths is that it tailors its program to the individual needs of a student by tailoring each program based on prior education, graduate degree objectives, and a common body of knowledge. Business undergrads, for example, might be required to take fewer courses. They can also pursue the MBA full-time and complete degree requirements in only one calendar year by attending both summer sessions and the January session as well as the fall and spring semesters.

The MBA program consists of four components: prerequisite courses for students who lack an undergrad business degree or specific course work, core courses that cover common business knowledge, specialization electives that allow a student to concentrate in an area of business, and the option of either a master's thesis or graduate research seminar. The thesis or research seminar trains students in research design and in the preparation of sophisticated business reports. Seven areas of concentration are offered.

The program exposes to traditional learning experiences as well as innovative exercises and simulated business situations. Particularly noteworthy is the program's emphasis on hands-on computer learning, which is enhanced by Hofstra's state-of-the-art computer facilities. Again and again, students raved about these facilities. Hofstra is "one of only a few non-doctoral programs which subscribes to the Center for Research in Security Prices (CRSP) database" and makes these data available to students. The database provides "daily and monthly information for over 8,000 firms" and is considered "essential for conducting financial event and market efficiency studies." A unique opportunity is found in the school's Small Business Management Institute, through which students serve as consultants to small businesses who have sought assistance from the government's Small Business Administration (SBA). The SBA provides small stipends to this group, which helps the businesses avoid defaulting on their SBA loans.

Describing the faculty, one student said "Professors are not just your teachers, they are your friends." Most Hofstra MBAs agree, profs have wide open, welcoming doors. As for their teaching abilities, the reviews are more mixed. Students wish they would use case studies more. According to our survey, students feel best prepared by their classes in marketing and finance (school strong suits) and say "The accounting courses are particularly tough." Claimed one MBA "Regional reputation is excellent. Outside of NYU and Columbia its the strongest program. But the bottom line is that we are still second tier when competing for national positions!"

PLACEMENT AND RECRUITING

The Career Development Office offers students assistance with resume preparation, interviewing skills, and job search strategies. Students may also place their resume in Hofstra's MBA resume book, which is distributed to Fortune 500 firms and smaller financial institutions in the New York City area.

In 1994, forty-five companies recruited on campus. Of all the students, 84% had a job within three months of graduation (four percent go on for additional education). The average starting salary for grad is $48,897. Forty-six percent of the class heads into finance where the starting salary is higher than the average: $51,000. This is followed by marketing, with 15% of the class and salaries at the average mark. The big hires: KPMG Peat Marwick, Chase Manhattan, Citibank, Andersen Consulting. Despite these stats, students said they're not satisfied with the range of companies recruiting.

HOFSTRA UNIVERSITY SCHOOL OF BUSINESS

STUDENT LIFE/CAMPUS

Hofstra is located in Hempstead, New York, twenty-five miles from New York City. Situated right on the Hempstead Turnpike, the campus itself is lovely—tree-lined and dotted with sculpture. It even houses an arboretum. Less lovely is the parking situation, which students say can be next to impossible. This is a daily headache, since the school is dominated by Long Island commuters (a small number live on-campus in the modern high-rise dorms). Classes are small, with an average of ten to twenty-five students in each. Students rate themselves as competitive, but hardly the type to mow someone down. Instead, there is a sense of camaraderie, and students solve problems in a team environment. Hofstra MBAs bring diverse and interesting work perspectives to the classroom experience. They also bring their smarts. But according to our survey, students don't necessarily like to hang out with or intend to keep each other as long-term buddies. Indeed, the social scene is subdued here because students commute and aren't around on weekends. Commented one MBA "School does not cater to full-time students. " Unsurprisingly, school spirit is largely absent. However, students agree that Hofstra is well run. Wrote one student, "The administration is accessible, including the Dean of the school." However, there are many school activities. There's an active seminar program and lots of "Career Forums" to attend. Students also organize tailgate parties before Hofstra football games, a spring picnic, and a graduate cruise around Manhattan. A newsletter keeps everyone connected to campus. Although this school tends to be attended by Long Island commuters, one student warned, "parking is sparse." A small number live in the high-rise dorms.

ADMISSIONS

According to the admissions office, the following are considered most important in your application: leadership, communication skills, and levels of increasing professional responsibility. After that, in descending order of importance, are your college GPA, GMAT score, work experience, essay, letters of recommendation, and extracurricular activities. "Admission processes," writes the school, "tend to be very similar to the selective to highly selective schools in the United States. All [application] materials are evaluated carefully by a committee comprised of faculty and administrators. We offer perhaps one of the more timely application turnarounds among the group of selective schools; once an application is complete, we generally notify the applicant of a decision within four weeks." Members of American minority groups, e.g., African-Americans, receive special consideration as do those students whose native language is not English."

Applicants may defer admission up to one year for medical reasons or to accrue additional work experience. There is an admission deferment program for college seniors.

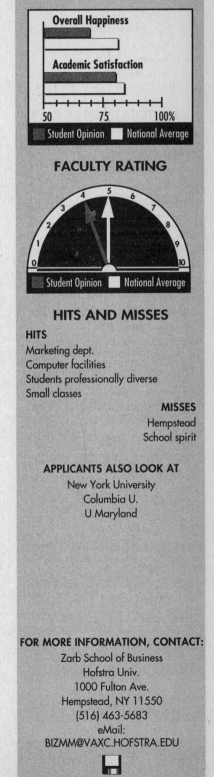

STUDENTS' OVERVIEW BOX

Overall Happiness

Academic Satisfaction

50   75   100%

Student Opinion   National Average

FACULTY RATING

Student Opinion   National Average

HITS AND MISSES

HITS
Marketing dept.
Computer facilities
Students professionally diverse
Small classes

MISSES
Hempstead
School spirit

APPLICANTS ALSO LOOK AT
New York University
Columbia U.
U Maryland

FOR MORE INFORMATION, CONTACT:
Zarb School of Business
Hofstra Univ.
1000 Fulton Ave.
Hempstead, NY 11550
(516) 463-5683
eMail:
BIZMM@VAXC.HOFSTRA.EDU

UNIV. OF ILLINOIS AT CHAMPAIGN-URBANA COLL. OF COMMERCE AND BUSINESS ADMINISTRATION

ADMISSIONS FACTS

Type of school	Public

Demographics

No. of men	403
No. of women	167
No. of minorities	66
No. of int'l students	200

EQUAL TREATMENT GRAPH

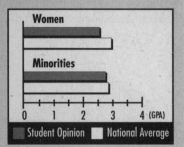

Admissions Statistics

Avg. GMAT	600
Avg. undergraduate GPA	3.4
Avg. age at entry	24
No. of applicants	832
No. accepted	534
No. enrolled	252

Deadlines and Notifications

Regular application	rolling (5/1 Rec.)
Regular notification	within 2 weeks
Special dates	N/A

Focus of Curriculum

General Management

Academic Specialties

Marketing, Finance

Special Programs

Chief Financial Officer Lecture Series, Business Advisory Council, Executive in Residence Program

FINANCIAL FACTS

In-state tuition	$6,300
Out-of-state tuition	$12,180
On-campus housing	$4,000

ACADEMICS

The curriculum at the University of Illinois (UI) B-school consists of three components: foundations, managerial functions, and professional concentrations. Six core courses provide a basic foundation—statistics, quantitative methods, production and operation management, organizational behavior, and micro and macro economics. Another six introduce students to the functional areas—marketing, managerial accounting, financial management, business law, and strategic management. During the second year, students take a capstone course in strategic management that integrates and applies previous course work. It teaches corporate strategy from a CEO's point of view. Electives create areas of specialization. The three newest are: Health Care Management, Food and Agribusiness Management, and the Management of Technology. Students may also take electives in other university departments. Wrote one student, "The MBA program is very flexible in terms of elective course work, unlike other schools which force you to take a track of courses." For those who need to juice up their computer skills, a required computer competency course gets students cranking through spreadsheets, database management, and business graphics.

The majority of MBAs report they feel well prepared in the following areas: general management, marketing, finance, teamwork, quantitative methods, and computing. A sizable number feel less confident about their accounting and operations skills. As for the faculty, students told us teaching at U of I can be spotty. Professors do garner rave reviews for their after-class accessibility. Although some students told us UI is not meeting their academic expectations, the majority said taking time off to get an Illinois MBA is well worth it. Several students said they chose this program because of its "high value/low cost." Enthused one student: "Great school. Overshadowed because Northwestern and Chicago are so close."

PLACEMENT AND RECRUITING

The Placement Office is common property here, shared by both undergrads and MBAs in the College of Commerce and Business Administration. However, they provide special services to MBAs. For example, a full-time resume book is distributed to hundreds of firms, and seventy-two companies recruit on-campus for MBAs. A program that distinguishes UI is the Alumni Networking File, a database of alumni grouped by geographic location, industry, and job title, who have made themselves available to field questions about their industries. Still, students aren't satisfied with what they perceive to be a less-than-aggressive MBA placement office. They'd like the school to beef up the range and number of companies recruiting from outside the Chicago area. But according to one student, "Career placement is improving. The resources are there, it just takes some digging." Of 1993 MBAs, seventy-four percent had been placed within three months of graduation. Companies doing the most hiring: Ford Motor Company, Arthur Andersen, Andersen Consulting, NBD Bank, Citibank, and Proctor & Gamble.

UNIV. OF ILLINOIS AT CHAMPAIGN-URBANA COLL. OF COMMERCE AND BUSINESS ADMINISTRATION

STUDENT LIFE/CAMPUS

Students report a heavy first-year workload and spend roughly twenty to thirty hours a week preparing for class. Although many students skim or blow off an occasional case, the majority feel it's necessary to read all or most of it. Wrote one student, "The case load may be intense, but it gives the school its strong academic reputation." To maintain their sanity, students look to their pre-assigned study groups for help. Said one, "The study group concept enhances interpersonal skills" as well. In terms of competitiveness, students observe there are some sharks but also some helpers. Overall, teamwork and a supportive learning environment prevail. As one student put it, "I was apprehensive about the competitive nature of B-schools. But my fears have been put to rest. The maturity and diversity of my classmates foster a cooperative spirit throughout this program." Another student, though, doesn't think much of Illinois MBAs: "I have the feeling that some students came here merely because they couldn't find a job, not necessarily because they definitely wanted to get an MBA."

One student's comments typified the prevalent feeling here: "Illinois boasts excellent facilities. The library is the third largest in the nation." In particular, Illinois MBAs are big fans of the athletic facilities—which house four entire gymnasiums—a monument to sweat. Equal in stature, the Krannert Center for the Performing Arts is a monument to the arts. More than 300 public performances of theater, music, ballet and opera are held annually. Students report both on- and off-campus housing is plentiful and attractive, although the majority opt to live off-campus in apartments. Social events are orchestrated through the MBA Association. They organize activities such as career forums, the annual spring banquet, and barbecues on football weekends.

ADMISSIONS

The admissions office considers your college GPA to be most important. After that, in descending order, they consider your GMAT scores, work experience, essays, and letters of recommendation. Work experience and extracurricular activities are "preferred" but not required. Students also present projects, portfolios, theses, and the like for review. Because of the quantitative components of the curriculum, applicants are advised to have completed a college-level calculus course. Writes the school, "The admissions program is client-oriented. An applicant can track his/her application through a 1-800-MBA-UIUC number."

Decisions are made on a rolling admissions basis. Applicants are notified of a decision ten days from receipt of the completed application. Waitlisted students are notified of a spot by June 15.

STUDENTS' OVERVIEW BOX

Overall Happiness

Academic Satisfaction

50   75   100%

■ Student Opinion   ☐ National Average

FACULTY RATING

0 1 2 3 4 5 6 7 8 9 10

■ Student Opinion   ☐ National Average

HITS AND MISSES

HITS
Quantitative skills
Library
Ethnic & racial diversity

MISSES
Accounting dept.
Placement
Lack diverse work experience

APPLICANTS ALSO LOOK AT

Northwestern U.
U Iowa
Indiana U-Bloom.
U Wisconsin-Madison
U Michigan
Washington U.

FOR MORE INFORMATION, CONTACT:
Jane G. White
MBA Program, 15 Commerce West
1206 South 6 St.
Champaign, IL 61820
(217) 244-8019

INDIANA UNIVERSITY GRADUATE SCHOOL OF BUSINESS

ADMISSIONS FACTS

Type of school	Public

Demographics

No. of men	402
No. of women	144
No. of minorities	72
No. of int'l students	74

EQUAL TREATMENT GRAPH

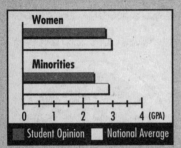

Women

Minorities

0 1 2 3 4 (GPA)

■ Student Opinion □ National Average

Admissions Statistics

Avg. GMAT	610
Avg. undergraduate GPA	3.2
Avg. age at entry	27
No. of applicants	1,334
No. accepted	642
No. enrolled	252

Deadlines and Notifications

Regular application	3/1
Regular notification	4/15
Special dates	N/A

Focus of Curriculum

Specialized

Academic Specialties

Finance, Marketing, Human Resources Management, International Business

Joint Degrees

MBA/JD

Special Programs

Deloitte & Touche and Procter & Gamble sponsored and judged case analysis competition, Foreign Study in eight foreign countries

FINANCIAL FACTS

In-state tuition	$7,179
Out-of-state tuition	$14,364
On-campus housing	$3,500

ACADEMICS

Indiana University has enhanced its reputation as one of the best B-schools in the nation with a thorough overhaul of its curriculum. The new program incorporates modern-day themes such as cross-functional learning, globalization, leadership, and multiculturalism. In an unusual break from tradition, the first-year courses are grouped in "cores." During the first semester there is a foundations core, a professional core, and a week-long "immersion" seminar on total quality management. During the second semester, there is a functional core and an immersion seminar on environmental management. The second year is devoted to specialization. The most novel innovation is that students receive only two grades in the first semester—one for each of the cores and one for the remaining core in the second semester. According to IU MBAs, approximately sixty percent of students get a B-plus, thirty percent A or A minus, ten percent B minus or worse. To enhance teamwork, the school year kicks off with a one-week orientation replete with team-building exercises and head-start classes in computers and accounting. The entering class is then divided into cohorts of sixty-five students each. Cohorts take first-semester courses together and are then reshuffled to introduce students to as many classmates as possible. Four faculty members oversee each core, creating a personal learning environment. But their involvement with the students extends beyond class. Students unanimously praise professors for their generous accessibility and fine teaching.

Although the program is only a year old, students already reported, "The new program is a great success." Added another, "The new curriculum is well thought out and offers a great team learning experience." Overall, students reported they felt well prepared in accounting, finance, and general management. Given the emphasis on collaborative learning, it's not surprising that students rate their teamwork and interpersonal skills as extremely strong. But there are weak spots: Students feel less confident about their skills in marketing, operations, and computing. Although some MBAs seemed to agree with the student who told us, "The administration is very customer oriented. It shields students from the inefficiencies and bureaucracy of the university as a whole." A sizable number say the school might be better run. For example, it can be difficult to get into popular courses. Still, most students echoed this last sentiment: "Overall, a great program at a bargain price." Prominent alumni who would agree: Harold Poling, Former Chairperson and CEO - Ford Motor Company; James Lipate, CEO - Penzoil, Frank Popoff, CEO - Dow Chemical.

PLACEMENT AND RECRUITING

Fully 223 companies recruited on-campus in 1994. Ninety-four percent of grads had secured a position within three months of graduation. Most MBAs headed into marketing. The average starting salary at Indiana is $53,620. Companies making the most offers: Intel, Ford, NBD, Eli Lilly, Proctor & Gamble, Federal Express, Pizza Hut, Whirlpool, Kraft, Andersen Consulting, Kimberly Clark, and Allied Signal. Wrote one student, "This is a Midwest school with a majority of job recruiters coming from Midwest companies (including Chicago)."

INDIANA UNIVERSITY GRADUATE SCHOOL OF BUSINESS

STUDENT LIFE/CAMPUS

Students agree that during the first year the pace and breadth of learning at IU can be frightening. Indeed, an "extremely demanding workload" requires students to study/prepare an average of thirty-five to forty hours each week. Few corners can be cut; the majority of students report it's important to do all or most assigned reading. Since the professionally diverse student body is also intelligent, they're well equipped to make it through the program. Still, one IU MBA said the trick is to learn how to "master balancing the demands of the program and your social life, so that you can enjoy the experience immensely." Good advice. According to students we surveyed, there's plenty to enjoy at IU. Students are laid back and friendly. Explained one MBA, "IU is an extremely cooperative place. Students are not cutthroat or too competitive."

Added another, "This is Indiana's culture—real and genuine." Not surprisingly, students are strong believers in extending a helping hand. MBAs say their social life is "BIG." They go out a lot, but in groups, not on dates. A favorite destination on Thursday nights (there's no class on Friday) is the designated bar of the week. Organized social events are also popular— picnics, barbecues, and the spring banquet. The majority of students become involved in the student-run career clubs, such as the Graduate Women of Business or Finance Club.

As for IU's hometown of Bloomington, writes the school, it's a "little like a mix of Ann Arbor, Berkeley, and Cambridge with a dash of Main Street, USA thrown in." Students report that housing, whether on- or off-campus, is cost-effective and extremely attractive. The majority opt to live off-campus in apartments in Bloomington or surrounding neighborhoods. Public transportation is easily accessible. A car is helpful if you want to go exploring on the weekend, but according to students, parking is the pits.

ADMISSIONS

According to the school, Indiana does not prioritize its admissions criteria "but weighs GMAT scores, the undergraduate record, and work experience most heavily. There are no cutoffs for GMAT scores or GPAs. Leadership experience is also an important factor." An interview is recommended, but not required. Applicants to Indiana University must have completed a course in calculus and received a grade in it of "C" or better. The school does not review applications on either a rolling admissions or rounds basis. There is one final deadline: April 15. All applicants are notified of a decision during the first two weeks of April. Students may request deferments for up to two years.

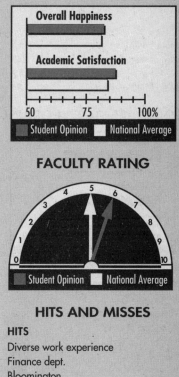

STUDENTS' OVERVIEW BOX

Overall Happiness

Academic Satisfaction

50   75   100%

■ Student Opinion □ National Average

FACULTY RATING

0 1 2 3 4 5 6 7 8 9 10

■ Student Opinion □ National Average

HITS AND MISSES

HITS
Diverse work experience
Finance dept.
Bloomington
Helping other students
Accounting dept.
Teamwork
School clubs

MISSES
Off-campus housing

APPLICANTS ALSO LOOK AT
U Michigan
UNC-Chapel Hill
Duke U.
Northwestern U.
U Texas
U Chicago

FOR MORE INFORMATION, CONTACT:
Graduate School of Business
10th and Fee Lane RM 254
Bloomington, IN 47405
(812) 855-8006

UNIVERSITY OF IOWA: IOWA BUSINESS SCHOOL

ADMISSIONS FACTS

Type of school	Public

Demographics

No. of men	165
No. of women	75
No. of minorities	12
No. of int'l students	55

EQUAL TREATMENT GRAPH

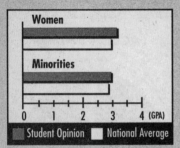

Admissions Statistics

Avg. GMAT	590
Avg. undergraduate GPA	3.2
Avg. age at entry	26
No. of applicants	640
No. accepted	238
No. enrolled	102

Deadlines and Notifications

Regular application	7/1
Regular notification	rolling
Special dates	3/1 (international)

Focus of Curriculum

General Management

Academic Specialties

Finance, Human Resources

FINANCIAL FACTS

In-state tuition	$3,713
Out-of-state tuition	$9,922
On-campus housing	$4,470

ACADEMICS

As one student puts it, "The Iowa MBA program is in transition and is still making adjustments in order to educate efficiently." Indeed, the school is instituting many changes to secure its position as one of the nation's best. One notable change is the spanking-new $36 million state-of-the-art building, which boasts a modern library, U-shaped lecture rooms, and high-tech computer labs. Iowa MBAs are positively fired up over these facilities, which they describe as "conducive to learning," "architecturally beautiful," and "a fantastic asset." Now students also hope that Iowa "establishes firmer ties with area corporations for classroom study, not just placement." Certain components of the MBA program are already in place. Chief among them are a commitment to first-rate academics and a general management education. Students described Iowa as a "gem in the rough" with "top-twenty potential." The first year consists of a highly structured sequence of core courses and has a quantitative bent. However, students explained, "The curriculum during the second year allows students to choose the majority of their classes. Many students pursue joint degrees in law, hospital administration, MIS, or accounting." One standout program, unique to Iowa, is the Emerging Free Market Economy Program, which sends teams of MBAs to act as consultants in eastern Europe during the summer. Shared another MBA, "Iowa is a place that welcomes student involvement and lets you build a portfolio of skills. The IMPACT program is a wonderful example. It starts during orientation week with an Outward Bound–like course and continues with workshops on communications skills, etc." Practical skills are acquired in one of the many consulting projects available to students in the local business community.

Professors garner high marks for their accessibility, but get mixed reviews for their teaching. One MBA told us, "There are excellent professors in the finance and management departments." Enthused another, "Profs are wonderful; I'll keep in touch with them long after I leave." But a sizable number of students had complaints. Griped one, "The biggest problem is the variability in the quality of teaching. Also, not enough have had serious business experience before becoming a prof." Moaned another, "Teachers place such an emphasis on class participation, people talk just to hear themselves speak." On the upside, students say the dean and faculty are responsive to student concerns. Overall, students say this program is on the move. Summed up one happy MBA, "The bottom line for the University of Iowa is this—what can we do for you?"

PLACEMENT AND RECRUITING

Eighty-three companies recruited on-campus in 1993. Eighty-two percent of graduating students were placed within six months of commencement. Leading recruiters are Andersen Consulting, Ford Motor Company, Kimberly Clark, Shell Oil, and Principal Financial Group.

University of Iowa: Iowa Business School

Student Life/Campus

Students report a moderately heavy workload and spend an average of fifteen to twenty-five hours a week preparing for class. Core classes have roughly fifty students per class, electives twenty-five to thirty. Seventy percent of all classes are taught by case study. The majority of students work in a study group. As one MBA put it, "One of the best things about this school is its small size. Only 120 students in each entering class, so you get to know everyone!" Students report a "FANTASTIC student community" and an "unbelievable amount of school pride." As one might expect in this kind of environment, students are competitive, but in a spirited way. The vast majority say classmates are very interested in helping others. As for the student body, Iowa MBAs say there are an "interesting cross-section of nonbusiness types with good insights." Claimed one, "The high percentage of international students has had a major impact on my perspective and ideas about people." But another griped, "Since there is no work requirement for this school, the average student is young with little or no experience. So the diversity is not what it should be."

At the center of all extracurriculars is the MBA Association. It orchestrates everything from Tailgaters and Holiday Fling educational programs to faculty/student mixers. Highlights are once-a-semester trips to cities like Chicago, St. Paul/Minneapolis for corporate site visits. Community service is also popular—Iowa MBAs volunteer to Habitat for Humanity. Student-run clubs such as the Minority MBA Association and Graduate MBA Association also play a big part in campus life. Every Thursday night they head to Fitzpatrick's, the unofficial MBA pub. Iowa offers civilized city living, although with a population of 50,000 this pace feels more like a small town. MBAs live off-campus in apartments in Iowa City and Coralville. The bus system is good, but most students bring a car.

Admissions

According to the admissions office, the following components are all weighed equally: essays, college GPA, letters of recommendation, extracurriculars, work experience, and GMAT scores. The school advises, however, "Applicants are encouraged to pay particular attention to the essay component of the application process. In addition to considering quantitative factors such as GMAT scores and the undergraduate transcript, we look at prior work experience (responsibilities, not just titles) career focus and ambition, maturity, and individuality." The school recommends that applicants have some quantitative proficiency (i.e., calculus) before matriculating. Admissions decisions are made on a rolling basis until the final deadline. Students may defer admission for up to one year. Roughly forty percent of all applicants are admitted.

STUDENT'S OVERVIEW BOX

Overall Happiness

Academic Satisfaction

50 75 100%
Student Opinion | National Average

FACULTY RATING

Student Opinion | National Average

HITS AND MISSES

HITS
Quantitative skills
On-campus housing
Helping other students
On-campus housing

MISSES
Accounting dept.
Diverse work experience

APPLICANTS ALSO LOOK AT
Ohio State U.
U Texas-Austin
U Illinois-C.U.
U Wisconsin-Madison
U Minnesota
Indiana U.
Washington U.
Purdue U.
Tulane U.

FOR MORE INFORMATION, CONTACT:
School of Business
108 Pappajohn Bus. Admin. Bldg.
Suite C140
Iowa City, IA 52242
(319) 335-1039
eMail:
uiowasom@scout-po.biz.uiowa.edu

UNIVERSITY OF KANSAS SCHOOL OF BUSINESS

ADMISSIONS FACTS

Type of school	Public

Demographics

No. of men	297
No. of women	174
No. of minorities	18
No. of int'l students	51

EQUAL TREATMENT GRAPH

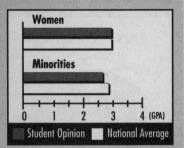

Admissions Statistics

Avg. GMAT	584
Avg. undergraduate GPA	3.30
Avg. age at entry	27
No. of applicants	322
No. accepted	161
No. enrolled	114

Deadlines and Notifications

Regular application	5/1
Regular notification	rolling
Special dates	N/A

Focus of Curriculum
General Management

Academic Specialties
Accounting, Finance

Jiont Degrees
JD/MBA

FINANCIAL FACTS

In-state tuition	$2,512
Out-of-state tuition	$7,390
On-campus housing	$3,232

ACADEMICS

Students we surveyed repeatedly emphasized two themes: first, that "KU's MBA program provides low cost/high value" and second, that it "emphasizes what the business world wants—teamwork/interpersonal skills and total quality management (TQM)." KU offers a generalist perspective; students pursue a broad study of the major business disciplines. Coursework features a global slant and "a TQM people-as-assets mentality." Students elect to specialize in one of several areas, including international business and human resources. Standout departments include accounting and finance. According to our survey this year, students were decidely less enthusiastic about the program and surprisingly, a majority of the comments we received were negative. We heard comments like "There is no real focus to the overall program. I don't believe the School has an idea of what a graduate of this school should really know" and "The Business School is becoming more and more cut throat. The students are too competitive and the teachers encourage it." The School is implementing a revised MBA program none too soon. On the Lawrence campus for full-time MBAs, students will enter a program enphasizing team work starting with an orientation week business simulation contest. During the first year all students will take the same foundation core of required classes and will work in teams of 5 with a faculty mentor assigned to each team. During four immersion weeks over the first year, students will focus completely on topical subjects like market based management or TQM. In the second year students will have an option to pursue a concentration in one of eleven fields.

The evening MBA program, designed for more experienced managers, will reduce the core hours in favor of electives. A student who worked on the team overhauling the programs says "Except for Finance and Accounting, there is too much of a theoretical emphasis in the program. I feel that the MBA program will emerge as the most competitive in the area in terms of price, location, breadth of course courses, and depth of knowledge in functional areas." But Kansas MBAs most decidedly feel this school is not weathering it's transition to a new program well. Also in the complaint department, one student wrote "senior faculty are 'Poor.'" On the other hand, profs are highly regarded for their accessiblity after class and interest in students. Class particpation, we're told, counts heavily toward the grade. And here's something that's working right: it's easy to get into required courses and popular electives. No matter how unsure Kansas MBAs feel about their academic preparedness, they still feel the MBA is a hot ticket. An overwhelming majority still see it as the ticket to success.

PLACEMENT AND RECRUITING

According to the school, over 150 national, regional and local firms recruit on campus, although these firms come as much for the undergraduates as they do for the MBAs. Over ninety percent of the class of '94 had secured a position by July. Top recruiters at KU: Andersen Consulting, Deloitte & Touche, and Payless Shoesource.

UNIVERSITY OF KANSAS SCHOOL OF BUSINESS

STUDENT LIFE/CAMPUS

The workload is heavy; the pressure can be intense. Students hit their books an average of twenty to thirty hours a week—sometimes more, sometimes less. Students rave about the benefits of KU's small size. Praised one MBA, "Classes are small, especially in the electives—twenty to twenty-five students in each." As one might expect in a small program, "Students are close and extremely helpful." They're also competitive. But as for how this affects relationships, it depends on who you ask. The majority of students report a vibrant social life. As for the student body itself, MBAs describe a program filled with "bright, talented students who have a lot of ambition." Praised one, "KU has done a great job with international students and relations." But one intolerant type wrote, "Too many foreign students get special privileges in class because of their so-called lack of English."

According to KU MBAs, "Computer technology is antiquated, as is the access to network services." These are gradually being updated. As for UK's hometown, just ask any MBA about Lawrence and she/he'll tell you "it's a great place to go to school." It's small and civilized, and just a forty-minute drive from the bright lights of Kansas City. One MBA observed, "The campus is beautiful and school spirit abounds (how 'bout them Hawks!)." But parking is difficult during sporting events and, in general, expensive. Most MBAs live off-campus in apartments and rental homes in Lawrence. The Graduate Business Council sponsors activities such as weekly beer busts and twice a year hosts a faculty roast and toast. One student told us this council "provides nice activities and leadership. They rounded up a micorwve and refrigerator for the graduate lounge." Nothing stands in the way of progress.

ADMISSIONS

According to the school, your college GPA, GMAT scores, letters of recommendation, and work experience are all weighted equally. Your extracurricular activities are also considered. Writes the admissions office, "There are no minimum scores for GPA/GMAT when considering candidates. The admissions board will also consider extra submissions, such as r_sum_s and extra letters of recommendations." Decisions are made on a rolling admissions basis. Students are notified of a decision approximately three weeks after all application materials are received. Notes the school, "The application form, supplemental data form, and check for $50.00 must be received by the deadline. Other materials (GMAT, transcripts, letters of recommendation, TOEFL) can come in after the deadline, but a student will not be admitted without all. We have no auditing of classes for noncredit, no exceptions." Students may defer admission for up to one year with a written request.

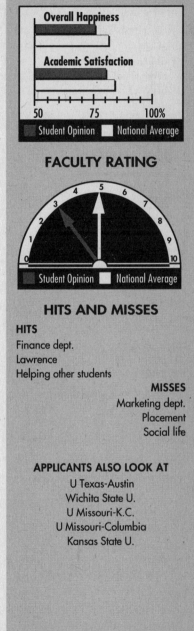

STUDENT'S OVERVIEW BOX

Overall Happiness

Academic Satisfaction

50   75   100%

Student Opinion   National Average

FACULTY RATING

Student Opinion   National Average

HITS AND MISSES

HITS
Finance dept.
Lawrence
Helping other students

MISSES
Marketing dept.
Placement
Social life

APPLICANTS ALSO LOOK AT
U Texas-Austin
Wichita State U.
U Missouri-K.C.
U Missouri-Columbia
Kansas State U.

FOR MORE INFORMATION, CONTACT:
Business School
206 Summerfield Hall
Lawrence, KS 66045
(913) 864-4254

UNIVERSITY OF KENTUCKY COLLEGE OF BUSINESS AND ECONOMICS

ADMISSIONS FACTS

Type of school	Public

Demographics

No. of men	202
No. of women	105
No. of minorities	12
No. of int'l students	39

EQUAL TREATMENT GRAPH

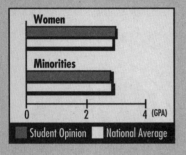

Women

Minorities

0   2   4 (GPA)

■ Student Opinion □ National Average

Admissions Statistics

Avg. GMAT	598
Avg. undergraduate GPA	3.34
Avg. age at entry	25
No. of applicants	272
No. accepted	98
No. enrolled	55

Deadlines and Notifications

Regular application	7/21
Regular notification	rolling
Special dates	N/A

Focus of Curriculum

General Management

Academic Specialties

General Management

Joint Degrees

MBA/JD, BS ENG/MBA

FINANCIAL FACTS

In-state tuition	$2,400
Out-of-state tuition	$7,200
On-campus housing	$2,592

ACADEMICS

Across the board, students feel more positive about their B-school experience at the University of Kentucky than they did in a previous survey for this book. Over and over, they enthused about the schools "excellent buy" in education, and told us "all students are here because they *want* to be here." Indeed, relative to other schools in this book, UK features one of the lowest tuitions.

In terms of academics, UK has recently completed a revision of its MBA program. Three new courses in Global Business Management, Leadership in the Contemporary Business Environment, and Information Systems have replaced older core courses. According to the school, the revised program is considered tow-track: "One track, the business track, is designed for business undergrads and emphasizes the development of a concentration in one of several areas: finance, Real Estate and Banking, Marketing and Distribution, MIS, International Business, Accounting/Finance, and Production and Manufacturing." The other track, is for those with non-business undergrad degrees who already have a concentration such as engineering. The big news: the program is no longer a two-year program, but a three semester program. Reported one MBA, "Program offers course work which is relevant to current developments in business." Electives may also be taken in other university departments. Although the marks students gave themselves for their academic preparedness were above average in all the major disciplines, the three highest were in general management, quantitative methods, and accounting. Still, students should do just fine when they take the B-school's required four-hour comprehensive exam in their final semester. No one has ever failed it.

As for the faculty, one impressed student wrote, "Very tough, teachers are demanding and do not allow slackers." Advised this MBA "Dr. Kelley's marketing class shouldn't be missed. Dr. Donnelley's marketing class and Dr. Poe's accounting class are particularly stimulating." Also in the good news department: "The administration is easy to work with, staff are accessible, and scheduling is smooth." MBAs appreciate the school's state-of-the-art computers, and new class facilities. Said one, "Excellent computer lab help." The only complaints we heard, and they don't reflect the majority: too many part-time students who seem distracted; and a lack of diverse professional experiences among classmates. All in all, the majority of students say taking time off to get a UK MBA is well worth it. And UK MBAs expect to be leveraging their degree long after that first job out of school.

PLACEMENT AND RECRUITING

In 1993, the school asked the special assistant to the dean to improve what students rated as a lackluster placement center. Raved one current MBA, "the program is possibly the most friendly and helpful placement office I have ever dealt with." Here are the current stats: In 1994, 80% of the grads were placed by gradation, 100% within three months of that date, strong numbers. The average starting salary of newly minted MBAs was $38,000. 93 companies recruited on-campus. The school reports that the top employers were predominantly financial institutions, accounting firms, consulting firms, and local corporations. Adds the school, "typically our students seek employment within the state of Kentucky, or the surrounding states, Ohio, Indiana, West Virginia, Tennessee.

UNIVERSITY OF KENTUCKY COLLEGE OF BUSINESS AND ECONOMICS

STUDENT LIFE/CAMPUS

The workload is moderate, the pressure is light. The majority of students report they hit the books an average of fifteen to twenty-five hours a week. The overwhelming majority of students utilize on the collective expertise of their peers by working in study groups. In most courses, exams count heavily toward the grade. As for those previously overstuffed classes, the administration has reduced class size dramatically, a critical improvement. Class participation also weighs heavily in the grading.

MBAs rate their classmates as smart. One MBA said this makes, "the learning environment fun and interesting." Bonus points go to UK for working to admit students from a variety of foreign countries, including the newly independent states of the former Soviet Union and from eastern Europe. Approximately twenty-five percent of the 100 students admitted each fall are international. Yet one MBA griped, "Too many students don't have enough work experience to make valuable contributions." What about competitiveness? It depends on whom you ask. Some say yes, some say no, with most answers falling in between. As for the social scene, the majority say it's lacking. There's only one student club, the MBA Association, which sponsors activities like student orientation, an MBA newsletter, a Thursday night supper club and a few intramural sports. The association also recently established an e-mail network for all MBA students. Students say the gym is pretty good and the "business lab and new classrooms are excellent." Other school attributes: a newly constructed Electronic Business and Economics Information Center, excellent computing facilities, an expansive library, and a summer-abroad program in Vienna, Austria.

As for the town of Lexington, students like it. A short road trip away is the city of Louisville. International students tend to live in on-campus housing, which is considered decent. The majority of MBAs opt for off-campus living in the town of Lexington. Parking is difficult. Most students drop their cars at the football stadium and shuttlebus in.

ADMISSIONS

According to the admissions office, your GMAT score, college GPA/transcript, and university attended are considered most important. After that, in descending order, are your letters of recommendation, work experience, essays, and extracurricular activities. Notes the office of admissions: "Undergraduate degrees in engineering or science are considered a plus. The one hundred best applications are accepted every year.

STUDENT'S OVERVIEW BOX

Overall Happiness

Academic Satisfaction

50   75   100%

Student Opinion   National Average

FACULTY RATING

Student Opinion   National Average

HITS AND MISSES

HITS
Quantitative skills
On-campus housing
Classmates are smart

MISSES
Finance dept.
Placement
Don't stay in touch

APPLICANTS ALSO LOOK AT
U Tennessee-Knox
Indiana U.-Bloom
U Cincinnati
Ohio State U.
U Louisville

FOR MORE INFORMATION, CONTACT:
Graduate Center
237 Business and Economics Building
Lexington, KY 40506-0034
(606) 257-3592
eMail: drball∅@ukcc.uky.edu

LOYOLA UNIVERSITY: CHICAGO GRADUATE SCHOOL OF BUSINESS

ADMISSIONS FACTS

Type of school	Private

Demographics

No. of men	505
No. of women	323
No. of minorities	58
No. of int'l students	76

EQUAL TREATMENT GRAPH

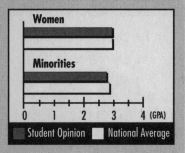

Admissions Statistics

Avg. GMAT	541
Avg. undergraduate GPA	3.22
Avg. age at entry	26
No. of applicants	489
No. accepted	340
No. enrolled	189

Deadlines and Notifications

Regular application	7/15
Regular notification	rolling
Special dates	N/A

Focus of Curriculum

Specialized

Academic Specialties

General Management, Accounting

Joint Degrees

MBA/JD, MBA/MSN

Special Programs

Foreign Study at Loyola's Rome Center Campus, Multicultural advisors for minority students

FINANCIAL FACTS

In-state tuition	$18,060
Out-of-state tuition	$18,060
On-campus housing	N/A

ACADEMICS

Loyola University—Chicago is a private Jesuit Catholic university fully accredited by the AACSB. Although religion is not carried over into the classroom, the university describes itself as committed to the development of "socially responsible leadership." Most recently, the school revamped its curriculum and added a required ethics course. According to the school, this "provides an analytical framework for integrating the personal values of the manager with the functional areas of business decision-making." Another new addition is an international business course. But beyond this, there's nothing especially different or innovative about this program. First-year students take a traditional lineup of ten core courses, four of which can be waived for undergraduate business course work. During the second year, students may specialize by taking electives in one of the following fields: accounting, health care management, financial management, marketing management, personnel management, production and operations management, management science and computers. Any deviation from the prescribed course of study is met with rigid sequencing rules. You can't take certain courses before others, and no more than two electives may be taken in any field of study beyond the area of specialization. Most courses are taught with a global perspective. The school also notes, "Socially Responsible Leadership" is not a buzzword here, but explored in each business discipline. The majority of students surveyed reported they feel well prepared in the areas of accounting, general management, and quantitative methods. Students feel their computer and presentation skills are far weaker.

Loyola students agree that the faculty are the backbone of this program. Professors are widely regarded as good teachers. Exclaimed one student, "Some profs are outstanding." In particular, professors are praised for their accessibility. Reported one Loyola MBA, "I have never had a TA here. Most of my professors are very accessible and even give out their phone numbers." A point of fact: Loyola delivers its program using only full-time, full-fledged professors. As for how well this school is run, it depends on whom you ask. A number of students agreed with the MBA who described the administration as "caring and responsive." An equal number of students agreed with this MBA: "The administration leaves a bit to be desired." Other complaints were about the inadequate library hours and difficulty of getting into popular courses. Loyola's spanking-new 300,000-square-foot facility providing modern classrooms, a new library, and state-of-the-art computer support have gone a long way to resolving these complaints. One of the biggest gripes was about the lack of class discussion hardly—a surprise, given how little class participation counts toward the grade. But for some students this school was a hot ticket to success. Notable alumni include: Michael Quinlin, President of McDonalds, Brenda Barnes, COO of Pepsi-Cola, and John Scott, Chairman, Kemper Life Insurance.

PLACEMENT AND RECRUITING

The Graduate School of Business has its own placement office. Advisors are available to help with resume and cover letter writing, as well as career planning. While the school stresses that students are responsible for securing their own jobs, the placement office does publish a resume book and schedules on-campus interviews. But the numbers tell it all: 68% of grads have a job within three months of graduation. The average starting salary is $41, 621. In 1994, 25 companies recruited on-campus. The major hirers: Ameritech, Andersen Consutling, Merrill Lynch, Motorola, Abbott Labs, Baxter HealthCare, Harris Trust, Kemper Financial. the majority of students (41%) head into finance.

LOYOLA UNIVERSITY: CHICAGO GRADUATE SCHOOL OF BUSINESS

STUDENT LIFE/CAMPUS

Loyola's program is especially designed for both full- and part-time students, and this pervades almost every aspect of the school. For example, classes meet one night a week for three hours. In addition, both full- and part-time students may begin the program at any of the four quarters during the year. One student wrote, "Moving between part-time and full-time is easy." Perhaps because almost eighty-five percent of students attending this program hold down a full-time job, the workload is manageable. The majority of students spend only ten to twenty hours on schoolwork, because they take only a one- or two-course load per semester. As for competition, it depends on who's in your class. Half of the students surveyed rated classmates as very competitive; the other fifty percent said they're only moderately so. Students were in agreement, however, that their classmates are professionally diverse.

The overwhelming feel to this school is commuter. As one student put it, "There is not much of a school-related social life for full-time students. The majority come to school part-time and therefore are not very interested in socializing. The location in Chicago somewhat makes up for this." All MBA classes are held at the downtown Water Tower Campus.

ADMISSIONS

Despite its generous fifty percent acceptance rate, Loyola places some exacting demands on its applicants. Academic strength, GMAT scores, work experience, recommendations, quality of undergraduate institution and difficulty of major and extracurricular activities are considered, in that order. These fairly ordinary criteria become somewhat more daunting when you consider that the average Loyola MBA candidate has *four* years of work experience before enrollment—twice that of most other schools' applicants.

STUDENT'S OVERVIEW BOX

FACULTY RATING

HITS AND MISSES

HITS
Chicago
Diverse work experience

MISSES
Marketing dept.
Off-campus housing
Don't stay in touch
Social life
Teamwork
Gym

APPLICANTS ALSO LOOK AT
Northwestern U.
U Illinois-C.U.
U Chicago

FOR MORE INFORMATION, CONTACT:
Graduate School of Business
Loyola University Chicago
820 N. Michigan Ave.
Chicago, IL 60611
(312) 915-6120
eMail: MBA-Loyola@LUC.EDU

UNIVERSITY OF MARYLAND COLLEGE OF BUSINESS AND MANAGEMENT

ADMISSIONS FACTS

Type of school   Public

Demographics

No. of men	188
No. of women	92
No. of minorities	59
No. of int'l students	56

EQUAL TREATMENT GRAPH

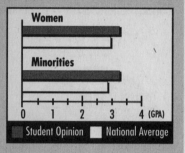

Women	
Minorities	

0   1   2   3   4 (GPA)

☐ Student Opinion ☐ National Average

Admissions Statistics

Avg. GMAT	622
Avg. undergraduate GPA	3.26
Avg. age at entry	26
No. of applicants	1,034
No. accepted	254
No. enrolled	120

Deadlines and Notifications

Regular application	5/15
Regular notification	6–8 weeks
Special dates	2/15 (early decision)

Focus of Curriculum

General Management

Academic Specialties

Entrepreneurship, Transportation and Logistics, International Business, Management Science

Joint Degrees

MBA/JD, MBA/Masters of Public Management

Special Programs

Part-time MBA program available

FINANCIAL FACTS

In-state tuition	$6,300
Out-of-state tuition	$10,950
On-campus housing	$2,899

ACADEMICS

The University of Maryland (UM) MBA program kicks off with an intensive orientation week. If you missed out on summer camp, you've got one more chance in this Outward Bound—oriented program. Management skills seminars and get-to-know-you sessions with faculty and classmates are also held. With new relationships in hand, you're ready for B-school.

UM offers a generalist MBA but has recently retooled its curriculum to include experiential learning modules. Thus far, students pronounce this up- and-coming program "outstanding" and say "everyone takes great pride in the changes being made here." A highly structured first year provides students a grounding in the functional areas. Team building and a global perspective are heavily emphasized through the coursework. During the second year, students choose electives based on their interests. UM is part of a consortium of Washington universities, so students often take courses at member schools such as Georgetown and George Washington. Within the B-school, a popular option is the field study project. Students offer their consulting services to real organizations on actual projects. Another value-added feature is the "How-to" Management Workshops Series. Topics are generated by students and cover issues such as leadership and communication skills. Participation is required. Students must also take one elective on international business. All in all, students say UM is well worth the investment of time and money. Indeed, the vast majority of UM MBAs say it is meeting or exceeding their expectations. Backing this up, students report they feel well prepared by their studies in marketing, accounting, finance and general management. They also report a high level of confidence in their teamwork and quantitative skills. In only one area do a sizable minority report average skills—computers. Professors are well regarded for their excellent teaching and accessibility. But several students expressed this sentiment: "Some professors are well known as authors, but lack good classroom skills. Some appear to have no formal teaching training." As for the administration, the reviews are mostly positive. The vast majority of students say the school runs like well-oiled gears and "the new dean has been a positive influence." Proclaimed one Maryland MBA, "The administration is really trying to improve the programs. They are very responsive to students." Students say getting into popular courses is unusually easy. Summed up one student, "Maryland is a great MBA program for the price. It's not Harvard, but it doesn't charge Harvard's tuition."

PLACEMENT AND RECRUITING

The majority of students report they are satisfied with the placement office and the range of companies recruiting. Wrote one MBA, "The school has recently turned more of its attention to the placement department. The new placement staff are well seasoned and knowledgeable about recruiting MBAs." Still, a sizable number of students can't wait until placement revs up.

UNIVERSITY OF MARYLAND COLLEGE OF BUSINESS AND MANAGEMENT

STUDENT LIFE/CAMPUS

UM divides its entering class into sections of forty to forty-five student each, affording its students lots of personal attention. Section mates take all their required courses together and develop a support system early in the program, when they need it most. The demanding first-year curriculum translates into twenty-five to thirty-five hours of work a week. Wrote one MBA, "The workload comes in waves." As one might expect with the case-study method, the majority of students say it's important to do all or most of the assigned reading. Students say classmates are very smart. They also bring a wealth of work experience to their B-school studies. Students also praise Maryland for recruiting a high number of international students who broaden classroom discussions.

Students are competitive. But cooperation, not confrontation is the basic theme here. "This is a down-to-earth, non-cut-throat program where the importance of working effectively with others is stressed," explained sever collegial MBAs. Indeed, UM MBAs are an extremely happy friendly group of students. They really enjoy each other's company. The expect to stay friends long after graduation. And they report an active, involved social life. The B-school has just moved into brand-spanking-new, state-of-the-art facilities which boast an interactive ATT teaching computer lab. As for the University of Maryland, it's huge—21,500 students. The B-school keeps to itself and maintains a small-school feel. There is almost no on-campus housing, but students say off-campus digs are attractive and affordable. A university shuttle bus carts students on- and off-campus, but if you live too far away you may be in for some hassles. As one unhappy commuter groaned, "Commuting to campus from outside College Park is a nightmare." The Social Committee fills up everyone's calendar with weekly happy hours, football/lacrosse tailgate parties, and golf tournaments. A popular extracurricular is community service.

ADMISSIONS

According to the admissions office, your GMAT score, college GPA, and work experience are considered "very important." Your essays, interview, letters of recommendation, and extracurricular activities are considered "important."

Decisions are made on a rolling admissions basis. Applicants are notified of a decision eight weeks after the completed application has been received. Accepted applicants may defer admission for up to one year.

STUDENT'S OVERVIEW BOX

Overall Happiness

Academic Satisfaction

50   75   100%

■ Student Opinion □ National Average

FACULTY RATING

0 1 2 3 4 5 6 7 8 9 10

■ Student Opinion □ National Average

HITS AND MISSES

HITS
Accounting dept.
Marketing dept.
Library
Diverse work experience
Teamwork
Classmates are smart

MISSES
On-campus housing

APPLICANTS ALSO LOOK AT
U Virginia
UNC-Chapel Hill
Georgetown U.
George Washington U.
American U.
U Texas
U Penn
Penn State U.
New York University
U Pittsburgh
Columbia U.
Duke U.
Ohio State U.

FOR MORE INFORMATION, CONTACT:
Management and Business Affairs
Building RM 2308
College Park, MD 20742
(301) 405-2278

UNIVERSITY OF MASSACHUSETTS: AMHERST SCHOOL OF MANAGEMENT

ADMISSIONS FACTS

Type of school	Public

Demographics

No. of men	40
No. of women	30
No. of minorities	2
No. of int'l students	20

EQUAL TREATMENT GRAPH

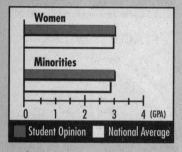

Women

Minorities

0 1 2 3 4 (GPA)

▬ Student Opinion   ☐ National Average

Admissions Statistics

Avg. GMAT	580
Avg. undergraduate GPA	3.2
Avg. age at entry	28
No. of applicants	310
No. accepted	75
No. enrolled	40

Deadlines and Notifications

Regular application	3/1
Regular notification	4/1
Special dates	N/A

Focus of Curriculum

General Management

Academic Specialties

Accounting, Finance

FINANCIAL FACTS

In-state tuition	$5,510
Out-of-state tuition	$11,300
On-campus housing	$2,116

ACADEMICS

If getting to know fellow classmates is of prime importance, the University of Massachusetts School of Management (SOM) is the program for you. Only forty students entered this year's class. In a day you can know everyone's name. SOM used to enroll ninety students a year, but down-sized the enrollment so the administration could perform a review of the program. There's no word on when they'll re-inflate to their previous size.

The SOM trains its students to be general managers. During the first year, students take eight required courses in the functional areas of business and have one elective. During the second year, students have up to four electives to specialize in fields such as accounting, finance, marketing, human resources management, and management information systems. Because courses emphasize quantitative methods, all students are expected to be proficient in math and to have previously taken a statistics and microeconomics course. In a unique program twist, students can supplement classwork with research and public service. "The curriculum is flexible with regard to independent studies and outside work," notes one MBA.

According to our survey, students report they feel well prepared in general management, quantitative methods, accounting, and finance. Perhaps because teamwork is emphasized, or because the whole school is no bigger than an extended study group, (in which the overwhelming majority elect to study) students also said they possess strong teamwork skills. They feel less confident of their computer and presentation skills. A sizable majority of those students surveyed said this program is meeting their academic expectations, an improvement from last year's more negative rating. However, new in the complaint department come these comments: "the facilities are mediocre," "the school lacks sophisticated technology necessary to teach in today's atmosphere," and "the administration needs to run the school more smoothly." Indeed, if a program drops two thirds of its capacity to focus its energies on an overhaul, you can be sure the entering forty are not going to be a top priority. On the other hand, students are guaranteed a high student/faculty ratio. And students here praise their professors for their teaching skills and accessibility: "The quality of teaching is quite good." The vast majority say taking time off to pursue a U Mass MBA is worth it. Considering the unmatched bargain in education U Mass offers, that may the understatement of this book: "Ninety-nine percent of full-time students are fully-funded. Tuition is waived and we receive a modest stipend. Where else can you get a graduate degree for that price - plus access to all the other graduate programs across the campus?"

PLACEMENT AND RECRUITING

The placement office conducts workshops on resume preparation and interview skills, and hosts recruiters from over a hundred firms. According to the students in our survey, the placement office is one notch above the bottom of the barrel. As one student rather politely put it, "Internship placement needs to improve." Students are equally unhappy about the range of companies recruiting on campus. However, not all the blame can be shunted on the placement office. With only forty students to pick from, most recruiters don't have the time or resources to visit this campus.

UNIVERSITY OF MASSACHUSETTS: AMHERST SCHOOL OF MANAGEMENT

STUDENT LIFE/CAMPUS

What it lacks in size this school makes up for in academic rigor. A demanding and challenging curriculum keeps most students buried in their books an average of twenty to thirty hours a week. Although the majority of students say it's important to do all or most of the reading, a significant number regularly skip or skim assignments. But students are certainly up to the workload; their peers consider them "extremely intelligent" and "professionally very diverse."

As for competition, students are keen on doing well, but not at the expense of a classmate. In such a tightly knit group, aggressive behavior would be unseemly. Students are friendly and team oriented. This intimacy breeds easy friendships that students expect to maintain long after graduation.

Amherst is located in a quintessential college town in suburban Massachusetts. Students report both on- and off-campus housing is more than adequate and affordable.

ADMISSIONS

The admissions office considers your work experience most important. After that, in descending order, are your GMAT score, letters of recommendation, college GPA, and essays. Extracurricular activities and interviews are not considered. It is recommended that applicants have completed courses in microeconomics and statistics before applying. Writes the school, "We are willing to make a number of academically 'high-risk' admissions decisions if we feel an individual has the potential to make a significant contribution to the business community. The strength of our program lies in its small size. Each student receives a great deal of individual attention from faculty and administrators."

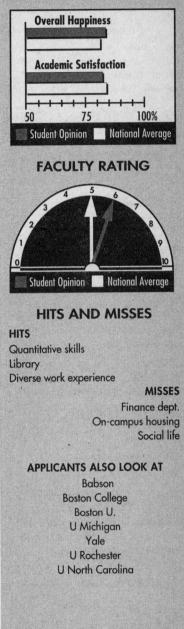

STUDENTS' OVERVIEW BOX

Overall Happiness

Academic Satisfaction

50   75   100%

■ Student Opinion   ■ National Average

FACULTY RATING

■ Student Opinion   ■ National Average

HITS AND MISSES

HITS
Quantitative skills
Library
Diverse work experience

MISSES
Finance dept.
On-campus housing
Social life

APPLICANTS ALSO LOOK AT
Babson
Boston College
Boston U.
U Michigan
Yale
U Rochester
U North Carolina

FOR MORE INFORMATION, CONTACT:
Masters Programs
School of Management
Amherst, MA 01003
(413) 545-5608

MASSACHUSETTS INSTITUTE OF TECH.: SLOAN SCHOOL OF MANAGEMENT

ADMISSIONS FACTS

Type of school	Private

Demographics

No. of men	390
No. of women	123
No. of minorities	75
No. of int'l students	194

EQUAL TREATMENT GRAPH

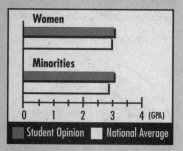

Women	
Minorities	

0   1   2   3   4 (GPA)

■ Student Opinion   □ National Average

Admissions Statistics

Avg. GMAT	650
Avg. undergraduate GPA	3.5/4.0
Avg. age at entry	28.5
No. of applicants	1,671
No. accepted	387
No. enrolled	298

Deadlines and Notifications

Regular application	2/3
Regular notification	3/31
Special dates	N/A

Focus of Curriculum

Specialized

Academic Specialties

International Business, Manufacturing/ Production, Transportation Logistics, Finance, Management of Technology, Information Technology

Joint Degrees

MS MGMT/Masters in Engineering

Special Programs

The MIT-Japan Program in Science, Technology and Management

FINANCIAL FACTS

In-state tuition	$21,690
Out-of-state tuition	$21,690
On-campus housing	$7,200

ACADEMICS

While few schools want to be stereotyped, at MIT the "techie" stereotype not only fits but is a badge worn with pride. The Sloan School has a well-deserved international reputation for excellence in quantitative and technical disciplines. Wrote one student, "MIT typically attracts a specific type of student—science, math, and engineering types—which enhances the school's position as a niche player. For people who know what they want to get out of school and have a focus on what they want to do jobwise, this is a great place." Proclaimed another, "MIT is very good at teaching you to think and understand the forces that drive business." Standout departments include finance, international studies, and operations management. In the latter area, students may participate in Leaders in Manufacturing, a twenty-four-month program whereby students earn a masters in both management and engineering. Here students spend six months interning with one of fourteen sponsoring industries, as for example Eastman Kodak or Boeing.

Like many B-schools, Sloan recently restructured its masters program and delivery. It kicks off with what students describe as a "fantastic" three-day, team-building seminar in Cape Cod (all expenses paid!). During the first semester, students are placed in tightly structured cohorts for the first semester and take all core courses together. However, after the first semester, students enjoy unprecedented flexibility. As one student wrote, "The level of freedom to design one's program of study is outstanding." Specialized management tracks, such as that for Product Development and Management, have also been introduced, and all students must now take a leadership/team building seminar led by second-years. Serious problems that still need to be addressed: teaching quality in the core is uneven, classrooms are crowded, the library needs improvement, and campus and learning facilities—from buildings to blackboards—are substandard. Some of the problems are due to the fact that the school has grown by thirty-five percent over the last seven years. To ease up crowded conditions, Sloan is building a new auditorium, classrooms, student lounge space, and a corporate information center. Summed up one MBA about comparisons to a too-close-for-comfort neighbor, "In contrast to Harvard, MIT Sloan is much more internationally focused, the students help each other, and the atmosphere is very antielitist. Practicality pervades everyone's thinking." But one MBA wanted this last word: "We make the most money—that's the bottom line! Who cares if we like it here or not?"

PLACEMENT AND RECRUITING

A summary of 1994 stats: 96% of the class had a job by graduation and the average starting salary was $68,000. Students who went into consulting and MIS snagged the highest salaries. Recruiters doing the most hiring were Hewlett-Packard, McKinsey, A.T. Kearney, Intel, Booz-Allen & Hamilton, Motorola, Citibank, Merrill Lynch, Lehman Brothers. Some MBAs feel Sloan needs a greater diversity of companies recruiting on campus—consulting and I-banking dominate. True, 35% of grads go into consulting. But Sloan's placement stats still beat out most other schools. And how many other schools can boast this roster of alums? Judy Lewent, CFO - Merck; John Reed, Chairman - Citicorp; Richard Avers, Chairman & CEO - Stanley Works.

MASSACHUSETTS INSTITUTE OF TECH.: SLOAN SCHOOL OF MANAGEMENT

STUDENT LIFE/CAMPUS

As one student put it, "Academics are very rigorous." Added another, "Students tend to take many courses and overwork themselves." Self-imposed or not, Sloan students report a killer-heavy workload. They hit the books an average of thirty-five to forty-five hours per week, making them one of the most hard-working, driven groups of all those surveyed in this book. Although the majority of students report it's important to do most of the reading/assignments, a large number say taking shortcuts is the key to survival. As for the pressure, it depends on whom you ask. Fifty percent said it's extremely intense, the other fifty percent said they can deal with it. Classes tend to be small. The majority of students work in study groups.

The often intense academic pressure does not corrupt an amiable atmosphere both in and out of the classroom. Sloan students rate themselves more cooperative than competitive. There are no fixed grading curves, no setting anyone apart for distinction based on grades alone. Wrote one, "Students can be difficult—but are basically laid back, warm, and friendly." Claimed another, "Students here help each other out." Partly because the environment is friendly, and partly because classmates have a lot in common, Sloan students like to hang out with each other and expect to maintain their strong friendships after graduation. As for the student body, students describe it as off-the-Richter-scale smart and professionally diverse.

Students agree Cambridge is a great town to live in. But MIT itself is not located in a pretty or residential section. Located only a couple of miles from resort-styled Harvard, the aesthetics of this campus make it seem a distant cousin. Offers this Sloanie, "It's not a pretty school, but the ugly buildings are full of life." New grad apartments have added to the on-campus housing capacity, but eighty percent of students live off-campus all over Boston and Cambridge. A nearby subway station provides access to the Boston area, although off-peak service is erratic and trains are slow. But they're safe. As for the social scene, it's dominated by the Graduate Management Society, which sponsors barbecues, weekly "Consumption Functions," and lots of international theme parties. But according to our survey, students aren't overwhelmed by their social life.

ADMISSIONS

Incoming students are expected to have completed calculus and economic theory before matriculating. If you wind up taking these courses at MIT, as one student put it, expect "math hell!"

Gaining admission to MIT is no walk in the park. From an applicant pool of over 1,500, Sloan fills a class just over strong. The admissions committee considers GMAT score, undergraduate GPA, quality of undergraduate school and coursework, recommendations, essays, and interview. The interview is recommended, and the admissions committee will have a written record of the meeting. And, yes, successful applicants to the Massachusetts Institute of Technology MBA program must have two semesters of college-level calculus.

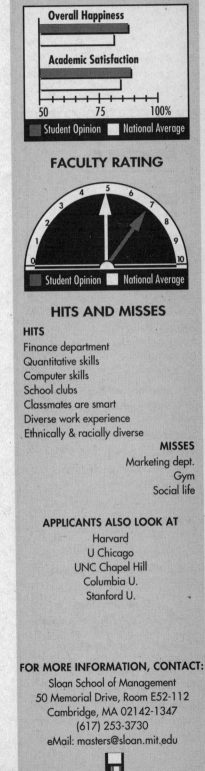

STUDENTS' OVERVIEW BOX

Overall Happiness

Academic Satisfaction

50   75   100%

■ Student Opinion   □ National Average

FACULTY RATING

■ Student Opinion   □ National Average

HITS AND MISSES

HITS
Finance department
Quantitative skills
Computer skills
School clubs
Classmates are smart
Diverse work experience
Ethnically & racially diverse

MISSES
Marketing dept.
Gym
Social life

APPLICANTS ALSO LOOK AT
Harvard
U Chicago
UNC Chapel Hill
Columbia U.
Stanford U.

FOR MORE INFORMATION, CONTACT:
Sloan School of Management
50 Memorial Drive, Room E52-112
Cambridge, MA 02142-1347
(617) 253-3730
eMail: masters@sloan.mit.edu

UNIVERSITY OF MICHIGAN: THE MICHIGAN BUSINESS SCHOOL

ADMISSIONS FACTS

Type of school	Public

Demographics

No. of men	624
No. of women	229
No. of minorities	242
No. of int'l students	126

EQUAL TREATMENT GRAPH

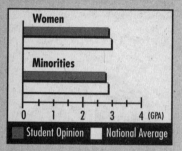

Admissions Statistics

Avg. GMAT	630
Avg. undergraduate GPA	3.3
Avg. age at entry	26
No. of applicants	2,700
No. accepted	N/A
No. enrolled	426

Deadlines and Notifications

Regular application	3/1
Regular notification	2–8 weeks
Special dates	12/1 (early decision)- early notification 2/15

Focus of Curriculum

General Management

Academic Specialties

General Management, Finance, Marketing, Accounting

Joint Degrees

Available with nineteen minorities, university departments/schools

Special Programs

Executive Skills, Workshops, International Studies, Center for International Business Education, International Exchange

FINANCIAL FACTS

In-state tuition	$12,359
Out-of-state tuition	$19,635
On-campus housing	$7,200

ACADEMICS

The University of Michigan has a well-deserved reputation as one of the best B-schools in the nation, boasting strong academic programs across the board and a general management focus. But Michigan has decided to go one step further and teach students what they'll need to know in the coming decades. Proclaimed one MBA, "It's very future oriented." The result is a new and progressive curriculum that incorporates interdisciplinary approaches, team-teaching, action-based learning, and '90s themes like global business and citizenship. A cornerstone of the new program is the Multidisciplinary Action Project (MAP), a six-week business apprenticeship that puts first-year students to work for real-life companies doing a multi-disciplinary exercise in process analysis. The MAP exercise often ends with a presentation to the CEO and other top executives. To judge by the comments in our survey, students are wild about MAP: "It offers the most excellent hands-on training I could ever conceive of." They're also wild about their dean, whom students credit with the trail-blazing direction of the school: "Michigan is incredibly innovative since Dean White came on board. His strong vision and high goals have produced many new programs that are making this school more competitive, attractive, and fun!" An added bonus: Students tell us insights and knowledge gained from Michigan's executive education programs (ranked by corporations as one of the best in the nation) quickly transfer to MBA classrooms and MBA executive skills workshops.

The school year kicks off with an orientation that emphasizes public service. Students take a field trip into Detroit to work on a community project. During the remainder of the year, through the Global Citizenship Program, students perform community work in teams. There are four academic "sessions" in the calendar year. During the second year, only one core course is required, the remainder being electives. Some of these may be taken in other university programs, such as the Law School and School of Natural Resources. Michigan also offers seventeen joint degree programs in fields such as law and music.

Students told us Michigan had prepared them well in subjects across the board. The one weak spot: operations. Complained one, "The program is too focused on 'soft' skills. There is too little emphasis on quantitative analysis." MBAs are unanimous, however, in their overall opinion of this program: This is a top-flight program more than meeting their needs.

PLACEMENT AND RECRUITING

Distinct to Michigan is a unique career tool called "M-Track." This state-of-the-art computer database allows students to network and access listings of open positions, recruiter presentations, and student/faculty information.

In 1994 360 companies recruited on-campus for permanent positions. Ninety-five percent of graduating MBAs reported accepting a position by July. Students received an average of two job offers each..

UNIVERSITY OF MICHIGAN: THE MICHIGAN BUSINESS SCHOOL

STUDENT LIFE/CAMPUS

The Michigan B-school boasts a sleek, modern, multi-building structure and amazing facilities. To foster strong academic and social relationships, Michigan sections the entering class of 400 into a more manageable size of six groups of roughly seventy students each. Students take all their first-year classes with their section mates, and travel in packs from classroom to classroom. Popular classes are reportedly easy to get into. Students endure a heavy workload and spend an average of thirty to forty hours a week studying. Despite this academic intensity, students report an "unpretentious environment" and "a positive, humble attitude." Students say their class-mates are competitive, extremely smart, very friendly and genuinely inter-ested in helping each other. Commented one MBA, "Lots of New York people who didn't get into Harvard or Wharton. Depending on your mood, it's either a plus or a minus."

As for Michigan's home town of Ann Arbor, commonly referred to as A2, students told us "it's the best place to go." Wrote one married MBA, "It's great for a family." About the only drawback is that "winters here are dismal." You'd better like football and basketball. Or at least have some Michigan spirit. "GO BLUE!" appeared several times on our survey ques-tionnaires. Always popular are the pre-game tailgate parties. In addition, an active student body get involved in intramural sports such as football, rac-quetball, and soccer. Two favorite events are the B-school Faculty Auction and the Spring Swing formal. Michigan offers more than 22 student clubs that focus on practical business issues. Whether it's arranging a panel discussion with Apple Computer founder Steven Jobs or organizing a fund-raiser for developing countries, students learn as much outside of the class-room as they do in it.

Students say, "The school spirit really takes you by storm and you feel that this place is home." Students also told us they appreciate and benefit from Michigan's diversity. If you're looking to broaden your experiences and go to school with a diverse and happily integrated student body, this is the place. This school attracts more minorities than any other B-school profiled in this book.

ADMISSIONS

According to the admissions office, the following criteria are considered: essays, college GPA, letters of recommendation, extracurricular activities, work experience, interview, and GMAT score. A college-level calculus course must be completed before enrollment. Applicants are strongly en-couraged to interview. The school asks applicants to note alumni ties in their applications, but does not reserve places in the class for those related to alumni. The school notes, "We do not use any 'formulas' or numerical cutoffs in admitting students. Because we use rolling admissions, there is an advantage to applicants who apply well before the March 1 deadline." Applications past the deadline are considered on a space-available basis. There is not a fixed allocation of space for in-state and out-of-state stu-dents.

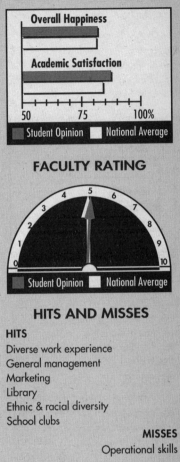

STUDENTS' OVERVIEW BOX

Overall Happiness

Academic Satisfaction

50 75 100%

Student Opinion   National Average

FACULTY RATING

Student Opinion   National Average

HITS AND MISSES

HITS
Diverse work experience
General management
Marketing
Library
Ethnic & racial diversity
School clubs

MISSES
Operational skills

APPLICANTS ALSO LOOK AT
Stanford U.
U Chocago
Northwestern
U Penn

FOR MORE INFORMATION, CONTACT:
Admissions Office
701 Tappan St.
Ann Arbor, MI 48109-1234
(313) 763-5796

UNIVERSITY OF MINNESOTA: CURTIS L. CARLSON SCHOOL OF MANAGEMENT

ADMISSIONS FACTS

Type of school	Public

Demographics

No. of men	188
No. of women	64
No. of minorities	28
No. of int'l students	42

EQUAL TREATMENT GRAPH

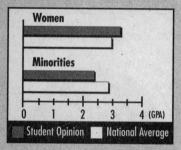

Women

Minorities

0   1   2   3   4 (GPA)

■ Student Opinion   □ National Average

Admissions Statistics

Avg. GMAT	580
Avg. undergraduate GPA	3.29
Avg. age at entry	28
No. of applicants	537
No. accepted	282
No. enrolled	97

Deadlines and Notifications

Regular application	April 1
Regular notification	4–6 weeks after deadline
Special dates	Dec. 1 for fellowship consideration

Focus of Curriculum

General Management with specialization

Academic Specialties

General Management, Information Systems

Special Programs

International Study in France, Germany, Sweden, Japan, Italy, Spain, Australia; International Management Exchange

FINANCIAL FACTS

In-state tuition	$8,268
Out-of-state tuition	$12,617
On-campus housing	$4,000

ACADEMICS

A big advantage of going to the Carlson School of Management is that it has close ties with the local Minnesota business community—a veritable hive of Fortune 500 companies. Through internships, field projects, and executive forums, students have extraordinary opportunities to learn by doing. Indeed, so many courses feature field work, at any given time Carlson MBAs are likely to be applying their skills in real-life corporate settings. This emphasis on both theory and application is one of the reasons the majority of students say taking off time to pursue a Carlson MBA is worth it. They also report Carlson has provided them a thorough and balanced B-school education.

Carlson has joined the ranks of other top B-schools by recently implementing a new, '90s curriculum. Students say because the program is in a state of flux, it's too soon to rate it. So far, "It's considerably better than the previous years." During the first year, students take an extremely structured series of core courses. These are integrated to reflect a cross-functional perspective. In addition, they take a lab in Managerial Communications, which provides students with personalized assessments of their oral and written communications skills and focuses on business writing and presentations. In the second year, students pursue a chosen field of study. They also take a fourteen-week field project—another chance to consult in one of those Minnesota companies.

The faculty here gets mixed reviews. Students give them good but not outstanding marks. In addition, there's a downside to going to a school that produces cutting edge research—many professors are holed up in their ivory towers. Students wish they had more interaction with them. As for their business training, students told us they feel reasonably well-prepared by their courses in marketing, operations, MIS, finance, and accounting. They gave themselves sky-high marks for their teamwork skills, but felt somewhat less confident of their quantitative and computer skills.

PLACEMENT AND RECRUITING

With the exception of a few B-schools, no group of MBAs reported they are satisfied with the services of career placement. But Carlson MBAs are particularly disappointed. According to our survey, the majority complain that the number and range of companies recruiting on-campus is inadequate. Explained one frustrated MBA, "Placement efforts seem to focus on regional area only." This won't be news to the school. They've already begun an internal audit and plan on making improvements soon.

UNIVERSITY OF MINNESOTA: CURTIS L. CARLSON SCHOOL OF MANAGEMENT

STUDENT LIFE/CAMPUS

Core courses have an average of fifty students each. Concentration courses are much smaller, fifteen to twenty per class. Currently, students report a very heavy workload. They say this has increased under the new curriculum, which compresses more learning into the calendar year. Relief comes in the form of study groups, which provide students academic as well as social support, and in skipping some of the work. A sizable number of students say it's not necessary to do all of the reading.

Like many small schools (roughly 115 in the entering class), Carlson provides its students a supportive learning environment. Students are non-competitive. They're extremely interested in helping each other. Perhaps because twenty-five percent of the student body is married, a not insignificant minority report they're not into hanging out with fellow MBAs. But this may just be the social climate here; fifty percent of the students we surveyed report a lackluster social scene. Of the professionally diverse student body, seventy percent have undergraduate degrees in areas other than business administration.

Currently the B-school is housed in several buildings shared with undergraduates and other departments. Students want improved facilities, as well as their own building. You ask—sometimes you get: Ground breaking for the new B-school is planned for 1994. As for residential housing, students say it's very affordable and very nice. Most opt for off-campus living in the nearby communities of Dinkytown and St. Paul. Many students share a duplex in one of the old divided homes on the lake. The MBA Association sponsors events such as intramural sports, barbecues, and a charity golf outing. Due to classless Fridays, every other Thursday is TGIT night.

ADMISSIONS

The admissions office considers your GMAT score, work experience, and college GPA most important. Then, in descending order, they consider your letters of recommendation, essays, and extracurricular activities. Applications are processed in semibatches. According to the school, "Applications are reviewed when they become complete. Those not offered admission at the time at which they are received are reviewed again within six weeks of the April 1st deadline." Students may defer admission for one year.

STUDENTS' OVERVIEW BOX

Overall Happiness

Academic Satisfaction

50   75   100%

Student Opinion   National Average

FACULTY RATING

Student Opinion   National Average

HITS AND MISSES

HITS
Location

MISSES
Quantitative skills
Ethnic & racial diversity
Placement

APPLICANTS ALSO LOOK AT
U Texas-Austin
U Iowa
U Chicago
Northwestern U.
U Illinois-Chicago
U Wisconsin-Madison
U Illinois-C.U.

FOR MORE INFORMATION, CONTACT:
Curtis L. Carson School of Management
271-19th Ave South
Minneapolis, MN 55455
(612) 624-0006

NEW YORK UNIVERSITY: LEONARD N. STERN SCHOOL OF BUSINESS

ADMISSIONS FACTS

Type of school	Private

Demographics

No. of men	N/A
No. of women	N/A
No. of minorities	N/A
No. of int'l students	N/A

EQUAL TREATMENT GRAPH

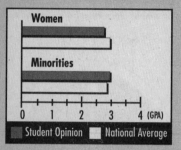

Women

Minorities

0   1   2   3   4 (GPA)

■ Student Opinion   □ National Average

Admissions Statistics

Avg. GMAT	N/A
Avg. undergraduate GPA	N/A
Avg. age at entry	N/A
No. of applicants	N/A
No. accepted	N/A
No. enrolled	N/A

Deadlines and Notifications

Regular application	N/A
Regular notification	N/A
Special dates	N/A

Focus of Curriculum

General Management

Academic Specialties

International Management, Finance, Information Systems

Joint Degrees

JD/MBA, MBA/MA in French studies, MBA/MA in Journalism, MBA/MA in Politics

FINANCIAL FACTS

In-state tuition	$19,500
Out-of-state tuition	$19,500
On-campus housing	$9,000

ACADEMICS

NYU's international management and finance departments are widely regarded as among the best in the country. With eighteen foreign exchange programs and international research centers of worldwide renown in their arsenal, the study of international business is especially strong. As for the finance department, one student wrote, "In interviews with financial services firms, a Stern finance major is on equal footing with students from Ivy League schools." But one student complained, "Finance is very good at NYU, but the other subjects are not taught as well." Noted another, "The school is too focused on churning out Wall Street finance types." However, one student advised, "NYU is ideal for someone with a liberal arts background in need of a formal quantitative base."

The first year consists of a prescribed program of eleven core courses in the functional areas of business. Because of the newly integrated curriculum, all have a global bent. Two minicourses are mandatory: ethics and management communication. A year-end capstone course, in the form of a team project, pulls together learning from all the core courses. The second year is more flexible—only two required courses: Legal, Social and Ethical Aspects of Business, and Business Strategy. Students take eight electives and declare a major, a double major, or even a co-major. For would-be-entrepreneurs, there are appealing courses from the Center for Entrepreneurial Studies. Particularly noteworthy is the Management Consulting Program, in which corporations such as Reebok, Campbell Soup, and IBM hire teams of students to do consulting work. Raved one student, "This is for course credit and a great real-life experience."

Equally impressive is the emphasis on environmental study. Several core marketing and product development courses integrate "environmental" concerns. The career placement office has even compiled a "green" directory of organizations looking for MBAs with an environmental orientation.

Overall, students we surveyed told us NYU had prepared them very well in the following areas: finance, accounting, general management, teamwork, and quantitative skills. Students reported weaker skills in marketing, operations, presentation/interpersonal, and computer skills. But students claim the marketing department is a rising star.

PLACEMENT AND RECRUITING

More than 250 corporations annually recruit Stern students, both on- and off-campus. In all, more than 5,000 interviews were held at Stern in 1990. Their 1993 placement rate was around eighty-seven percent.

Still, students in our survey said they weren't satisfied with the efforts of OCD. Complained one student, "The Placement Center could be a *lot*, *lot* better." Many students feel the companies come for the school, not because of the efforts of the placement center. On a more positive note, students were enthusiastic about the school's alumni, whom the majority of them contacted and found responsive. Reported one Stern MBA, "Access to alumni is very easy and very helpful."

NEW YORK UNIVERSITY: LEONARD N. STERN SCHOOL OF BUSINESS

STUDENT LIFE/CAMPUS

NYU boasts one of the largest international enrollments among B-schools—thirty percent! Unfortunately, only seventeen percent of the students are female. But according to one student, "The women are so tough, they demand more attention and respect than any group of women I've ever encountered!" NYU divides the entering class into "blocks" of about sixty students each who spend the first two semesters together. This creates a school within a school and allows students to develop the academic and social bonds early on.

"NYU is a great place to combine the merits of an outstanding university and the excitement of a cosmopolitan city," wrote one student. The social scene depends on the activities of the student-run clubs, which organize parties and outings. This being New York, there are a million things to do. Students cluster in small groups and hit the town.

Students describe a heavy workload and spend an average of twenty to thirty hours a week studying. Classes tend to be large, with an average of fifty to sixty students in each. Several students complained: "Too big classes, too many people, too much irrelevant material." Stern MBAs rate themselves as fairly competitive, but also willing to help each other. As for congeniality, NYU doesn't win any awards. While the majority of students say they enjoy hanging out with classmates, a surprisingly large number say they don't. The school is basically campusless, which causes students to feel detached from each other. Almost no one lives on-campus, and school housing is in scant supply. Priority is given to foreign students. Most would do better to locate their own digs in nearby Greenwich Village, Chelsea, or Tribeca. NYU is primarily a commuter school. Compounding this commuter feeling is NYU's huge part-time program—1,800 students who can easily switch to full-time status or vice versa. The total effect is a lack of the *esprit de corps* that fires up so many of the other B-schools.

But the campus is by no means without its merits. As one student cited, "The new Management Education Center building has enhanced the school greatly. It has state-of-the-art presentation equipment, comfortable lecture halls, and small meeting rooms. The new uptown location creates a much friendlier and collegiate atmosphere," although one student complained, "There is no adequate cafeteria on premises and no decent places to study in the building." This MBA should venture out of the facilities. Located in the heart of Greenwich Village, the immediate neighborhood boasts Chinese food, sushi, a street vendor's hot dog, pizza, and several diners.

ADMISSIONS

According to the admissions office, the following criteria are considered (in order of importance): essays, college GPA/transcript, letters of recommendation, extracurricular activities, work experience and GMAT scores. The interview is optional.

STUDENTS' OVERVIEW BOX

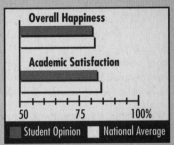

FACULTY RATING

HITS AND MISSES

HITS
Finance
Quantitative skills
Ethnic & racial diversity
New York City

MISSES
Marketing
Off-campus housing
Student community
Large classes

APPLICANTS ALSO LOOK AT
Columbia U.
Northwestern U.
Carnegie Mellon U.
U Connecticut

FOR MORE INFORMATION, CONTACT:
Stern School of Business
44-West 4th Street
New York, NY 10003
(212) 998-0900

UNIV. OF NORTH CAROLINA AT CHAPEL HILL: KENAN-FLAGLER BUSINESS SCHOOL

ADMISSIONS FACTS

Type of school	Public

Demographics

No. of men	291
No. of women	92
No. of minorities	48
No. of int'l students	48

EQUAL TREATMENT GRAPH

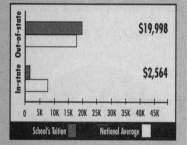

$19,998

$2,564

| 0 5K 10K 15K 20K 25K 30K 35K 40K 45K |

School's Tuition ▓ National Average ☐

Admissions Statistics

Avg. GMAT	622
Avg. undergraduate GPA	3.2
Avg. age at entry	27
No. of applicants	1,933
No. accepted	387
No. enrolled	196

Deadlines and Notifications

Regular application	3/1
Regular notification	4/29
Special dates	N/A

Focus of Curriculum

General Management

Academic Specialties

General Management

Joint Degrees

JD/MBA, MBA/MRP in Real Estate Development and Urban Planning, Master of Accounting

Special Programs

The Board of Visitors, The MBA Enterprise Corps, International Exchange, The Washington Campus

FINANCIAL FACTS

In-state tuition	$2,557
Out-of-state tuition	$10,092
On-campus housing	$6,300

ACADEMICS

Kenan-Flagler (KFBS) is one of the nation's most highly regarded state B-schools. Students say it's best "for those who want a broad perspective which is what most company's want." Backing this up is a rigorous program of academics.

KFBS's innovative curriculum focuses on business issues and problems, not functional areas,. The initial week of the first year sets the tone for the entire program. Through the combined efforts of the first-year faculty and corporate executives, students learn how the analytical and functional tools presented in the curriculum fit together. The curriculum is designed around seven-week modules ("mods"), four per year. The approach allows KFBS to offer a greater variety of topics—such as consulting or environmental issues—not possible under a semester system. Because the multi-functional courses cram so much learning into one program, students told us KFBS is not for lightweights. Wrote one, "We think our workload is heavier than that at most other top B-schools." Further, a student advised, "This school is great for people with nonbusiness backgrounds."

As one student put it, "Teamwork is the cornerstone of the school. You either like to work in teams or you learn to." To begin with, students are pre-assigned mandatory study groups organized around members' experience and backgrounds. Ninety-eight percent of the class also participates in the optional MBA Adventure, an Outward Bound-style exercise designed to enhance the team approach to problem solving. Again, during the fall, a two-day "Time Out for Team Building" exercise is held. But according to one MBA, "Teamwork is sometimes overemphasized. Sometimes you don't get enough of a chance to do individual work and develop individual skills.". As for the faculty, it's regarded as A+. Check out hot professors David Ravenscraf (microeconomics), David Hartzell (finance), and Robert Connolly (international finance and winner of the 1992 MBA teaching award). Students say, "the faculty are passionate about their teaching and consider the students their first priority, both in and out of the classroom."

Students raved about all the academic opportunities. Wrote one, "There are excellent opportunities to get in 'real' work situations—practicums, case development, consulting." For example, second-years participate in "The Art of Negotiation," a one-day workshop and role play. Electives feature student consulting projects to real companies. At less than $10,000 a year in tuition for out-of-state residents, happy KFBS students say this program offers "high value for the low money!" Summed up one, "If you're looking for a top-ten public university in the South, this is it."

PLACEMENT AND RECRUITING

In 1994, ninety percent of grads had a position within three months of graduation. Over 133 companies recruited on-campus. Those hiring the most MBAs: Merrill Lynch, Frito Lay, Citicorp, and Johnson & Johnson. Students here are renowned for their self-initiated "phonathon" to massive numbers of alumni for job leads. The majority of students reported they were only moderately satisfied with the career placement office. As for the range of companies recruiting, the typical response was that it's okay, not great. Students wish there were more technology-oriented companies recruiting.

UNIV. OF NORTH CAROLINA AT CHAPEL HILL: KENAN-FLAGLER BUSINESS SCHOOL

STUDENT LIFE/CAMPUS

Core classes average sixty students per class, electives thirty-five. Grading is based on a combination of tests, papers, class participation, and project-based work. As one student wrote, "UNC is about cooperation; the cut-throat tactics that exist at some schools are not seen here." Indeed, "The quality of your team can affect your grades." Students reported classmates are extremely smart and have varied and interesting work experiences. A typical comment was, "Great combination of appropriate competitiveness and true friendship of this school will lead us to excellent managers." There are complaints about the school's push for diversity: "I think minorities are given overly favorable treatment by the school. There is a big emphasis on diversity, some of it is fake." The facilities don't have many fans either, as one MBA illustrated by saying, "The only bummer is that we're waiting for the new building to be constructed. Our relatively modest structure causes this school to be underrated." Otherwise students describe "an ideal college setting." UNC/Chapel Hill boasts a stately, tree-lined campus and buildings listed with the National Historic Register. Because Chapel Hill is a university town with extensive apartment developments, it's a renter's market. Public bus lines make off-campus living especially convenient.

Sports, particularly the Tarheels basketball team, are popular. Students describe an active student community. There's a "high level of participation, involvement in school functions, and a commitment to community service." The annual mini-biathlon sponsored by the MBA Student Association raises thousands of dollars for charities, as does a student golf tournament at the prestigious Governor's Club course. The social scene is active and extends into town on the weekends. A short road trip away are coastal beaches to the east, the Appalachian mountains to the north and west. Students' relations with the administration are reportedly excellent. Shared one MBA, "I've been impressed by the impact student's suggestions have had on the curriculum and administrative processes in a very short time."

ADMISSIONS

According to the admissions department, "Evidence of strong leadership capabilities" is considered most important. After that, the following criteria are weighed equally: essays, work experience, college GPA, GMAT scores, letters of recommendation, interview, and extracurricular activities. The admissions office notes that "because of our large applicant pool, applicants are encouraged to apply as early as possible." Only seventeen percent of those who apply are accepted, establishing KFSB as one of the five most selective schools profiled in this book. Applicants are strongly encouraged to schedule an on-campus interview, sit in on classes, and meet with current MBA students.

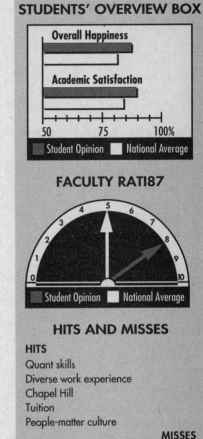

STUDENTS' OVERVIEW BOX

Overall Happiness

Academic Satisfaction

50   75   100%

■ Student Opinion   □ National Average

FACULTY RATI87

■ Student Opinion   □ National Average

HITS AND MISSES

HITS
Quant skills
Diverse work experience
Chapel Hill
Tuition
People-matter culture

MISSES
Marketing
Ethnic & racial diversity
Facilities

APPLICANTS ALSO LOOK AT
Duke U.
U Virginia

FOR MORE INFORMATION, CONTACT:
Anne-Marie Summers
CB# 3490, Carroll Hall UNC-CH
Chapel Hill, NC 27599-3490
(919) 962-2395

NORTHEASTERN UNIV. GRADUATE SCHOOL OF BUSINESS ADMINISTRATION

ADMISSIONS FACTS

Type of school	Private

Demographics

No. of men	57%
No. of women	43%
No. of minorities	15%
No. of int'l students	40%

EQUAL TREATMENT GRAPH

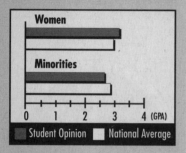

Admissions Statistics

Avg. GMAT	range 440–690
Avg. undergraduate GPA	2.5–4.0
Avg. age at entry	26
No. of applicants	801
No. accepted	483
No. enrolled	269

Deadlines and Notifications

Regular application	5/1
Regular notification	1 month
Special dates	N/A

Focus of Curriculum

General Management

Academic Specialties

Finance, Accounting

Special Programs

Part-time MBA Program; Executive MBA Program

FINANCIAL FACTS

In-state tuition	$16,800
Out-of-state tuition	$16,800
On-campus housing	$6,500

ACADEMICS

A hallmark of Northeastern's business program is that it provides opportunities to combine paid professional work with study. There are five different MBA programs: a part-time program, an Executive MBA, the two-year full-time MBA, the Cooperative Education MBA, and the High Technology MBA. The High Tech MBA is the first of its kind in the nation. In this program, technical professionals take classes one night a week and on alternate Saturdays, and focus on management in the high-tech industry. Perhaps the most popular and unique of the five programs is the Cooperative Education MBA which begins in January and June. It offers students paid MBA-level employment for six months—and the chance to earn over $15,000—during twenty-one months of accelerated study. Raved one student, "This is an excellent opportunity for those who continue straight from undergrad. I bolstered my resume by gaining MBA-level experience with a Fortune 500 Company!" Especially noteworthy is the MS-MBA in accounting, which enjoys corporate support from the major accounting firms. The Coop MBA boasts a 100 percent placement rate for its most recent classes students.

Northeastern's MBA programs offer generalist perspectives and contain a core of the basic business subjects. Electives are used to broaden or deepen the course of study. Prior to class, a three-day residency jump-starts the programs with a team-building exercise and a foray into case study. Among the extras: an executive mentoring program that allows students to form personal relationships with CEOs and the like.

Northeastern's generalist formula appears to work. The overwhelming majority of MBAs say this program is worth the investment of time and money. They also say it's meeting their academic expectations. Reported one, "The MBA program is excellent and very practical—coursework involves lots of 'real life' examples and cases." Wrote another, "We are constantly reminded that there is a balance between analysis and good instinct, and analysis and action. We are better prepared to face the reality of business life than most Ivy Leaguers!" Students feel well prepared by their studies in finance, accounting, general management, and quantitative methods. But close to fifty percent feel far less confident of their marketing and computer skills. Other weak spots—students say it can be difficult to get into popular courses. They also wish the school ran more efficiently and the faculty were more consistent. Students gave professors higher marks for their wide availability after class. Northeastern also earns high marks for its equitable treatment of women and minorities.

PLACEMENT AND RECRUITING

Students feel the Office of Career Development and Placement is long on talk and short on delivery. They criticize it for providing them minimal on-campus recruiting and few leads. For some extra help, students suggest you head over to the university's main career office in Ryder Hall. Here are 1994 stats: Over 100 companies recruited on-campus. Sixty-six percent of grads had a job by graduation; eighty-one percent three months later. The majority of students go into finance and consulting. The average starting salary is $39,789. The major recruiters: Texas Instrument, Fidelity, Kraft, Ocean Spray. Alumni role models: Dennis J. Picard, Chairman and CEO, Raytheon Co; J. Philip Johnson, President and CEO, CARE; Richard Egan, Chairman of the Board, EMC Corporation.

NORTHEASTERN UNIV. GRADUATE SCHOOL OF BUSINESS ADMINISTRATION

STUDENT LIFE/CAMPUS

Northeastern relies on the case study method, which tends to produce late-night, intensive study sessions. Students here study an average of twenty-five to thirty-five hours a week. Observed one student, "Since this school is quarterly, the workload is heavier than at other schools which are semesterly (as compared to my friends in B-school elsewhere.)" The vast majority report there are few corners to cut; it's important to do all or most of the assigned reading. Depending on the program you're in, the pressure ranges from manageable to formidable. Fortunately, study groups play an integral part in case preparation. Typically, students analyze cases on their own, then meet to share ideas and prepare comments for the next day's class. Class participation counts for twenty to forty percent of the grade. Classes are generally kept to twenty-five to fifty students.

Students are fairly competitive, but rarely into one-upmanship. Cooperation is the accepted mode of behavior. Northeastern MBAs say the student body is both professionally and racially diverse, a claim that most B-schools can't make. Wrote one student, "I'm amazed by the diversity of the students, which has changed my opinion of B-schools for the better. This is how it should be." They also say fellow students are bright. However, a sizable number report that classmates aren't the type of people they like to hang with. In all likelihood, this has to do with the influx of part- and semi-full-time attendees who tend to be focused on their own thing. Still, the majority report an active social life.

B-school classes are held in Dodge Hall, a recently unveiled, gleaming new facility which features state-of-the-art classrooms, high-tech computer facilities, a student lounge, case rooms, and a modern Career Center office. As for Boston, everyone loves this preppy East Coast city (but finding affordable housing is difficult, and almost no one lives on campus). For extracurriculars, the MBA Association sponsors corporate speaker events, as well as barbecues. Students advised: "This is a great school if one gets involved."

ADMISSIONS

The admissions office considers the following criteria (in no particular order): essays, college GPA, letters of recommendation, work experience, and GMAT scores. The office of admissions notes, "Decisions are made by small committees after an application has been read by at least three professionals who independently assess several factors: academic preparation (GMAT scores and transcripts), maturity, motivation, and direction (essays, recommendations, and work experience). These factors are considered equally important."

STUDENT'S OVERVIEW BOX

Overall Happiness

Academic Satisfaction

50   75   100%

Student Opinion   National Average

FACULTY RATING

Student Opinion   National Average

HITS AND MISSES

HITS
Ethnic & racial diversity
Location
Small classes
Library

MISSES
Marketing
Student community
Placement
On-campus housing

APPLICANTS ALSO LOOK AT
Boston U.
Boston College

FOR MORE INFORMATION, CONTACT:
Graduate School of
Business Administration
350 Dodge Hall
360 Huntington Ave.
Boston, MA 02115
(617) 373-2714

NORTHWESTERN UNIV.: J. L. KELLOGG GRADUATE SCHOOL OF MANAGEMENT

ADMISSIONS FACTS

Type of school	Private

Demographics

No. of men	833
No. of women	344
No. of minorities	177
No. of int'l students	294

EQUAL TREATMENT GRAPH

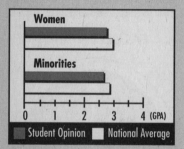

Admissions Statistics

Avg. GMAT	640
Avg. undergraduate GPA	3.3
Avg. age at entry	27
No. of applicants	4,393
No. accepted	970
No. enrolled	582

Deadlines and Notifications

Regular application	March 30
Regular notification	May 30
Special dates	Dec. 1(early decision)

Focus of Curriculum

General Management, students may select major(s)

Academic Specialties

General Management, Nonprofit Management, Transportation Management, Production Management, Health Care Management, International Business, Entrepreneurship

Joint Degrees

MM/JD, MM/MD, MM/MS in nursing at Rush University, Master of Management in Manufacturing

Special Programs

Pre-enrollment math "Prep"; Foreign study in nine countries

FINANCIAL FACTS

In-state tuition	$19,698
Out-of-state tuition	$19,698
On-campus housing	$7,812

ACADEMICS

Kellogg, an extremely popular B-school in the last five years, offers the Master of Management (MM) degree. Students pursue a general management curriculum and "specialize in one or more of the professional fields: general business, public and nonprofit, health services, transportation, and real estate management." First-years take nine required core courses and three electives. Students who have completed prior study in a core course may apply for a waiver. Students with enough prior coursework may even complete their MBAs in one year. Group work dominates everything at Kellogg—studying, classwork, even social life—giving students their well-earned reputation as team players, although a common complaint was that the "teamwork thing" gets tiresome. Kellogg has a seemingly unshakable reputation as a marketing school, although more students enroll for finance classes than any other department. But the program actually has many other strong suits, notably: transportation management, real estate management, public and nonprofit management, and manufacturing. Tons of international business courses and nine foreign study programs in Europe and Thailand make the study of international business a priority. An exciting new area of formal study is entrepreneurship. And students rave about the MMM program, designed primarily for engineers who are in manufacturing/operations.

Kellogg has a reputation of being an easy school. Students describe the workload as only moderately heavy; the majority spend an average of twenty to thirty hours per week studying, a leisurely pace by top B-school standards. Claimed one student, "People complain that Kellogg is too easy, but it can be as challenging as you want it to be. I took several five-course loads and am planning to take only three a couple of times just to enjoy life." Added another, "Even though you don't have to work as hard here as you do at other B-schools, most people do. Students are high achievers." The academic year at Kellogg is divided into three quarters. Most classes are kept to twenty-five to fifty students. The first year kicks off with Conceptual Issues in Management (CIM), a week-long orientation organized by returning second- years; CIM features get-to-know-you, teamwork exercises but, thankfully, no high-anxiety ropes courses. Faculty and administration come out to press the flesh and greet new students. Overall, students said they were moderately satisfied with their quantitative and computer skills. But on the plus side, they said they "have a lot of say or control in how the school is run. This is very good—and unique." As for their profs, students rated them as good, but this rating falls well below the ratings faculty received at comparable schools. Most of the less than eloquent teaching occurs in core courses. On a happier note, students said faculty are very accessible.

PLACEMENT AND RECRUITING

More than 300 companies recruit on-campus. As for placement rates, in 1993 more than eighty-seven percent of the graduates had reported placement three months after graduation. Students are happy with the quality and number of companies recruiting on-campus and satisfied with the Office of Career Development itself.

NORTHWESTERN UNIV.: J. L. KELLOGG GRADUATE SCHOOL OF MANAGEMENT

STUDENT LIFE/CAMPUS

Like many schools, Kellogg uses sectioning to foster social and academic relationships. The 440 entering students are divided into eight sections, creating a "homeroom" of about fifty-five students each. This lasts for the fall quarter only. After that, disbanded sectionmates keep in touch via numerous planned events.

Reported one MBA, "Excellent classroom interaction and dynamics." But in the complaint department, students moaned, "Emphasis on grades is somewhat excessive. A graduate school should be more *professional*," and "Kellog is not internationally inclined. Many students are more insular than I would have expected from such a top-tier school."

Much of the social scene revolves around activities successfully sponsored by the Graduate Management Association (GMA). These range from the academic (they compile quarterly teacher-course evaluations) to the social (weekly Friday afternoon beer bashes and parties like the Halloween Bash). The GMA also coordinates Kellogg's two largest social events: the Charity Ball in February and the Black Tie Spring Fling. Advised one MBA, "Time management is essential due to the number of clubs, social activities, the job search, and academic load." Explained others, "This is a small community, you're under a microscope," and "Social life centers around alcohol." The Northwestern campus itself is beautiful, located along a half-mile stretch of Lake Michigan, twelve miles from downtown Chicago in the suburb of Evanston.

On-campus housing is fair, with space available to 250 single students and fifty apartments for the wedded.

Students say, "Meeting people at Kellogg is an education in itself. People are amazingly friendly, helpful, and smart." More than one enthusiastic student wrote, "I love it here!" The atmosphere is midwestern laid back and "nurturing." Shark alert: Students who enjoy the rigor of a competitive environment might be better off elsewhere. Then again, if they transferred they might not be able to say, "I'm having much more fun than my friends at Harvard Business School and have no fewer job offers." Well, maybe—on average, Harvard MBAs are placed sooner and earn more. But one Kellogg student says the bottom line is this: "It's getting tougher to separate the people who really want to be here from the people who apply because of the school's ranking."

ADMISSIONS

According to the Kellogg admissions office, your GPA, GMAT score, essays, work experience, extracurricular activities, recommendations and interviews (which are required) are all "equally important." GMAT scores of applicants are typically high, undergrad grades are strong, and applicants have several years of impressive work experience. Applications are reviewed in rounds. As for when to apply, applicants are advised, "The earlier the better." Admission deferrals are considered on a case-by-case basis, but professional circumstances may be considered.

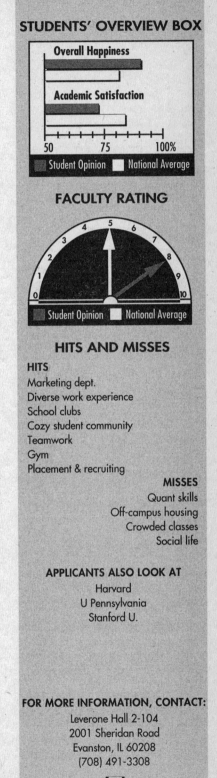

STUDENTS' OVERVIEW BOX

Overall Happiness

Academic Satisfaction

50   75   100%

Student Opinion   National Average

FACULTY RATING

Student Opinion   National Average

HITS AND MISSES

HITS
Marketing dept.
Diverse work experience
School clubs
Cozy student community
Teamwork
Gym
Placement & recruiting

MISSES
Quant skills
Off-campus housing
Crowded classes
Social life

APPLICANTS ALSO LOOK AT
Harvard
U Pennsylvania
Stanford U.

FOR MORE INFORMATION, CONTACT:
Leverone Hall 2-104
2001 Sheridan Road
Evanston, IL 60208
(708) 491-3308

UNIVERSITY OF NOTRE DAME COLLEGE OF BUSINESS ADMINISTRATION

ADMISSIONS FACTS

Type of school   Private

Demographics

No. of men	206
No. of women	64
No. of minorities	17
No. of int'l students	62

EQUAL TREATMENT GRAPH

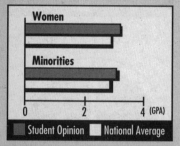

Women

Minorities

0   2   4 (GPA)

■ Student Opinion ■ National Average

Admissions Statistics

Avg. GMAT	557
Avg. undergraduate GPA	3.06
Avg. age at entry	24.8
No. of applicants	400
No. accepted	N/A
No. enrolled	106

Deadlines and Notifications

Regular application	5/13
Regular notification	4 weeks
Special dates	5/13 (early decision)
	replies early to mid Dec.

Focus of Curriculum

General Management, Students can specialize

Academic Specialties

General Management

Joint Degrees

JD/MBA

Special Programs

The London and Santiago Program: Notre Dame has its own campus and faculty in the heart of each city. The 3-Semester Taxation Program

FINANCIAL FACTS

In-state tuition	$16,400
Out-of-state tuition	$16,400
On-campus housing	$4,150

ACADEMICS

Notre Dame offers two MBA programs: the traditional two-year program and an accelerated three-semester MBA. The two-year program is "designed for students with little or no academic background in business." Students in this program must have completed a calculus and/or advanced algebra class prior to matriculation. First-years in this program take twelve required core courses. Second-years have flexibility and tailor coursework to their career goals.

The three-semester MBA is designed for students who hold an undergraduate degree in business. This program kicks off with a nine-week summer semester in which students attend review sessions of the courses in the first year of the two-year MBA program. After completing these sessions, which are graded, students join the second years in the other program. But this doesn't always work. Reported one student, "There are two flavors here—two-year and twelve-month. The school promotes them as one integrated program, but competition and animosity between the two can be high." A few students complained about the three-semester program itself: "The review sessions cram information down your throat. You don't learn—you survive." Still, many others were satisfied. Wrote one, "It provides an excellent opportunity to take time out from your profession and look at things from a new perspective. I would highly recommend the program."

Overall, students gave good marks to both programs for the rigor of academics. Professors are widely regarded as "excellent" and "accessible." Students appreciated the international focus in the curriculum, the opportunities for foreign study, and Notre Dame's intensive language classes. Over twenty percent of the student body is foreign, further promoting the international perspective. Group work is standard practice; team projects make up many of the class assignments. Given Notre Dame's Catholic tenor, a huge emphasis is on ethics, which is featured in several stand-alone courses.

PLACEMENT AND RECRUITING

Ninety-five firms recruited on campus last year. In June 1993, eighty percent of all graduating students had secured a job within three months after graduation. Leading recruiters were Arthur Andersen, Ford, Andersen Consulting, Proctor & Gamble, Ford Motor Company, and National Bank of Detroit.

Students were fierce in their criticism of the placement center, firing off comments like, "Employers come for the undergraduates, not the MBAs!" and "They do nothing." Students are optimistic, however, that things will improve under new placement director Joyce Manthey. Said one student, "They've made great strides and are positioning themselves to do better." Students absolutely raved about the alumni network. "I have contacted a number of alumni in very senior positions and all of them have offered more help than I could ever have asked for." One student put it more bluntly, "Alumni are *everything*; don't even bother going to the placement office."

UNIVERSITY OF NOTRE DAME COLLEGE OF BUSINESS ADMINISTRATION

STUDENT LIFE/CAMPUS

Like their undergrad counterparts, Notre Dame MBAs enjoy their football games and sports. Students told us they have a great social life. Planned activities are organized by the MBA Student Association and include welcome-back parties, football tailgaters, student/faculty mixers, the Christmas Dance and the Spring Formal. Community service projects (a natural extracurricular at this ethics-heavy school) include the Urban Plunge, Big Brothers/Sisters program, and a food drive at Thanksgiving. Student clubs such as the Marketing Club and Technology Group allow students to organize networking events such as career nights and executive visits. Students also enjoy the small school environment (the student body numbers only 500) where "a family atmosphere pervades everything." Raved one MBA, "The environment is not competitive. Everyone helps each other through the program." However, complaints about the facilities and the administration were common. Respondents wrote, "The school's dedication to the B-school is suspect," "the MBA administration is pathetic," and "the administration focuses on undergrad hand holding." There seems to be a link between the problems with the administration and a lack of improvement in problem areas. More than one student said the typical response to suggestions was, "We don't have the money" or "Wait for the new building" (completion date: 1995). Still, one student's remarks typified the prevalent attitude here: "I chose the school for where it's going and what it will become. A $50-million new building with library will create real confidence and a new identity." Help is on the way, but not soon enough for some students. In the meantime, though, students will continue to enjoy each other: "Things are intimate here; you really get to know your professors and classmates."

A note on housing: On-campus digs are available in a new modern graduate complex. There's a married student complex, but at present demand is greater than supply. Most folks head off-campus, where housing is more plentiful. Campus parking is available at a nominal fee.

ADMISSIONS

The admissions committee considers the following criteria (not necessarily in order of importance): college GPA, GMAT scores, extracurricular activities, letters of recommendation. According to the admissions office, "Our criteria are not weighted. We prefer, but do not require, work experience. An undergraduate business degree is required for our three-semester program, but there are no specific curricular requirements for our two-year MBA. We highly recommend interviews; we conduct interviews at all the United States MBA Forum sites, as well as schedule on-campus interviews, followed by a class and tour, if requested. Applicants should choose their recommendations carefully. Family, friends and colleagues should be avoided. Supervisors and managers are preferred for those applicants with work experience; if still in school, faculty members or supervisors from internships are appropriate." Students are advised to apply as early as possible and to take the GMAT in October.

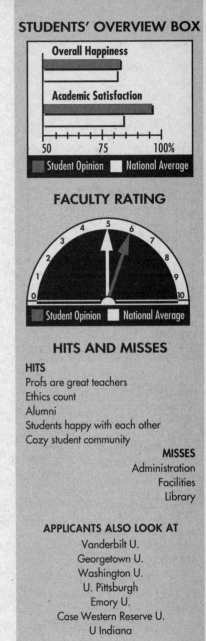

STUDENTS' OVERVIEW BOX

Overall Happiness

Academic Satisfaction

50   75   100%

Student Opinion   National Average

FACULTY RATING

Student Opinion   National Average

HITS AND MISSES

HITS
Profs are great teachers
Ethics count
Alumni
Students happy with each other
Cozy student community

MISSES
Administration
Facilities
Library

APPLICANTS ALSO LOOK AT
Vanderbilt U.
Georgetown U.
Washington U.
U. Pittsburgh
Emory U.
Case Western Reserve U.
U Indiana

FOR MORE INFORMATION, CONTACT:
MBA Admissions
110A Hurley
Notre Dame, IN 46556
(219) 631-8488
FAX (219) 631-8800

OHIO STATE UNIVERSITY COLLEGE OF BUSINESS

ADMISSIONS FACTS

Type of school	Public

Demographics

No. of men	154
No. of women	76
No. of minorities	27
No. of int'l students	61

EQUAL TREATMENT GRAPH

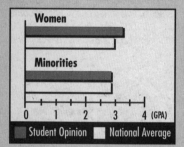

■ Student Opinion	□ National Average

Admissions Statistics

Avg. GMAT	608
Avg. undergraduate GPA	3.23
Avg. age at entry	27
No. of applicants	777
No. accepted	346
No. enrolled	113

Deadlines and Notifications

Regular application	6/1
Regular notification	rolling
Special dates	N/A

Focus of Curriculum

General Management

Academic Specialties

Finance, Real Estate, Transportation, Logistics

Special Programs

Business Solution Team (BST); Student Investment Management (SIM); Executive Luncheon Series; Foreign Study

FINANCIAL FACTS

In-state tuition	$4,842
Out-of-state tuition	$12,000
On-campus housing	$5,354

ACADEMICS

Ohio State has a well-deserved reputation as one of the best B-schools in the country. To ensure that entering students begin on equal footing and can tackle this rigorously quantitative program, a pre-enrollment program provides students a review of skills in accounting and number-crunching. The school also offers students three computer literacy modules. The first of these takes place a week before classes begin and focuses on hardware, operating systems and word processing.

The first-year core curriculum is highly structured. In true '90s style, courses are tightly integrated and feature group projects. But this is basically a rigorous, meat-and-potatoes program. The second year is extremely flexible and devoted to specialization. Operations and Logistics Management, Finance, and Real Estate are reportedly excellent departments. Wrote one student, "The first year provides a solid grounding in the fundamental concepts. The second year is more interesting and practical." Said another, "I will not be competent in all of the functional areas—but I will be competent in my areas of concentration." Apparently this is so for many students. Ohio MBAs report uneven skills in several areas. The overwhelming majority of students feel well-trained in finance, general management, operations, and quantitative methods. This is evidenced by their success in running and managing $5 million of the university's endowment. MBAs participating in the Student Investment Management Program boast a portfolio growth of over $2 million in just two years. They also give themselves sky-high marks for teamwork which the program is obviously successful at teaching. A sizable number report they're less than confident about their abilities in marketing.

Regardless of their own academic strengths and weaknesses, students give their professors good grades for their teaching. Explained one MBA, "During the first year, half of the teachers are very good to stellar. During the second year, this increases to three fourths of the faculty." As for accessibility, with a student-to-faculty ratio of 8:1, students report they get plenty of individual attention from professors. According to one MBA, "They even participate in student events."

PLACEMENT AND RECRUITING

The Career Development Office works with other MBA placement offices to coordinate the Big Ten job fairs in major U.S. cities and participate in the MBA Consortium held in Chicago. Still, like the students at most B-schools, Ohio MBAs say it isn't enough. One student's comments seemed to typify the prevalent feeling here: "The quality of companies recruiting on campus needs to improve. "Still, students say there are opportunities to network: "The local business community is very receptive to student requests for participation in speeches and luncheons." In 1994, 110 companies recruited on-campus. Eighty-seven percent of grads had an offer by graduation; ninety-eight within three months of that date. The average starting salary was $43,500. Making the most offers: Andersen Consulting, BankOne, the Limited, AT&T, Caterpillar Logistics, Citibank, CompuServe, General, Huntington Bank, NBD Bank.

OHIO STATE UNIVERSITY COLLEGE OF BUSINESS

STUDENT LIFE/CAMPUS

Students report a heavy workload and moderate to high anxiety levels, although one MBA qualifies this: "A great deal of the pressure is self-imposed." Self-imposed or not, students here study hard. They hit their books an average of thirty to thirty-five hours a week and do all or most of the required reading. As one might expect, the result of this intensity is that students are fairly competitive. But according to our survey, they're also "team oriented and friendly." Students want to succeed, but not at the expense of a classmate. As one student put it, "One of the benefits of going to a small school (only 130 students in each class), is everyone knows each other and there is a supportive atmosphere." This also extends to the social scene. Raved one MBA, "All the students are friends and go out together frequently."

A favorite watering hole is Street Scenes. Extracurricular activities include whitewater rafting and ski trips. Student clubs such as Women in Business, the Black MBA Association, and the MBA Council offer career and networking activities. One of the most popular events is an annual MBA/corporate golf day, in which a foursome of executives and students share a game of golf. Reported one student, "The golf facilities are excellent." Students are less pleased with the school's facilities. Most agreed with the MBA who said they're "horrible." But a new $62 million B-school complex is in the works and should go a long way toward creating a campus befitting a top school. One student has even higher hopes: "Once the new facility is built, I expect the MBA program to be the best in the nation." Fortunately, students don't have to wait that long to find decent housing. Both on- and off-campus, accommodations are affordable, available, and attractive. The majority of students opt to live off-campus in shared apartments in Columbus. Several students alluded to "a feeling of excitement here" and told us, "The program is on the move, trying to implement changes that will improve the program." Some of the changes may come in the form of a revamped curriculum, which is currently under review. Some of the changes may be administrative. Students said the school needs to be run more efficiently and the library needs a facelift.

ADMISSIONS

The admissions office at Ohio State considers your managerial/leadership potential most important. The school then considers, in descending order of importance, your GMAT scores, college GPA, work experience, letters of recommendation, essays, and extracurricular activities. Decisions are made on a rolling admissions basis. The school adds, "Our self-completing application allows applicants to manage their files. Once they submit a completed application, an admission decision will be sent to them within four weeks. Early application completion is strongly recommended."

STUDENTS' OVERVIEW BOX

Overall Happiness

Academic Satisfaction

50   75   100%

■ Student Opinion   □ National Average

FACULTY RATING

■ Student Opinion   □ National Average

HITS AND MISSES

HITS
Finance
Operations/logistic management
Ethnic & racial diversity
School clubs
Tuition
Student community

MISSES
Placement
Facilities

APPLICANTS ALSO LOOK AT
U Pennsylvania
U Michigan
Indiana U.
U Texas-Austin
Case Western Reserve U.
U Virginia
U Pittsburgh

FOR MORE INFORMATION, CONTACT:
MBA Programs
Hagerty Hall
1775 College Rd.
Columbus, OH 43210
(614) 292-8511
eMail: cobgrad@ohio-state.edu

UNIVERSITY OF PENNSYLVANIA: THE WHARTON SCHOOL GRADUATE DIVISION

ADMISSIONS FACTS

Type of school	Private

Demographics

No. of men	N/A
No. of women	N/A
No. of minorities	N/A
No. of int'l students	N/A

EQUAL TREATMENT GRAPH

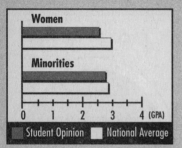

Admissions Statistics

Avg. GMAT	N/A
Avg. undergraduate GPA	N/A
Avg. age at entry	N/A
No. of applicants	N/A
No. accepted	N/A
No. enrolled	N/A

Deadlines and Notifications

Regular application	N/A
Regular notification	N/A
Special dates	N/A

Focus of Curriculum

Specialized, with a major declared

Academic Specialties

Finance, Marketing, Accounting

Joint Degrees

MBA/JD, MBA/MD, MBA/DMD-dental, MBA/MSE Engineering

Special Programs

Wharton's Sol C. Snider Entrepreneurial Center. The Lauder Institute's Program in International Studies: Paid consulting available, Summer Pre-enrollment "Prep," Foreign Study

FINANCIAL FACTS

In-state tuition	$21,000
Out-of-state tuition	$21,000
On-campus housing	$7,982

ACADEMICS

Long considered a bastion of finance, Wharton now boasts first-rate academics in general management, marketing, accounting, real estate, entrepreneurship, nonprofit business management, insurance/risk management, and business law. Equally important is the emphasis on global study. This is supported by an international student body (almost thirty-two percent), international courses, two international joint-degree programs, and a global immersion program in Russia, China, Japan, or Brazil. Courses at Wharton have a quantitative orientation and require well-developed math skills. Advised one student, "It helps if you were quantitative before coming to this program."

Wharton recently overhauled its MBA program to create a "curriculum for the twenty-first century." The traditional two-term academic year has been replaced with four intensive six-week modules. Single-discipline instruction has been scrapped for "team-taught courses and integrative case study projects which draw together cross-functional insights." Reported one student, "Wharton is working very hard to change, incorporating leadership, teamwork, and increasing teaching quality through constant feedback." Entering first-years kick off with a four-week preterm in August. Students are "prepped" in courses such as economics and statistics so that all first-years begin on an equal footing. Although the new program has been in pilot stages, thus far students report a heavier workload and more papers/exams, due to the more compact schedule of modules.

First-years take nine core courses and must complete a Management Communications course and demonstrate proficiency in LOTUS and basic math before progressing to the second year. The second year offers students a choice of nearly thirty majors in ten departments. A dizzying collection of 200 electives offers opportunities for specialization or eclectic sampling. Here are some favorites: Innovation and Entrepreneurship, Geopolitics, Risk and Crisis Management, and Environment of the Firm.

A hot topic: teaching quality, which has reportedly been subpar in the last few years. Here's what we found: Superstars and duds walk the same hallways. Wrote one student, "The best researchers don't mean the best teachers."

PLACEMENT AND RECRUITING

Students are quite happy with the quality, range, and number of companies recruiting on campus. Students also gave high marks to the career placement center itself, and rated the alumni network as vital and helpful. In 1992–1993, a total of 674 firms, representing over fifty industries, made offers to Wharton graduates and summer interns. Despite this, Wharton's eighty-four percent placement rate (1992) is low by Ivy League standards.

Leading recruiters were financial and consulting heavyweights such as Booz Allen, McKinsey, Bankers Trust, and Goldman Sachs. But Proctor & Gamble stole away a fair number of hires as well. Average starting salaries were sky-high, among the top five of the B-schools profiled in this book.

UNIVERSITY OF PENNSYLVANIA: THE WHARTON SCHOOL GRADUATE DIVISION

STUDENT LIFE/CAMPUS

Each fall, 750 students enter Wharton, making it the second-largest MBA program in the nation. To create a more intimate environment, the entering class is now divided into "cohorts" of sixty students each who are named by alphabetical letter and remain together through the core courses. Classes are held in amphitheater-style rooms where students are identified by their name plates, known as "tents." An average class numbers forty to fifty. Students are competitive. However, given the school's emphasis on group work, competitive students are at a disadvantage: shark behavior is frowned on, and pegs someone as undesirable for group projects. "The best part of Wharton is the student body," says a typical student. Exclaimed one student, "Great people here—much more helpful than I thought they would be." "They're bright, conscientious, and interesting." Still, as one student complained, "Wharton students like to complain."

Part of the University of Pennsylvania's 260-acre campus, Wharton is bordered by historic buildings and spacious lawns. The official Wharton building is Vance Hall, an outdated four-story structure. (Stay tuned—Vance should receive a facelift in the near future.) The new Steinberg-Deitrich Hall is shared with (and really home to) Wharton undergrads. It's hard to characterize a Wharton type. Traditionally, the school has been described as a feeder to the financial community but, in recent years, students have been as likely to go into management consulting or marketing as investment banking. Despite the diverse student body, Wharton has an East Coast, Ivy League feel. But that doesn't mean students don't know how to go crazy. There is a HUGE social scene here. Example: The Walnut Walk (in which students don boxer shorts and bar-hop down Philly's Walnut Street), cohort theme parties such as the "Kentucky Derby," weekly all-you-can-eat pizza nights at the pub, the Holiday Ball and Spring Ball, and "ding" night at Cavanaugh's, where an employment rejection letter gets you free beer. In between are the Wharton Follies, intramural sports, and the activities of over 100 student clubs. As for housing, married or single students can live in the Graduate Towers, in which twelve floors have been set aside for MBA students. Many students opt to live off-campus in Center City or West Philly, where apartments are plentiful and reasonably priced.

ADMISSIONS

The admissions office considers the following criteria (in no particular order): essays, GMAT score, college GPA, letters of recommendation, extracurricular activities, and work experience. The interview is optional. Writes the school, "The admissions committee evaluates applicants individually. Selection of students is not driven by categories or quotas. Applicants should represent themselves as they truly are versus what they may feel Wharton wants to hear. Applicants should also help the committee fully understand any unusual or nontraditional aspects of their candidacy." It is advisable to apply early in the admissions period.

STUDENTS' OVERVIEW BOX

FACULTY RATING

HITS AND MISSES

HITS
Finance dept.
Diverse work experience
School clubs
Student smarts
Teamwork
Placement

MISSES
Banker types
On-campus housing

APPLICANTS ALSO LOOK AT
Dartmouth College
U Virginia
Duke U.
Harvard
Stanford U.
Northwestern U.

FOR MORE INFORMATION, CONTACT:
The Wharton School
102 Vance Hall
Philadelphia, PA 19104
(215) 898-3430

PENN STATE UNIV.: MARY JEAN AND FRANK P. SMEAL COLLEGE OF BUSINESS ADMINISTRATION

ADMISSIONS FACTS

Type of school	Public

Demographics

No. of men	156
No. of women	74
No. of minorities	45
No. of int'l students	57

EQUAL TREATMENT GRAPH

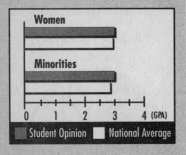

Women

Minorities

0   1   2   3   4 (GPA)

☐ Student Opinion ☐ National Average

Admissions Statistics

Avg. GMAT	N/A
Avg. undergraduate GPA	3.17
Avg. age at entry	27
No. of applicants	1,106
No. accepted	288
No. enrolled	114

Deadlines and Notifications

Regular application	rolling
Regular notification	rolling
Special dates	N/A

Focus of Curriculum

Specialized

Academic Specialties

Transportation logistics

Joint Degrees

Manufacturing/Engineering
Health Care Adm./Science

Special Programs

The Center for International Business Education and Research (CIBER), The Center for Finance and Real Estate, The Center for Technology Management, Classless Fridays meant for internships

FINANCIAL FACTS

In-state tuition	$5,554
Out-of-state tuition	$11,326
On-campus housing	$2,380

ACADEMICS

The Smeal College of Business is highly regarded for its rigorous academics, team-building approach, emphasis on communication skills, and small, personal program. Not content to rest on its laurels, Smeal has revised its curriculum to reflect the latest in trendy B-school offerings: an international focus has been built into all the core courses, the semester has been regrouped into seven-week blocks, and team teaching and the integration of functional areas have been introduced. Off-campus corporate experiences have become integral to the learning process. Students feel a truly unique part of the Penn State program is MBA Action - an outward bound type of program. "It's a 2-day outdoor experience during orientation week designed to break down social and ethnic barriers. The program helps band the class together early in the semester. "

Due in part to the new seven-week sessions (there are four per academic year), first-year students take a whopping nineteen core courses and have room for one elective. But since some of these courses last for all four of the seven-week sessions, they're really more like one epic course, rather than four minis. One of these courses is the Communications Skills for Managers Course, which happens to be a hallmark of the program. Most students agree that "Communication skills - written, oral, and visual are an integral part of the program. They are focused on intensely. The 3 sub disciplines are highly and effectively coordinated."

The core courses are offered in a predetermined schedule. Translation: You've got no flexibility here. During the second year, however, it's all electives. Some of these are used to pursue an area of emphasis, such as accounting, insurance, or international business. According to the school, dual concentrations are popular. In addition, students can select electives from any of the 125 departments at the university.

Students in our survey judged their marketing, operations, general management, quantitative, presentation, and teamwork skills to be particularly strong. Areas needing strengthening were finance, accounting, and computer skills. As for the faculty, profs get mixed reviews, although several students said those teaching in the communications department are terrific. Complained one "I sense little passion on the part of profs in teaching, and a great deal of passion for research and consulting." Still, according to our survey, MBAs are unanimous: the Penn State sheepskin is going to take them places.

PLACEMENT AND RECRUITING

Under the auspices of the MBA Association, students are provided workshops on goal clarification and time management. They also put together both a Corporate Guide and a Resume Book which it mails to more than 750 companies. According to the school, "The most intensive recruiting takes place during the Career Interview Program, organized and directed by second-year MBA candidates. In this program, interviews are assigned by computer through a mutual company/student selection process. Over one hundred companies recruit on campus annually for MBAs. In 1994, eighty-nine percent of grads found themselves with an offer within three months of graduation. Stealing away the most hires were Goldman Sachs, Ford , AT&T, American Management Systems, Johnson & Johnson, GTE, and Hewlett-Packard.

PENN STATE UNIV.: MARY JEAN AND FRANK P. SMEAL COLLEGE OF BUSINESS ADMINISTRATION

STUDENT LIFE/CAMPUS

The total entering class of 160 students is divided into four sections of forty students each to create an intimate learning environment and afford students a low student-to-faculty ratio. Students like the intimate size of the school: "Small classes and assigned teams provide maximum integration of the student body." Penn State utilizes a range of teaching methods: lectures, case studies, readings, management simulations, games, and role playing. Group work and team building are emphasized through the program. The majority of students work in study groups, but play it solo in the classroom. In many of the courses, class participation is weighed most heavily in the grade. Students report a heavy, though not killer, workload. On average, they study twenty to thirty hours a week. Outside of class they attend one of the numerous extracurricular recruiting and social events hosted by the MBA Association. Popular student clubs include the Investment Association, the Marketing Club, and Women in Business.

Students here say they're competitive, and despite a strong desire to help each other, ambivalent about whether their classmates are the type of people they'll want to stay in touch with after graduation. One student wrote, "They may not be the brightest MBA students, but they are very down-to-earth and helpful." Others noted they do have scholarly appeal. We also heard mixed reviews on the success of diversifying the student body: "Very little is done to bring the various races and different ethnic backgrounds closer together socially, "and "we have an extremely diverse group of students here in terms of race and nationality. I think the administration tries too hard to diversify the student body." An important note: Penn State sponsors the Executive Panel Presentation, a simulated business exercise that invites executives from a wide range of companies to participate as review panel members. Participants have included Malcolm Forbes Jr., Mark DuMars, president of Inglewood Associates, and John Rawley, assistant to the chairman of Hershey Foods. The exercise formally culminates thirty weeks of first-year instruction. The entire class is divided into small consulting groups to review a complex business case that calls on technical concepts learned in the first year. They have seventy hours within which to arrive at solutions and make a presentation to faculty serving on the review board. Winning teams go on to present to the visiting executives.

ADMISSIONS

According to the admissions office, your GMAT score, work experience, and college GPA are considered most important, and then, in descending order, your interview, essays, and letters of recommendation. They note, "Interviews are strongly encouraged and considered on a par with work experience." Applications are handled on a rolling admissions basis. It generally takes two to six weeks "depending on the backlog" for a student to be notified of a decision after receiving the completed application. Students may defer admissions for up to two years for personal reasons.

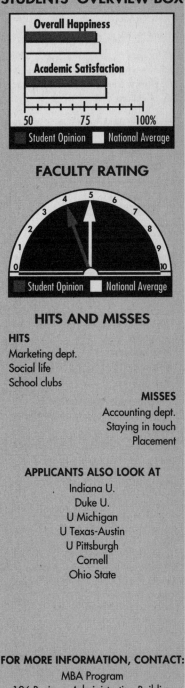

STUDENTS' OVERVIEW BOX

Overall Happiness
Academic Satisfaction
50 75 100%
Student Opinion / National Average

FACULTY RATING

Student Opinion / National Average

HITS AND MISSES

HITS
Marketing dept.
Social life
School clubs

MISSES
Accounting dept.
Staying in touch
Placement

APPLICANTS ALSO LOOK AT
Indiana U.
Duke U.
U Michigan
U Texas-Austin
U Pittsburgh
Cornell
Ohio State

FOR MORE INFORMATION, CONTACT:
MBA Program
106 Business Administration Building
University Park, PA 16802-3000
(814) 863-0474
FAX (814) 863-8072
eMail: GXP4@PSUVM.PSU.EDU

UNIV. OF PITTSBURGH: JOSEPH M. KATZ GRADUATE SCHOOL OF BUSINESS

ADMISSIONS FACTS

Type of school	Public

Demographics

No. of men	286
No. of women	129
No. of minorities	36
No. of int'l students	108

EQUAL TREATMENT GRAPH

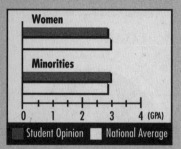

Women

Minorities

0 1 2 3 4 (GPA)

▨ Student Opinion   ▢ National Average

Admissions Statistics

Avg. GMAT	605
Avg. undergraduate GPA	3.2
Avg. age at entry	27
No. of applicants	1,061
No. accepted	463
No. enrolled	301

Deadlines and Notifications

Regular application	wait list after 5/15
Regular notification	4-6 weeks
Special dates	N/A

Focus of Curriculum

General Management with specialization in nine concentration areas

Academic Specialties

Finance, International Business

Joint Degrees

MBA/MS in areas of specialization such as East Asia, Latin America, and eastern Europe, MBA/Masters International Business, MBA/Information Systems

Special Programs

Foreign Study in Prague and Budapest; Intensive foreign language instruction

FINANCIAL FACTS

In-state tuition	$12,897
Out-of-state tuition	$21,651
On-campus housing	$10,000/R&B

ACADEMICS

The Katz School "offers an MBA program that is unique, enabling you to earn your MBA in eleven months, over three terms of study rather than in the two years usually required elsewhere." This is made possible by the program's pace, breadth of study, and its integrated curriculum, which prevents duplication of course material. The obvious advantages of an 11-month program are: 1) you get quick reentry into the working world, and 2) tuition and other costs are cut in half. The disadvantages are you miss out on a summer internship and have little time to digest what you've learned. Nonetheless, many students agree that "one of the most valuable assets you gain at Katz is the ability to effectively manage complex business problems under extreme time constraints." This year Katz has revamped its program. Over and over, students raved about the new, self-organized "Learning Organizations" which consist of fourteen students each. According to our survey, the new program has been well received: "Learning Orgs have considerably changed my learning experience by demonstrating the complexities of group cohesion and effectiveness." Another recent addition is the transition module. To prepare for the July through June sprint, students can take optional pre-program workshops to improve their skill in areas they are weak in. Still another highlight of the program is the Project Course, in which students solve actual corporate problems and see their solutions implemented.

International content is integrated into a majority of the courses. Wrote one student, "The professors incorporate new issues from the international business community into curriculum." All students take a "strategy envelope" of three courses: Competing in a Global Environment, Organizational Transformation, and Managing Strategic Performance. Summed up this happy MBA "Katz is a 21st century school."

According to one student, "Faculty are dedicated." Apparently so—students doled out high marks to their profs for spending quality time with them. As for their teaching abilities, the reviews were decidedly mixed.

PLACEMENT AND RECRUITING

The efforts of Katz's placement office are among the most ambitious of schools profiled in this book. They offer sessions with image consultants on everything from etiquette to interview attire. Katz begins its program in the summer and ends it in June to stay in sync with recruiting efforts at other schools.

Of last year's MBA class, seventy-five percent had a job by graduation, eighty-seven percent forty-five days later, and over ninety percent within six months. Twenty percent of students accepted positions in Pittsburgh and twenty percent elsewhere in Pennsylvania. One hundred companies came on campus for Pittsburgh MBAs. Hiring the most were Ford, the Big Six CPA firms, Pittsburgh National Bank, National Bank of Detroit, AT&T, Merck, and Swiss Bank. Thirty-four percent of grads went into finance; twenty-one percent of the class headed into marketing jobs.

UNIV. OF PITTSBURGH: JOSEPH M. KATZ GRADUATE SCHOOL OF BUSINESS

STUDENT LIFE/CAMPUS

Everything here is defined by the breakneck pace of the program, which isn't comfortable. One tired MBA explained, "I'm not a virgin, but these seven-week courses are tough." Advised another, "Academics in some areas get compressed. This one-year program is a great jumping board for people who just need a degree for the next job switch." As for the new program, several students expressed this feeling: "I cant help but feel like a guinea pig. It seems this year's class was used as a testing group for many theoretical concepts. However, the administration receives high marks for smoothing out bumpy parts."

Students noted that their classmates are somewhat competitive, smart, and interested in helping fellow classmates: "Students are a big part of what makes Katz exceptional. This is definitely not the ultra-competitive cutthroat environment you might find at some MBA schools." Not surprisingly, learning, not grades, is emphasized here.

According to our survey, "Katz facilities are very modern and technologically advanced." The campus itself is located in Oakland, a small, college-town part of Pittsburgh. Hard to believe, but Pittsburgh is consistently ranked as one of the most livable cities in the United States. Students say it's clean, safe, and full of things city folk love to do. Favorite on-campus activities include weekly happy hours, intramural sports, and going to watch U. of Pittsburgh's nationally rated football and basketball teams. Community service ranks high on the scorecard of favorite extracurriculars. A large number of students are involved in ABBEY (Going ABove and BEYond).

A value-added program for students is the Executive Briefings series, hour-long presentations held several times a month at which chief executives from major corporations come to Katz to speak on career and industry issues. Afterward, a handful of students join the exec and the dean for lunch. Equally exciting is the American Assembly Dialogue, which brings business leaders to campus to discuss major economic and social issues of the day. Katz is the only school in the nation to hold this event. Past participants include Ivan W. Gorr, Chairman of Cooper Tire and Rubber Co., Ted Turner of Turner Broadcasting System, and Robert Maloney, Chairman, Diebold, Inc.

A final note: The real secret behind Katz's one-year MBA is that many of its students enroll in one of the joint degree programs and earn two degrees in two years, a solid return on one's time and money.

ADMISSIONS

Katz first considers your work experience and then in descending order, GMAT score (TOEFL for international students), college GPA, essays, interview, letters of recommendation, and extracurricular activities. According to the school, "Quantitative information is important, but a student's work background and experiences through their college years can be as important as actual performance numbers on the GMAT or academic record." Minorities, international, and handicapped students are given special consideration. Each application is individually considered, then evaluated in groups of 100 or more.

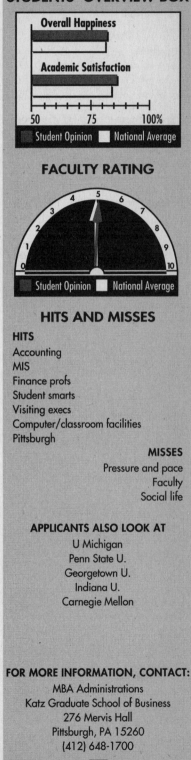

STUDENTS' OVERVIEW BOX

Overall Happiness
Academic Satisfaction
50   75   100%
Student Opinion   National Average

FACULTY RATING

Student Opinion   National Average

HITS AND MISSES

HITS
Accounting
MIS
Finance profs
Student smarts
Visiting execs
Computer/classroom facilities
Pittsburgh

MISSES
Pressure and pace
Faculty
Social life

APPLICANTS ALSO LOOK AT
U Michigan
Penn State U.
Georgetown U.
Indiana U.
Carnegie Mellon

FOR MORE INFORMATION, CONTACT:
MBA Administrations
Katz Graduate School of Business
276 Mervis Hall
Pittsburgh, PA 15260
(412) 648-1700

PURDUE UNIVERSITY: KRANNERT GRADUATE SCHOOL OF MANAGEMENT

ADMISSIONS FACTS

Type of school	Public

Demographics

No. of men	84
No. of women	47
No. of minorities	13
No. of int'l students	26

EQUAL TREATMENT GRAPH

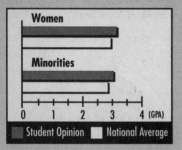

Admissions Statistics

Avg. GMAT	607
Avg. undergraduate GPA	3.24
Avg. age at entry	26
No. of applicants	1,060
No. accepted	326
No. enrolled	159

Deadlines and Notifications

Regular application	4/15
Regular notification	rolling
Special dates	3/1 int'l students

Focus of Curriculum

General Management with specialization in an "option(s)" area

Academic Specialties

Production/Operations Management, Finance, Strategic Management, Technology

Special Programs

Washington Campus Program, Externship Program, Big Ten MBA Job Fair, MS in Human Resources Mgmt

FINANCIAL FACTS

In-state tuition	$4,050
Out-of-state tuition	$11,040
On-campus housing	$5,860

ACADEMICS

Krannert offers two basic graduate management degrees: one in Industrial Administration (MSIA) and one in Management (MS). MSIA students complete their program in eleven months, including a summer session. Students in both programs share the same core course requirements. However, MSIAs take three electives. By contrast, MSs take up to nine, and they must declare an "options area." Both programs emphasize a quantitative and analytical approach and also rely heavily on computer modeling.

The school seeks out students "who are comfortable with using technology, understanding their potential for competitive advantage and being able to enhance the adoption of technology in corporations." Not surprisingly, they then attract students with technical and/or quantitative backgrounds.

One of the assets that draws students to Krannert is a national reputation in operations management. Raved one, "Krannert deserves to move into the top twenty B-school rankings." But another complained, "The Operations program is overrated, although it's seeking to reposition itself." Core and elective courses offer coverage in the areas of Total Quality, International Management, Management of Technology and Information, and Information Management for Competitive Advantage.

Students at Krannert gave the administration good marks. Wrote one, "The school now considers students' concerns and problems. Decision-makers are accessible and they're genuinely concerned." This sense of satisfaction apparently has much to do with the newly restructured curriculum, which now features two eight-week modules instead of the traditional sixteen-week semester. The shorter modules lighten up the core requirement load, provide students greater exposure to a variety of courses, and permit them to take more electives during the first year. One area that remains a problem: the faculty, which students rated below the national average.

High marks went to the administration for their efforts to involve students in shaping Krannert. We also heard a few moans and groans about the percentage of students accepted directly from undergraduate school. Summed up this MBA, "The program is making a definite, concerted effort to: increase the size of the class, bring in more faculty, and start an advertising campaign so that the school can gain more of the respect it deserves."

PLACEMENT AND RECRUITING

According to the school, in 1994 eighty percent of the student body was placed by graduation, ninety percent within three months. The majority of grads went into operations and finance. Leading recruiters were: Ford, TRW, Allied Signal, Intel, IBM, Merck, and Ernst an Young. Wrote one would-be tycoon, "I doubled my salary with my MBA." As a reference point, the average starting salary is $50,000.

PURDUE UNIVERSITY: KRANNERT GRADUATE SCHOOL OF MANAGEMENT

STUDENT LIFE/CAMPUS

Krannert is located in West Lafayette, Indiana, in a semi-urban community two hours from Chicago and an hour from Indianapolis. The B-school computers/classrooms are state-of-the-art. Krannert students work out at the "Co-Rec," an impressive gym featuring amusement-park-like facilities—from bowling to golf courses to archery. Although the social scene is below average, it does exist. Planned events include school picnics in the fall and the annual alumni/student banquet. Weekends are spent catching up on sleep, playing in the intramural sports leagues, and attending informal get-togethers. Wrote one student, "Krannert draws primarily from the Midwest—Minnesota down to Texas. But a surprisingly large group of students come from California, New York, and abroad." Wrote another, "People are great—must be that Midwest charm! But it ain't life in the big city."

The Krannert School is, by design, a small program with approximately 150 students in the entering class each fall. This fosters a cooperative team atmosphere. Wrote one, "The small size facilitates a group atmosphere both in and out of the classroom." It makes "class participation more animated, group projects more fun, social life more accessible." First-years take core courses together so they have a "cohort experience." Study groups further draw them together and are considered the "nucleus" of case preparation and schoolwork. Students are competitive "but don't have a killer mentality." This may have something to do with the new emphasis on ethics and touchy-feely skills, as well as the school's unique Personal Leadership Development Plan. Interested students sign up for the program during orientation week and design a personal program of coursework and leadership experiences. Krannert also boasts a "no-nonsense, hard-work atmosphere," although at times, students say this borders on the excessive. Said one MBA "Stress is pretty high." Added another, "You learn time management and stress management very quickly with the heavy workload, company receptions, and work assistantships. This is not a program for the faint at heart." Perhaps that's why recruiters attribute a Midwest work ethic to Krannert grads: newly minted MBAs don't expect to start at the top, they expect to work hard to get where they want to go.

ADMISSIONS

The admissions office reports, "Although applicants come from diverse backgrounds in terms of education, experience, and cultures, they tend to have in common a strong analytical and problem-solving background." Krannert first considers an applicant's GPA, then in descending order of importance: GMAT scores, work experience, interview, letters of recommendation, essays, extracurriculars. Applications are handled on a rolling admissions basis; students are notified of a decision three to six weeks after their file is completed. Students can defer admission up to two years, and twenty to twenty-five percent of applicants are accepted with no work experience. Krannert uses a self-managed application (you accumulate documents and submit them all together) so applicants know the application is complete at the time of submission.

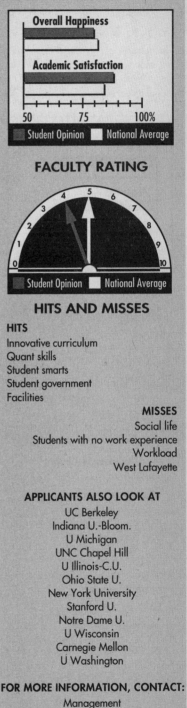

STUDENTS' OVERVIEW BOX

Overall Happiness

Academic Satisfaction

50   75   100%

Student Opinion   National Average

FACULTY RATING

0 1 2 3 4 5 6 7 8 9 10

Student Opinion   National Average

HITS AND MISSES

HITS
Innovative curriculum
Quant skills
Student smarts
Student government
Facilities

MISSES
Social life
Students with no work experience
Workload
West Lafayette

APPLICANTS ALSO LOOK AT
UC Berkeley
Indiana U.-Bloom.
U Michigan
UNC Chapel Hill
U Illinois-C.U.
Ohio State U.
New York University
Stanford U.
Notre Dame U.
U Wisconsin
Carnegie Mellon
U Washington

FOR MORE INFORMATION, CONTACT:
Management
1310 Krannert Center, RM 104
W. Lafayette, IN 47907-1310
(317) 494-4365
eMail: patz@mgmt.purdue.edu

RENSSELAER POLYTECHNIC INSTITUTE SCHOOL OF MANAGEMENT

ADMISSIONS FACTS

Type of school	Private

Demographics

No. of men	139
No. of women	46
No. of minorities	14
No. of int'l students	70

EQUAL TREATMENT GRAPH

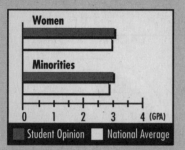

Women

Minorities

0   1   2   3   4 (GPA)

■ Student Opinion   ■ National Average

Admissions Statistics

Avg. GMAT	590
Avg. undergraduate GPA	3.1
Avg. age at entry	26
No. of applicants	278
No. accepted	164
No. enrolled	64

Deadlines and Notifications

Regular application	5/01
Regular notification	6-8 weeks
Special dates	N/A

Focus of Curriculum

Specialized

Academic Specialties

Management of Technology, Technological Entrepreneurship, MIS, Health Systems Management

Joint Degrees

JD/MBA, MBA/MS in Engineering and other fields of study

Special Programs

3–2 Undergraduate MBA, International Exchange in seven countries, Summer "Bridge" Program for Minority Students

FINANCIAL FACTS

In-state tuition	$15,750
Out-of-state tuition	$15,750
On-campus housing	$6,000

ACADEMICS

Rensselaer Polytechnic Institute (RPI) School of Management offers two degrees: a traditional MBA and its newest complement, the Management & Technology (M&T) MBA. The traditional MBA offers the basic two-year formula with a technical/quantitative slant. The M&T program, which students talk most about, emphasizes the integration of the traditional business areas with each other and with technology. Explained one student, "RPI has moved from a traditionally based MBA to a more entrepreneurial/general management program utilizing technology." As one might expect, the program also features a heavy technical/quantitative slant and attracts engineering types with strong math and computer backgrounds. To bolster "softer" skills, RPI requires its techie types to take a leadership seminar. Students also reported, "Group work is a very important part of the program." According to one M&T MBA, plenty of English majors make it here too: "Not having a technical background has not hindered my status in the program." The single most exciting aspect about the program, wrote one MBA, is that "it involves lots of student consulting in technological areas" and is a "hotbed for new ventures." Enthused one student, "The strongest contribution to my education has been the yearlong, team-based, product development program." Explained one student, "RPI is very much involved with entrepreneurial activities through the Incubator Project and Technology Park, which provides students real-life experience in working with start-up, high-tech companies." But students also said the school offers other less technologically oriented programs. The Health Systems Management Concentration is reportedly excellent.

Professors received good grades. Explained one student, "The good ones are awesome," although there are some not-so-eloquent teachers. More impressive, given the dedication to cutting-edge research, is that "faculty are very accessible and assist students outside of class." Raved this techie, "One professor is a world authority in the Business Incubator concept. Through my work with him and other faculty, I've obtained a summer position doing consulting in the Ukraine." All in all, students agreed, "RPI's new M&T program is one of the most innovative programs around." Nevertheless, "the program is still in its infancy and rough around the edges."

PLACEMENT AND RECRUITING

A rare find—a group of B-school students who report they're reasonably satisfied with their placement office and the range of opportunities available. This may be due to the truly *unique* offerings of an RPI MBA. Its high-tech ingredients provide students a competitive edge. And as more companies become technology driven, the M&T MBA becomes more appealing. Summed up one student about employment potential through RPI: "What this school needs more than anything else is a full-time placement coordinator for the B-school. Otherwise excellent." Seventy-three percent of RPI MBAs had been placed within three months of their 1992 graduation.

RENSSELAER POLYTECHNIC INSTITUTE SCHOOL OF MANAGEMENT

STUDENT LIFE/CAMPUS

With only 200 students in the whole school of management, RPI is defined by high student/faculty interaction and small classes, although core classes tend to be larger. The workload is a killer. The vast majority of students study outside of class a whopping thirty to forty hours a week. Study groups provide some relief. During the second year, the academic workload levels off. But second-years take a practicum in a local industry, which requires fifteen to twenty-five hours a week. At least it's not homework. Class participation and presentation count as a high percentage of the grade in many courses.

RPI students are intensely competitive and driven. But students appreciate a helping hand from their peers and frequently reciprocate. The emphasis on teamwork lightens up the industrious mentality of the scientific types. Reports one student, "The program is so group oriented, it's difficult not to hang around classmates because I spend so much time with them." While the majority agreed they like and enjoy each other, the social scene is hindered by all the academic activities both in and outside the classroom. Most events are scheduled through the MBA Association and include happy hours, barbecues, golf events, and guest speaker series. The majority of students live off-campus in Troy and Peekskill. About thirty percent of the students live on campus in graduate housing, which is considered extremely attractive.

A final note: Students agree the student body is both professionally and ethnically diverse. There's a large percentage of international students, almost forty percent, and minority students—roughly forty percent.

ADMISSIONS

The admissions office considers your college GPA most important. After that, in descending order, the office considers your GMAT score, work experience, extracurricular activities, interview, letters of recommendation, and essays. A TOEFL of 580 or greater is required of those who speak English as a second language. The school favors applicants with a technically oriented undergraduate background: "Our focus is the intersection of management and technology. Everything we do begins with the conviction that for all firms in all future markets, sustainable competitive advantage is built upon a technological foundation."

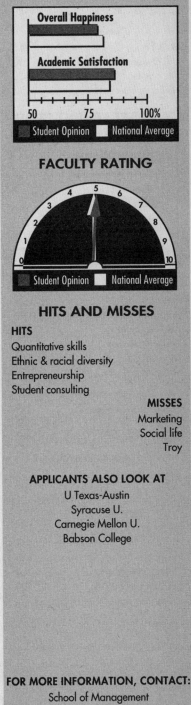

STUDENTS' OVERVIEW BOX

Overall Happiness

Academic Satisfaction

50   75   100%

■ Student Opinion   □ National Average

FACULTY RATING

■ Student Opinion   □ National Average

HITS AND MISSES

HITS
Quantitative skills
Ethnic & racial diversity
Entrepreneurship
Student consulting

MISSES
Marketing
Social life
Troy

APPLICANTS ALSO LOOK AT
U Texas-Austin
Syracuse U.
Carnegie Mellon U.
Babson College

FOR MORE INFORMATION, CONTACT:
School of Management
Lally Management Center
Troy, NY 12180-3590
(518) 276-6789

RICE UNIVERSITY: JESSE H. JONES GRAD. SCHOOL OF ADMINISTRATION

ADMISSIONS FACTS

Type of school	Private

Demographics

No. of men	165
No. of women	63
No. of minorities	30
No. of int'l students	33

EQUAL TREATMENT GRAPH

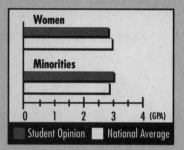

Admissions Statistics

Avg. GMAT	623
Avg. undergraduate GPA	3.25
Avg. age at entry	27
No. of applicants	882
No. accepted	304
No. enrolled	120

Deadlines and Notifications

Regular application	3/1
Regular notification	3–5 weeks
Special dates	N/A

Focus of Curriculum

Specialized

Academic Specialties

Accounting, Finance, Entrepreneurship

FINANCIAL FACTS

In-state tuition	$11,300
Out-of-state tuition	$11,300
On-campus housing	$5,800

ACADEMICS

As one student put it, "Within Houston, Rice is acknowledged as the 'Harvard of the Bayou.'" Indeed, Rice is well known for its top-flight program and high-quality students. According to the school, "Legal and governmental analysis is stressed, both as a first-year course and as a perspective from which to view business activity." An international perspective and the development of strong communication skills are also pervasive components in the curriculum. Wrote one student, "The Jones School is small relative to other top MBA programs, and non-accredited. For this reason, I imagine it does not get the national credit it probably deserves." Perhaps because the MBA program was originally an offshoot of the school's master's in accounting program, the curriculum strongly emphasizes quantitative skills. Observed one, "The quantitative skills required here are more intense than at the engineering programs at my last masters program."

First-year students take thirteen required courses, which make use of team projects, case study, and oral presentations. Wrote one MBA, "The school emphasizes the articulation of ideas over book-type learning." Indeed, oral presentations feature heavily in a student's total class grade. During the second year, students devote their electives to one or two concentrations.

A few students complained of a lack of variety in the courses offered. Explained one, "There tends to be an over-concentration on certain areas." However, across the functional areas of business, students rated their skills as very strong. There was only one notable weak spot—operations. But the school is addressing this with a special faculty recruiting committee: "We are currently recruiting a senior level operations person to redevelop our operations program."

Professors are highly regarded for their teaching and generous after-class accessibility. This is helped by a low student/faculty ratio of 7:1. But over and over students told us, "The single most important thing about the school is the use of adjunct professors from the local business community. They are extraordinary and bring a sense of reality to the academic world." One criticism popping up, though, is "Too many first-time teachers teaching core courses."

PLACEMENT AND RECRUITING

Wrote one student, "If you want to work in the Southwest, Rice is the school to go to." Still, like the students at most of the other B-schools, Rice students would like to see a larger range of companies recruiting on campus. Offers one student, "Because Jones doesn't get the national recognition it deserves, the number and array of company's recruiting on campus is severely limited relative to schools of comparable quality." We also heard: "The placement office works extra hard" and "The office is very accessible and aggressive." One happy camper reports, "I came here earning $35K a year and have accepted a position at $100 plus a year already!"

RICE UNIVERSITY: JESSE H. JONES GRAD. SCHOOL OF ADMINISTRATION

STUDENT LIFE/CAMPUS

Rice boasts a highly demanding academic program. There is a steep learning curve in many of the core courses. Unsurprisingly, students report a heavy workload. "The first year is *very* tough," wrote one, "but the second year is more practical and interesting." Another reported "The coursework is difficult but substantive and mostly well-planned and well-integrated. "Outside of class, students spend an average of thirty-five to forty-five hours doing school work/studying. The majority say it's very important to do most or ALL of the assigned reading.

One student's comments typified the prevalent feeling here: "Rice's small size contributes to much of the successful MBA experience." With only 100 students in the entering class, the benefits of the program's small size draw nothing but praise:" Interaction between students is both frequent and substantial. I know everyone in my MBA class at Rice" and "The small size affords terrific interaction with professors." While students are competitive, we also heard "I have been most impressed by my fellow students - far from being the cut throat, money grubbers I expected, they are uniformly friendly, enthusiastic, and very team oriented." However, one second year, is more critical, "The spirit of cooperation is hampered by the unofficial grading policy of 50% A's maximum in core courses and the brittle egos around here."

Of Rice's home city, one student wrote, "Being located in Houston is an advantage." The student clubs take advantage of the city's offerings and organize visits to Houston area businesses. Reported another, "Coming from out of state, I found Houston a comfortable and friendly town." For an urban environment, Rice offers a surprisingly tranquil and beautiful campus. A tree-lined, three-mile jogging path encircles the campus. On- or off-campus, students report that housing is affordable and very attractive. Both intramural sports and golf are popular. Favorite watering holes are Valhalla (the campus pub) and Kay's. Monthly parties on Herring Hall's patio are also popular.

A final note: Students at Rice agree that theirs is not an ethnically and racially diverse community. Wrote one student, "The school should work to recruit more minority students into the program. Blacks make up less than one percent of the class. This is not representative of the real world."

ADMISSIONS

The Jones admissions department considers the following criteria most important: essays, college GPA, letters of recommendation, and work experience. Extracurricular activities are also considered. An interview is not required. According to the school, "Each applicant receives a comprehensive evaluation due to the composition of our admissions committee, which includes two graduating MBA students, a recent alumnus or alumna, a tenured faculty member, and the admissions director. We do not select or reject an applicant based solely on his or her academic record or GMAT score; instead we evaluate each applicant in the context of the entire application." Decisions are made on a rolling basis.

STUDENTS' OVERVIEW BOX

Overall Happiness

Academic Satisfaction

50   75   100%

Student Opinion   National Average

FACULTY RATING

Student Opinion   National Average

HITS AND MISSES

HITS
Finance dept.
Classmates are smart
Library

MISSES
Marketing dept.
Ethnic & racial diversity

APPLICANTS ALSO LOOK AT
U Texas-Austin
U Houston

FOR MORE INFORMATION, CONTACT:
Jones Graduate School
P.O. Box 1892
Houston, TX 77251
(713) 527-4918

UNIV. OF ROCHESTER: WILLIAM E. SIMON GRADUATE SCHOOL OF BUSINESS ADMINISTRATION

ADMISSIONS FACTS

Type of school   Private

Demographics

No. of men	308
No. of women	97
No. of minorities	40
No. of int'l students	170

EQUAL TREATMENT GRAPH

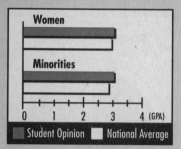

Women

Minorities

0 1 2 3 4 (GPA)

■ Student Opinion   □ National Average

Admissions Statistics

Avg. GMAT	604
Avg. undergraduate GPA	3.22
Avg. age at entry	26
No. of applicants	960
No. accepted	370
No. enrolled	152

Deadlines and Notifications

Regular application	6/1
Regular notification	rolling
Special dates	N/A

Focus of Curriculum

Specialized, 11 concentrations, options to pursue a double or triple major

Academic Specialties

Accounting, Finance, Marketing, Operations, Information Systems

Joint Degrees

MBA/MS in Microbiology and Immunology (Biotechnology), MBA/MS in Nursing, MBA/Masters in Public Health, MS in Manufacturing Mgmt, MS in MIS, MS in Mgmt. of Manufacturing Info. Systems

Special Programs

VISION Broaden Your Horizons Intercultural Seminar Series, The Executive Seminar Series, International Exchange Programs

FINANCIAL FACTS

In-state tuition	$19,950
Out-of-state tuition	$19,950
On-campus housing	$6,750

ACADEMICS

Simon is a school with strong potential, renowned for its academic research, scholarly faculty, and finance and accounting programs. The curriculum is oriented around the basic concepts of microeconomics. Price theory is emphasized and used as a framework for understanding how firms operate in a free-market system. First-year courses are a mix of case studies and lectures, and coursework is integrated to enhance decision-making and problem-solving skills. A required, first-year, third quarter "capstone course" called "Practicum in Management" allows students to evaluate a diverse range of business cases. Students gain experience in identifying the major problems of a case, assembling relevant data and applying the tools and specialized knowledge gained in other core courses. The nationally acclaimed student-managed VISION Program, established in 1993 and required for all first-year students, is a year-long series of management modules that emphasize skills like interviewing, time management, and diversity awareness. Corporate sponsors have included AT&T; Bausch & Lomb; Eastman Kodak Company; IBM; PepsiCo, Inc.; and Procter & Gamble Company. Although students build general management skills, students are encouraged to complete one concentration in a functional area of business.

Overall, students said the program stresses quantitative methods. Claimed one, "While they're trying to become less of a quant school, there is still too much emphasis on quantitative subjects." But one MBA advised, "Someone with a nonquantitative background can survive." Students' self-assessment of their skills showed erratic strengths. For example, while students rated their finance, accounting, and teamwork skills as sky - high, they were less confident about their marketing, and operations skills. General management skills were rated above-average, but not stellar. Simon students are taught by senior, tenure-track faculty who rank among the nation's top five in academic journals. Wrote one MBA "The idea that they are unavailable due to their commitment to research is a rumor. The research keeps them on the cutting edge, yet they are on a first name basis with most of the students. They are available as often as you need them." Professors are highly regarded for their after-class accessibility.

PLACEMENT AND RECRUITING

Students may interview in Manhattan through the New York Recruiting Program. In 1994, "Twenty-eight percent of the class obtained positions with New York City-area businesses." Over ninety companies interviewed on-campus. Seventy-five percent of the graduating class had a job by graduation, ninety-four percent within three months. The big recruiters were Xerox Corporation, Bausch & Lomb, Proctor and Gamble, and Bank of Nova Scotia. Students said they were moderately happy with the placement office itself, on their wish list is a wider range of on-campus recruiters. Complained one "I plan to get my own job. If I had to rely on career services and the companies that come, I wouldn't be as pleased. The school name is not widely known and the school needs to do more PR." An overwhelming number of students utilized alumni contacts in their job search and found them helpful.

UNIV. OF ROCHESTER: WILLIAM E. SIMON GRADUATE SCHOOL OF BUSINESS ADMINISTRATION

STUDENT LIFE/CAMPUS

A hallmark of Simon's program is the cohort and study group experience. Entering students are grouped together in sections, or cohorts, which stick together for the first three quarters of the program. The school also pre-assigns students to study groups constructed to operate as mini-management teams. Some students complained about this emphasis on group work. Complained one, "Everything is done in groups. I feel it's overemphasized here; I wish there were more individual work." Students say they're competitive: "Students that come here actually want to learn. They're not here just for the three letters, MBA." However, competition is not cutthroat; students say their classmates are cooperative and interested in helping each other.

Students agree that the student body is ethnically and racially diverse. A whopping forty percent of students are international, twenty-five percent women. One of the more popular events on-campus is the bimonthly Broaden Your Horizons, lunchtime presentations by foreign students about their country. It's standing room only when Brazilians defend their country's inflation, Canadians discuss their health care system, and the presenters offer classmates a buffet of their native foods.

Simon boasts a brand-spanking-new B-school building. Inside it features state-of-the-art facilities and computers, and an elegant, clubby atmosphere. Wrote one student, "Aside from the fact that it's a snow magnet, this campus is perfect." Some of the brutal weather can be avoided by using the indoor tunnels beneath the campus. As for the town of Rochester, it offers the quintessential college-town experience. Students doled out high marks for the affordability and comfort of both on- and off-campus housing. On-campus townhouses are especially nice for married students with families. Off-campus, students opt for shared Victorian homes in the trendy Park Avenue section of town.

ADMISSIONS

Three-fourths of the full-time graduating class starts in September; the remaining one fourth start in January and complete the program in an accelerated eighteen-month schedule.

The admissions committee considers the following criteria (not listed in order of importance): Quality of undergraduate school; academic accomplishments and ability; essays, college GPA, letters of recommendation, and GMAT. Interviews are required of applicants with fifteen months or fewer of prior full-time work experience. For all others, interviews are strongly encouraged. Decisions are made on a rolling admissions basis. Applicants are notified of a decision within three weeks of applying.

Accepted students may defer admission for up to two years.

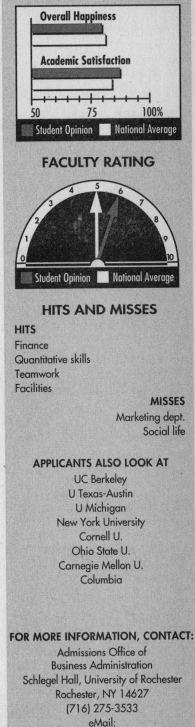

STUDENTS' OVERVIEW BOX

FACULTY RATING

HITS AND MISSES

HITS
Finance
Quantitative skills
Teamwork
Facilities

MISSES
Marketing dept.
Social life

APPLICANTS ALSO LOOK AT
UC Berkeley
U Texas-Austin
U Michigan
New York University
Cornell U.
Ohio State U.
Carnegie Mellon U.
Columbia

FOR MORE INFORMATION, CONTACT:
Admissions Office of
Business Administration
Schlegel Hall, University of Rochester
Rochester, NY 14627
(716) 275-3533
eMail:
MBAADM@ssbfacstaff.ssb.rochester.edu

UNIV. OF SOUTHERN CALIFORNIA GRADUATE SCHOOL OF BUSINESS ADMINISTRATION

ADMISSIONS FACTS

Type of school   Private

Demographics

No. of men	283
No. of women	112
No. of minorities	62
No. of int'l students	59

EQUAL TREATMENT GRAPH

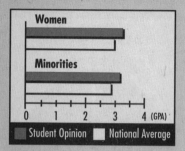

Admissions Statistics

Avg. GMAT	610
Avg. undergraduate GPA	3.1
Avg. age at entry	28.1
No. of applicants	1,266
No. accepted	440
No. enrolled	195

Deadlines and Notifications

Regular application	4/15
Regular notification	rolling
Special dates	12/1 (early decision)

Focus of Curriculum

Specialized

Academic Specialties

Accounting, Finance, Entrepreneurship, Organizational Behavior

Joint Degrees

JD/MBA, MBA/MS in Industrial and Systems Engineering, MBA/Master of Planning, MBA/Master of Real Estate Developement, Doctor of Pharmacy/MBA, MBA/MS in Nursing, MS in Gerontology/MBA, Doctor of Dental Surgery

FINANCIAL FACTS

In-state tuition	$18,246
Out-of-state tuition	$18,246
On-campus housing	$5,500

ACADEMICS

A revamped curriculum at use emphasizes the '90s themes seen at many progressive B-schools: globalization, leadership, communication skills, ethics, the use of technologies in problem solving, and, according to the school, "the interrelatedness of management issues." Like many programs, USC organizes the first-year core courses sequentially so that concepts and skills build upon earlier ones. What's unique about USC is that they employ a staggered model; not all courses begin and end at the start or conclusion of a semester. Courses segue from one functional area to another to create an integrated learning experience. Two times a semester, a core faculty member "exports" him- or herself into a colleague's class to team-teach an issue related to more than one functional area, for example finance and marketing. During the second year, students have up to four electives to specialize and one requirement—the field consulting project.

USC offers a lot to the would-be business leader. A recent raid on hot professorial talent from other B-schools has beefed up several departments. Standouts include Finance, Real Estate, Health Care Advisory Services, and Organization Behavior, the latter of which is nationally known. Particularly strong is Accounting and Entrepreneurship. As for where students judge their strengths to be, accounting, finance, marketing, and general management seem to be the areas in which USC MBAs feel they're getting their best training. Students feel less confident about their computer skills. An unusual find at a top-flight school, students say getting into the most popular courses is a breeze. Reported one MBA, faculty members who design the program are "very responsive—willing to adapt program accordingly." They're also terrific teachers. But students say "incompetent teachers" roam the same halls.

PLACEMENT AND RECRUITING

The school reports an average of 174 companies recruiting on campus in 1994 - ninety on-campus; eighty-four in the "Just-in-Time" program. The latter responds to a company's request within three days with an appropriate candidate at the recruiter's office. Seventy-five percent of the class has a job offer by graduation; ninety-two percent three months later.

Recruiters with the biggest appetite: Ernst and Young, Deloitte and Touche, Standard Chartered Bank, Citibank, Mattel, Arthur Andersen, Price Waterhouse. Students are most enthusiastic about the power and reach of the alumni network. Wrote one student, "Big school. Big alumni base, over 9,000 people." Explained another, "I came here for the West Coast Trojan alumni network."

UNIV. OF SOUTHERN CALIFORNIA GRADUATE SCHOOL OF BUSINESS ADMINISTRATION

STUDENT LIFE/CAMPUS

USC boasts a 150-acre park-like campus sitting right in the middle of L.A. On the plus side, it's a short ride to the bright lights of downtown L.A. On the minus side, it's just a short ride to Watts, one of L.A.'s less appealing neighborhoods. However, for an urban school USC boasts a lower crime and violence rate than most other large research universities located in or near urban areas. Despite the relative safety of the campus, most students opt to take advantage of the L.A. lifestyle and live in the beach communities of Manhattan, Hermosa, and Redondo Beach about a thirty-minute drive away. There is rarely a shortage of things to do on campus, or in L.A. As one student put it, "USC is a great school in many ways—academics, extracurricular activities, sports, etc." Social activism is extremely popular. Shortly after the L.A. riots in the spring of 1992, USC entrepreneur students provided mentoring to owners of stricken businesses and helped them apply for disaster loans.

Like most B-schools, USC takes its entering class of 200 students and divides them into smaller sections of fifty students each. Section mates take all the first-year courses together and, according to USC MBAs, do a lot of "first-year bonding." They also do a lot of work. Students spend approximately thirty to forty hours a week studying outside of class. This tapers off by the second year. Apparently the school's emphasis on teamwork has paid off. Over and over, students praise USC for its "healthy balance on competition and teamwork." There's competition, but this is mostly self-driven. Teamwork and the desire to help a classmate is the overriding ethic. But all this touchy-feely stuff doesn't come at the expense of smarts. Students say classmates are bright and professionally diverse. Wrote one, "People here are of high caliber and bring a lot of their work background into the classroom."

USC attracts a twenty-one percent international population, but it falls short in attracting minorities—only eight percent make up the student body.

ADMISSIONS

According to the school, USC considers essays, college GPA, letters of recommendation, extracurricular activities, work experience, GMAT scores, leadership, and interviews. USC recommends that applicants be proficient in mathematics, through calculus. USC goes by rolling admissions. Students are notified of a decision approximately three weeks after receipt of the completed application, including test scores. The final deadline for applicants is April 1. Students who are placed on a waitlist decision are notified of a post by June 30. On a case-by-case basis, students may defer admission for one year.

According to the school, "We are a member of the Consortium for Graduate Study in Management, offering fellowships for talented minorities."

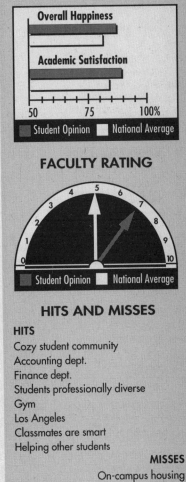

STUDENTS' OVERVIEW BOX

Overall Happiness

Academic Satisfaction

50   75   100%

■ Student Opinion □ National Average

FACULTY RATING

■ Student Opinion ■ National Average

HITS AND MISSES

HITS

Cozy student community
Accounting dept.
Finance dept.
Students professionally diverse
Gym
Los Angeles
Classmates are smart
Helping other students

MISSES

On-campus housing
Library

APPLICANTS ALSO LOOK AT

UC Berkeley
Northwestern U.
UC Los Angeles
Stanford U.
New York University
Columbia U.
U Pennsylvania
U Chicago

FOR MORE INFORMATION, CONTACT:

Annette Loschset
Ass't Dean of Admissions
Bridge Hall, 101 MC 1421
Los Angeles, CA 90089-1421
(213) 740-7846
eMail: USCMBA@SBA.USC.edu

SOUTHERN METHODIST UNIVERSITY: EDWIN L. COX SCHOOL OF BUSINESS

ADMISSIONS FACTS

Type of school	Private

Demographics

No. of men	166
No. of women	70
No. of minorities	13
No. of int'l students	53

EQUAL TREATMENT GRAPH

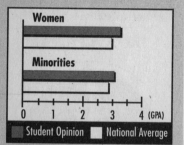

Women

Minorities

0 1 2 3 4 (GPA)

■ Student Opinion   □ National Average

Admissions Statistics

Avg. GMAT	612
Avg. undergraduate GPA	3.05
Avg. age at entry	25
No. of applicants	409
No. accepted	274
No. enrolled	114

Deadlines and Notifications

Regular application	5/15
Regular notification	rolling
Special dates	N/A

Focus of Curriculum

General Management

Academic Specialties

Accounting, Finance

FINANCIAL FACTS

In-state tuition	$17,000
Out-of-state tuition	$17,000
On-campus housing	$2,476–$3,394

ACADEMICS

As one student put it, Southern Methodist University (SMU) has long been known for its "outstanding ties to the Dallas business community." More recently, SMU has become known for its progressive curriculum, a result of the school's transformation from a one-year to a two-year program. The most exciting part of this change has been the addition of the Business Leadership Center (BLC), through which students tailor their learning to their individual needs. According to the school, the BLC builds students' skills in four areas: Preparing for Academic and Career Success; Communication Skills; Team Work and Team Building; and Coaching, Developing, Motivating, and Influencing. Over and over, students told us this program is a huge plus. Explained one, "The BLC fulfills many other aspects of preparing the student for the real world. Seminars, speakers, and consultants help round out the edge where the classroom leaves off."

The first-year curriculum consists of ten core courses and runs concurrently with BLC seminars to allow students opportunities to practice new skills in the classroom. Second-year students take just five required courses. By all reported, the curriculum is demanding. It's underlying themes are international business and issues in leadership. Again, BLC seminars are interwoven throughout the program, as are career enhancement workshops. One program, the Executive Mentor Connection, matches a professional mentor with five students each. Students might find themselves invited by the mentor to attend a senior management meeting where they grapple with a thorny issue. Students appreciate this program and say, "It's of incredible personal and professional value."

The majority of students told us SMU doesn't just pay lip service to administrative responsiveness and student involvement. One student wrote, "Excellent program. Very proactive approach from staff and faculty seeking constant improvement." Overall, students gave themselves high marks for their skills in the functional areas, a strong indicator that the trendy topics have not come at the expense of the basics. Students rated themselves sky-high in their interpersonal, and presentation skills. Strong marks also went to their general management, finance, accounting, and computer skills. All in all, students agree: SMU is providing them an excellent education. Plus: few schools profiled in this book felt as confident as SMU grads about the boost they feel the MBA will give them both short and long term.

PLACEMENT AND RECRUITING

The majority of students report they are not satisfied with the efforts of the career services office nor the range of companies recruiting. Complained one student, "Career placement is almost non-existent." Students say alumni are very helpful in the job search but that "few graduates move throughout the country and thus SMU's reputation is very localized." This might explain why SMU places only sixty percent of it's MBAs at graduation, and only seventy-seven percent three months after. Companies with the biggest take of SMU grads are Andersen Consulting, EDS, American Airlines, Ernst and Young, and Deloitte and Touche.

SOUTHERN METHODIST UNIVERSITY: EDWIN L. COX SCHOOL OF BUSINESS

STUDENT LIFE/CAMPUS

SMU MBAs give themselves high grades for teamwork: "The cooperation among students is great. We also have many community service activities so we can interact with the community while improving our skills." Adds another, "We aren't cutthroat like at some other institutions." However one student's wish list contains a request for more team - *building* skills: "The classes have a lot of team projects. These can be frustrating. Some facilitation to help us learn to work together more than just heaving projects at us would have been very successful." Class participation counts heavily towards the grade. Although students say it's critical to do all the assigned reading, the workload is manageable, the pressure moderate.

The SMU B-school is housed in a three-building complex. The facilities in these buildings got high marks across the board. Reported one student, "The classroom facilities are first rate (multi-media, comfortable furnishings) and the electronic resources of the Business Information Center are the best in the nation." Students are also pleased with the library and the state-of-the-art gym. Both off-campus and on-campus housing is reportedly attractive and readily available.

Students at SMU spend their time outside of class playing intramural tennis and volleyball. A favorite event is the spring golf tournament. Every Thursday night is drink-and-be-happy hour. On weekends, groups of students venture off-campus to enjoy the city delights of Dallas. But the dating scene is light: "Given our age group in grad school, most people are married or in steady relationships."

Although SMU is located in a major metropolitan area, it lacks the diversity of an urban school. Students we surveyed agreed—the student body is not ethnically and racially diverse. However they agreed that they are professionally diverse and smart.

ADMISSIONS

The SMU admissions office told us that a strong GMAT is most important, and then in descending order, interview, GPA, work experience (not required), extracurricular activities, and essays. Non-U.S. applicants must take the TOEFL exam. The school writes, "Admissions staff evaluate all facets of an application and are subjective with their evaluations." They look for students who are "focused and highly motivated." Rolling admissions decisions begin to be made in January for the full-time entering class. The final deadline for filing an application is May 15. Students are notified of a decision within four to six weeks of receipt of the completed application. On a case-by-case basis, students may be placed on a waitlist.

STUDENTS' OVERVIEW BOX

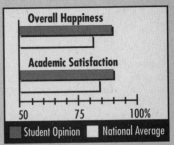

FACULTY RATING

HITS AND MISSES

HITS
Accounting dept.
Helping other students
On-campus housing

MISSES
Marketing dept.
Ethnic & racial diversity
Placement

APPLICANTS ALSO LOOK AT

U Texas-Austin
Vanderbilt U.
Tulane U.
Emory U.

FOR MORE INFORMATION, CONTACT:
Keith Pendergrass, MBA Office
Cox School of Business
282 Crow Building
Dallas, TX 75275-0333
(214) 768-2630; (800) 472-3622
FAX (214) 768-4099
eMail: mbainfo@mail.cox.smu.edu

STANFORD UNIVERSITY: STANFORD GRADUATE SCHOOL OF BUSINESS

ADMISSIONS FACTS

Type of school	Private

Demographics

No. of men	530
No. of women	196
No. of minorities	133
No. of int'l students	177

EQUAL TREATMENT GRAPH

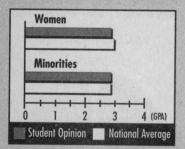

Admissions Statistics

Avg. GMAT	N/A
Avg. undergraduate GPA	N/A
Avg. age at entry	27.2
No. of applicants	6,000
No. accepted	N/A
No. enrolled	360

Deadlines and Notifications

Regular application	3/15
Regular notification	6/1
Special dates	N/A

Focus of Curriculum

General Management

Academic Specialties

Accounting, Finance, General Management, Marketing, Strategic Management, Nonprofit Management

Joint Degrees

MBA/Ph.D.-School of Engineering, MBA/MS-Manufacturing Systems Engineering, JD/MBA, MBA, MBA Public Management

Special Programs

Health Services Management option, The Speakers Platform, Global Management Program

FINANCIAL FACTS

In-state tuition	$21,189
Out-of-state tuition	$21,189
On-campus housing	$8,600

ACADEMICS

The Stanford Graduate School of Business is indisputably one of America's great B-schools. If you study here, you will study among the nation's best and brightest, learn from Nobel Prize-winning faculty, and gain access to power employers. The first-year curriculum features a quantitative orientation and is extremely demanding, so much so that students frequently complain that it causes a synaptic meltdown. It's common for first-years to experience panic attacks about whether they'll make it or not. Despite their fears, almost no one flunks out.

Stanford breaks its year into three quarters: fall, winter, and spring. First-years are required to take eleven core courses on four broad areas: organizational behavior; business and the changing environment; economics; functional areas such as accounting, finance, marketing, operations; and computer modeling, decision analysis/statistics. Students can take exemption exams to place out of cores. During the second year, students may choose from over 100 electives. Wrote one student, "Elective classes often work with local businesses; it's great to see real-world applications of knowledge." Favorites are: Strategic Management in the Nonprofit Environment, Personal Creativity in Business, Strategy and Action in the Information Processing Industry, and Power and Politics in Organizations. The interest in nonprofit topics is related to the popularity of the school's Public Management Program (PMP), which students describe as excellent. PMP is a certificate which is earned by taking three public management electives in addition to their required courses. Stanford also offers a Global Management Program within the MBA. Of the professors, students report: "Although there are outliers on the faculty—duds along with the truly outstanding teachers—on average they get the job done." Less-than-exciting teaching tends to occur in core courses. Some of the best learning experiences are found in the visiting speakers program. Wrote one student, "This is a great place to meet entrepreneurs such as Scott McNealy, CEO of Sun Microsystems."

PLACEMENT AND RECRUITING

In 1994, 194 companies interviewed on-campus. A large number of graduates go to work for smaller, high-growth ventures in both Silicon Valley and elsewhere. Ninety-six percent of the class had a job within three months of graduation. Average starting salaries were among the three highest of schools profiled in this book—$70,000 (which does not include sign-on bonuses)—a solid return on one's investment. The only complaint was about the recruiting grind, which students said is "unbelievably pressure-packed, especially when classmates have offers and you don't."

STANFORD UNIVERSITY: STANFORD GRADUATE SCHOOL OF BUSINESS

STUDENT LIFE/CAMPUS

As one student put it, several factors make Stanford stand out: "The absolute irrelevance of grades, which includes a nondisclosure policy, the entrepreneurial spirit of the class, the supportive and comfortable atmosphere, the emphasis on social life, and the access to Silicon Valley." Much of student life revolves around the student clubs, of which there are over 100, including one for spouses and partners, The High Teach Club, and the "I Have a Dream Program," unique to the Stanford Business School. To judge by the responses to our survey, students are wild about each other. Raved one, "The most valuable resource is the student body, 670+ energized folks who love to have fun." Located in suburban Palo Alto, Stanford is what California dreamin' is all about: sunny days, breathtaking views, hot tubs, year-round swimming in the school's outdoor pool and, just a few hours' drive away, skiing in Lake Tahoe. A sprawling golf course on campus makes golf clubs *de rigueur*. Friday afternoons are reserved for Liquidity Preference Functions (LPF)—a veritable beerfest. Tuesday nights it's the "Friends of Arjay Miller" a.k.a. FOAM (which includes everyone). As for the campus, it's beautiful. Spanish-style buildings feature red-tiled roofs, "a Stanford trademark." Raved one student, "We also have a fabulous research center. I'm amazed at the breadth and depth of data available on-line or on CD-ROM. This is almost worth the price of tuition alone!" On-campus housing is available, but dorm-like. Most students opt to rent shared houses in the hilly communities nearby. Many of these belong on the cover of *Architectural Digest* and are expensive (a four bedroom runs $1,800-$2,400 per month). But house/hot tub parties are one of the chief forms of social entertainment.

Unsurprisingly, students agree the student body is super-smart. But they also say they're ethnically and socially diverse. Claimed one, "Diversity is more than recruiting rhetoric at Stanford. There are plenty of former I-bankers and consultants. But classmates also include a professional soccer player, a labor union leader, an air-force pilot, and professional triathlete." All in all, students are unanimous: "Stanford is an absolutely wonderful place to go to school."

ADMISSIONS

Notes the admissions office, " We do not interview individual applicants. We ask that you treat your essay as an interview on paper. We have tried to design our essays to elicit the same type of information that you would share in a face-to-face meeting. Focus on the essays. We want to get to know you, so don't simply reiterate information we find elsewhere in your application. We use the nation's most selective admissions process to admit students who represent a broad range of professional and personal achievement." Affirmative action is considered for Native Americans, Mexican-Americans, African-Americans, and Puerto Ricans. Applications are batched in one of three rounds. According to the school, "The earlier you apply, the better." College seniors are admitted with a mandatory two-year deferral.

STUDENTS' OVERVIEW BOX

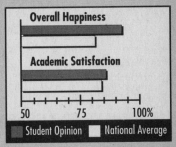

Overall Happiness

Academic Satisfaction

50   75   100%

■ Student Opinion □ National Average

FACULTY RATING

■ Student Opinion □ National Average

HITS AND MISSES

HITS
Gen. management
Teamwork skills
Classmates are smart
Cozy student community
Library
Placement

MISSES
Gym
Getting into popular courses

APPLICANTS ALSO LOOK AT
Cornell U.
UC Los Angeles
U Chicago
U Texas-Austin
U Michigan
UNC Chapel Hill
U Virginia
Dartmouth College
U Pennsylvania
Harvard

FOR MORE INFORMATION, CONTACT:
MBA Admissions
Stanford University
Stanford, CA 94305-5015
(415) 723-2766

SYRACUSE UNIVERSITY SCHOOL OF MANAGEMENT

ADMISSIONS FACTS

Type of school	Private

Demographics

No. of men	165
No. of women	85
No. of minorities	20
No. of int'l students	90

EQUAL TREATMENT GRAPH

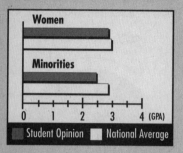

Admissions Statistics

Avg. GMAT	550
Avg. undergraduate GPA	3.1
Avg. age at entry	25
No. of applicants	650
No. accepted	300
No. enrolled	125

Deadlines and Notifications

Regular application	4/20
Regular notification	rolling (3 weeks)
Special dates	EDP 11/15
	notification 12/5

Focus of Curriculum

General Management

Academic Specialties

General Management

Joint Degrees

JD/MBA, MBA/MS in Nursing Management, JD/MS in Accounting

Special Programs

The Innovation Management Program, MS in Accounting, Part-time availability

FINANCIAL FACTS

In-state tuition	$12,586
Out-of-state tuition	$12,586
On-campus housing	N/A

ACADEMICS

Like many B-schools, Syracuse has responded to the obvious weaknesses of theory-based programs and retooled its curriculum to reflect the times. The updated curriculum addresses topics such as globalization, social responsibility, ethics, technology, diversity and managing total quality. Distinct to Syracuse, and worthy of an honorable mention, is the "management and the natural environment" theme, which focuses on the responsibilities of business in environmental issues. Also new and exciting: the Entrepreneurship and Emerging Enterprises Center and a distinguished lecture series. A lot of credit goes to Syracuse's new dean who spearheaded much of the change and a focus on curriculum quality. Said one satisfied MBA "Syracuse has put considerable time and effort into improving the MBA experience."

The first-year curriculum is extremely regimented. You have to take what they tell you. This consists of the unifying theme courses, personal skills development courses such as "teamwork and groups" and "computer proficiency," and professional core courses. During the second year, students choose from seven elective courses and complete their remaining core courses. Electives can be used to specialize, or pursue a general management program. Areas of study include human resources, innovation management, law and public policy, managerial statistics, and transportation and distribution. Students can also pursue interdisciplinary studies - from law to engineering and computer science, a bonus for MBAs who want to broaden their marketability by studying at Syracuse's top-rated Newhouse Graduate School of Public Communications.

In the complaint department: not enough senior, tenured faculty teach the core courses. There's "forced group work, not teamwork," and the school "needs improved computer facilities." We also heard that too many students are accepted directly from undergrad school. On the plus side, students praise the faculty for their enthusiasm and feel "the student/faculty ratio is excellent."

Several students told us they chose Syracuse because it is the designated B-school in their army controller program. Non-military MBAs said this adds to the diversity of the school.

PLACEMENT AND RECRUITING

The Career Center offers services such as a resume book, a mock interview day, and a uniquely valuable program—counseling on networking. Syracuse is responding to the Career Center's mediocre grades (awarded by its students in prior surveys) with significant new funding, additional computers, job-posting databases, and software to increase accessibility to recruiter info. Placement rates are solid: seventy-nine percent of the class of '94 had been placed three months after graduation, a significant increase from two years ago. The average starting salary: $47, 600.

SYRACUSE UNIVERSITY SCHOOL OF MANAGEMENT

STUDENT LIFE/CAMPUS

A small program to begin with—only 130 in each class—Syracuse makes the program even smaller by sectioning students into groups of forty each. Over and over, students raved about how this school "has made major changes over the last two years—all for the better!" They also described Syracuse as "student-centered," "diverse," and overall, "a great experience."

Students report they are burdened with a heavy workload. This is the result of the pace and breadth of the new curriculum. They study an average of twenty-five to thirty hours a week and report a moderate, not killer, amount of pressure. Papers and class participation are the preferred instruments of the grading system. A fairly competitive atmosphere prevails, although overriding this is a student body interested in helping others. Agreed the majority of MBAs, "Syracuse is very teamwork oriented." Added one business type "The upper twenty-five percent of the second years are highly competitive. I fall in this category and find the pressure stimulating."

Students report they're satisfied with the school's facilities. The campus itself is beautiful—a 200-acre spread of grassy lawns and historical-landmark buildings. The town of Syracuse has a secluded, rural feel. The weather in winter: misery. A decent though not robust social scene exists here. Particularly noteworthy is Syracuse's "Friday Shared Experience" program, which is a lot less touchy-feely than it sounds. Also garnering star reviews: Orange Consulting Group, a student-run organization that arranges for MBAs to consult with area corporations. Students are paid for their consulting work, but altruism is taught early here; all monies go to a scholarship fund for other students. Fridays are classless, held open for job fairs, debates, reviews of exam topics with profs, or just goofing off.

ADMISSIONS

The admissions office considers (not listed in order of importance) your essays, college GPA, letters of recommendation, extracurricular activities, work experience, and GMAT score. An interview is encouraged. Writes the school, "We use a subjective process to evaluate candidates. Admissions formulas or models are not used. Each candidate is evaluated based upon his or her individual qualifications. Weaknesses in some areas can be offset by strengths in other areas. Personal interviews are very important and can be conducted in Syracuse and major cities throughout the U.S." Decisions are made on a rolling admissions basis. Candidates may defer admission for up to two years.

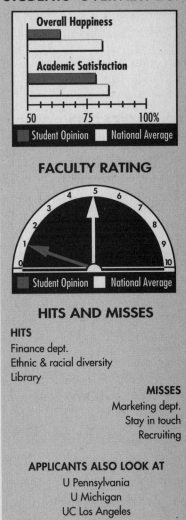

STUDENTS' OVERVIEW BOX

FACULTY RATING

HITS AND MISSES

HITS
Finance dept.
Ethnic & racial diversity
Library

MISSES
Marketing dept.
Stay in touch
Recruiting

APPLICANTS ALSO LOOK AT
U Pennsylvania
U Michigan
UC Los Angeles
U Arizona
Rensselaer P.I.
SUNY Buffalo
New York University
U Rochester

FOR MORE INFORMATION, CONTACT:
School of Management
Crouse-Hinds School of
Management Building
Syracuse, NY 13244
(315) 443-3850

UNIV. OF TENNESSEE AT KNOXVILLE COLLEGE OF BUSINESS ADMINISTRATION

ADMISSIONS FACTS

Type of school	Public

Demographics

No. of men	109
No. of women	46
No. of minorities	7
No. of int'l students	8

EQUAL TREATMENT GRAPH

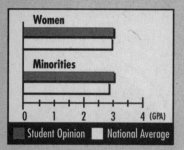

Admissions Statistics

Avg. GMAT	601
Avg. undergraduate GPA	3.33
Avg. age at entry	28
No. of applicants	540
No. accepted	156
No. enrolled	82

Deadlines and Notifications

Regular application	4/1
Regular notification	rolling
Special dates	N/A

Focus of Curriculum

Technology

Academic Specialties

Technology

Joint Degrees

JD/MBA, BA/MBA in five years

Special Programs

The MBA Symposia, TOMBA, The Oak Ridge National Library (ORNL)

FINANCIAL FACTS

In-state tuition	N/A
Out-of-state tuition	N/A
On-campus housing	$1,725

ACADEMICS

The University of Tennessee at Knoxville (UTK) B-school has overhauled its program to introduce a new paradigm for learning: cross-functional courses, team-teaching, team-building, global study, and experiential exercises. This roll-up-your-shirtsleeves, activity-based program offers students more real-world experience than they could hope to find at most other B-schools. Indeed, UTK is the most innovative program in its regional area, and students rave about the new curriculum. Here's what they say: "Our focus is on customer service and quality, rather than learning the individual functions." "UTK's new MBA program is both innovative and comprehensive. We will be well prepared to serve as cross-functional leaders."

According to the school, "The centerpiece of the core curriculum is a yearlong case experience where students run their own business. Working in teams and focusing on the themes of customer values and organizational systems, students make the management decisions necessary to keep the business in operation. They solve large and complex problems and then give formal presentations to executives who have faced similar problems."

Distinct to UTK is the Oak Ridge National Laboratory (ORNL), which offers students access to pioneering technology. According to the school, "Students develop marketing strategies for commercializing technologies developed by ORNL. Selected students from any concentration may serve as consultants and market analysts who work with scientists from ORNL to identify, research and, when possible, market technologies with commercial potential."

As structured as the first year is, the second year is unstructured. Students take eight specialized electives to build an area of concentration. This allows them to tailor a course of study to their career objectives. Up to four electives may be taken in a single area; the remaining electives may be used to form a second concentration or support the major one. Overall, students told us they've struggled with finance and accounting. A dozen or so say their quantitative skills also need bolstering. Complained one, "Those without business backgrounds should have programmed learning modules to catch up in accounting, computers." However, they judge their skills in marketing, general management, operations, interpersonal skills, teamwork, and presentation skills to be quite strong. Students report the "key learnings here have been how to think—not what to think."

PLACEMENT AND RECRUITING

Particularly noteworthy is the one-semester mandatory business placement course designed to provide students strategies for an independent job search. Its effectiveness is reflected in Tennessee's 1994 placement of ninety percent of it's grads within 3 months of their graduation. Recruiters grabbing the most MBAs: Philips Consumer Electronics, Burlington Northern, Wachovia Bank of Georgia, Morgan Keegan Investment Bank, Procter and Gamble, Andersen Consulting, Eli Lilly, Frito-Lay, Hoechst Celanese Group.

UNIV. OF TENNESSEE AT KNOXVILLE COLLEGE OF BUSINESS ADMINISTRATION

STUDENT LIFE/CAMPUS

UTK features a very small program. A maximum of 100 students are admitted each year. These are divided into two sections of fifty each. All entering students participate in the same yearlong first-year program. Students describe a heavy workload and hit the books an average of thirty to forty hours a week. This results in a fair amount of pressure, though not enough to provoke an anxiety attack. To lighten the load, the majority of students work in study groups.

Observed one student, "The focus here is on learning and not on competition." A unique grading system also encourages cooperation in which "grading is based on team and individual performance and comprehensive written evaluations, NOT exams."

Students report a high quality of life. This is due in part to the terrific social scene and in part to a campus that boasts state-of-the-art facilities. TOMBA, the Tennessee Organization of MBAs, is the professional and social association for full- and part-time MBA students. The heart and soul of student life, TOMBA not only organizes the social events for students but organizes the network of UTK MBA alums, runs a professional speaker series, and orchestrates a major community service project. All MBA students are expected to join. As for UTK's hometown, one student wrote, "Knoxville is a great town to go to school in, but you wouldn't want to live here full-time." Known for its great basketball and football teams, one Big Orange supporter wrote, "Sports are huge."

A note on diversity: Although students agree that interaction among ethnic groups is easy and relaxed, there are unfortunately few minority students with whom that assertion can be tested.

ADMISSIONS

According to the admissions office, your GMAT scores are considered most important. After that, in descending order, your college GPA, work experience, interview, essays, extracurricular activities, and letters of recommendation come into play. "Since the UTK program is relatively small," writes the office of admissions, "we can give a good deal of individual attention to our applicants in order to determine whether ours is the right program for them and whether they are right for our program. As often as possible, we invite students to visit the campus, sit in on classes, and talk with current MBA students. In addition, we involve the faculty and administration in the admissions process."

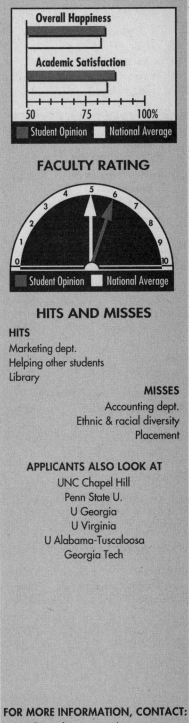

STUDENTS' OVERVIEW BOX

Overall Happiness

Academic Satisfaction

50   75   100%

Student Opinion   National Average

FACULTY RATING

Student Opinion   National Average

HITS AND MISSES

HITS
Marketing dept.
Helping other students
Library

MISSES
Accounting dept.
Ethnic & racial diversity
Placement

APPLICANTS ALSO LOOK AT
UNC Chapel Hill
Penn State U.
U Georgia
U Virginia
U Alabama-Tuscaloosa
Georgia Tech

FOR MORE INFORMATION, CONTACT:
College of Business Administration
527 Stokely Management Center
Knoxville, TN 37996-0550
(615) 974-5033

UNIVERSITY OF TEXAS AT ARLINGTON COLLEGE OF BUSINESS ADMINISTRATION

ADMISSIONS FACTS

Type of school	Public

Demographics

No. of men	N/A
No. of women	N/A
No. of minorities	N/A
No. of int'l students	N/A

EQUAL TREATMENT GRAPH

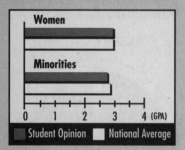

Women

Minorities

0 1 2 3 4 (GPA)

■ Student Opinion □ National Average

Admissions Statistics

Avg. GMAT	N/A
Avg. undergraduate GPA	N/A
Avg. age at entry	N/A
No. of applicants	N/A
No. accepted	N/A
No. enrolled	N/A

Deadlines and Notifications

Regular application	N/A
Regular notification	N/A
Special dates	N/A

Focus of Curriculum

Specialized

Academic Specialties

Finance, Accounting, Information Systems

FINANCIAL FACTS

In-state tuition	N/A
Out-of-state tuition	N/A
On-campus housing	N/A

ACADEMICS

Most students would agree with the one who wrote, "The University of Texas-Arlington (UTA) offers the 'most bang for the buck' of any MBA program in North Texas. It's just as good as, if not better than Southern Methodist University or Texas Christian University." Wrote another, "I chose UTA because of its affordability *and* flexibility." Indeed, if you're a working student, UTA is a natural first choice. Students may begin the program in either the fall, spring, or summer semester—part-time or full-time. The majority of classes are offered at night. Students with prior academic work in business may waive out of equivalent foundation courses or simply go on to the "advanced" courses. Expect loads of math: The curriculum has a strong quantitative slant. Concentrations are available in one of the following areas: accounting, economics, finance, information systems, management, international management, management science, marketing, and real estate. The majority of students report they feel well-trained by their studies in accounting and finance—UTA power subjects— and report above-average quantitative skills. Students were less confident of their skills in marketing, operations, and presentations/communications. "The program is very good at the basic tools," wrote one student, "but is weak in application via simulations and experiential activities." Nonetheless one student says, "School is continually trying to stay with current trends and technology, especially information technology courses."

As for the faculty, one student commented, "Most of the professors make learning relevant to the 'real world'; not just theory. They're also willing to help you one-on-one outside of class." As for their teaching methodology, one MBA wrote, "Professors and lectures place lots of emphasis on research papers and presentations." But as pleased as students are with their profs, students are displeased with the school's administration. One student complained, "I have been frustrated by the bureaucratic 'policies and procedures' that the school operates under." A frequent complaint was about the facilities—the library, computers, and campus—which are considered inadequate. Still, one MBA countered, "UTA is striving to improve and has improved things since I began."

PLACEMENT AND RECRUITING

According to the school, "Seventy-six of the 131 students who graduated in 1988–89 responded to the College's annual salary survey. Almost ninety-five percent of the respondents were employed. The average salary was $38,824. The salary range was $22,000 to $90,000." Explained one student, "Starting salaries are lower than some of the other MBA schools in the state since recruiting is not a strength." Added another, "This school is not well thought of across the country. However, in the Dallas/Fort Worth metro area, the school is very respected and carries a lot of weight with local companies."

UNIVERSITY OF TEXAS AT ARLINGTON COLLEGE OF BUSINESS ADMINISTRATION

STUDENT LIFE/CAMPUS

UTA is geared toward the commuter/part-timer. Wrote one typical student, "UTA is close to home and work. I wouldn't give up working full-time to attend school." The majority of students are married. All of this translates into a commuter school atmosphere: the student body is less than cohesive, the on-campus social life dead. Wrote one student, "I sorely miss the camaraderie that my undergrad university provided." Explained another, "Student organizations are in great numbers but student apathy towards them is just horrible." This is a large school, with a large student body. And there isn't much interaction outside of the classroom." Still many MBAs weren't bothered by the lack of *esprit de corps*. Huffed one, "This is a commuter school. I'm not interested in the social activities it has to offer."

On a happier note, UTA MBAs agreed the student body is both professionally and ethnically diverse. Roughly eighteen percent of the student body is foreign. Reported one, "Nice mix of working, non-working, foreign and domestic students." Although one student noted, "There are more geeks here than at any other school in America," another wrote, "this school is proudly homophobic!" As for their smarts, one MBA noted, "UTA students have appreciable academic skills." According to our survey, students are moderately competitive. As one student put it, "Constructive competition is encouraged." This means that students aren't the note-stealing type. On the other hand, they're not the most helpful either. A large number of students say their teamwork skills aren't the kind to win anyone Mr. or Ms. Congeniality. Still, the majority work in study groups. The workload is considered reasonable given students' nine to five workday schedule.

A final note: For the rare student who wants to attend full-time and live on-campus, one student told us, "School housing is almost unavailable. You have to wait for a very long time, and the opportunity to get something is zero."

ADMISSIONS

While it accepts more applicants than it rejects, Arlington does expect its entering class to have a great deal of work experience to draw from. GMAT scores rank next in importance, followed by undergraduate GPA and letters of recommendation.

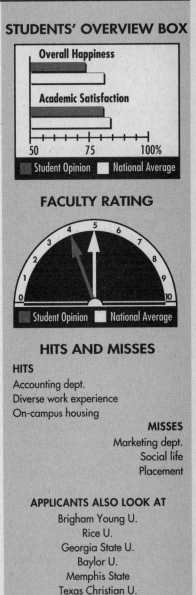

STUDENTS' OVERVIEW BOX

Overall Happiness

Academic Satisfaction

50   75   100%

■ Student Opinion   □ National Average

FACULTY RATING

■ Student Opinion   □ National Average

HITS AND MISSES

HITS
Accounting dept.
Diverse work experience
On-campus housing

MISSES
Marketing dept.
Social life
Placement

APPLICANTS ALSO LOOK AT
Brigham Young U.
Rice U.
Georgia State U.
Baylor U.
Memphis State
Texas Christian U.
U Dallas
Southern Meth. U.

FOR MORE INFORMATION, CONTACT:
College of Business Administration
P.O. Box 19376, UTA Station
Arlington, TX 76019
(817) 273-3004

UNIVERSITY OF TEXAS AT AUSTIN GRADUATE SCHOOL OF BUSINESS

ADMISSIONS FACTS

Type of school	Public

Demographics

No. of men	306
No. of women	152
No. of minorities	101
No. of int'l students	82

EQUAL TREATMENT GRAPH

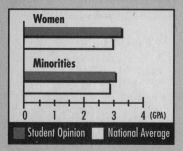

Admissions Statistics

Avg. GMAT	625
Avg. undergraduate GPA	3.36
Avg. age at entry	27
No. of applicants	2,700
No. accepted	794
No. enrolled	458

Deadlines and Notifications

Regular application	3/15 (domestic)
Regular notification	within 8 weeks
Special dates	2/1 (international)

Focus of Curriculum

Specialized

Academic Specialties

Accounting, Management Information Systems, Marketing, Human Resources, Entrepreneurship

Special Programs

Foreign Study, The Masters in Professional Accounting Program, Joint degree programs

FINANCIAL FACTS

In-state tuition	$3,480
Out-of-state tuition	$15,360
On-campus housing	$7800-8800

ACADEMICS

The University of Texas at Austin (UT) is one of the nation's finest public B-schools. Students say the "bang for the buck" is unbeatable. Among the academic strengths of the school are accounting, human resources, and information systems management (ISM), the last of which is supported by a major grant from IBM and utilizes CLASSROOM 2000, a special facility designed for advanced ISM study. Particularly noteworthy is the marketing department, which focuses on brand management and consumer and trade promotions. Praises one MBA, "Alliances between UT and industry are numerous. Marketing students have opportunities to partner with companies such as Proctor and Gamble and Nestle to get real world experience."

The first year is extremely structured. The second year is flexible—students tailor their programs by choosing from over 170 electives. Students give high marks to the information technology concentration: "The school offers a wide variety of excellent courses in information technology ranging from basic systems info to database design." Also singled out for excellence is the school's "entrepreneurship focus." Distinct to UT is the Quality Management Consortia, which are made up of fourteen small companies that make a two-year commitment (via funding and sponsoring internships) to classroom education and on-site implementation of Total Quality Management (TQM). Equally exciting is MOOT CORP, a venture competition program offered as part of the technology management and entrepreneurship concentration. Students develop detailed, business plans and then match them against those of their peers at schools such as Harvard, Purdue, and Wharton.

The program has made big strides in improving the quality of it's faculty over the last two years. Adjunct professors are widely claimed to be terrific: "Program has extraordinary adjunct professors who bring stellar real world experience to the academic world." Exciting program enhancements include a new $1.6M MBA investment fund intended to give "participants real experience in money and management and security analysis." The most common complaints were about lightweight academics, assignment of busywork, and placement. But according to students, the administration has begun a campaign to correct these deficiencies. The administration has supported research at corporations across the country to determine what skills are needed in the marketplace—both short- and long-term.

PLACEMENT AND RECRUITING

Over 300 companies interviewed on-campus. Roughly eighty percent of the graduating class had a job within three months of graduation. The hot recruiters: American Airlines, GTE, United Airlines, Lotus, IBM, Xerox, 3M, Proctor & Gamble, Ford Motor Company, the Big Six accounting firms, major I-banks, Wells Fargo, and McKinsey. Nonetheless, we're told "All students aren't interested in climbing the traditional corporate ladder. I've met a lot of people who want to work with non-profits, the government, or start their own small companies."

UNIVERSITY OF TEXAS AT AUSTIN GRADUATE SCHOOL OF BUSINESS

STUDENT LIFE/CAMPUS

UT is housed in the George Kozmetsky Center for Business Education, a 350,000-square-foot complex of four inter-linked buildings containing classrooms, research centers, and computer laboratories. As for Austin itself, students ranked UT's hometown as one of the nation's best. Close to the midway point between Dallas, Houston, and San Antonio, Austin boasts a mixture of high culture, tropical weather, and outdoorsy vacation activities such as boating, rock climbing, fishing, and horseback riding. And just in case you were concerned, one Texan we surveyed assured us, "Austin does not have cows walking down the street." Indeed, Austin is home to dozens of entrepreneurial, high-tech companies. Much of student life revolves around the Graduate Business Council, which sponsors activities such as sports events and informal get-togethers. Students also plan their orientation week, graduation week events, and host the Friday night Distinguished Lecturer Program. Professional and student groups worth joining include the Marketing Network, Environmental Management Concern, and the Graduate Finance Association.

From class assignments to consulting projects, group work dominates UT. Not surprisingly, students rated themselves as outstanding team-players. Students here are competitive, but "supportive and willing to help others." High ranking also went to classmates' "smarts."

Minority enrollment is particularly high because UT participates in an eleven-school consortium which recruits and funds gifted minority candidates. Ford Motor Company recently asked the school to put together a team of Hispanic students to develop a plan to recapture market share in the Hispanic automobile purchasing category. Ford was so impressed with the proposal that they flew the students to Dearborn headquarters for a two-day series of presentations to top brass.

ADMISSIONS

The admissions office uses the following criteria to evaluate applicants (not listed in order of importance): GMAT scores, essays, academic record and college GPA, work experience, and letters of recommendation. An interview is not required, but strongly encouraged. Writes the school: "Although grades and GPA are important, other areas receive substantial consideration. Personal and professional goals, achievements, extracurriculars, community involvement, and evidence of leadership and management abilities are considered in the admissions decision." The school places a high priority on increasing the representation of qualified women and minorities in the program. Decisions are made on a rolling admissions basis. Advises the school, "Apply as early as possible." Applicants are notified of a decision within six to eight weeks. On a case-by-case basis, the admissions committee allows students to defer admission for up to two years.

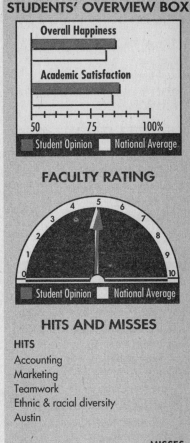

STUDENTS' OVERVIEW BOX

Overall Happiness

Academic Satisfaction

50   75   100%

■ Student Opinion   □ National Average

FACULTY RATING

■ Student Opinion   ■ National Average

HITS AND MISSES

HITS
Accounting
Marketing
Teamwork
Ethnic & racial diversity
Austin

MISSES
Placement

APPLICANTS ALSO LOOK AT
Northwestern U.
Dartmouth College
Cornell U.
Rice U.
Columbia U.
Tulane U.
U Rochester
New York University

FOR MORE INFORMATION, CONTACT:
Graduate School of Business
P.O. Box 7999
Austin, TX 78713
(512) 471-7612

TEXAS A&M UNIVERSITY COLLEGE OF BUSINESS ADMINISTRATION

ADMISSIONS FACTS

Type of school	Public

Demographics

No. of men	341
No. of women	168
No. of minorities	39
No. of int'l students	103

EQUAL TREATMENT GRAPH

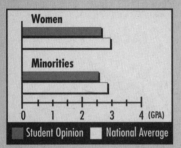

Women

Minorities

0 1 2 3 4 (GPA)

■ Student Opinion □ National Average

Admissions Statistics

Avg. GMAT	602
Avg. undergraduate GPA	3.25
Avg. age at entry	25
No. of applicants	843
No. accepted	435
No. enrolled	226

Deadlines and Notifications

Regular application	rolling
Regular notification	rolling
Special dates	N/A

Focus of Curriculum

General Management

Academic Specialties

General Management, International Business

Joint Degrees

MBA/MA in International Management with Johannes Kepler University, MBA with École Superieur de Commerce, Master of Science in five business fields

Special Programs

Study Abroad in five countries

FINANCIAL FACTS

In-state tuition	$2,077
Out-of-state tuition	$6,181
On-campus housing	$3,150

ACADEMICS

Plenty of Texas A&M B-school students agreed with the Aggie (as they like to call themselves) who wrote, "A bargain!" Even for out-of-state residents, this school offers one of the lowest tuition rates in the country.

But Texas A&M has more than price going for it. It also boasts a national reputation and, according to students, "a great location." The school's new updated curriculum starts off with an Outward Bound-style orientation, followed by an integrative three-week course called Markets and Corporate Strategy, which describes how businesses operate with diverse stockholders such as customers, the public, and investors. Students also take a two-semester leadership and development program, which focuses on ethics, cultural diversity, and leadership. A Cross Discipline Project (the CDP) gets student hands working on real-world problems and solutions. MBA teams study an existing company and then do an analysis on each of its functional areas. Unique to Texas A&M is a required summer term in which students focus on international business and work in an internship. Elective hours can be earned through internships, study abroad, or foreign language classes. Everything here features a global slant. The latest addition to the program is "Aggies on Wall-Street" which according to the school is a "3-week program beginning in the Summer of 1995." Students get to travel to the Big Apple, glad hand industry leaders, and tour the major exchanges and commercial banks.

Not everyone appreciates Texas A&M's new program. Griped one , "The new schedule cuts out people like myself who can no longer work part-time to pay for school." The marks students gave themselves for academic preparedness in all the major disciplines were above average. High scores were in the areas of accounting, general management, and teamwork. Lower scores were in marketing and operations. As for the faculty, professors receive average grades for their teaching. Students award them much higher marks for their after-class accessibility. Overall, Aggies say this school is meeting their academic needs and a providing them a career-enhancing boost.

PLACEMENT AND RECRUITING

Aggie MBAs share their placement center with the undergraduate school, which makes them unhappy. Unsurprisingly, students gave this department below-average grades. But the school has recently dedicated a full-time position in the placement center to help MBAs in their job search. Reports the school, "There was a 37% increase over last year in the number of companies recruiting MBAs on campus in the 1994-95 academic year. Additionally, we had a 100% success rate from alumni whom we requested support in locating internships for students. Indeed, Students compliment the "Aggie network" and say alumni are responsive. This last may explain A&M's ninety-three percent placement rate for 1994. Top employers: Exxon, Andersen Consulting, Arthur Andersen, and Price Waterhouse.

TEXAS A&M UNIVERSITY COLLEGE OF BUSINESS ADMINISTRATION

STUDENT LIFE/CAMPUS

By all accounts, the workload is heavier under the new program and in the first year, but it's not overwhelming. The majority of students study an average of twenty to twenty-five hours a week. In most classes, exams and class participation count heavily toward the grade.

Students here are competitive, but also cooperative. Wrote one, "Hospitality and friendliness are pervasive characteristics of peers and the community." In the complaint department Aggies feel the student body lacks diverse professional experience, a complaint we heard over and over. Students agreed that Aggies are not racially diverse. Wrote one, "Like everywhere, there is a need for more minority representation (Hispanics, blacks, and females). On the upside, students moved into a new B-School building in January 1995 which boasts excellent facilities and computer labs, and "executive-style" classrooms, although students want longer computer center hours and their own business library. As for the town of College Station, students say it's okay. The majority live off-campus in housing that is affordable, though not especially beautiful. Extracurriculars are sponsored by the MBA/MS Association, which holds a case competition, executive lecture series, and recruiter/faculty/student golf tournament. An alumni mentor program quickly gets Texas students hooked into the famed "Aggie alumni network," providing them a competitive advantage in the job search. Of course, sports are big—football, basketball, and baseball. A new recreational center opens in Fall 1995 that features an olympic size pool, weight and fitness room, aerobics, room, indoor track, and for those with no fear of heights, an indoor climbing wall—a first among B-School athletic centers.

ADMISSIONS

While Texas A&M has no cut-and-dried formula for selecting MBA applicants, they do hold them to fairly rigorous standards. Above all, your GPA and GMAT score ought to be well above average. Beyond those, your work experience (they like to see a resume), personal essay, recommendations, and the quality and rigor of your undergraduate program are all taken into consideration. Leadership in any pursuit plays well. There are no set math requirements, but A&M appreciates a strong quantitative background in its applicants. Decisions are made on a rolling admissions basis. Funds are available to cover airfare for minority student who wish to visit the campus.

STUDENTS' OVERVIEW BOX

FACULTY RATING

HITS AND MISSES

HITS
Accounting dept.
Classmates are smart

MISSES
Marketing dept.
Lack diverse work experience
Placement

APPLICANTS ALSO LOOK AT
U Texas-Austin

FOR MORE INFORMATION, CONTACT:
Masters Program Office
413 E.L. Wehner Building
College Station, TX 77843-4117
(409) 845-4714

235

TEXAS CHRISTIAN UNIVERSITY: M. J. NEELEY SCHOOL OF BUSINESS

ADMISSIONS FACTS

Type of school — Private

Demographics
No. of men	176
No. of women	85
No. of minorities	26
No. of int'l students	33

EQUAL TREATMENT GRAPH

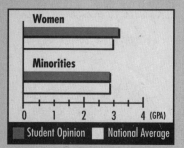

Women

Minorities

0 1 2 3 4 (GPA)

■ Student Opinion □ National Average

Admissions Statistics
Avg. GMAT	550
Avg. undergraduate GPA	3.1
Avg. age at entry	26
No. of applicants	293
No. accepted	219
No. enrolled	122

Deadlines and Notifications
Regular application	4/30
Regular notification	rolling
Special dates	N/A

Focus of Curriculum
General Management

Academic Specialties
Finance, Marketing, Management

Teaching Methodology
Case Study, Lecture

FINANCIAL FACTS
In-state tuition	$7,320
Out-of-state tuition	$7,320
On-campus housing	N/A

ACADEMICS

As one student put it, Texas Christian University (TCU) is "under recognized. By far, it has been improving its standards and courses over the past few years." Perhaps, but we heard students concerns about the program's recent struggles loud and clear: "TCU's MBA program seems to be in an adolescent stage. The majority of the MBA students have raised questions and issues to the faculty and Dean. These have been unanswered." Several students told us TCU has already begun to make it's way out if its transition. And not everyone was negative about the experience: Wrote one, "First-year students are required to participate in integrative team projects at end of each semester that is case-based and incorporates skills developed during that semester's classes—excellent "real world" experience." As for the faculty, some, but not all of the complaints were limited to that troubled, transition semester: "The first semester classes were below expectations in teaching and material covered." On a positive note, another wrote, "Faculty are ALWAYS available for discussion outside of class."

TCU offers students a two-year generalist MBA. During the second year of the program, students can concentrate their studies in one of five areas: decision sciences, finance, management, management information systems, or marketing. Across the board, students report they feel well prepared by their training in areas such as marketing, finance, accounting, general management, and teamwork. TCU is one of a select few schools that boasts a Center for Productive Communication. Raved this MBA "The Center is a wonderful facility for writing and speaking skills and is very receptive to assisting students with their many team projects and presentations." Another major asset, literally, is the Educational Investment Fund, with cash and securities totaling $1.2 million—one of the largest student-run portfolios in the nation. Here students are offered incomparable hands-on experience in investment management. For more hands-on experience, students can participate in the Student Enterprises Program, whereby teams of students act as paid consultants to various profit and not-for-profit organizations.

PLACEMENT AND RECRUITING

According to students, TCU is the best school to go to for "GREAT connections to businesses in the Dallas/Fort Worth area." Although one student groused, "Placement opportunities are only available through a campus wide career center." Stats for 1994: Seventy percent of the class had secured a position within three months of graduation. The biggest recruiters: PepsiCo, American Airlines, F.D.S. Andersen Consulting, F.D.S., Harris Methodist Health Systems. An impressive roster of grads to meet on the alumni circuit: John Roach, Chairman, CEO and President - Tandy Corporation; Webb Joiner, CEO - Bell-Helicopter-Textron; Roger King, Senior Vice President, Personnel, Pepsico; Gordon England, CEO, Lockheed-Fort Worth.

TEXAS CHRISTIAN UNIVERSITY: M. J. NEELEY SCHOOL OF BUSINESS

STUDENT LIFE/CAMPUS

TCU is a small school. Total enrollment is kept to 300 students—half the size of the national average. Classes are small too—core classes average thirty-five students, electives twenty. The workload can be substantial. One dissatisfied MBA complained, "Emphasis is on the quantity of workload instead of quality."   But another countered, "If you want unbelievable academic pressure, you won't find it here." Indeed, the majority of students study only fifteen to twenty-five hours a week. The bottom line for one MBA: "The program was a little more challenging than expected."

Enthused one MBA, "The best part of TCU is the friendliness and accessibility of the people: students, faculty, administration, and community." Raved another, "It's easy to get to know people and get help with problems." As one might expect, students here are competitive, but not into backstabbing. The school's emphasis on teamwork creates a supportive and friendly atmosphere. Though one student wrote, "Personally, I'm disappointed that 'slackers' or less-than-serious students are not screened by the first year."

Most students would agree with the one who wrote, "I enjoy the company of my fellow classmates." As for the makeup of the student body, TCU MBAs said classmates are smart and professionally diverse, but, unfortunately, not racially diverse.

Much of the social whirl is handled through the MBA Association, which organizes parties and a designated eatery/bar of the week for Thursday night get-togethers. Reported one student, "Socially all students seem to participate actively. There are many organized and casual social activities." As for TCU's hometown of Fort Worth, students think it's terrific. Most MBAs live off-campus in apartment complexes in the Hulen area of Fort Worth, a ten-minute commute by car from campus. Only one apartment complex is within walking distance of school. The average for living expenses is $8,500 per year.

ADMISSIONS

According to the school, your work/life experience is considered most important. After that, in descending order, come your extracurricular activities, college GPA, GMAT scores, essays, letters recommendation, and interview. Prerequisites include: quantitative proficiency, and a foundation in macroeconomics and microeconomics. Writes the school, "Consistent with TCU's emphasis on the individual, our admissions staff looks closely at the specific merits of each application. No single admissions formula is used. Our goal is to select applicants from a variety of backgrounds who possess a balanced set of credentials: strong academic aptitude, demonstrated leadership skills, and meaningful work and lifetime experiences." Accepted applicants are not permitted to defer admission. In state applicants do not receive extra consideration.

STUDENTS' OVERVIEW BOX

Overall Happiness

Academic Satisfaction

50   75   100%

■ Student Opinion   □ National Average

FACULTY RATING

■ Student Opinion   ■ National Average

HITS AND MISSES

HITS
Finance dept.
Classmates are smart
Safety

MISSES
Ethnic & racial diversity
Gym
Library

APPLICANTS ALSO LOOK AT
U Texas-Austin
U Texas-Arlington
Baylor U.
Southern Meth. U.
Texas A&M
Rice U.

FOR MORE INFORMATION, CONTACT:
MBA Admissions
P.O. 32868
Fort Worth, TX 76129
(817) 921-7531
(800) 828-3764
eMail: conway@zeta.is.tcu.edu

TULANE UNIVERSITY: A. B. FREEMAN SCHOOL OF BUSINESS

ADMISSIONS FACTS

Type of school	Private

Demographics

No. of men	169
No. of women	60
No. of minorities	25
No. of int'l students	72

EQUAL TREATMENT GRAPH

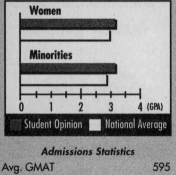

Women

Minorities

0   1   2   3   4 (GPA)

■ Student Opinion   □ National Average

Admissions Statistics

Avg. GMAT	595
Avg. undergraduate GPA	3.1
Avg. age at entry	25
No. of applicants	525
No. accepted	318
No. enrolled	118

Deadlines and Notifications

Regular application	5/1(dom.), 4/1(Intenat'l)
Regular notification	rolling 3–4 weeks
Special dates	N/A

Focus of Curriculum

General Management, students have option of specializing

Academic Specialties

International Business, Marketing, Finance

Joint Degrees

MBA/JD, MBA/Master of Public Health, MBA/MA in Latin American Studies, part-time MBA program available

Special Programs

Study Abroad, International Internships

FINANCIAL FACTS

In-state tuition	$18,760
Out-of-state tuition	$18,760
On-campus housing	$2,700-$4,945

ACADEMICS

Touted as an "up and comer," Tulane has retooled its curriculum to focus more on global business, the managerial role, and the social and political environment in business. The result is a unique course of study. First-years now take two "focus modules" which encourage collegial bonding among students. The first module is called the Job of the Executive and is delivered during the first two weeks of school. Students learn why they need to study all the disciplines and how that multifunctional knowledge is used in the workplace. The module also establishes student identification with the school and promotes interaction with faculty and other students. The second module is called Business Perspectives, which sharpens students' understanding of the social and value contexts in which businesses function. Along with the modules, first-years take the more traditional core courses, which are theoretical and lecture oriented. Second-years go on to modules three and four, which focus on Total Quality Management and Leadership. Case analysis, computer simulations, videotape sessions, and field assignments are heavily utilized. Popular B-school electives include Cases in Finance and Negotiations, International Business, and Strategic Marketing, which features a business simulation game. Students told us the finance and entrepreneurship departments are particularly strong.

To judge by the responses to our survey, Tulane manages to create a strong international environment not just with coursework and foreign study but with the very makeup of its student body. Again and again students told us this makes for a complete learning experience. Wrote one, "The high percentage (thirty-four percent) of international students in the first-year class offers a fantastic perspective in the global business environment." Agreed another, "International students facilitate continuous cultural interaction." To assist international students in their transition to American studies, the school offers a special International Student Orientation Program. But there were a few weak spots: not enough tenured faculty teach the core courses, and students say their marketing skills are sub-par. On the plus side, they gave themselves high marks for their proficiency in general management, finance, accounting, and operations.

PLACEMENT AND RECRUITING

Fifty-nine organizations interviewed on campus in 1993. A new placement director was appointed in June 1993. According to students, the placement office is headed on the right track and "help is easily accessible." They also report that faculty are eager to help students in their job search. Tulane enjoys solid placement rates. In 1994, seventy-six percent of the class had a job by graduation, eighty-seven percent had one within three months. Leading recruiters were Arthur Andersen, Bankers Trust, Carnegie International, and Citicorp.

Tulane University: A. B. Freeman School of Business

Student Life/Campus

According to the school, Tulane's location in New Orleans plays a critical role in the success of the program. Students strongly agree. Wrote one, "New Orleans is an extremely broadening experience." Ready yourself for a diet of crawfish, po' boys, and a night life that undergrads regularly travel thousands of miles to partake in.

Like most B-schools, Tulane is housed in just one building. But in this case, it's spectacular. Goldring/Woldenberg Hall is a newly built (1986) seven-story complex featuring an auditorium, group study rooms, classrooms, and a three-story atrium. Hangout time is enhanced by a second-floor outdoor patio which surrounds the entire building. The building also houses a state-of-the-art technology/computer center, a library, an audio visual studio complete with television studio and editing and viewing room, a computer classroom with forty-four networked laptops, and a computer-integrated manufacturing laboratory used for simulating manufacturing processes. Wrote one student, "The physical facilities—building, classrooms, services—are advanced."

The majority of students work in study groups. Class participation and papers count heavily towards grade. As for the pressure, it's moderately heavy during the first year, then like most schools, tapers off during the second year.

One student's remarks typified the prevalent attitude here: "The best students here are on par with the smartest you'll find anywhere, and a great deal cheaper to hire than those from some of the top schools." They rated each other as smart and highly diverse. Students also said, "There is a very strong emphasis on team work." and students are friendly and cooperative. Reported another, "We help each other with homework, projects, and studying for tests." The overwhelming majority of students rated classmates as highly competitive. Yet one student countered, "Even though Tulane has a very competitive environment, students help each other." One student added, "The administration and faculty know you by name." And that's not all. One grateful MBA told us he was driven around the area for two hours by the Assistant Director of Admissions when the student was seen looking for an apartment on foot. Now that's a responsive administration!

Admissions

The admissions committee considers work experience, GMAT scores, and college GPA most important, and then, in descending order of importance, the interview (required for all domestic applicants); letters of recommendation, essays, and extracurricular activities. Undergrad coursework is highly recommended, but not mandatory. Tulane uses a rolling admissions process. All applicants are automatically considered for merit-based fellowships at the time of admission. College seniors who are admitted may defer for up to two years. Tulane features a combined five-year baccalaureate/MBA program. Wrote one student, "The five-year program is excellent and extremely competitive. Students in this program were among Tulane's best undergraduates."

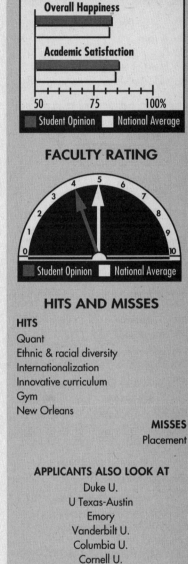

STUDENTS' OVERVIEW BOX

Overall Happiness

Academic Satisfaction

50   75   100%

Student Opinion   National Average

FACULTY RATING

Student Opinion   National Average

HITS AND MISSES

HITS
Quant
Ethnic & racial diversity
Internationalization
Innovative curriculum
Gym
New Orleans

MISSES
Placement

APPLICANTS ALSO LOOK AT
Duke U.
U Texas-Austin
Emory
Vanderbilt U.
Columbia U.
Cornell U.

FOR MORE INFORMATION, CONTACT:
Office of Admissions
A. B. Freeman School of Business
New Orleans, LA 70118-5669
(800) 223-5402
(504) 856-5410

VANDERBILT UNIVERSITY: OWEN GRADUATE SCHOOL OF MANAGEMENT

ADMISSIONS FACTS

Type of school	Private

Demographics

No. of men	276
No. of women	101
No. of minorities	33
No. of int'l students	84

EQUAL TREATMENT GRAPH

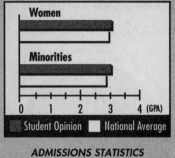

ADMISSIONS STATISTICS

Avg. GMAT	530–680
Avg. undergraduate GPA	2.6–3.8
Avg. age at entry	25.2
No. of applicants	1,048
No. accepted	495
No. enrolled	197

Deadlines and Notifications

Regular application	5/1
Regular notification	within 6 weeks
Special dates	12/1 (early app.)
	1/31 (early app. notification)

Focus of Curriculum

General Management

Academic Specialties

General Management, Human Resources, Services Marketing

FINANCIAL FACTS

In-state tuition	$19,650
Out-of-state tuition	$19,650
On-campus housing	$4,500

ACADEMICS

Although for years this school has been known as a southern powerhouse, the Owen Graduate School of Management has only recently burst onto the national B-school scene. Indeed, several students said they chose Owen because of its "up-and-coming attitude." From the get-go, Owen delivers a solid education. A first-year, noncredit course called Mathematics for Managers bolsters rusty skills with a rapid review of algebra, calculus, and linear equations. Professors teach the major disciplines from a cross-functional point of view. A yearlong course, Managerial Problem Solving and Communication, serves up the kind of fare that allows managers to translate ideas into actionable programs. But the icing on the cake is the chance to take electives from two of the school's research centers—the Operations Roundtable and the Center for Service Marketing—which students say provide cutting-edge insights. During the second year, students can opt to add an "international emphasis" by taking three international electives. One of the international electives, International Management and Issues, features a visit to a foreign country with the dean and several faculty. Each year students in this course decide where they want to go, and whom they want to meet with. The most recent class traveled to Korea and Taiwan. Owen MBAs may also earn degree credit for advanced language study. Much praise was also heaped on the school's human resources management program, which students say is "tops."

Distinct to Owen is an elective track of Services Marketing Courses, which addresses issues of customer satisfaction and service quality management. Students in these tracks work as apprentices for companies such as AT&T, American Airlines, and the National Symphony on their services marketing and customer relationships.

Owen MBAs are happy with the high level of interaction between faculty and students, a factor bolstered by small classes (an average of twenty-five to thirty-five students in each). Owen MBAs feel very well prepared by their studies in marketing, finance, human resources, quantitative methods, computers, and presentation skills. The administration garners positive reviews, and, overall, students say this program is exceeding their expectations.

PLACEMENT AND RECRUITING

In 1993, 200 companies interviewed Owen students. Ninety-five percent of the class had a permanent job offer within three months of graduation. The major recruiters were: AT&T, American Airlines, Andersen Consulting, MCI, GE, PepsiCo, Northern Telecom, Deloitte & Touche, Eli Lilly, Taco Bell, Federal Express, Sara Lee and Proctor & Gamble. One student reported, "Average starting salaries starting to rise, but could be better. Remember though, a large number of students stay in the South with low cost of living." Reported another, "Owen has just hired a full-time staff member to tackle international placement and recruiting."

VANDERBILT UNIVERSITY: OWEN GRADUATE SCHOOL OF MANAGEMENT

STUDENT LIFE/CAMPUS

Like many small schools, Owen provides its students with an intimate learning environment. With only 180 students in each entering class and an average class size of thirty-five, Vanderbilt MBAs receive a highly personalized education and get to know each other well. Wrote one student, "One key aspect of Owen is its personal culture. Everyone is a person here, not a number." Adds another, "Tight group of students. Everyone helps each other." Students rate themselves as competitive, and the workload, while not up-all-night impossible, can be tough. Students hit the books roughly thirty hours a week. The overwhelming majority utilize study groups to get the benefit of many heads applied to a single problem. Students are intelligent and professionally diverse. Observed one MBA, "Everyone brings something to the table."

Owen offers one-stop schooling. Everything is located in one building, which students describe as "outstanding." Equally awesome is the athletic center, which, in addition to every piece of exercise equipment you can imagine, also features an indoor climbing wall. As for Owen's hometown, students say Nashville is great. Ninety percent of the students live off-campus and find the cost of living reasonable. On-campus, the student-run clubs sponsor many activities: a lecture series, community service work, student-consulting projects, baseball games, a golf tournament, and the Fall Ball.

ADMISSIONS

The admissions office considers your work experience most important, then, in descending order, your college GPA, interview, GMAT scores, essays, letters of recommendation, and extracurricular activities, although the school adds, this order "differs according to the background of various candidates."

The interview is an "integral part of the admissions process," advises the school. "It allows a candidate to present key aspects of their background, character, and aspirations that are not easily conveyed in writing. The primary objectives in the interview are to assess career aspirations and explore motivation and clarity of purpose." Students must take a calculus course to demonstrate strong quantitative skills. The school goes by rolling admissions. The final deadline is May 1.

Applicants with two or more years' work experience getting their application in by the first Friday in December will have a decision by the end of January. Applicants who would benefit from additional work experience may defer admission for up to two years. Keep in mind that applications are up by twenty percent at this school.

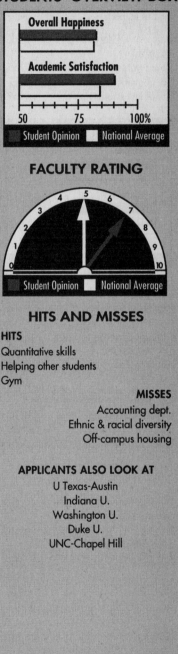

STUDENTS' OVERVIEW BOX

Overall Happiness

Academic Satisfaction

50   75   100%

Student Opinion ■ National Average

FACULTY RATING

Student Opinion ■ National Average

HITS AND MISSES

HITS
Quantitative skills
Helping other students
Gym

MISSES
Accounting dept.
Ethnic & racial diversity
Off-campus housing

APPLICANTS ALSO LOOK AT
U Texas-Austin
Indiana U.
Washington U.
Duke U.
UNC-Chapel Hill

FOR MORE INFORMATION, CONTACT:
Admissions
401 21 Avenue S.
Nashville, TN 37203
(615) 322-6469

UNIV. OF VIRGINIA: COLGATE DARDEN GRADUATE SCHOOL OF BUSINESS ADMINISTRATION

ADMISSIONS FACTS

Type of school	Public

Demographics

No. of men	320
No. of women	165
No. of minorities	77
No. of int'l students	62

EQUAL TREATMENT GRAPH

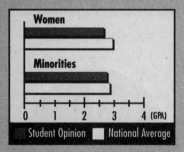

ADMISSIONS STATISTICS

Avg. GMAT	627
Avg. undergraduate GPA	3.19
Avg. age at entry	27
No. of applicants	2,192
No. accepted	564
No. enrolled	252

Deadlines and Notifications

Regular application	3/15
Regular notification	4–6 weeks
Special dates	N/A

Focus of Curriculum

General Management

Academic Specialties

General Management

FINANCIAL FACTS

In-state tuition	$9,000
Out-of-state tuition	$16,000
On-campus housing	$2,004–$4,640

ACADEMICS

Darden is part of a state-affiliated university with a well-deserved reputation as one of the best B-schools in the nation. Leo I. Higdon Jr., the new dean, who brings twenty years of Wall Street experience with him, is already proving to be very popular: "Leo has brought with him energy, enthusiasm, commitment, and power." The program the new dean oversees provides a general management education for individuals who expect to be "general managers later and strong functional managers early in their career," although one student added, "The school is very entreprenurial. Over forty percent of Darden grads start or buy their own businesses." The foundation for this is the case study method. Notes the school, "In analyzing each case, students learn how to define important issues, when and how to apply analytical techniques, and how to make decisions after evaluating alternatives." With fifty percent of the grade based on class discussion, one student exclaimed, "We have terrific and lively discussions. Darden classes are routinely interrupted with laughter and applause." As for the quality of education, students describe Darden's program as "a top-notch learning experience." The curriculum features a heavy emphasis on quantitative applications and is known for it's heavy workload: "Darden is a boot camp, but it's well worth the effort—you are never left out to dry. There's a lot of support."

First-year MBAs take nine required courses, but this feels more like one nine-month multifunctional course. Alas, no electives allowed. Second-years take three required courses and can choose from among sixty-five electives. A major component of the second year is the Directed Study, which involves working with a faculty member on a managerial issue involving field research.

Students noted several reasons for choosing Darden: low cost combined with prestige, cozy student community, and the case study method. A surprising number of students said they selected Darden because of its tough-as-nails reputation. Many mentioned the school's long-standing emphasis on values and ethics as a drawing card. As for the faculty, Darden tops the charts.

PLACEMENT AND RECRUITING

Exactly 173 companies recruit on-campus. The major recruiters in 1994-5: American Airlines, Chase, Chemical Bank, Citibank, Coopers & Lybrand, Gemini Consulting, JP Morgan, MCI, Merrill Lynch. By August 15, ninety-nine percent of students were placed. Commented one student, "Corporate recruiting is very strong in marketing, finance, and consulting, but hi-tech and manufacturing are scarce." One MBA warned, "Incoming students need to realize that the current alumni network is less established than it is at other top tier schools." But all agree, that alumni network is very supportive.

UNIV. OF VIRGINIA: COLGATE DARDEN GRADUATE SCHOOL OF BUSINESS ADMINISTRATION

STUDENT LIFE/CAMPUS

Students told us Darden offers "a happy environment." Located in the college town of Charlottesville, the UVA campus is beautiful. But the B-school buildings are not. The good news is a state-of-the-art facility, designed by Robert A. M. Stern, that will be completed in 1995. Nearly fifty percent of the first-year class lives in a nearby apartment complex, christened Darden Gardens. Several other apartment complexes are within walking distance, which alleviates some of Darden's parking problems. Many students rent shared farmhouses near the Blue Ridge Mountains (a ten-minute commute) for roughly $600 per month.

Students complain about the lack of ethnic diversity. "Darden needs to be more proactive in widening the base of the student body in term of ethnicity and nationality." However, relative to other top B-schools, Darden fares well in the diversity of its demographics. Another student says, "The percentage of minority students at the school is paltry." Make of this what you will.

Students perform eighty to one hundred hours of schoolwork every week. A typical complaint was that a three-night caseload leaves little time for student clubs and activities. Wrote one, "Married with children, time management can be a problem." Although this MBA countered, "Darden is great for married students and one's with children—very supportive, great town. The workload limits the social scene for singles." Still, another reported, "Darden is not as difficult as people say. You have to be disciplined and keep up with the work so as not to be killed by cold calls. Second year is a lot less stressful." Students are pre-assigned to study groups intentionally structured to create a mix of skills and expertise, as well as offer support.

Students are competitive, but not cutthroat. Darden's small size fosters a close-knit, homey atmosphere. Wrote one MBA, "Classmates are bright and supportive. They're not out to get each other." Observed another, "Students here are genuinely nice, genuinely down-to-earth. I like 99.9% of people here." Summed up this Dardenite, " Southerners don't dominate here, but they do soften the destructive forms of competition that appear at some grad schools—they're less uptight."

ADMISSIONS

Each of the following components count for roughly one-third in the admissions decision: Academics (GPA, GMAT); work/professional experience; and personal attributes (essays, interview, extracurriculars). The interview is strongly encouraged but not required. The committee explains, "We look for evidence of competitive academic performance, intellectual ability, significant work and life experiences, as well as other qualities of character that cannot be quantitatively measured. Factors such as breadth of perspective, international exposure and diversity are also taken into consideration." Applications are processed in one of three rounds. Students are rarely granted a deferral; possible reasons for one are military obligation or visa restrictions.

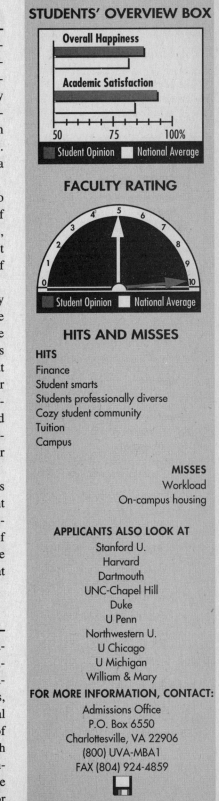

STUDENTS' OVERVIEW BOX

Overall Happiness

Academic Satisfaction

50   75   100%

Student Opinion   National Average

FACULTY RATING

0 1 2 3 4 5 6 7 8 9 10

Student Opinion   National Average

HITS AND MISSES

HITS
Finance
Student smarts
Students professionally diverse
Cozy student community
Tuition
Campus

MISSES
Workload
On-campus housing

APPLICANTS ALSO LOOK AT
Stanford U.
Harvard
Dartmouth
UNC-Chapel Hill
Duke
U Penn
Northwestern U.
U Chicago
U Michigan
William & Mary

FOR MORE INFORMATION, CONTACT:
Admissions Office
P.O. Box 6550
Charlottesville, VA 22906
(800) UVA-MBA1
FAX (804) 924-4859

WAKE FOREST UNIVERSITY: BABCOCK GRADUATE SCHOOL OF MANAGEMENT

ADMISSIONS FACTS

Type of school	Private

Demographics

No. of men	180
No. of women	59
No. of minorities	2
No. of int'l students	28

EQUAL TREATMENT GRAPH

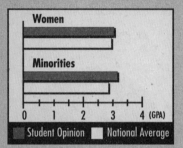

Women

Minorities

0 1 2 3 4 (GPA)

Student Opinion National Average

Admissions Statistics

Avg. GMAT	603
Avg. undergraduate GPA	3.2
Avg. age at entry	26
No. of applicants	439
No. accepted	238
No. enrolled	109

Deadlines and Notifications

Regular application	4/1
Regular notification	rolling
Special dates	EDP 12/1
EDP final notification 12/3	

Focus of Curriculum

General Management

Academic Specialties

General Management, International Business

Joint Degrees

MBA/JD; MBA/MD

Special Programs

Babcock Leadership Discussions Series; Partners in Education; Babcock World Business Games

FINANCIAL FACTS

In-state tuition	$17,500
Out-of-state tuition	$17,500
On-campus housing	$5,550

ACADEMICS

Wake Forest (WF) stresses a general management perspective in a program that is as grounded in the traditional basics as it is in the experiential aspects of business education. Extensive use is made of case study analysis and presentation. But the program is also peppered with role plays, field projects, teamwork exercises, and business simulation games. In particular, oral and written skills are emphasized. The first-year curriculum immerses students in the major disciplines and is extremely structured. Courses are organized in such a way as to present the field of management as a unit rather than as a series of stand-alone subjects. As the school explained, "For example, an organizational behavior exam may be based on cases taught in accounting, marketing, and analytical methods." A course on interpersonal behavior brings in the soft skills. Of primary importance is the study of international business. Many students participate in the East Asia Management Program, which includes a trip to Pacific Rim countries, or join the large number of MBAs who opt for a summer job abroad. During the second year, students specialize or develop an "elective, yet coherent" course of study. One valuable stepping stone at WF is the Mentor Program, which matches students with executives who have similar career interests. WF MBAs rave about this program, which allows them to make important contacts in the business community.

Professors are widely praised for their exceptional teaching skills and extraordinary accessibility. Compared to other schools in this survey, students at WF are among those reporting the highest rate of academic expectations being met or exceeded. Across the board, students say WF has provided them a stellar education, particularly in the areas of marketing, finance, and general management. The only weak spot, and even here the grade was above average, is operations. This includes the functional areas of business as well as soft and quantitative skills. The single area in which self-rated competency was not unanimous was operations; one-fourth of the students felt their skills needed bolstering. The administration garners mixed reviews.

PLACEMENT AND RECRUITING

Like most B-schools, WF's Career Planning and Placement Office serves up a full plate of career services. The office distributes a resume book of second-year students to hundreds of corporations. They also participate in the MBA Consortiums in Atlanta and New York to present students to organizations not recruiting on campus.

Still, while students say the career office is not horrible, they certainly don't think it's operating at peak efficiency. In particular, students are disappointed with the range of companies recruiting. The smart move at WF is to utilize alumni and mentor relationships. The overwhelming majority of students said they did just that and found the individuals they contacted helpful. The record for 1994: Fifty employers recruited on-campus. Seventy-five percent of grads had offers by graduation; ninety-percent three months later. Twenty-two percent of grad went into marketing/adv/sales where the average starting salary was $43,475. Ten percent of students went into consulting where the average starting salary was $50,900.

WAKE FOREST UNIVERSITY: BABCOCK GRADUATE SCHOOL OF MANAGEMENT

STUDENT LIFE/CAMPUS

Depending on the next day's case load, students spend anywhere from four to six hours a night preparing their insights for in-class discussion. Class participation typically counts for forty to fifty percent of the grade. To emphasize teamwork and provide WF MBAs with an academic support system for the case method, WF pre-assigns students to study groups. This reduces much of the anxiety. The overriding culture is supportive. As one might expect, WF MBAs like each other. Indeed, classmates intend to stay friends long after that last case is cracked. Students say the intelligent student body is also professionally diverse and enriches their learning experience.

According to our survey, the library and gym are great. Indeed, the same holds true for all the facilities. The B-school just moved into the Professional Center for Law and Management—a brand-new building shared with the law school—although the verdict's not in on how these two will fare as roommates. Expect powerful alliances. Students say the local area and campus is beautiful. Most students opt for off-campus living in nearby apartments. International students are provided housing on-premises in the Wake Forest MBA International House. The social scene teems with activity. Surprisingly, students here, unlike students at other B-schools, date a lot. Those law school collaborations may already have begun. Group activities include picnics, intramural sports, and anything involving the great outdoors. Many of these are sponsored by student-run associations such as the Entrepreneur Club, Women in Business, Student Government Association, and International Business Club., and Mentor Club.

Former students who walked this campus include: James Steeg, Executive Director of Special Events - NFL; Steven Lineberger, President - Sara Lee Knit; Ann Morrison, President - New Leaders Institute; Ronald Marstik, Vice President - Ciba-Giegy.

ADMISSIONS

Work experience tops the list of admissions criteria at Babcock, followed by quality of undergraduate curriculum and GPA, GMAT scores, reputation of undergraduate school, personal statement, interview and recommendations. Think about two years of full-time labor before applying to the program. Writes the school "Wake Forest does not employ minimums, cut-off scores, or formulas when reviewing applicant files. While interviews are not required, they are highly recommended. Applicants who schedule interviews are matched with student host who take them to class, give them a tour of the facility, and take them to lunch."

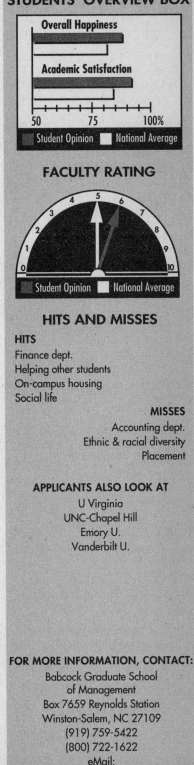

STUDENTS' OVERVIEW BOX

Overall Happiness

Academic Satisfaction

50 — 75 — 100%
Student Opinion — National Average

FACULTY RATING

Student Opinion — National Average

HITS AND MISSES

HITS
Finance dept.
Helping other students
On-campus housing
Social life

MISSES
Accounting dept.
Ethnic & racial diversity
Placement

APPLICANTS ALSO LOOK AT
U Virginia
UNC-Chapel Hill
Emory U.
Vanderbilt U.

FOR MORE INFORMATION, CONTACT:
Babcock Graduate School
of Management
Box 7659 Reynolds Station
Winston-Salem, NC 27109
(919) 759-5422
(800) 722-1622
eMail:
patricia-divine@mail.mba.wfu.edu

UNIV. OF WASHINGTON GRADUATE SCHOOL OF BUSINESS ADMINISTRATION

ADMISSIONS FACTS

Type of school — Public

Demographics

No. of men — 268
No. of women — 132
No. of minorities — 52
No. of int'l students — 80

EQUAL TREATMENT GRAPH

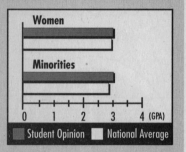

Admissions Statistics

Avg. GMAT — 622
Avg. undergraduate GPA — 3.24
Avg. age at entry — 28
No. of applicants — 800
No. accepted — 300
No. enrolled — 180

Deadlines and Notifications

Regular application — 3/1/95 (dom.)
4/1/95 (intl.)
Regular notification — 4/1/95
Special dates — N/A

Focus of Curriculum

General Management

Academic Specialties

Marketing, Finance, Entrepreneurship, International Business, Environmental Management

Joint Degrees

MP Accounting, JD/MBA, MBA/MAIS, MBA/MHA Health Administration

Special Programs

Overseas Study, Engineering and Manufacturing Management, Environmental Management Program, International Management Fellows Program

FINANCIAL FACTS

In-state tuition — $4,050
Out-of-state tuition — $9,963
On-campus housing — $4,650

ACADEMICS

The University of Washington (UW) is ideal for students who have no prior academic coursework in business. The first year consists of introductory level courses in the major disciplines. A new curriculum integrates interrelationships of these disciplines in a single, yearlong course which also stresses ethics and international business. Students also take modules on leadership, diversity, and communications. These modules are taught by both B-school faculty and Seattle-area business executives. According to students, the first year core is mandatory, but "outstanding!" During the second year, students work on satisfying the international business requirement. Wrote students, "UW is very Asian Rim and Computer-Industry oriented," the latter probably due to the influence of high-tech Seattle companies such as Microsoft and Physio Control. Expect a lot of math: The curriculum is numbers oriented. There's also a heavy-duty research requirement.

Enthused one student about this school, "Best plus—every class incorporates total quality management (TQM) issues. Everyone had to do a twenty-minute video on TQM." Many students raved about another plus, the Business Diagnostic Center, which matches student volunteers with local companies in need of management expertise. Distinct to UW is the new environmental management (EM) program, (which students rave about) the first of its kind in any MBA program in the nation. Here students earn an EM certificate by taking a series of team-taught environmental courses. As part of the program, students are placed in internships with companies such as Amoco and PepsiCo. There's also a new program in entrepreneurship and innovation which provides students with an opportunity to interact with some of Seattle's homegrown entrepreneurs. One student asserted, "This is a great experience; eighty percent of the first-year students were involved this year." MBAs have completed projects for Starbuck's Coffee, Boise Cascade, and the Seattle Theater Group. As for the faculty, one MBA wrote, "the UW program is excellent because of the quality of the profs." Added another, "Strong, young professors." Professors are also said to be widely accessible and highly committed. By all accounts, the new program at UW is already a huge hit. Unsurprisingly, students say this program is worth the investment of time and money. Exclaimed another, "Best value in the northwest!!"

PLACEMENT AND RECRUITING

In 1994, forty companies recruited on-campus. To interview with a greater number of companies, students participated in several job fairs. By graduation, seventy percent of the class had been placed in a full-time position; eighty-two percent three months later. The average starting salary is $44,060. The majority of grad go into accounting, finance, consulting, and marketing. Top employers: Deloitte and Touche, Hewlitt- Packard, Intel, Andersen Consulting, Micorsoft, Tektronix, Ore-Ida, Ernst and Young. Wrote one MBA, "Our reputation is not as high because of poor employment. Nobody wants to leave Seattle. That's why the reputation has not improved."

UNIV. OF WASHINGTON GRADUATE SCHOOL OF BUSINESS ADMINISTRATION

STUDENT LIFE/CAMPUS

Students report a moderate to heavy workload and study an average of twenty-five to thirty hours a week. The vast majority of MBAs say they don't take shortcuts; it's important to do all or most of the reading. But students don't feel like they're in a pressure cooker. Study groups, which were recently introduced in the program, allow students to leverage off members' expertise and collaborate on schoolwork. The entering class of 180 is divided into cohorts of forty-five students each who take all the first-year courses together with the same faculty. According to students, this provides an intimate learning environment and encourages cooperation. Indeed, the best part of life here is the sense of community and camaraderie among students. UW MBAs are good friends. They intend to stay friends long after graduation. Enthused one MBA "Everyone works together to help each other out. You don't find the competition among students that you do at other MBA programs." A new grading system of High Pass, Pass, Low Pass, and Fail helps this along. In the upcoming year, students will receive individual performance evaluations from the faculty. Students reported their classmates are very bright and professionally diverse.

One student's comments capture the prevalent feeling here: "New facilities are badly needed, especially a larger student lounge, although the computer lab is pretty good." A new business building is currently in the works and the library is being renovated. Students say the "administration goes out of it 's way to respond to student's problems."

As for Seattle, students noted, "UW is located in a great city," and they enjoy "the scenery and lifestyle of Western Washington." Indeed, UW is paradise for outdoorsy types. Just an hour away are the Cascade Mountains. The university itself sits on Lake Washington and is surrounded by Puget Sound. As one might expect, biking, hiking, and skiing are favorite activities, so it's no surprise that the school attracts recreation-oriented folk. It's not unusual for there to be an Olympic medalist in the entering class. For the less athletically inclined, there are plenty of student club activities. Two favorites: international theme parties, and comfort food night.

ADMISSIONS

The admissions office considers the following criteria (in no particular order): essays, college GPA, extracurricular activities, work experience, the interview, and GMAT scores. Letters of recommendation are not considered. Notes the school "We look closely at GPA and GMAT scores, but high quantitative measures do not ensure admissions—strong work experience or extensive extracurricular or community activities can significantly improve an applicant's chances of admission." Decisions are made on a rolling basis. "We strongly encourage early application. Students must complete a college-level calculus course before enrollment," writes the office of admissions. The MBA Director personally calls applicants who have been admitted to the program.

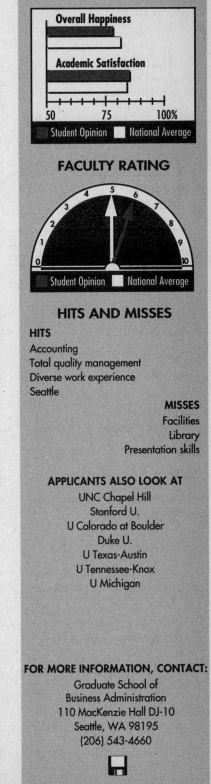

STUDENTS' OVERVIEW BOX

Overall Happiness

Academic Satisfaction

50   75   100%

■ Student Opinion   □ National Average

FACULTY RATING

0 1 2 3 4 5 6 7 8 9 10

■ Student Opinion   □ National Average

HITS AND MISSES

HITS
Accounting
Total quality management
Diverse work experience
Seattle

MISSES
Facilities
Library
Presentation skills

APPLICANTS ALSO LOOK AT
UNC Chapel Hill
Stanford U.
U Colorado at Boulder
Duke U.
U Texas-Austin
U Tennessee-Knox
U Michigan

FOR MORE INFORMATION, CONTACT:
Graduate School of
Business Administration
110 MacKenzie Hall DJ-10
Seattle, WA 98195
(206) 543-4660

WASHINGTON UNIVERSITY: JOHN M. OLIN SCHOOL OF BUSINESS

ADMISSIONS FACTS

Type of school	Private

Demographics

No. of men	194
No. of women	77
No. of minorities	33
No. of int'l students	76

EQUAL TREATMENT GRAPH

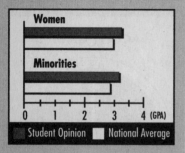

Women

Minorities

0 1 2 3 4 (GPA)

Student Opinion / National Average

Admissions Statistics

Avg. GMAT	606
Avg. undergraduate GPA	3.2
Avg. age at entry	25
No. of applicants	822
No. accepted	348
No. enrolled	138

Deadlines and Notifications

Regular application	3/30
Regular notification	rolling
Special dates	N/A

Focus of Curriculum

General Management

Academic Specialties

General Management

Joint Degrees

MBA/JD; MBA/MS in Social Work; MBA/MA in Architecture; MBA/MA in East Asian Studies; MBA/MSW; MBA/MA; MBA/Health Admin.; MBA/MA Int'l Affairs

Special Programs

The MBA Enterprise Corps; Foreign Study

FINANCIAL FACTS

In-state tuition	$19,100
Out-of-state tuition	$19,100
On-campus housing	N/A

ACADEMICS

While Olin has recently added innovative components to its program, the school's traditional, generalist formula remains intact. First-year students get a thorough grounding in the functional areas. Courses are sequenced to incorporate learning from prior courses. Still, nonquant types find it rough going here: There is a heavy emphasis on applied mathematics and microeconomics throughout the coursework. Second-years craft their own study with electives in the Olin School and other university departments. So far, standard fare. But the program that everyone talks about is Olin's Management Center. Here companies pay for teams of MBAs to come on-site and consult on matters ranging from marketing to strategy. At the conclusion of this practicum, students make a formal presentation to the client company. Thus far, Apple Computer and Monsanto have asked Olin students to advise them on select issues. Social responsibility is also promoted—student teams perform pro bono consulting to organizations in the nonprofit sector. The school is so committed to this program they suspend classes for a week so students can focus exclusively on their consulting. Another experiential learning program that has received a lot of press is TYCOON, a one-week simulated management program taught in conjunction with a strategy course. A new exciting program is the dual-degree MBA/MA in East Asian studies in which students study Japanese or Mandarin Chinese and complete a semester or internship in their target country (China, Taiwan, or Japan). Finally, a "close encounter" series brings small groups of students face to face with top executives such as John Pepper, president of Proctor & Gamble.

Olin is considered a go-getter school and, according to the students in our survey, it has begun to earn its stripes. The majority of Olin MBAs said this program is meeting their academic expectations, although a third said they're less than satisfied. One MBA asserted, "I think the educational and developmental experience at Olin is *very* underrated." The administration earns high marks this year, a quantum leap from their previous low ratings. This may be due to the efforts of MBAs working with the administration to develop a "continuous improvement process" for the school. Professors get decent grades for their teaching but better grades for their accessibility. Again, this depends on who you ask. Raved one student, "Intelligent faculty stimulate creative thinking and express a genuine concern for students." But another student complained, "The use of non-Ph.D. professors without business backgrounds seriously undermines the quality of education here."

PLACEMENT AND RECRUITING

Career placement gets mixed reviews. One satisfied job seeker wrote, "The career management system here is excellent." But another griped, "Their career strategies are ineffective." Olin boasts close ties with St. Louis–area businesses. In 1993, eighty-three percent of the graduating class was placed by August 15. The median starting salary was $45,000. Major recruiters were Andersen Consulting, NBD Bank, Towers Perrin, Ralston Purina, Procter & Gamble, and Ernst & Young.

WASHINGTON UNIVERSITY: JOHN M. OLIN SCHOOL OF BUSINESS

STUDENT LIFE/CAMPUS

Olin MBAs reported a steady, heavy dose of work, especially during the first year. Students prepare for class roughly twenty-five hours a week and describe the academic pressure as intense, forcing the efficient use of study groups, which are considered integral to student life. The small size of the school (150 students in each full-time class) offers many advantages: small classes, personal attention, and a supportive environment. Students say this school is competitive but, not surprisingly, teamwork is the overriding theme here. A three-day, student-run outdoor leadership program in the Ozarks facilitates students' bonding. Confirmed one MBA, "There's a strong familylike atmosphere." So much so, added another, that "if you don't like teamwork, you could wind up very lonely here." Olin MBAs described classmates as "high quality" and "realistic."

From classrooms to computing facilities, Olin MBAs enjoy top-notch, well-appointed facilities. As for the campus itself, it's amazingly beautiful. Students also say housing is plentiful and attractive. Most live off-campus in nearby apartments. The heavy social scene at WU ranges from weekly Friday afternoon keg parties to student fund-raisers such as the charity run for Florida Hurricane victims. For an unusual dining experience, students attend one of the many International Pot-Luck Dinners, sponsored by the International Business Council. Most recently, a student from Kazakhstan served a horse dish which converted more than one MBA into an avowed vegetarian. Other major clubs (not sponsoring horse dinners) are: Entrepreneurs Club, Business Minority Council, International Business Council, Operations and Manufacturing Club, Voluntary Action Committee, and Women in Management.

A final note: Students agree that WU is ethnically and racially diverse. As for equal treatment, WU practices what it teaches. The associate dean is one of the few women in her position in the nation. Over and over we heard about how WU "encourages American students to form groups with and act as a support to foreign students."

ADMISSIONS

According to the admissions office, your work experience is considered most important. After that, the school considers in descending order, your college GPA, GMAT scores, essays, letters of recommendation, extracurricular activities, and interview. Writes the school, "The interview is not required, but strongly recommended, and can be a determining factor." The school also requires students to submit a very detailed work history. Olin's Consortium for Graduate Study in Management is dedicated to funding fellowships for talented minorities. Admissions are handled on a rolling basis; students are notified of a decision three to five weeks after their application is received. Students may defer admission for up to one year for work or cost related situations. Students who defer must pay a deposit to hold a spot in the class.

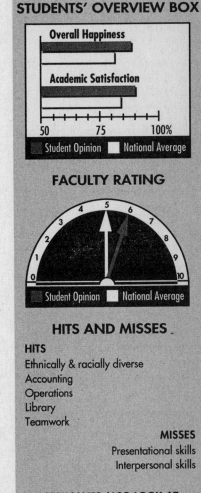

STUDENTS' OVERVIEW BOX

Overall Happiness

Academic Satisfaction

50   75   100%

■ Student Opinion   □ National Average

FACULTY RATING

■ Student Opinion   □ National Average

HITS AND MISSES

HITS
Ethnically & racially diverse
Accounting
Operations
Library
Teamwork

MISSES
Presentational skills
Interpersonal skills

APPLICANTS ALSO LOOK AT
Indiana U.-Bloom
U Michigan
Northwestern U.

FOR MORE INFORMATION, CONTACT:
John M. Olin School of Business
Campus Box 1133
St. Louis, MO 63130
(314) 935-7301
eMail: MBA@OLIN.WUSTL.EDU

COLLEGE OF WILLIAM AND MARY GRADUATE SCHOOL OF BUSINESS

ADMISSIONS FACTS

Type of school	Public

Demographics

No. of men	165
No. of women	51
No. of minorities	6
No. of int'l students	12

EQUAL TREATMENT GRAPH

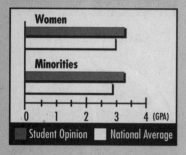

Women

Minorities

0 1 2 3 4 (GPA)

■ Student Opinion □ National Average

Admissions Statistics

Avg. GMAT	574
Avg. undergraduate GPA	3.03
Avg. age at entry	26
No. of applicants	317
No. accepted	188
No. enrolled	76

Deadlines and Notifications

Regular application	5/15
Regular notification	30 days past deadline
Special dates	12/3 (Early Decision)
	12/17 (E.D. notification)

Focus of Curriculum

General Management

Academic Specialties

General Management

FINANCIAL FACTS

In-state tuition	$4,945
Out-of-state tuition	$13,886
On-campus housing	$7,500

ACADEMICS

William and Mary (W&M) wins a "most improved" award for the progress it has made over the last three years. Interviews and surveys of over 100 plus students turned up almost no complaints and mostly praise for the administration's successful efforts to reinvent the program: "The administration is doing everything in their power to prove to the business world what we already know. We are the 'Pistol Pete' of B-Schools." Also, "This is without a question an up and coming program: the quality of the professors has improved and industry is recognizing the increasing prestige associated with the college with the oldest charter in the country."

William and Mary starts its program off with an innovative Outward Bound-type, three-day orientation. Approximately 100 entering students dangle and swim their way through a high-ropes course and raft-building exercise on the James River. Students are also divided into six-person study groups in which they will work for the first year. To get these future MBAs ready for school, a battalion of eighteen professors introduces them to the case study method.

During the first year, students take thirteen core courses. Computers are required in all courses (incoming students must bring one with them.) The first year also includes a topics program on issues such as business versus environmental concerns, cultural diversity, and the changing world of finance. The year ends with a week-long computerized simulation game in which student teams compete against one another in the international recreational shoe market. During the second year, W&M MBAs specialize or continue their generalist studies and perform a field study thatis now mandatory. Fortunately, the field study is popular.

Students say there is a good balance of case and other methods and that there is a "very quantitative course load." Classes and field work are intended to be integrated and complimentary and students feel the school is successful at this. "In operations, we routinely use concepts incorporated directly from our stat class. The operations prof waits until the process is taught in stat then just supplies his material. I immediately get feedback to see if I learned the material. Great coordination." One MBA says ""Faculty will bend over backwards to 1) get to know you personally, 2) make sure you do well in the program, 3) provide counsel in their particular area of expertise, 4) create an environment which is extremely conducive to learning and personal growth." Finally, the vast majority of students praised W&M for its extremely low cost.

PLACEMENT AND RECRUITING

The Office of Career and Employer Development offers extensive programs such as mock interviews and weekly seminars on developing effective contacts. A Mentor Program enables students to interact with a mentor chosen from a list of business leaders based in areas from New York City to Atlanta. While students complain that there aren't enough recruiters on campus, they feel they are well prepared for recruiting. Seventy percent are placed at graduation, eighty-three percent within three months.

COLLEGE OF WILLIAM AND MARY GRADUATE SCHOOL OF BUSINESS

STUDENT LIFE/CAMPUS

The most attractive aspect of life at W&M is the sense of community fostered by the school's small size. Students report "lots of individual attention," "small classes," and "a supportive environment." Close working relationships are practically inevitable thanks to the study groups. As one student put it, summing up the feelings of his peers, "There is an amazing feeling of unity among the first year students. Everyone is very open and willing to help. We are all in the same boat and we appreciate our differences and our contributions. It is a great team experience." Second year students are paired up with incoming students in the "CEO-Presidency Club" in which the second years serve as mentors. Of the professionally diverse student body, classmates told us they're "among the brightest around."

Students describe "A very tough workload, but the word from alums is that W & M MBAs are *very* prepared." Wrote another, "The first year classes truly push you to your limit." W&M's hometown of Williamsburg can be described as quiet and quaint, but some students find this less than exciting: "The only real problem is Williamsburg—it's boring." With easy access to Virginia Beach, Richmond, and D.C., students say they can get away when they need to. They also describe the campus as beautiful. New graduate housing right on campus offers great accommodations for both single and married students.

ADMISSIONS

According to the admissions office, work experience is considered most important. Then follow, in descending order, letters of recommendation and essays, GMAT scores, college GPA, and required interview (phone interviews are arranged for those unable to travel to Williamsburg.) William and Mary features a five-round admissions process and notes that it is advisable to apply in the first three. On a case-by-case basis, students can defer admission for up to one year.

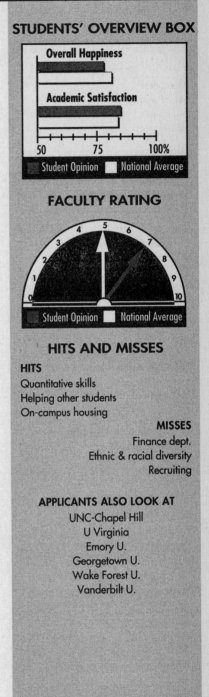

STUDENTS' OVERVIEW BOX

Overall Happiness

Academic Satisfaction

50 75 100%

Student Opinion National Average

FACULTY RATING

Student Opinion National Average

HITS AND MISSES

HITS
Quantitative skills
Helping other students
On-campus housing

MISSES
Finance dept.
Ethnic & racial diversity
Recruiting

APPLICANTS ALSO LOOK AT
UNC-Chapel Hill
U Virginia
Emory U.
Georgetown U.
Wake Forest U.
Vanderbilt U.

FOR MORE INFORMATION, CONTACT:
Lois V. Fraley
Graduate School of Business
Blow Memorial Hall RM 254
Williamsburg, VA 23186
(804) 221-2900

UNIVERSITY OF WISCONSIN-MADISON BUSINESS SCHOOL

ADMISSIONS FACTS

Type of school	Public

Demographics

No. of men	N/A
No. of women	N/A
No. of minorities	N/A
No. of int'l students	N/A

EQUAL TREATMENT GRAPH

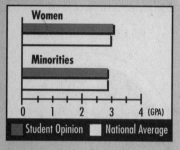

Admissions Statistics

Avg. GMAT	N/A
Avg. undergraduate GPA	N/A
Avg. age at entry	N/A
No. of applicants	N/A
No. accepted	N/A
No. enrolled	N/A

Deadlines and Notifications

Regular application	N/A
Regular notification	N/A
Special dates	N/A

Focus of Curriculum

General Management

Academic Specialties

General Management

FINANCIAL FACTS

In-state tuition	N/A
Out-of-state tuition	N/A
On-campus housing	N/A

ACADEMICS

According to UW MBA students, you will find excellent niche programs at Wisconsin, considered a top-tier public B-school by students who go there: "Applied Securities, Actuarial Programs, the A.C. Neilson Marketing Center, Real Estate, and the Distribution Management Program—most schools don't have outstanding programs like these!" Students are equally fired up about the quality and productivity curriculum, the innovative small business and entreprenuership courses, and the Joyce Erdman Center for Manufacturing and Technology.

Students expressed disappointment only about the core course program they're required to complete. Other than recent additions to the curriculum—including an infusion of hip courses on ethics, negotiation and bargaining, strategy and policy, and managing innovation and technology—students describe core courses as mediocre. Fortunately, there's a way out. Although first-years must complete a foundation core of thirteen courses, students who have completed relevant coursework may be waived into higher level (and presumably more interesting) courses. Electives can be taken as early as the first-year. A huge emphasis is placed on international business, which includes mondo courses on international topics, a summer abroad program, yearly student/faculty trips to destinations like the Pacific Rim and Latin America, and foreign language classes in other UW departments to prep for it all.

For most MBA's the first three semesters are spent fulfilling the core requirements which students say makes for a "rigid" first year. A warning to the mathematically disinclined: A heavy quantitative slant sends many students running for help. (The school strongly advises students bolster their number-crunching skills before applying.) Fortunately, students can find a helping hand at the Learning Center in the form of tutorial sessions that quickly redress forgotten concepts.

As for the faculty, students agree, faculty are "exceptionally accessible," but the quality of their teaching is inconsistent. A common sentiment: "You have great profs, but lots of terrible ones, too." But overall, students agree, Wisconsin is an "up-and-coming program on the verge of becoming an elite graduate business school."

PLACEMENT AND RECRUITING

138 employers interviewed master's students during the 1993-1994 academic year (an increase of twenty percent over last year). At graduation, twenty percent of the May 1994 graduates indicated they were still seeking employment. Generally twenty-five percent of the graduates accept positions in the manufacturing sector and seventy-five percent in the service sector. The average base salary reported by May 1994 graduates was $41,266 (does not include bonuses or commissions). Over seventy-five percent of the graduates accepted positions in the Midwest.

UNIVERSITY OF WISCONSIN-MADISON BUSINESS SCHOOL

STUDENT LIFE/CAMPUS

As one MBA put it, Wisconsin's best assets are its students and laid back culture. One typical remark was, "Students are very intelligent, inquisitive, and competitive with themselves—not each other." Wrote another, "Students don't flaunt their knowledge. They have a different attitude towards competition and class than most East or West schools." Students described themselves as "very friendly" and always willing to help each other out." Among Wisconsin's other assets is its diversity of students: "There is a *real* diversity of academic backgrounds, work experiences, and ethnic/cultural backgrounds." An unusually large and active international student body includes MBA's from countries such as India, Indonesia, France, Germany, Morocco, Asia, and South America. Unfortunately, this diversity is not adequately reflected in the makeup of the faculty. Most students felt there were not enough female professors. As for social activities, they abound. During the long winters, parties proliferate, especially for the majority of students who live on-campus. When it warms up, everyone hangs out at Memorial Union on "the Terrace" facing Lake Mendota. Thursday nights are accompanied by bands and beer. Intramural sports are popular: basketball, volleyball, and six-man football. Great golf is a priority—students get half off at the University Ridge Golf Course—one of the top courses in the state. But not everyone is a jock. Community service plays big here, too. In the past, UW MBAs wrote a report for the Mayor's Office on what business can do to solve community ills. Roughly eighty student clubs offer ample opportunity for group involvement, such as Women in Business, Marketing, and Toastmasters.

Over and over, students raved about their "awesome new $45 million school building" which is specially equipped with multimedia applications in the classroom. Gushed one MBA, "I've never seen a building where you can plug a laptop into the wall and access the school's databases." As for the town of Madison itself, one student offered this glowing report: "It's wonderful, sophisticated with many outdoor-oriented artistic, cultural, and athletic opportunities." Indeed everyone seems to agree, this is one of those quintessential college towns, where the quality of living is high. The only negative in this residential utopia—campus parking. It's a nightmare.

ADMISSIONS

UW considers a prospective student's work experience an important factor in the selection process. Wisconsin is also looking for students with strong GMAT scores, good grade point averages, good references, and a dynamite essay. The deadline for admission for the September 1995 class is June 1. The deadline for financial aid is January 1. The admissions office adds, "We urge students considering the UW School of Business to contact us and arrange for a visit. We feel if we can spend time with the prospective student, we will have a better chance to evaluate that applicant and give them a close-up look at the programs here."

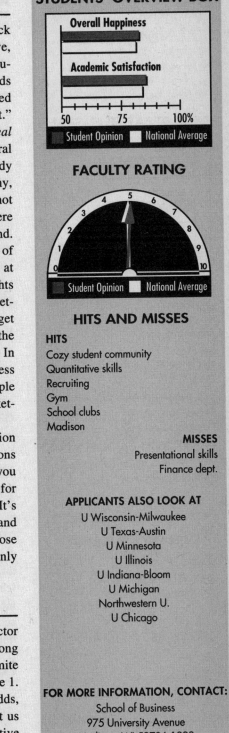

STUDENTS' OVERVIEW BOX

Overall Happiness

Academic Satisfaction

50   75   100%

Student Opinion   National Average

FACULTY RATING

Student Opinion   National Average

HITS AND MISSES

HITS
Cozy student community
Quantitative skills
Recruiting
Gym
School clubs
Madison

MISSES
Presentational skills
Finance dept.

APPLICANTS ALSO LOOK AT
U Wisconsin-Milwaukee
U Texas-Austin
U Minnesota
U Illinois
U Indiana-Bloom
U Michigan
Northwestern U.
U Chicago

FOR MORE INFORMATION, CONTACT:
School of Business
975 University Avenue
Madison, WI 53706-1323
(608) 262-1550
FAX (608) 265-4194

UNIVERSITY OF WYOMING COLLEGE OF BUSINESS

ADMISSIONS FACTS

Type of school	Public

Demographics

No. of men	14
No. of women	21
No. of minorities	22
No. of int'l students	11

EQUAL TREATMENT GRAPH

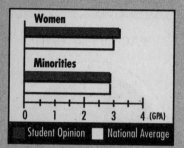

Admissions Statistics

Avg. GMAT	568
Avg. undergraduate GPA	3.2
Avg. age at entry	27
No. of applicants	71
No. accepted	58
No. enrolled	20

Deadlines and Notifications

Regular application	3/30
Regular notification	rolling
Special dates	N/A

Focus of Curriculum

General Management

Academic Specialties

General Management

FINANCIAL FACTS

In-state tuition	$2,425
Out-of-state tuition	$6,817
On-campus housing	$1,512

ACADEMICS

Beautiful, rugged, pristine: When University of Wyoming students describe the natural setting in which they're located, these are the words they use. But a room with a view won't cost you much. This state-run B-school is among one of the least expensive programs included in this book. As one student told us, it "offers the best bargain for academic education." That education includes small classes and a high level of student/faculty interaction. Said one student, "The most outstanding asset of this school is the student/teacher ratio. You really get to know your professors." Reported another, "Faculty members provide excellent examples of what it means to be a professor. They're good teachers. There's a fair balance between their research and commitment to students." The school offers both a full and part-time MBA program. The latter relies on "compressed video," which, notes the school is a "new technology that enables students in a number of different locations around Wyoming to see and hear each other and the instructor as if they were all in the same place. The system uses fiber optic telephone lines to transmit both audio and video signals thereby making possible two-way communications among selected sites in Wyoming."

Students with non-business undergraduate degrees must take Common Body of Knowledge (CBK) courses as prerequisites for the core MBA program, an unusual twist among B-schools. While this does get everyone on solid footing, one student gripes, "CBK classes are geared too heavily to quantitative aspects of business. More qualitative courses should be available to balance the two." Another twist: students have to maintain a 3.0 GPA (on a 4.0 scale). More than two C's, and it's probation time. After completing CBK requirements, students take core MBA courses and electives in an extremely unstructured program. For example, a student can take a psychology course in another graduate department and have it count toward the MBA degree. But several students told us this program is not as diverse in offerings as it appears to be. Wrote one, "Electives are scarce. There should be more grad-level international courses." Added another, "There should be required communications courses." There is one unusual requirement for graduation: Students must write a thesis to demonstrate their writing and research capabilities. As for skills, students report they feel well prepared by their studies in general management, quantitative methods, and computers. They're less confident of their marketing and accounting skills. Still, as one might expect, students are unanimous: Wyoming is well worth the investment of time and money.

PLACEMENT AND RECRUITING

Seventy-one companies recruit on campus each year. The average starting salary is $23,64.00. In 1994 the rate of placement was thirty-eight percent.

UNIVERSITY OF WYOMING COLLEGE OF BUSINESS

STUDENT LIFE/CAMPUS

As one MBA put it, "The program is not real high pressure, which makes it more enjoyable." Agreed another, "The workload is manageable." Two-thirds of the students report it's important to do all or most of the reading; the rest say shortcuts are fine. The majority work in study groups, although one MBA griped, "There should be more mandatory group work." What students seem to appreciate most at Wyoming is the small, homey atmosphere. Wrote one: "Students are warm and supportive. Everyone knows each other." This does, of course, have its downside. There isn't a lot of privacy in a graduate program of only sixty students. But there also isn't backstabbing competition.

Wyoming is paradise for the outdoorsy type. You are easily within an hour of rock climbing, hiking, skiing—any outdoor activity conceivable.

Steamboat is a frequent roadtrip destination. But bring more than ski pants—Wyoming winters are l-o-o-o-ng. As for the school's hometown of Laramie, students say it's safe and civilized, if more than a bit boring. Most students live on campus in affordable, accessible housing. There are few social outlets on campus or in the town of Laramie. The primary student club is the Graduate Business Council, which sponsors career-related events as well as Friday afternoon get-togethers at the campus beer garden. Wrote one MBA, "We certainly party," but much of this occurs in informal gatherings over a potluck dinner.

ADMISSIONS

Wyoming accepts about two-thirds of its MBA applicants (about half of whom wind up enrolling) on the basis of GPA, GMAT score, personal interviews, work experience, quality of undergraduate curriculum, and essays. Approximately one-third are from Wyoming. Writes the school, "The others are dispersed evenly throughout the U.S., China, and Germany."

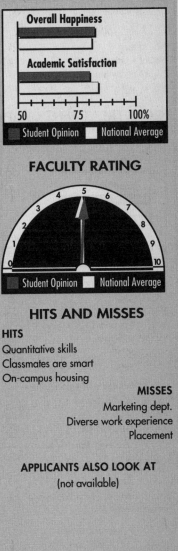

STUDENTS' OVERVIEW BOX

Overall Happiness

Academic Satisfaction

50   75   100%

Student Opinion   National Average

FACULTY RATING

Student Opinion   National Average

HITS AND MISSES

HITS
Quantitative skills
Classmates are smart
On-campus housing

MISSES
Marketing dept.
Diverse work experience
Placement

APPLICANTS ALSO LOOK AT
(not available)

FOR MORE INFORMATION, CONTACT:
College of Business
P.O. Box 3275 University Station
Laramie, WY 82071-3275
(307) 766-6858
eMail: LHIME@UWYO.edu

YALE UNIVERSITY SCHOOL OF MANAGEMENT

ADMISSIONS FACTS

Type of school	Private

Demographics

No. of men	292
No. of women	141
No. of minorities	70
No. of int'l students	123

EQUAL TREATMENT GRAPH

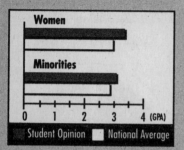

Admissions Statistics

Avg. GMAT	656
Avg. undergraduate GPA	3.4
Avg. age at entry	27.5
No. of applicants	1,258
No. accepted	465
No. enrolled	217

Deadlines and Notifications

Regular application	3/27
Regular notification	rolling
Special dates	N/A

Focus of Curriculum

Specialized

Academic Specialties

Finance, Mgmt. in the Public and Non-profit sectors

Joint Degrees

MBA/JD; MBA/Master of Arch.; MBA/Master of Divinity; MBA/Master of Drama; MBA/Master of Epidemiology and Publ. Health; MBA/Master of Forestry and Envt. Studies; MBA/Master of East Asian Studies; MBA/Master of Internat'l and Developement Economics; MBA/Master of Internat'l Relations

Special Programs

The Outreach Mgmt. Consulting Group; Externship Program; Internship Fund

FINANCIAL FACTS

In-state tuition	$20,990
Out-of-state tuition	$20,990
On-campus housing	$7,560 est. R&B

Note: Most SOM students live off-campus and share apts.

ACADEMICS

The Yale School of Management (SOM) doesn't offer an MBA. It offers a Master's in Public and Private Management (MPPM), which one student describes as "the true master's of management degree, an MBA-plus." Whatever the description, SOM's primary mission is to "educate managers for business *and* government *and* nonprofit organizations." However, as one Yale student said, "It seems public/non-profit because so many (over seventy percent) come from that background." Nonetheless, Yale places an emphasis on the interrelatedness of the public, private and non-profit sectors. Given the historical interconnectedness of business and government, Yale considers its integrated, multi-sector approach to management simply more pragmatic than a strict MBA curriculum.

In addition to their sector studies, first-year students take an intensive group of core classes in the typical, functional areas of business; hence the description "MBA-plus." There is a strong emphasis on quantitative as well as soft skills. Second-year students focus on a specialization and take up to seven electives. An outstanding department is finance. Overall, students describe a rigorous and intellectually challenging program that meeting their academic expectations. Students praise the quality of their education and Professors garner rave reviews. Adds one student, "Regular review sessions and personal tutors are available if needed (free of charge)." Despite all this, there are academic weak spots, especially by an MBA's standards. A large number of students report they feel only adequately prepared in operations management and computer skills.

PLACEMENT AND RECRUITING

Yale offers an on-line contacts database and an aggressive alumni network program that includes job postings from within alumni companies. Overall, Yale students are dissatisfied with the range of companies recruiting on campus. But one student explained, "Our placement office has the daunting task of finding jobs for 400 people who have 400 different career goals. We are hurt by the fact that companies aren't going to come here and find a lot of people who fit their molds." Still, according to one student, "Yale has had tremendous success in placing banking and finance people, due to the reputation of its finance department and faculty." The school's niche positioning in other areas hasn't hurt either. In 1994, 134 companies recruited on-campus and seventy-eight percent of grads had a job by graduation, ninety-one percent within three months. The average starting salary was $58,564. Major recruiters were Booz Allen, CS First Boston, Chemical Bank, Citicorp, Goldman Sachs, Coopers and Lybrand, IBM, Mckinsey, Morgan Stanley, and Procter and Gamble.

YALE UNIVERSITY SCHOOL OF MANAGEMENT

STUDENT LIFE/CAMPUS

According to our survey, students are the heart and soul of this program. As one Yalie put it, "The student body is one of the school's great strengths—tremendous geographic, academic, and professional diversity—both in terms of background and objectives. This range of perspectives makes classroom discussion especially interesting." Agreed another, "Since group work is emphasized, the high quality/diversity of students adds to the learning experience."

Students report a demanding workload and spend an average of thirty-five to forty hours a week preparing for class. Wrote one student, "There is a heavy infusion of weekly problem sets during the first year, requiring in-depth analysis and complete write-ups." No doubt this requires hard work, but students aren't competing for grades. SOM's noncompetitive scale of grading (proficient, pass, and fail) de-emphasizes student-against-student competition. Still, like many MBAs, Yale students report a fair amount of academic pressure, although one says this "varies because it's self-imposed." Students rave about the support they get from classmates. One student gushed, "The small size (200 per class) allows for a true sense of community. We *really* enjoy and work well with each other." Exclaimed another, "Our student body is warm, friendly, cohesive—I love it here!" Apparently these warm feelings will continue after graduation. Shared one student, "Classmates will be friends and assets for life."

As for Yale's hometown of New Haven, students say, "It's a crime-ridden city with nothing going for it." Still, the majority of students opt to live off-campus in apartments in the city's residential neighborhoods, inland or along the Long Island Sound. Students say off-campus housing is both attractive and reasonably priced. Wrote one student, "We don't rely on public transportation but on Yale University shuttles which are very convenient, efficient, and free." One student boasted that SOM has the "best golf course of any B-school in the country." Beyond golf, students report an active and varied social life, though this doesn't include dating. Students tend to socialize and travel in packs.

A note on the student body: Thirty-six percent of the students are international and represent twenty-six different countries. Wrote one student, "This makes Yale culturally stimulating. Also impressive is the integration of the international students into all school activities." Reported another, "Above average number of married students, and those with children."

ADMISSIONS

Applicants to Yale had better have excellent GPAs and GMAT scores if they hope to attract the attention of the admissions committee, which accepts less than a quarter of those who apply to the MBA program. Work experience, letters of recommendation, and a strong background in mathematics complete the list of admissions criteria. Yale goes by a rounds admissions process. According to Yale the round you apply in "does not impact admissibility." Students may defer admission for up to two years.

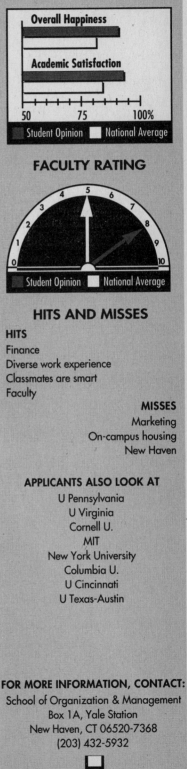

STUDENTS' OVERVIEW BOX

Overall Happiness

Academic Satisfaction

50   75   100%

Student Opinion   National Average

FACULTY RATING

Student Opinion   National Average

HITS AND MISSES

HITS
Finance
Diverse work experience
Classmates are smart
Faculty

MISSES
Marketing
On-campus housing
New Haven

APPLICANTS ALSO LOOK AT

U Pennsylvania
U Virginia
Cornell U.
MIT
New York University
Columbia U.
U Cincinnati
U Texas-Austin

FOR MORE INFORMATION, CONTACT:
School of Organization & Management
Box 1A, Yale Station
New Haven, CT 06520-7368
(203) 432-5932

Index

Index

ABOUT THE AUTHOR

Nedda Gilbert is a graduate of the University of Pennsylvania and holds a master's degree from Columbia University. She has worked for The Princeton Review since 1985. In 1987, she created The Princeton Review corporate test preparation service, which provides Wall Street firms and premier companies tailored educational programs for their employees. She currently resides in Chicago.

CULTURESCOPE

The
Princeton Review

Guide to an Informed Mind

Has this ever happened to you?

You're at a party. An attractive person who you have been dying to meet comes over and says, "Man, does that woman have a Joan of Arc complex, or what?" and you, in a tone that is most suave, say "Uh," while your mind races wildly, "*Joan of Arc, OK, France, uh...damn,*" as the aforementioned attractive person smiles weakly and heads for the punch bowl.

No? How about this?

Your boss finally learns your name and says, "Ah, good to have you aboard. Do you like Renaissance painting?" You reply with an emphatic "Yes! I do!" to which she returns, "What's your favorite fresco?" You start stammering, glassy-eyed, your big moment passing you by as visions of soda pop dance through your brain.

CULTURESCOPE can help.

If you have gaps of knowledge big enough to drive a eighteen-wheeler through, The Princeton Review has the thing for you. It's called CULTURESCOPE. It's a book that can make people think you've read enough books to fill a semi, even if you haven't.

CULTURESCOPE covers everything: history, science, math, art, sports, geography, popular culture—it's all in there, and it's fun, because along with all of the great information there are quizzes, resource lists, fun statistics, wacky charts, and lots of pretty pictures.

It's coming soon to a bookstore near you.

You won't go away empty-headed.

THE
PRINCETON
REVIEW